DUKE ELLINGTON

DUKE ELLINGTON

James Lincoln Collier

MICHAEL JOSEPH
London

MICHAEL JOSEPH LTD

Penguin Books Ltd, 27 Wrights Lane, London W8 5TZ (Publishing and Editorial)
and Harmondsworth, Middlesex, England (Distribution and Warehouse)
Viking Penguin Inc., 40 West 23rd Street, New York, New York 10010, U.S.A.
Penguin Books Australia Ltd, Ringwood, Victoria, Australia
Penguin Books Canada Ltd, 2801 John Street, Markham, Ontario, Canada L3R 1B4
Penguin Books (N.Z.) Ltd, 182–190 Wairau Road, Auckland 10, New Zealand

First published in Great Britain 1987

Printed in Great Britain by Billings & Son Ltd, Worcester

British Library Cataloguing in Publication Data

Collier, James Lincoln
   Duke Ellington.
   1. Ellington, Duke 2. Jazz musicians –
   United States – Biography
   I. Title
   785.42′092′4   ML410.E4
   ISBN 0–7181–2821–4

For Robert Andrew Parker

Preface

The jazz world has always been filled with interesting personalities: gunslingers and saints, the beautiful and the damned. Few, however, have embodied in one personality as many contradictions as Duke Ellington. He was gregarious and, as one of his friends said, a "devourer of relationships." But he was also reserved, a private man whom few people knew well. He could be unstintingly generous; but he could also argue with his musicians over petty amounts of money. He was infinitely loyal and kept on his payroll people who had outlived their usefulness; but he could manipulate the people around him ruthlessly for his own ends. Who the real Duke Ellington was is a mystery that fascinated even those who knew him well.

In this book I have tried to open, at least a little, this extraordinary man to view. His impact on twentieth-century music is large, and it is only through understanding who he was that we can know how he made so major a mark on our times. I have tended to emphasize the earlier portions of Ellington's life and career. There are several reasons for this. For one, a number of books published after his death covered the later stages of his career fairly thoroughly. For another, it is my view that Ellington's most important music came before he was fifty, and I wished to concentrate on that work. Perhaps most critical, the forces that shape any artist's work generally appear early. Such was the case with Ellington, and I had necessarily to look at his early days to find the roots of his art.

A book like this is not created by one person but is built on the work of many other people who have gone before. I have depended for discographic details on the superb compilations of Benny H. Aasland, D. Bakker, and the Italian team of Massagli, Pusateri, and Volonté. Where biographical detail was otherwise lacking, I have used Leonard Feather's standard work *The Encyclopedia of Jazz* and the ever-reliable John Chilton's *Who's Who of Jazz*. Previous biographies are discussed in the text, and readers will discover my opinions of them there.

I have found particularly useful dozens of oral histories of people associated with Ellington, and I would like to thank the following for guiding me to them and helping me in other ways: Dan Morgenstern and the staff of the Institute for Jazz Studies at Rutgers University; Vivian Perlis and her associates Harriet Milnes and Jan Fournier at the Duke Ellington Oral History Project at Yale University; and the staff at the Schomburg Center for Research in Black Culture, in New York City. Herb Gray supplied me with some pictures and other material from his private collection. Fran Hunter generously shared with me her memories of the Ellington family. Rob Darrell supplied me with early letters and his memories of Duke. Francis "Cork" O'Keefe also shared his memories of Duke with me. Andrew Homzy gave me the benefit of his insights into Ellington's music. Geoffrey L. Collier helped me with analyses of certain Ellington pieces. Edward Bonoff in particular checked many of the musical analyses and offered valuable suggestions and criticisms.

I am especially grateful to John L. Fell, who provided me with a number of Ellington items I could not locate, spent many hours running for me Ellington films from his private collection, and read the manuscript in its entirety, offering many valuable suggestions and comments. I cannot thank too much Stanley and Helen Dance, who spent hours of their time talking to me about Ellington, again and again answering questions and offering their criticisms and comments on the manuscript. Their aid was invaluable. Needless to say, the help provided me by the Dances and any of the others aforementioned does not constitute an endorsement by them of my interpretations and critical opinions of Ellington and his music, which are my own responsibility.

I must also thank my editor, Sheldon Meyer, always supportive, sensitive, and forbearing. Finally, I am grateful to Wiley Hitchcock and the Institute for Studies in American Music at Brooklyn College for providing a fellowship that, in part, supported the research for this book.

New York   J. L. C.
January 1987

Contents

DUKE ELLINGTON

1

Childhood

To most of the people who knew him, Duke Ellington was unique, a person who resembled no other they had met, somehow more spacious, grander in design, than ordinary people. Although they would admit that Ellington was a private person who was difficult to know, they again and again insisted that there was something special about him. Barney Bigard, his star clarinetist for some fifteen years, said, "Everyone in that band knew they were working with a genius."[1] Cootie Williams, who was with Ellington for even longer, said, "Duke was the greatest guy I ever met in my life. Musician and man."[2] He was charismatic almost from childhood, and by the end of his life he seemed to some, at least, to possess a majesty that nobody would affront.

He was, then, somewhat different from most other important jazz artists—or artists in general—who usually, apart from their special talents, turn out to be quite ordinary people, with tics and foibles that seem incongruous, or even unnerving, when seen against the shining honesty of their work and the magic of their talent.

But with Duke Ellington the character and the talent were one. And in this he was rare. Most artistic achievement of a high order depends, in the end, not on training and analysis but on the possession of a gift, a given, of a skill of some kind greater than that granted to most people: an ability to rapidly describe in novel terms events and feelings; a flow of association so that one idea brings in train a raft of others; a talent for seeing relationships between very disparate entities.

Gifts of these kinds are inexplicable and lie at the core of most artistic success, where they escape analysis, defying attempts to attribute them to the artist's character or upbringing or to the influences of other artists.

Duke Ellington had no such gift. He lacked the melodic inventiveness of a Bix Beiderbecke, a Johnny Hodges; many of his most famous melodies were supplied to him by members of his band. His sense of larger form, of musical architecture, was notoriously weak; the most persistent criticism of his longer works, where lack of form would be most noticeable, was that they were "rambling" and "incoherent." And although his sense of time was sure and although he was considered by people who played with him an excellent band pianist, he did not have the exquisite rhythmic sense of a Louis Armstrong, a Benny Goodman, a Lester Young, that makes even the simplest and most direct of melodies swing.

Yet, at his death in 1974 Duke Ellington left what is possibly the most significant body of work in jazz, and thus, if we take jazz to be an important part of the music of our time, one of the most significant bodies of music of the twentieth century. How can this be? How can a man with no easily discernible gift produce a body of work so important?

The answer lies in his character. Ellington carved his creations not so much with raw talent, as did the Armstrongs and Charlie Parkers, but with the chisel of his character. Who Duke Ellington was is critical to the work he produced. If he had been different in this way or that, his work would have been different and might not even have existed.

Most jazz musicians make their greatest impact and frequently create their best work in their early twenties, and many have added little to their reputations after the age of thirty. Ellington showed no such precocity. He was twenty-eight before he created any music worth listening to for any except historical reasons; he did not begin to make a name for himself until he was almost thirty; and he was in his forties, a relatively old age for a jazz musician, when he came to musical maturity. As I have pointed out elsewhere, had Ellington died at the age Beiderbecke did, he would be remembered as an obscure bandleader of the 1920s who cut half a dozen records of some interest. Had he died when Charlie Parker did, he would be remembered as a challenger to Fletcher Henderson's crown as leader of the best black band of the early days of the big bands, and as author of a dozen or so first-rate jazz pieces. Had he died at Fats Waller's age, he would be a figure of consequence in jazz history, creator of a substantial body of brilliant jazz, but not to be classed with Armstrong, Parker, Miles Davis, and a few others at the top of the jazz pantheon.

But he did not die young; and he left a body of work so large and so gripping that I can map only a fraction of the territory in a book this size. To understand that work, we must understand who Duke Ellington was.

To begin with, Duke Ellington was black. To be a black in America is a condition nearly unique in human history. There has never been anything quite like it. The English, French, and Spanish who established slavery in the New World, and the Americans who continued it, hardly invented the institution, which appears to be as old as civilization itself. But in America the end result was a subculture spread through the social body that was neither entirely of it nor entirely out of it. American blacks exist in a side culture running parallel to the mainstream, very similar to, at times joining, but never entirely part of the central culture. As a consequence blacks have always been seen by the white majority as somewhat different, somewhat exotic, somewhat threatening. Blacks in turn have been forced to view the mainstream culture with two eyes—the one coveting the advantages whites seem to possess, the other angrily trying to reject a culture they have trouble laying claim to. The friction engendered by the rubbing together of these two branches in the culture has had profound and obvious effects, one of which was the creation of a style of entertainment that played a major role in defining Duke Ellington's music.

With Emancipation, blacks innocently supposed that they would suddenly be allowed access to everything they had been denied before: education, political office, jobs, careers, wealth. For a time during Reconstruction, when the northern armies occupying the South were opening doors for blacks, it seemed that it might happen. Optimistic blacks, determined to make ways for themselves, began educating themselves and learning politics. As they tried to push themselves into the mainstream, they took for their cultural model the white middle class. The ideal, according to Joel Williamson's major study of the period, "would prove to be deeply and persistently Victorian."[3] Upwardly mobile blacks cultivated the genteel mode endemic to the Western world; it demanded a rather formal manner of dress and deportment, coupled with an abhorrence of sexual display, drunkenness, and the open emotionalism thought to characterize "foreigners," lower-class blacks, and working people in general. Of particular importance to Ellington's development was the presence in this Victorian culture of a genteel interest in the arts. The "best" art—the music of the "Three B's," the painting of the academic formalists, Greek statuary, the plays of Shakespeare, and the novels of Scott—was thought to be "uplifting" and to turn the mind to higher things and away from depravity and debauchery. Art, and especially good music, had moral connotations to the Victorians. It was this view of art that the new black middle class of the post-Emancipation period adopted.

But as Ellington's parents were growing up, conditions for blacks were changing. In the North, and to some extent in the South, it was coming to be recognized that the newly enfranchised blacks constituted an important body of voters, who might profitably be courted. As a consequence, some places were opened in the government and the political establishment in general for black politicians, who were then given a few grubby handfuls of patronage to dispense. The door into the mainstream opened a little farther.

In the South, however, there was a growing attempt, through the 1880s and 1890s, to slam the door shut. A powerful movement to shove blacks back into serfdom, quite explicit in its aims, was swelling; it brought with it an epidemic of lynching that peaked in 1892 when 156 blacks, mostly men, were lynched. Williamson says, "The sudden and dramatic rise in the lynching of black men in and after 1889 stands out like some giant volcanic eruption on the landscape of Southern race relations. There was, indeed, something new and horribly palpable on earth. It was signalized by the mob, the rushing, swelling fury of a mass of struggling men, the bloody and mangled bodies, and the smell of burning flesh."[4]

Among black leaders the consequence was despair and the end of the optimistic illusion that blacks could find a way into the mainstream through ambition, hard work, and education. They began to turn away from the white model, and out of this view, espoused especially by W. E. B. DuBois, would grow the precursor of the "black is beautiful" movement, a sense that the black destiny was different from the white. This new attitude would play a role in producing the Harlem Renaissance of the World War I period and later, and that too would have profound effects on Duke Ellington's music.

But the change in attitude was, as Williamson points out, felt more by the leadership than by the mass of blacks, who were still hopeful of entering the mainstream. Ellington's parents lived by the ideal of Victorian gentility until they died, and they raised Duke to it.

Duke's paternal great-grandfather came from North Carolina, his great-grandmother from Virginia.[5] They were presumably slaves, and both were taken, or sold to South Carolina, where Duke's grandfather, James, was born in about 1840. This was a normal pattern for the time: slave-holding was unprofitable in the upper states of the South, especially Virginia, and surplus slaves were frequently sold into South Carolina and Georgia, where conditions along the miasmal coastline made the life of a slave short.

James Ellington formed an alliance with Emma, born in 1844 in South Carolina, possibly on the same plantation as James was. James was light-skinned and possibly had a white father; Emma was darker. She bore her first child when she was fourteen, and she would go on bearing more for another twenty-two or so years. Not long after the Civil War, probably in 1868 or 1869, the family moved to Lincoln County, in the northwestern part of North Carolina. At some point they settled in the Rock Hill area of Lincolnton, according to one report. It was a hilly patch, with a creek running through it, where there was a small black enclave.

At first James worked at casual labor, and Emma as a domestic. However, the family appears to have acquired a farm of some kind. James, unhappily, became paralyzed sometime in the 1870s, and was confined to a wheelchair for the rest of a long life, but he still managed to run the farm, with the help of his numerous progeny. Furthermore, he saw to it that his children got an education, at least as much as black children of that time and place were able to get. What seems clear, in any case, is that the Ellingtons were above the average lot—more intelligent, better educated, and more ambitious than many of the blacks around them. John, a brother close in age to James Edward, taught in a local school for a period, it is said.

It was, however, not a very good time for ambitious blacks. Race relations were worsening, and the tide of lynching rising. In the years after 1890, Lincoln County—and the South in general—was economically depressed. There were good reasons for blacks to move north, and in the early 1890s, just when both the recession and the wave of lynchings were at their worst, a group of Ellington men began to emigrate to Washington, D.C.

The city of Washington had a special place in the minds of American blacks. For one thing, as a consequence of Reconstruction, southern blacks had for decades seen the federal government as their protector against state and local governments. Black rights were not a high-priority item with most federal governments, but at least Washington was committed to the concept of equality and did, to a degree, feel obligated to do something for blacks. For example, various kinds of bills designed to ensure that blacks could vote were introduced into Congress from time to time, and some came close to passing. Washington was thus seen by many blacks as a place of refuge, the castle on the hill to which they could repair at the approach of the enemy.

For another thing, the search for black votes required the opening of those doors into government, and by the 1890s certain posts in the Treasury Department and the Government Printing Office, especially, were seen as the preserve of blacks. The effect was to create in Washington a relatively large black elite with money and a degree of power. To this were added the faculty of Howard University and the black doctors and lawyers who, by and large, issued from it. This black upper crust thought well of itself and was admired by blacks elsewhere. Some of the prestige flowed down to the blacks in the middle ranks, so that Washington blacks, at the time when Duke Ellington was growing up, saw themselves as special, members of the leading social group in the black culture.

There was, to be sure, another side to black Washington. Directly behind some of the most elegant mansions on the most charming streets lay a horrendous alley culture filled with an "overpowering stench." "A person who had never ventured down the alley openings could scarcely believe the tales of what he would find."[6] When Ellington was a boy, some twenty thousand blacks lived in these alleys. Conditions, according to Jacob Riis, were worse than they were in New York's slums.[7]

Between alley dwellers and the elite of doctors and bureaucrats lay two or three other ill-defined social classes, and black children were not encouraged to mix with inferiors. Ellington himself said, "I don't know how many castes of Negroes there were in the city at that time, but I do know that if you decided to mix carelessly with another you would be told that one just did not do that sort of thing."[8]

Duke Ellington thus did not grow up as did, say, Louis Armstrong, a member of a despised minority whose sense of inferiority was so ingrained that it was barely conscious; rather, he was part of a social group whose members had risen through genuine achievements and were vested with pride and a sense of superiority, not merely over lower blacks, but over a good many whites as well. Ellington said that his teachers emphasized self-respect:

> When we went out into the world, we would have the grave responsibility of being practically always on stage, for every time people saw a Negro they would go into a reappraisal of the race. [They] taught us that proper speech and good manners were our first obligations, because as representatives of the Negro race we were to command respect for our people. . . . They had pride there, the greatest race pride, and at that time there was some sort of movement to desegregate schools in Washington, D.C. Who do you think were the first to object? Nobody but the proud Negroes of Washington, who felt that the kind of white kids we would be thrown in with were not good enough.[9]

Anyone who knew Duke Ellington as an adult could see the results of this teaching in his every move: the good manners and proper speech carried to an extreme; his unyielding insistence that he be respected; the racial pride that led him, long before the "black is beautiful" movement of the 1960s, to insist that he was writing Negro music; and his need always to mingle with the "best" people, which led him so far as to avoid bringing certain members of his own band into his home to mix with his family.

Washington, D.C., was thus a magnet for blacks, especially for those from North Carolina, only a few hours away by train. At least four Ellington men came to the city in the early 1890s: James Edward, who would become Duke Ellington's father; his brother John; and two others, William G. and another James, whose relationship to James Edward and John is obscure. By 1893 they were living in a house, probably a rooming house, at 1735 H Street, N.W. Over the next few years they worked primarily as waiters. But they were intent on moving up: in 1897 John was running some sort of small restaurant, possibly an oyster bar, and James was working as a coachman.

By this time they had been joined by two other Ellington men, James Edward's brother George and Edward, whose relationship to the others is again obscure. It is clear from the record that these six men formed a tight-knit group, two or three of them usually living together and frequently, we can assume from the fact that several of them worked at the same occupation at times, getting each other jobs. The Ellingtons, then, were a group of intelligent and energetic young men—some of them still teenagers in the late 1890s—who were determined to make something of themselves.

Duke's father, James Edward, or J.E., as he was frequently called, got his big chance in 1897 or 1898 when he went to work for Dr. M. F. Cuthburt, reputedly a society doctor who tended Morgenthaus and Du Ponts. J.E., not yet twenty at the time, started as a coachman for Cuthburt, living on the premises, probably in a room in the barn or over the carriage house, as was the custom at the time.

J.E. would stay with the Cuthburt family for some twenty years. From coachman he moved up in stages to become the family butler. Precisely what the job was is not known, but the butler in a wealthy household held a position of some importance, overseeing some of the other servants and taking primary charge of the elaborate entertaining that was a regular feature of life with such people. J.E. had already acquired his florid manner of speech, apparently from his own father, who, according to Duke's sister, Ruth, was a "flirt" and was still reaching out for girls when he was paralyzed and in a wheelchair.[10] He handed around overripe compliments to women like bonbons—"Pretty can only get prettier, but beauty compounds itself" was typical. He dressed as elegantly as he could afford to, and he lived as high as he could. Duke said, "J.E. always acted as though he had money, whether he had it or not. He spent and lived like a man who had money, and he raised his family as though he were a millionaire."[11] Given this attitude, the young J.E. would have been quick to emulate the style of the family. He learned about wines and food and about the most renowned makes of flatware and china. As his competence grew, he and various of the Ellington men began catering at some of the great houses around Washington; once he even served at the White House. Not only was he able to bring home from these affairs the most elegant sorts of food, but he was given by the Cuthburts and others odds and ends of china and silverware, which he put into use at home. J.E. knew what a gentleman was, and he was determined to be one. There was an element of pretentiousness in this, but we can only respect his insistence that he was as good a man as any. Duke Ellington was not raised in a wealthy home; at times money was tight, in part because of J.E.'s desire always to have the best. But he grew up, paradoxically, knowing a good deal more about champagne and Wedgwood than most youngsters do, and it is clear that J.E.'s feeling for the elegant, however superficial, became part of Ellington's way of seeing the world. Throughout his life Duke always felt that he was somehow degraded if he did not go first-class. He did not judge himself on how much money he had; frequently he did not even know. It was the *style* in which he lived that mattered.

At about the time when he went to work for Dr. Cuthburt, J.E. met Daisy Kennedy. Daisy came from a higher stratum of black Washington society than J.E. did. J.E., after all, had begun life as a day laborer. Daisy's father, James William Kennedy, was a captain of police, a job that suggests that he had political connections, power in the black community, and some kind of relationship with the white establishment.

There is a family legend that he was born a slave on a plantation in Virginia, the illegitimate son of the plantation master and a slave woman. He fell in love, so the story goes, with a fellow slave, herself of mixed blood, part black and part Cherokee. His master freed him, as slave owners sometimes did in cases of their half-caste sons, and he emigrated to Washington. After Emancipation he returned to Virginia to claim his love, and brought her back to Washington, where they proceeded to bear nine, ten, or twelve children, depending on which source you choose. Kennedy was light-skinned, and his daughter, Daisy, more so, and the story is possible in terms of the dates involved.

Kennedy died when Duke was young, and Duke did not remember him, but he remembered well his Kennedy grandmother, Alice, who lived on for years. The family called her Mamma, and she ran a house filled with children and grandchildren coming and going.

Daisy Kennedy grew up with a strong religious bent and with the Victorian moral views that were part of her culture. According to a family friend, Fran Hunter, Daisy was "genteel" and "dignified."[12] Ruth said, "My mother was quite puritanical."[13] She would not wear lipstick, used a pince-nez, and was, again according to Ruth, "a real Victorian lady."[14]

Daisy came to adulthood with what would have been called at the time "advantages." She was light-skinned, pretty—even beautiful—cultivated for her time and place, and the daughter of a man with important connections. Socially, she stood only a short distance below the daughters of the doctors, lawyers, and college professors at the top of black Washington society. She would have been an extremely desirable catch in her own social group, and it is surprising that she chose—and was permitted to choose—James Ellington, an ill-educated coachman only recently arrived from the hills of North Carolina. The match appears even odder when we realize that J.E., for all his elegance and courtly ways, was no puritan. Ruth said flatly that he was a womanizer.[15] Duke's son, Mercer, who knew J.E. well, said that he "always liked to live it up."[16] In later life he was a heavy drinker, and possibly an alcoholic. He was clearly the wrong sort of person, both socially and temperamentally, for Daisy; and yet she married him. We do not know why; we can only guess that she was taken by J.E.'s courtly manner, which presumably obscured his lack of education and his other social defects. In any case, the marriage seems to have been reasonably successful. There were strains later on, probably occasioned by J.E.'s love of the high life; but Duke insisted that J.E. was at pains to see that Daisy had a lifestyle she deserved—a nice home, summers at the shore, proper attire. Duke said, "The best had to be carefully examined to make sure it was good enough for my mother."[17]

Daisy and J.E. were married on January 5, 1897, a day after Daisy's eighteenth birthday. They began married life in the bride's home on Twentieth Street. A son was perhaps born in the year they were married, or early 1898, one who died in infancy, but that is not certain. It is sure, however, that on April 29, 1899, a son was born at the Kennedy house and named Edward Kennedy Ellington. He would be an only child until he himself was nearly an adult.

The young family continued to live in the Kennedy house until about 1900, when Duke was a year or so old. At about this time, J.E. was promoted to butler in the Cuthburt household, and it is reasonable to suppose that an increase in salary allowed him to set up his own home. It was probably nothing more than a few rented rooms: for the first ten years after leaving the Kennedy house, the Ellingtons moved almost every year from one place to another in an area heavily populated by blacks lying roughly between Dupont Circle and Howard University. Frequently in these years Daisy helped out at the Cuthburt house, at times as a sort of receptionist, at others as a preparer of food for the Cuthburt parties. The implication of all this is that, whatever airs J.E. put on, the family was struggling financially.

Nonetheless, Duke had a comfortable boyhood. The area today is in the main dilapidated, but in Duke's youth it was a pleasant place of three- and four-story brick houses set on wide streets. There were trees in the backyards, and plenty of light and air. It is probable that the family had at least a floor in one of these houses.

Duke's childhood was uneventful and happier than most. Cousins, uncles, and aunts came and went. The house was regularly filled with relatives; there were also visits to the Kennedy place, where there would be more relatives, and to the houses of uncles and aunts. There was always plenty of food, always fun. Summers J.E. sent his wife and child to "the shore," as many city-dwelling families did, on the grounds that hot city summers were breeding grounds for disease and risky to children. Daisy and Duke made extended stays with relatives in Atlantic City, Philadelphia, Asbury Park. At home he climbed the pear tree in the Kennedy backyard, went through the ordinary illnesses of childhood, played sports, especially baseball. (In his memoirs Ellington speaks of being an enthusiastic baseball fan, but since as an adult he showed no interest in any sport—indeed, hated fresh air so much that he kept his windows closed—this professed love of baseball needs to be viewed skeptically.)

His boyhood was characterized more than anything by his being a well-loved member of a large, extended family and, especially, by the extraordinary attention paid to him by his mother. He said, "My mother never took her eyes off precious little me, her jewel, until I was four years old. . . ." When he was sick with pneumonia, she prayed at his bedside "night and day."[18] When she sent him off to Patterson Elementary School at five, she would discreetly follow him until she saw him go through the school door, and when school was out she would frequently be waiting for him there.

The relationship between Ellington and his mother went beyond the ordinary. Why Daisy so doted on her children we cannot know. If it is true that Daisy had lost an earlier child, it is understandable that she would be fearful of losing another, an only child for most of his youth. Whatever the cause, Duke grew up secure in the unending love of his mother, a certitude that he would always be first in her eyes. Few children are this lucky; and it left Duke with the sense that he was special. "You are blessed," Daisy would tell him, meaning that he was beyond the ordinary, and Duke believed her.[19] He came to feel that he was, in the precise sense of the word, a little prince. As a boy he would stand on the steps of his house and make his cousins bow and curtsy to him. "I am the grand, noble, Duke; crowds will be running to me."[20] His younger cousin Bernice Wiggins remembered how angry she would get when Duke made her stand at attention while he announced, "Mother dear, your son is going to be the greatest, the grandest, the glorious Duke."[21]

He actually practiced being not merely celebrated but royalty itself. Late in his career Duke was introduced to Queen Elizabeth of England. Irving Townsend, for a period Duke's record producer, reported, "According to accounts of their meeting, Ellington met compliment with greater compliment, charming the Queen with his sweet talk."[22] As a tribute, he composed for her a piece called The Queen's Suite. Townsend said, "Ellington went about the composition of 'The Queen's Suite' with greater concentration than he displayed for any other music with which I was associated."[23] Only a single copy was pressed, to be presented to the queen for her enjoyment, and was kept private until after Duke's death. It is clear from the whole episode that Duke saw himself as worthy of mingling with royalty.

This view that he was special was cut into Duke's consciousness when he was very young, and it was to remain a salient element of his character for all of his life. It manifested itself in his behavior in numberless ways: his refusal to scuffle in the muck with lesser men, even when they had badly wronged him; his ability to accept even the most fulsome praise without a blush; his willingness to aspire to anything without fear; his commanding presence and ability to rule wherever he went.

Duke Ellington came into his teens, then, as a protected and well-loved child, growing up in an orderly household where decorous behavior was simply part of the air he breathed; he was confident in manner and sure that he had, despite everything, been born to high estate.

2

Introduction to Music

As Duke Ellington was growing into adolescence, the entertainment world he would soon enter was undergoing a rapid, violent change. This change was undergirded by a much deeper, pervasive shift in the American spirit, a shift so profound that even today few except specialists in the field recognize how significant it was. One of those specialists, Lewis A. Erenberg, in a study of New York nightlife, says, "Scholars have recognized that the period from 1890 to 1930 marked a profound reorientation in American culture, one that broke from older forms of gentility in which individuals were to subordinate themselves voluntarily to a social code. But starting in the 1890s, values became more informal, and the restrictions placed on the individual's personal desires and impulses were lessened."[1]

This subject is far too complex to be dealt with in any detail here. Suffice it to say that the new attitude would cast off the Victorian constraints on pleasure and self-expression in general, and allow people more freedom to enjoy themselves at the expense of self-discipline and social control. In practice, this meant a new freedom in sexuality, drink, and what might be called "good times"—the right to go out at night to dance, sing, and eat as you liked.

Inevitably, there arrived a group of entrepreneurs intent upon capitalizing on the new spirit, by selling the public what it needed to enjoy itself. They began by putting together the foundations of the great entertainment industry that has characterized, more than anything, the American twentieth century. It is no accident that the cabaret, the musical theater, the motion picture, the commercial music industry called Tin Pan Alley, the dance hall, and the nightclub all developed as major institutions in the first two decades of this century. Young middle-class people of Ellington's generation saw a brand-new and exciting world that stood in marked contrast to the smothering gentility of their homes, with their Landseer prints and dusty sets of Shakespeare and the Lake poets. To be sure, there was nothing surprising about this new world to children growing up in the black and immigrant ghettos of the big cities, many of whom had had firsthand experience before puberty with prostitution, alcoholism, and drug addiction. However, to youths like Duke Ellington, it was fresh and exhilarating. We must bear in mind that this new spirit was more than a simple desire for sensual pleasures: this young generation sensed that the new spirit was "right" and the old way "wrong." These young people brought a moral fervor to the enjoyment of the new freedoms; in going out to drink, dance, and copulate, they were insisting on their rights; it was a crusade. As a consequence, they felt they had almost a spiritual duty to be up on the newest thing—the newest dance steps, the newest drink, the newest music.

The newest music, as Duke was growing up, was ragtime. It had been created by black pianists, possibly the result of an attempt to transfer banjo strumming to the piano, probably sometime in the third quarter of the nineteenth century. It seems to have flowered most luxuriantly in the area around St. Louis, but by the 1880s it was being played all through the South, and into the North as well, especially in saloons and brothels. The music was characterized by an excessive use of syncopation, particularly in pianistic figures in the right hand, which were worked out to supply a counterrhythm to a strong 2/4 beat in the bass. By the middle of the 1890s formal rags were being composed, written down, and published, and very quickly they became immensely popular. Sheet music of rags like Scott Joplin's "Maple Leaf Rag" sold in the hundreds of thousands. By the first years after the turn of the century, when Ellington was a boy, ragtime had become so popular that famous bandmasters like John Philip Sousa had to include rags in their concert programs.

The ragtime boom was followed a decade later by a rising interest in another new form of music, the blues. Precisely when the blues were created is hard to know. However, statements that they date back well into the nineteenth century are suspect. W. C. Handy, "the father of the Blues," and Ma Rainey, "the mother of the Blues," both say they first heard the blues shortly after the turn of the century. Both had been traveling throughout the South in the preceding decade, and it is hardly likely they would have missed the blues had they been widely known. My own guess—and it can be no more than that—is that the blues developed out of the work song in the so-called Delta area of Mississippi, around Clarksdale, and spread out from there, moving especially downriver to New Orleans, where they were being played not long after 1900. In 1912 four blues were published, among them "Memphis Blues," which started W. C. Handy on the road to fame.

Unknown to Ellington, or indeed to virtually anybody else in Washington, during the years of his boyhood there was growing in New Orleans a hybrid music, made of a hard-to-untangle mix of ragtime, the blues, and popular forms. By 1910 jazz, still known as ragtime and sometimes as "playing hot," was well known in New Orleans. Jazz musicians were beginning to move out of the city by about 1910, but it was not until 1915, when a cadre of white musicians brought it to Chicago, that it made a significant splash. The stir it created there encouraged an entrepreneur to bring a jazz group, the Original Dixieland Jazz Band, to New York, where it also made a hit. In 1917 Victor recorded the band. The records became best-sellers, and the jazz boom began.

The interest in both jazz and ragtime was considerably fueled by a craze for dancing that swept over the country in 1912 but that had undoubtedly been developing slowly over the preceding decade. Before the turn of the century, in the decorous old days, nice people did not dance in public, and the dances they did tended to be the more formal reels and schottisches, which were fairly energetic and required a good deal of practice. However, down in the entertainment underworld of saloons and brothels, another type of dancing, probably developed by blacks in ragtime bars, was all the rage. There were a variety of them, but they can be lumped together as "the trots"—the turkey trot, the fox trot, the bunny hug, and more. The trots were rhythmic and simple and could be learned in fifteen minutes. Perhaps most important, they allowed couples to dance in as close an embrace as they chose to. The trots began to emerge from the saloons into polite society by around 1910. Within a couple of years the craze for dancing, spurred by the popularity of Vernon and Irene Castle as a dance team, had grown to the point where restaurants had to put in orchestras and permit couples to get up between courses and trot among the tables. From this period until the end of World War II, dancing of this kind was at the heart of American social life for young people, especially as a courtship ritual; for decades young males invited young women to "go dancing" as a first stage in mating, until going to a darkened movie theater gradually supplanted it. In the years after World War I, young people thought nothing of going dancing several times a week. As early as 1915 F. Scott Fitzgerald, sending his younger sister Annabelle some advice from Princeton on how to be popular, said, "Dancing counts as nothing else does."[2]

Dancing, of course, required music, and the trots seemed to call especially for the uneven, dotted rhythms. It is therefore not surprising that, according to Edward A. Berlin's excellent study of ragtime, "the most noticeable shift in ragtime of the 1910s is in the increased use of dotted rhythms. . . ."[3] The new jazz music, however, was virtually an exercise in dotted rhythms and very quickly replaced ragtime as a basis for dancing. By the early 1920s ragtime had become passé, still lingering on, but seen by the younger generation as something from an older day. The music of the new age would be jazz, so much so that the period of the 1920s came to be called the Jazz Age. It all happened very fast: not until 1917, with the Original Dixieland Jazz Band recordings, did the term "jazz" become widely known; by 1922 F. Scott Fitzgerald was already thinking of calling a collection of his stories "Tales from the Jazz Age."

An important factor in swelling the craze for the new music was the invention of mechanical systems of sound reproduction. The player piano, which allowed pianos to be played mechanically, was important in bringing ragtime into homes where nobody played, or at least nobody played well enough to handle the more complex rags of Joplin, James Scott, or Joseph Lamb. More important was the spread of the record player through the population during the period around World War I. Originally, it was an expensive toy available only to the rich, but cheap models had come onto the market by around the turn of the century and were flooding into American homes. Finally, in the early 1920s, the development of yet another means of sound reproduction, radio, began to bring live music, played in distant cities, to people's homes. Some jazz was being broadcast as early as 1923, and by the last years of the decade a torrent of the new music was in the air. Radio would have a major effect on the career of Duke Ellington.

During the years when Ellington was growing up, then, a whole array of currents in the social system—musical, mechanical, spiritual—were creating a welcome for the new entertainment, and especially for jazz. However, it would be some time before any awareness of the new music broke in on Duke Ellington. James and Daisy Ellington were aspirants after the genteel norms of the Victorian middle-class life, already under pressure even as they married. People like them, black and white, expected their children to do well in school, keep away from lower-class children, stay out of trouble, and deport themselves like little ladies and gentlemen. In particular, black people like the Ellingtons hated—it is not too strong a term—the blues and other forms of low-down music played by uneducated and, no doubt, immoral black working-class people. The black middle class was hanging on to its status by its fingertips, and even the slightest taint of lower-class immorality, as they saw it, might push them down the slope. Anything out of that culture was suspect, and especially its music. When Fletcher Henderson's middle-class parents learned that he was going to tour as a pianist and musical director for the blues singer Ethel Waters, they were sufficiently alarmed to travel to New York from Georgia to see what it was all about: Henderson was then in his twenties. Lil Hardin, a pianist who later married Louis Armstrong and appeared on many of the famous Hot Five series, reported that her mother called the blues "wuthless, immoral music played by wuthless, immoral loafers espressin' their vulgar minds with vulgar music."[4]

The key word was *vulgar*. The blues were vulgar and so were work songs and so was the shouting and hollering that went on in the sanctified church. What J.E. thought about this music is hard to say. He would not have heard the blues in his boyhood in North Carolina, but he must have heard at least some work song and gospel shouting. Daisy, however, would have had little experience of these forms of black folk music, and J.E., aspiring as he was to move upward, would have adopted the middle-class attitude that they were, indeed, vulgar. Years later, Duke's sister, Ruth, remembered sitting with her mother in the family living room in Washington, surrounded by Victorian furniture, the porcelain shepherds and shepherdesses that J.E. collected, the antimaccassars on the overstuffed chairs, listening to a radio announcer introduce "Duke Ellington and his Jungle Music."

> It was quite a shock. Here we were, my mother and I, sitting in this very respectable, Victorian living room in Washington, my mother so puritanical she didn't wear lipstick and the announcer from New York telling us we are listening to Duke Ellington and his Jungle Music! It sounded very strange and dissonant to us.[5]

As a consequence, Duke Ellington did not grow up hearing all around him the hand-clapping gospel music of the sanctified church, the work songs, or even the rough ragtime of the saloons out of which the popular versions grew. There was certainly music of this kind in the alley culture behind the great houses, but Ellington did not mingle with those people, and nowhere does he mention hearing this older black folk music. Ironically, Ellington was eventually to insist that he was writing "Negro" music and to include his version of work songs and church hymns in such pieces as *Black, Brown, and Beige*. In fact, most of what he knew of black folk music he got from books.

The musical tradition that Duke Ellington grew up in was the same European tradition that white middle-class children learned about. Daisy Ellington could, apparently, play the piano fairly well, and Duke speaks of her playing sentimental pieces from the standard semiclassical repertory. J.E. played piano by ear. Both Duke and Ruth have reported that he could play "operas"—possibly certain of the famous arias widely popular at the time like "Martha," or set pieces like the march from *Aida*. However, he seems to have spent more of his time organizing what were called barbershop quartets and teaching the other singers their parts from the piano. In addition, other members of the large Ellington and Kennedy cousinage played various musical instruments and sang. They, too, were drawing on the standard fare from the American song bag.

To be sure, Duke probably heard a certain number of the spirituals and plantation melodies, like those of Stephen Foster, that had been drawn from the black folk tradition. Middle-class blacks of the time nurtured a tradition of vocal music. In most big cities they supported musical societies built around choral groups, which frequently offered weekly concerts featuring a soloist, often a well-known one like Roland Hayes, brought in from the outside. Many black newspapers ran regular columns on the activities of these clubs and reviewed, almost always with enthusiasm, their concerts. The music at such concerts would include not only the standard vocal repertory but also the spirituals and plantation melodies that had, by the turn of the century, become an accepted part of the general American tradition. Ellington undoubtedly heard a certain amount of this music, derived from black folk music and Europeanized to suit the general taste, but most of the music he heard at home was strictly white and, in general, "artistic."

At some moment, around the time Duke was seven, eight, or nine, Daisy elected to give him piano lessons. This, too, was typical of the American middle-class home. There was no idea that he should ever play professionally, let alone with a dance band. It was simply that, according to the genteel notion, a cultivated person knew something about music: art, as we have seen, was supposed to be uplifting and an improver of morals, and music, which soothed the savage breast, was especially so. Moreover, before the era of radio and the record player, families needed at least one pianist in the house to entertain—and show off—for visitors and to accompany the singing that was an important part of home entertainment. In most middle-class American families it was customary for at least one of the girls to take piano lessons, but it was not unusual for boys to take them too; a common theme of the cartoons of the day was the forlorn boy seated at the piano with his baseball glove in his lap.

Duke's piano teacher was a woman named Clinkscales. The name is so improbable that there has always been some question about whether she really existed, but in fact Marietta Clinkscales lived at 739 Fourth Street, N.W., in the Ellington neighborhood, and gave piano lessons. (Stanley Dance, an Englishman who was close to Ellington for many years, has pointed out that Clinkscales is a not uncommon name in England, and it was some time before he got the joke.) Precisely what Marietta Clinkscales taught Duke we do not know, but we can suppose it was the sort of thing any child of the time would have learned: finger exercises and the simplest of pieces. Duke, however, had little interest in music and less in learning how to play it. He practiced as little as he could and wriggled out of the lessons as often as possible, and eventually Daisy, who doted on her son, gave up. How long the lessons lasted we do not know, either, but it could not have been more than a few months, and possibly no more than a few weeks. But they were important, for when Duke eventually became interested in music, he gravitated toward the piano, rather than, say, the drums, banjo, or trumpet. It is, obviously, a much shorter step to composing from the piano than from the drum.

He went to Garrison Junior High School for the seventh and eighth grades and then on to Armstrong Technical High School. Armstrong was not a top high school for blacks, like Dunbar, where the upwardly mobile wanted their children to go, but a vocational school that tended to send its graduates into the trades. It is clear enough from this and other things that Ellington, however bright, was not a very good student, was uninterested in his schoolwork, and did just enough to get along—and not always even that, for he failed to graduate from high school. What mattered to him more than anything else was having a good time for himself, and, when he finally developed a taste for music, assiduous attention to his homework stood little chance.

According to his own story, his interest in music was finally awakened by a pianist named Harvey Brooks, whom he heard in Philadelphia when he was about fourteen, on one of those summer visits to the seacoast at Asbury Park. Brooks, who was not much older than Duke, went on to become a competent professional pianist and had a minor career in jazz touring with the popular blues singer Mamie Smith and recording under his own name and that of others, including one session for Louis Armstrong. Ellington recalled, "[Brooks] was swinging, and he had a tremendous left hand, and when I got home I had a real yearning to play. I hadn't been able to get off the ground before, but after hearing him I said to myself, 'Man, you're just going to have to do it.' I went around to a couple of piano players, but I couldn't learn anything they were trying to teach me."[6]

Ellington was a late starter, and it was a struggle for him to catch up. According to his story, not long after he had been so impressed by Harvey Brooks, he was confined to his house for "a couple of weeks" with a cold. He used the time to "fiddle around" on the piano, building on what little he had learned from Mrs. Clinkscales.[7] In the course of this week he worked out a piece he called "Soda Fountain Rag," because he had been working as a soda jerk at the Poodle Dog Cafe, on Georgia Avenue, which appears to have been more of a cabaret than an ice cream parlor and which was one of three or four places during the period where the better-off black youth hung out. Shortly afterward, he worked out another composition, called "What You Gonna Do When the Bed Breaks Down?" and on the basis of these two tunes he began playing for little parties and events for his high school friends. These are both quite simple pieces, but pleasant enough, the sort of thing any adolescent might work out. "I was invited to many parties," he remembered, "where I learned that when you were playing the piano there was always a pretty girl standing down at the bass clef end of the piano."[8]

Then, at about fifteen, he began hanging around Frank Holliday's poolroom on T Street, between Sixth and Seventh, N.W., next door to Washington's celebrated black theater, the Howard. Holliday's attracted big-time gamblers, sports, and a lot of the local pianists. Some of these people were self-taught and could not read music, but several of them had a substantial amount of formal training. Ellington began listening, watching, and asking questions. Apparently, he was an ingratiating young man because several of the older men went out of their way, when Duke was fifteen, sixteen, and seventeen, to help him. One of these was Oliver Perry, called Doc, because he wore glasses. Perry was a proud man and carried himself with a dignity that impressed people. Duke knew Perry from Holliday's poolroom, but he would also run into him at dances for the high school students that Perry sometimes played. Ellington took it upon himself to visit Perry in his home frequently. Perry never charged him anything and, moreover, gave him something to eat during these sessions. Duke learned from him a system for recognizing chords from a piece of sheet music. This meant that, even if Duke could not actually play the notes on the sheet music as written, he could pick out the melody with his right hand and fit an approximately right set of chords to it with his left. It was certainly a poor way to learn the piano, because it gave Ellington a crutch to get along on without having to learn anything properly.

A second man who gave him substantial help was Henry Grant, who was something of a figure in black Washington musical circles. He taught music at Armstrong Tech and ran one of the musical organizations that were characteristic of middle-class black culture, the Afro-American Folk Song Chorus. Grant gave Duke some casual lessons in harmony in his home.

The instruction that Duke got from Perry, Grant, and other men he happened to buttonhole was quite informal, amounting more to tips and advice than to systematic schooling. There are a couple of things to be said about this. One is that Ellington, for all his life, was exceedingly resistant to formal study. He did not like the self-discipline it involved, and he liked even less having anyone tell him what to do. He got out of the lessons with Mrs. Clinkscales as soon as possible and never did particularly well in school; when he finally did become interested in music, instead of asking his parents for piano lessons, as most adolescents do, he managed things in such a way as to avoid the formal student-teacher relationship.

Later in life he would be scornful of formal teaching. Edmund Anderson, a friend, once suggested that he go to Juilliard and study formal theory. He replied, "Edmund, if I were to do that I think I'd lose everything else that I have. I would ruin everything."[9] He once discovered that Joya Sherrill, a singer with the band in the 1940s, was studying with a voice coach. "And he went through the ceiling. He said, 'Don't take any voice lessons. I don't want you to do that. . . . You have a natural style . . . and it will just destroy what you're doing naturally.' "[10]

Ellington, as will become clear, put a great deal of stock in letting the "natural" musical impulses of his musicians flow, even to the point of encouraging them to get drunk if necessary to do it, and this feeling unquestionably colored his attitude toward formal study. But there was more to it than that. He simply did not like to put himself beneath anyone else. "[Duke] would never ask you to show him something," Sonny Greer said. "No, his pride wouldn't allow that."[11] Mercer, who spoke frequently of how scornful Ellington could be about formal study, said, "The greater part of his knowledge was self-taught, by ear, and gradually acquired later by reading and application."[12] This was the hard way of doing it, but it was the way Duke preferred, even if it would take more time and cost him more energy.

One reason why he never worked harder than he did at his music was that, at this point, he saw music primarily as a way into the spirit of the new age—the high life, to put no fine point on it. Ellington was, in later life, taken to be somewhat more intellectually sophisticated than he actually was, and sometimes statements that he made about himself were considered ironic when, in fact, he meant them to be taken at face value. This is true of his remark that a lot of his interest in learning how to play the piano arose from his perception that women are attracted to piano players, something Mercer corroborated when he said, "I think that what put him into show business in the first place, more than anything else, was that it was a good way to get a girl to sit beside you and admire you as you played the piano."[13] As we shall see later on, when he had his own orchestra in New York, he was slow to do anything significant with his music, beyond what he had to do to keep the job. There is little in any of his memories of his youth to suggest that music as such meant a great deal to him; it was mainly a ticket to other goals. Many of the young people of Duke's generation who made careers in jazz were drawn—indeed, driven—to it by an intense feeling for the music itself, and to them the high life it was imbedded in was merely adjunctive: Bix Beiderbecke, Louis Armstrong, Fats Waller. For Duke music was simply part of the good times.

A consequence of this was that he tended to look for short-cuts, for ways to make an impression, to get by without having to put himself out a great deal. He said, "When I found that something I wanted to do was a little too difficult for the yearling that I was then, I would cop-out with something appropriate to my limitations. Naturally and eventually, sooner than I expected, I found my own musical self breaking through with fitting substitutions, some of which were good enough to attract the attention of my superiors."[14] The statement is a little bit disingenuous; at bottom it means simply that Duke was finding ways to slide by that sounded to the lay audience a good deal better than they would to professionals. In particular, Ellington seems never to have truly mastered the stride left hand that was the essence of the jazz piano style in the early days. For the beginner the principal difficulty in learning how to play stride is keeping both hands doing quite different things at once—the old rubbing-your-head-and-patting-your-belly-at-once trick. Although Ellington did develop a semblance of skill at it and did use the standard stride bass often in his playing later on, he more frequently avoided it, sticking with a simpler "comping" style, which requires less two-hand coordination. I do not wish to exaggerate Ellington's technical weaknesses as a pianist, but they were there nonetheless. Edmund Anderson, in all innocence, once handed Duke the sheet music to "My Funny Valentine" and was startled to discover that he had trouble reading it. Juan Tizol, for years a trombonist with the Ellington orchestra and one of the best-trained musicians Ellington ever employed, said, "You couldn't give Duke a piano part [score] and say, 'Play this piano part'; he was not that type of player. He couldn't play it. He played his own stuff because there was no part to it. But Duke Ellington wasn't a man where somebody could give him a piano part and say play that—no he couldn't do that."[15] Claude Hopkins, one of the youths of the black social circles Duke moved in (his father was a professor at Howard University, and Claude was conservatory trained), said, "Duke used to be one of the guys around then. We were friends all our lives. At first he wasn't too good—he was a very bad reader. But as time went on he developed of course."[16] Ellington himself said, "I could never catch on to what anyone else played so I developed my own stuff."[17]

This was another of those comments taken as clever irony, as Duke perhaps hoped it would be; but there was a substantial amount of truth in it. We can see even this early the effect of Duke Ellington's character on the way his music could go; for a variety of reasons, mostly having to do with his temperament, he was unwilling to do the hard work needed to acquire a sound piano technique. The lack of skill then forced him to invent, improvise, find ingenious solutions to problems, and it drove him early into a creativity a trained pianist, who could play off sheet music with ease, was not forced into. There was, of course, a little of the flimflam about all of this: Ellington, as we shall see, liked outslicking people. Mercer once said, "My father had great respect for people who might be classified as 'carney men.'" But even though Duke was to an extent putting one over on his listeners, he was also learning to put music together on instinct and his own ear.

Despite his shortcomings as a pianist, by the time he was seventeen or so Duke had become part of the black society of the period, going to dances and parties, playing when he could, and hanging around cabarets like the Poodle Dog, Jack's on Seventh, Mrs. Dyers' on R, "where all the society kids went,"[18] and the Ottaway House, many of them located in the S.W. area that was considered the "hot" place by Duke's group. He had acquired from his admired father the gentleman's deportment, dress, and florid style of speech that he continued to employ for the rest of his life. He also, at some point, picked up his nickname. He himself offered several versions of the story; but given his elegant style of presenting himself and his regal manner, "Duke" must have seemed obvious to his school fellows. "Duke" would be the name the world knew him by, and people around him, like the musicians, tended to call him that. His family and a few others called him Edward. Some of the longtime members of the band developed their own special names for him. Cootie Williams sometimes called him Dumpy— Duke was quite heavy at periods during the 1920s and 1930s. Others called him Piano Red or Sandhead, from the tinge to his hair caused by a hair straightener he used at one time. But "Duke" fit, and it stuck.

At some point, probably when he was at least sixteen, a few of the older pianists began sending him out to substitute for them on jobs they could not or would not handle. He was, by his own admission, not really qualified to play many of these jobs, but he was bold and he managed to skip and slide by. "I only knew three or four numbers. I played them slow, fast, medium."[19] He told a story of earning seventy-five cents for his first job and racing home to wake up his family and tell them about it.

He was also, during this period, working at various odd jobs to earn spending money: as a delivery boy, soda jerk, and, during the war, a messenger boy at the Navy Department. More important, he was studying commercial art at Armstrong Tech and showed some talent for it. He seems, at this stage, to have had a greater natural gift for painting and drawing than for music. He used his skills to pick up change by lettering signs and eventually painting backdrops for shows at the Howard Theatre. His interest in art would prove significant, for one of his greatest strengths as a composer was as a colorist: it was his "tone palette" that the early critics singled out for comment first.

Working out the details of the beginning stages of Ellington's musical career is extremely difficult. The dozens of partial accounts of them that Duke gave to various interviewers over his life conflict wildly, but they generally agree that they focused on a place called True Reformer's Hall, a meeting hall of some kind in the N.W. area. When Duke was near the end of high school he probably began rehearsing in Room 10 of True Reformer's Hall with a cadre of students roughly his own age. At the center of the group were the three Miller brothers, whose father taught music at Armstrong Tech and had got from him some training: Bill, who played saxophone and guitar; Felix, saxophone and drums; and Brother, or "Devil," who also played drums. In the group, too, were William Escoffery, guitar; Lloyd Stewart, drums; Sterling Conaway, banjo; Ted Nickerson, trombone; and a few others. The band that emerged out of this group was built around the Millers and included Duke. There is no indication that Duke was the leader; Bill Miller appears to have been the strongest of them musically, but decisions were probably made mutually. The group personnel shifted considerably from job to job, undoubtedly depending on who happened to be available.

We also cannot be entirely sure of what kind of music these teenagers were playing, but it is safe to assume that it was not jazz, which would not have been known to them until after the success of the Original Dixieland Jazz Band records in 1917. It was, almost certainly, popular tunes, often built around raggy syncopations, played for dancing by one or two horns, at times harmonized, supported by a rhythm section. The instruments would solo in turn, playing the melody more or less as written; there would be little improvisation. It would all have been jerry-built, rough-and-ready music.

Duke was by no means committed to a career in music at this point. It was all just fun, girls, and a source of spending money. Sometime during his senior year he won a poster contest sponsored by the National Association for the Advancement of Colored People. The prize was a scholarship to Pratt Institute in New York, an important art school that emphasized commercial art. How seriously Duke considered it we do not know, but events intervened. For one thing, he failed to graduate from high school on schedule in 1917. According to one source he "came within one French course of graduating." (Years later the school awarded him an honorary diploma.)

For a second matter, about 1917 he became involved with Edna Thompson, a neighbor and schoolmate. Edna was born on Ward Place, across the street from where Duke lived the first years of his life. She said she was Duke's playmate as a schoolchild and his classmate all the way through school, although Mercer says she went to Dunbar, a more classically oriented school than Armstrong. She claimed that she helped him learn how to read music when they were both in high school and that there they fell in love.[20] Whatever the case, in the summer of 1918 Edna became pregnant. They were married on July 2, 1918, and their son, Mercer, was born on March 11, 1919.

Duke now had a family to support. In partnership with Ewell Conaway, brother of the banjoist Sterling Conaway, he opened a small sign-painting business, turning out advertising posters for dances and whatever else anyone required. He continued to work as a musician as much as possible. At some point during this period he was sent on a job by one of the professional pianists he knew, Louis Thomas. It was a simple cocktail party or reception, and he would play only background music to conversation. Thomas told him to collect a hundred dollars for the job, keep ten for himself, and bring the rest to Thomas. Duke was astonished at these sums. He was aware that the big-band booking organizations, like Meyer Davis, took large ads in the yellow pages of the telephone book. The next morning, he always claimed, he took a similar ad for himself and, thereafter, was able to work continually, often sending out several bands on a single night.

He was beginning to do quite well financially for a young man, and he took a house at 2728 Sherman Avenue and moved the little family in. He could afford a car, and in 1919 Edna became pregnant again. This child, unfortunately, died in infancy. "It was too close to the first," Edna said. "We were very young then. Kids, really. I think we both thought Mercer was a toy."[21] Given all this, it would have been difficult for Duke to take up the Pratt scholarship.

But there was another, more significant current driving Duke Ellington into music. For intelligent and gifted blacks most routes into the professions were closed. One of the few ways to make money and fame was through show business and, in particular, through music. I will discuss the rise of black show business more fully later on. For the moment, I will say only that the dance boom produced a strong demand for musicians, so much so that anybody who could play at all was likely to find jobs. Boyd Bennett, a musician who was working during this period, said, "There weren't enough good readers around so a lot of people came into the business who played by ear."[22] Dance musicians were seen then less as professionals than as servants to be lumped together with waiters in restaurants and cabarets. Blacks were acceptable, and the effect, for a period, was to make dance music almost a black specialty, like Pullman portering. Tom Whaley, later a copyist for Ellington, said, "Well, you see, up till the first World War there was nothing but black musicians. White musicians didn't have a chance."[23] By 1919, whites were moving into the business wholesale, but blacks were still acceptable and, in some cases, preferred. The leading dance band in New York while Duke was in high school was a black band run by James Reese Europe, and other black leaders, including Tim Brymn, Will Vodery, and Ford Dabney, were in demand for dancing and in theater pits.

The consequence was that Ellington had little choice but to pursue a career in music once he had established himself in the business. He was hardly alone: jazz, in the early days, was filled with intelligent and educated blacks like Claude Hopkins, Don Redman, and Fletcher Henderson, some of them with college degrees, who had drifted into dance music because there was no room outside of day labor for them elsewhere. Duke Ellington did not have a high school diploma, much less a college degree. Music was virtually his only choice.

3

New York

One of Duke Ellington's greatest strengths as a composer, as I have pointed out, was his use of a rich "tone palette." His compositions are continually alive with shifts of color—now the soft azure of an alto saxophone, next the red slashes of a growling trumpet, then the burgundy of the baritone saxophone. Nor was it merely a matter of playing with the natural sound differences of the instruments of the orchestra: Ellington was very conscious of the different sound each of his instrumentalists got, and he would call for not just a trumpet at a given point but a specific trumpet player whose particular sound he wanted then. As a consequence, in order to understand how Ellington worked, we must know about the palette he had at his command.

Some of the players who produced it began to drift into his life haphazardly during his apprenticeship as a piano player. The first of these was Otto Hardwick. Hardwick insisted on pronouncing his name "Oh-toe," from which his friends eventually derived the nickname "Toby," by which he was invariably known. Toby lived in the same neighborhood as Duke and apparently attended some of the same schools Duke did. His father and J.E. were friends; as a result, Toby was, in a sense, family. He was, however, five years younger than Duke, and they cannot have had much of a relationship in boyhood.

Around the age of fourteen, when Ellington was rehearsing with the Miller brothers and others, and trying to break into the music business, Toby took up the string bass and began playing it at sessions at True Reformer's Hall. It was a heavy instrument for a boy to carry—his father reportedly often had to carry it for him to the hall—and he soon switched to C-melody saxophone and, eventually, the alto, possibly at the suggestion of Elling-ton. Quickly he became good enough to work now and then with the float-ing cadre of musicians around Ellington and the Millers, who were working jobs in Washington.

He could not at that point have been much more than an apprentice, able to play by ear the popular melodies of the time, more or less straight. He would, however, go on to be an important member of the Ellington band, especially in the early years, when the group was forming its musical style. He was never a great jazz improviser: a few rare, hot solos made in the 1940s, when he had been playing for some twenty-five years, show him to have been rhythmically stiff and unimaginative. But Hardwick possessed a rather pure tone devoid of the fullness and touches of harshness typical of jazz saxophonists; and he generally played a smooth, legato style. His manner contrasted considerably with that of other saxophonists in the El-lington band, and it was just what Ellington wanted in certain cases, espe-cially for the expression of the sweetish, wistful melodies Duke was fond of.

Hardwick, furthermore, contributed a lot of melody to the Ellington book. He was one of a group of "bad boys" who studded the band from beginning to end, fey and unreliable, the sort of boyish personality women liked to mother. Toby admitted as much: "I was never a serious money-making man. I preferred just being Toby."[1] Just being Toby frequently meant being absent from the band on a tear for three or four days at a time. Barney Bigard, who came into the band after Hardwick, once fol-lowed Toby around one night to see where he went. "All that man did was go from apartment to apartment, friends to more friends, girls to more girls. And at each place he'd go to drinking something."[2] According to Bigard, Toby dragged some of the other bad boys down with him and was a continual nail in Ellington's shoe. But all of that would come later.

A second musician who joined the group at True Reformer's Hall and went on to play an important role in later Ellington bands was Arthur Whetsol. Whetsol was quite a different piece of business from Hardwick. He was born in Punta Gorda, Florida, the son of a Seventh Day Adventist of Mexican descent. According to John Chilton, his original surname was Schiefe, but he adopted his mother's maiden name. He grew up in Wash-ington, the very model of propriety in most respects—in part, no doubt, be-cause of his religious background. He adopted the attitude common to many blacks of his time that they must earn the respect of white society by behaving honorably and with dignity. He was, as a result, a serious young man, scrupulous about his deportment and his use of English. Not surprisingly, he went to Howard University as a premedical student. He did not really intend to make music a career, but it was undoubtedly a way for him to help pay his college bills. Characteristically, he went about music in the correct manner, becoming one of the few good readers in the early Ellington band and developing a pure, accurate, almost dainty tone, analogous to what Hardwick was getting on the saxophone. He would not do much jazz soloing with the Ellington band, but when, in the absence of the principal jazz trumpeter, he had to play jazz solos, he proved to be a more than competent jazz musician, if a little rhythmically stiff. On occasion he even managed the growl and plunger style creditably. Ellington liked Whetsol's plaintive sound, which he said drew from audiences "great big ol' tears," and he used Whetsol frequently to expose the same sort of rueful melodies he sometimes gave to Hardwick.

A third addition to the group was the drummer Sonny Greer. He was born William Alexander Greer in Long Branch, New Jersey, in 1902. He was named for his father, who was, according to Greer, a master electrician for the Pennsylvania Railroad, with a gang of men under him. His mother was a modiste. He went to an integrated school, had a paper route, delivered groceries, practiced pool two hours a day, and developed a confident and outgoing personality that frequently allowed him to charm himself into positions his talents might not have gained for him. Nobody in his family was particularly musical—"including me," he said.[3]

He became a drummer almost by accident. The J. Rosamond Johnson Company, a black touring group, led by a successful black songwriter and producer of black musicals, came through Long Branch. The show's drummer, Eugene "Peggy" Holland, came into the poolroom where Greer hung out and played with him for the next several days. He was impressed by Greer's skill and offered to teach him to play the drums in exchange for instruction in pool. On the strength of these few lessons Greer joined the high school marching band and this way came into music. By the time he was in his late teens, he was gigging around Asbury Park with an integrated band in which he was the only black and rehearsing in New York with the famous Clef Club orchestra. He met Sterling and Ewell Conaway in Asbury Park, and they suggested he pay a visit to Washington, D.C. He went for three days and stayed for several years, because he found plenty of work there. He was, inevitably, drawn to Frank Holliday's poolroom, and he was playing pool there one day when somebody rushed in from the Howard Theatre next door and asked if there were any drummers in the house: the drummer with the Howard band had fled precipitously from an alimony subpoena. Greer grabbed the job and became the house drummer, doubling at the Dreamland Cafe with Claude Hopkins and the trombonist Harry White, who would later on be in the Ellington band briefly. The Dreamland Cafe, another local hot spot frequented by bootleggers and gamblers, had ten waitresses who sang the blues. Thus Sonny became part of the musical life of the city.

Such, in any case, is Sonny's story, filtered out of a number of interviews. Greer was, all of his life, as much a showman as a musician. Few critics have rated him one of the top jazz drummers of his day. But, in the early period, when records were strictly a side matter to musicians, the success or failure of a band depended on how audiences reacted to them in cabarets, dance halls, and theaters. Orchestras were part of a show, and visual effects were important. Sonny Greer had energy and confidence. He eventually acquired very showy equipment, which included huge gongs, bells, exotic temple blocks, and even at times kettledrums. He would do flashy routines with his sticks. He sang as well—for a time he was the band's principal vocalist—and, from the point of view of showmanship, he would in the early days be the most important member of the band. He was also generally thought to be an excellent drummer when accompanying show dancers, something the band would be called upon to do frequently, accenting along with them and firing them off with cracks and bangs.

Unfortunately, Sonny was another of the bad boys in the band. His particular problem was liquor, and many stories have been told of his falling with a crash among his drums. Once, in Los Angeles, Dusty Fletcher was on the bill and going through his hit routine, "Open the door, Richard," when Sonny went backward off his stool into the chimes. Fletcher fled and announced, "I'm not going back out there."[4] Nobody was able to change Greer. He was simply irrepressible. Years later, Cootie Williams, a star with the band for years who at times felt called upon to straighten out the bad boys, said, "I couldn't do anything with Sonny. No one could do anything with Sonny. . . . I remember an instance over in Europe. He got the DT's and I had to beat the drum."[5]

In 1933, when the Ellington orchestra made a visit to England, Sonny gave the *Melody Maker*, the British musicians' paper, an interview in which he talked about his musical principles. "The bass drum should be felt and not heard," he said, "and it shouldn't ring. The press roll is the 'drummer's daily bread.' " Using brushes, you would beat with one, feather with the other. "The only essential for a potential drummer is, I consider, a flair for 'effect' and a sense of 'rightness' at all times, which will enable him to gauge exactly even such minutiae as the dynamic force with which, say, a particular cymbal beat should be played."[6] The language of the interview was, obviously, dressed up by the *Melody Maker* writer, but, assuming that the content reflects Greer's thinking, we can see that his interest was "effect." Sonny got his first lessons from a show drummer, at a time when there was very little understanding of jazz outside of New Orleans and when the concept "swing" did not yet exist, which helps to explain why he played as he did.

Ellington, apparently, was as close to Greer as he was to anybody, at least in the early days before he began to separate himself from the sidemen. He said Sonny was "the nearest thing I ever had to a brother,"[7] and Greer recalled, "From the moment I was introduced to Duke, I loved him. It was just something about him. He didn't know it but he had it then. I've never seen another man like him. When he walks into a strange room the whole place lights up."[8] He added that Ellington was "like my brother." Duke, as we have seen, liked "carney men," and Greer was all of that—a zesty, sharp-dressing hipster with a line of jive that impressed Ellington. Indeed, Greer was seen by the Washington crowd as a New York sharp, and he whetted their appetites for a visit to the city to the north.

A final addition to the group that would become Ellington's first band was the banjoist Elmer Snowden. Snowden was born and raised in Baltimore. He took up the guitar and banjo when he was young and was working professionally around Baltimore as a teenager. The banjo, contrary to what is widely believed, was not used in the early New Orleans jazz bands. It was one of the few—perhaps the only—jazz instruments developed from an African model, and it was used primarily as an exotic specialty instrument in minstrel shows, vaudeville, and the like. By about 1918 it was beginning to be incorporated into dance bands for the novelty effect, and it remained in vogue until about 1930, when the guitar returned to favor for rhythm sections. At the time when the Ellington band was coalescing out of the musicians practicing at True Reformer's Hall, a banjo was essential to any up-to-date orchestra.

Snowden moved to Washington, a short distance from Baltimore, and very quickly established himself as a strong rhythm player. He had, even then, been a professional for several years and was more experienced than any other of the True Reformer's set. He soon replaced Sterling Conaway as the banjoist of choice among them. Conaway did not go on to have a significant career in jazz, but he was a competent enough musician to work in Paris in the 1920s with Eddie South, a conservatory-trained violinist who demanded good musicianship.

The pieces for what would be the first Ellington band were falling into place. These young men were by no means polished musicians, nor were they considered anything but fairly rough apprentices by the older musicians. Most of them read with difficulty, if at all; and even Elmer Snowden, who had been playing professionally for several years, was far from an accomplished pro.

Nor was Ellington the leader. Greer had more show business "personality" than Ellington did, and Snowden was booking a lot of the jobs. Ellington was just one among the group who worked when he could with whatever combinations were being put together at the time.

Nor, once again, were these apprentice musicians playing jazz. Although jazz was rapidly becoming popular, few young players had mastered it before 1920. A lot of the best players were still down in New Orleans, and those who came north were working mainly in Chicago and on the West Coast. It is therefore doubtful that these men had heard much, if any, live jazz. Jazz records, too, were only beginning to come out in quantity, and while they certainly would have been familiar with the Original Dixieland Jazz Band's hits, like "Livery Stable Blues" and "Tiger Rag," they may not have heard much else.

Again, we cannot be sure exactly what kind of music this embryonic Ellington band played. However, the jobs were mainly at dances, in cabarets where they backed singers, and at receptions and dinners where they were to supply quiet, background music. They would have been playing the popular ragtime songs of the day and waltzes for dancing, as well as very simple arrangements of the newest popular tunes. A good deal of the music would have been quite "sweet." The melody would be stated in straight fashion by the horns—Hardwick, Whetsol—either solo or harmonized or, alternatively, both. Piano and banjo solos would be fitted in for variety and to give the horns a rest. The beat would have been raggy but hardly a jazz beat. They were playing, in sum, the peppy, new dance music that hundreds of bands around the United States were playing.

Ellington had, by 1920 and 1921, been playing for money for four or five years, and he had improved. Like hundreds of other young pianists, he had learned James P. Johnson's classic "Carolina Shout" from the piano roll. (The roll caused the keys to go down automatically, and the student could slow the mechanism and follow the movements of the keys that way.) He and his friends spent a great deal of time hanging around places like Holliday's poolroom, the Dreamland, and the Poodle Dog. There they would hear tales of New York, especially Harlem, which hung in front of them like a golden cloud. It was the place, they all knew, where they would eventually have to go.

New York City had become the center of the American entertainment industry. The music publishing business, Tin Pan Alley, had developed there after 1885, and the Broadway theater was setting the pace for shows elsewhere. The new movie industry was still partly in New York.

It will astonish musicians today to realize that so strong was the demand for entertainment during the 1920s that leaders were competing desperately to hire good players. Abel Green, a reporter for the show business newspaper the *New York Clipper*, wrote in 1922, "According to the men who are booking orchestras all over the country there is an acute shortage of Class A dance orchestras at the present time. . . . The craze for dance organizations is just beginning according to indications."[9] Top men were making as much as three hundred dollars a week at a time when a haircut cost fifty cents, and even journeymen musicians could earn a hundred dollars a week.

Perhaps, even more significantly, there was growing, among music fans and especially among those who liked to dance, a feeling that some bands were better for the purpose than others. During the years around World War I the black bands of James Reese Europe and two or three others had developed followings among society people, but, in general, dancers took bands for granted and rarely knew anything more about them than they knew about the waiters in the restaurants they ate in. Bands tended to be pickup groups, thrown together for this job or that one; they did not often have distinctive styles and frequently were not known to dancers by name.

In the early 1920s, though, this began to change. In part this was due to the astonishing success of the Paul Whiteman orchestra after 1920. Whiteman was in the process of developing an enormous celebrity and growing rich, and there followed an increasing tendency for people booking bands for their parties, weddings, and proms to ask for specific bands that they thought would provide more danceable music or play the sort of tunes they wanted to hear. Abel Green said, "But the fact remains that, where in former years they were content to dance to any old tin band, they are usually particular in the sort of music they 'hoof' to."[10] By about 1925, according to Francis "Cork" O'Keefe, a young band booker would become a power in the dance orchestra business, college prom committees were actually demanding this or that star sideman with the group they hired.[11] The basis for the celebrated "name" band was being formed, and it would have consequences for Duke Ellington.

In addition, a strong black entertainment industry had developed as a segment of show business. A few blacks had made livings as entertainers as far back as the eighteenth century, but the tradition of the black entertainer really began after the Civil War, when blacks were free to travel and set up businesses of their own. They began by offering minstrel shows in imitation of the ones white entertainers had been presenting since the 1830s; when the minstrel show gave way to the variety theater in the 1880s, many black dancers, singers, and comics went along with it. By the 1890s black entertainers were an accepted part of show business.

Nor was it just entertainers: by the end of the century black writers and composers were beginning to create full-dress musical comedies for Broadway theaters. These shows frequently included white acts and, perhaps more surprising, played to mixed audiences, with the blacks seated either upstairs or in half of the orchestra seats. Indeed, by 1910 there had grown up a vogue for black shows written and directed by men like Rosamond Johnson, his brother James Weldon Johnson, Will Marion Cook, and Will Vodery, the last two of whom would act as tutors to Duke Ellington.[12] The music for these shows was generally "raggy"—that is, highly syncopated. Precisely what relationship these syncopated songs, as they came to be known, bore to ragtime itself has not been traced, but both forms certainly had their roots in the music of the plantation cabins. Syncopated songs had a considerable vogue around the turn of the century.

Black show business had its ups and downs; according to Thomas Laurence Riis, who has made a careful study of early black musical theater, these black shows at times had trouble getting bookings in the best houses and were forced into second-tier ones, which some refused to play.

Then, in 1921, a musical called *Shuffle Along*, cooked up by the black entrepreneurs Flournoy E. Miller and Aubrey Lyles, with music by Eubie Blake and Noble Sissle, became a smash hit. "Memories of You" came from that show. Josephine Baker was in the chorus, and it skyrocketed Florence Mills, on whose death Ellington would compose a tribute, to fame. The show started a renewed interest in black entertainment that would become a boom by the end of the decade. According to J. A. Jackson, a black columnist who reported regularly on black entertainment for *Billboard*, the show "began the renaissance of the Negro in musical comedy."[13] As early as 1923 Jackson would write, "Things are picking up very perceptibly for the colored group in this industry due to the increase in the numbers of pictures being made in the territory adjacent to New York. Another factor in the matter is that directors are desirous of having naturalness and have just about eliminated the madeup, white actor in the Negro characterizations."[14]

With the success of *Shuffle Along* and the dozens of black shows that followed over the decade, cabaret managers began booking black acts in white locations. By 1923 Florence Mills was the headliner at the Plantation Room on Broadway; in 1924 the jazz dancer Johnny Hudgins was at the Winter Garden; and in 1923, as we shall see, a group of young musicians from Washington would go into the Hollywood, also in the Times Square area.

Surprisingly, at some of these places audiences were mixed. Jackson reported, in regard to the Hudgins Winter Garden show, "A unique feature . . . was . . . that the house had an unusually large professional patronage, many being Negroes."[15]

To be sure, blacks in movies, in cabarets, and on the stage were not playing *Hamlet* or singing lieder, although there had been, in the post–Civil War period, black singers like Sissieretta Jones, who sang classical material. They were supposed, instead, to perform the blues, the jazz dances, and the stereotypical slapstick comedy, replete with references to watermelons, stolen chickens, and razors, that it was assumed they had a natural aptitude for. But at least the doors to careers in entertainment were open to blacks.

There was a converse to this rising black show business: white acts began playing to black audiences, to a degree, at least. A Puerto Rican, Marie Downs, in 1909 opened a small theater in Harlem for the local populace and, in 1915, built on the same site the Lincoln Theatre, where Fats Waller would begin his professional career playing theater organ. By 1924 Downs was booking white acts in the Lincoln. "Once there was a prejudice on the part of white acts against appearing before a Negro audience but that has just about disappeared."[16]

A consequence of all of this was that the entertainment industry became the cutting edge of the integration movement in the United States. Efforts to integrate blacks and whites had been made in America as early as the seventeenth century, but most of these movements were led by educated blacks and whites who, through principle or religious conviction, chose to make a stand on black rights. The integration movement in show business was grass roots, coming about naturally. Contact between performers inevitably led to acquaintanceships, friendships, and, in many cases, sexual affairs. A good many males in show business took affairs with black women, especially light-skinned women, for granted. Frenchy DeMange, one of the gangsters who ran the Cotton Club, had a fairly long affair with one of the chorus girls, who went on to become a famous entertainer. But the movement was not all in one direction: a surprising number of black males in show business had white girlfriends. Dicky Wells, the club owner, not the jazz musician, is reported to have had a whole following of white women.

The impulse to integrate in show business was hardly absolute: many places, especially large hotels, refused to book black entertainers, and many white professionals would not work with blacks if they could avoid it. But it was becoming increasingly hard to avoid: black singers, dancers, and composers were being hired to produce and direct one aspect or another of white producers' shows, which frequently put white entertainers in the position of taking instructions from blacks. Frank Montgomery, a black dancer, choreographed at least two white shows; Will Vodery was Florenz Ziegfeld's musical director from 1911 to 1932; and Leonard Harper worked with several white acts.

Back in Washington, Duke Ellington and his friends were hearing all about this from, among others, Sonny Greer, who claimed to be knowledgeable about what went on in New York and who told the others fanciful tales on that subject. They were all determined to get there. "Harlem," said Duke, "to our minds, did indeed have the world's most glamorous atmosphere. We had to go there."[17]

How the Ellington band eventually made its way to New York is a story that has been told differently by everybody involved. However, if the details are questionable, the general outline of the tale is clear enough. One piecing together goes like this. In the winter of 1922, Wilbur Sweatman, a black clarinetist, appeared at the Howard Theatre with his band. Sweatman was older and had come out of minstrelsy and ragtime and was trying now to convert to the new, hot music just at the moment it was really beginning to burst into wide popularity. His specialty, however, was playing three clarinets at once, and neither he nor his orchestra played jazz.

During the Howard stay he needed a drummer, and Greer, who was in the house band, was asked to join the band and travel with it to New York. Greer demanded that Sweatman take his pals Ellington and Hardwick. Ellington was loath to give up the lucrative work he had in Washington, but the wayward Toby was willing, so Greer and Hardwick left with Sweatman. Sometime later Ellington did join the band, and by March of 1923 all three were working with Sweatman at the Lafayette Theatre in Harlem, the premier black theater in the city.

According to Samuel B. Charters and Leonard Kunstadt, in their excellent survey of jazz in New York,[18] the Sweatman band was due to leave town, and the three young Washingtonians, infected by the glamour of the city, decided to stay and see if they could find work. They failed miserably—Duke jokingly spoke of sharing a hot dog three ways—and their inability to find work in booming times suggests they were still a long way from being accomplished musicians.

But Greer was both personable and fearless about walking up to important people and introducing himself, so they managed to spend a good deal of time in Harlem cabarets cadging drinks and talking to star pianists like Willie "the Lion" Smith, James P. Johnson, and Johnson's protégé, the young Fats Waller. Smith, in particular, was kind to the Washington men and did what he could to help them, which was not much more than buying them drinks and once giving Ellington money for a haircut. "I like you kids," he told them, "you're nice clean kids, and I want you to do well."[19] Smith undoubtedly was referring to the middle-class manners that Ellington and Hardwick, in particular, had grown up with.

Ellington took the Lion for his mentor and, eventually, composed a portrait of him. (Smith, in return, composed a portrait of Ellington.) Willie "the Lion" Smith was a bubbling and outgoing entertainer who liked to shout out comments from the piano as he played and challenged anybody to a musical duel. Unfortunately, he was badly underrecorded; he left no records from this period, and it is hard to say, exactly, what Duke got from him. However, Smith tended to be a somewhat "prettier" player than some of the other stride men, and he used more walking and comping basses than others who employed the ordinary stride pattern most of the time. Both of these tendencies would become characteristic of Ellington's piano style.

But the help that Smith gave the Washington musicians was not enough.

They could not find work, and one day Duke found fifteen dollars in the street and they took the train back to Washington.

Meanwhile, Edna and the baby had apparently moved into J.E.'s house at 1212 T, N.W., where he and Daisy had been living for a year or so. J.E. had not long before managed to get a job as a blueprint maker with the Navy. The new salary allowed him to buy or lease the T Street house and rent out rooms to help with the expense. He and Daisy would stay in the house for another ten years, and it would be Duke's base when he returned to Washington throughout the 1920s. J.E. and Daisy had also produced a second child, Duke's sister, Ruth.

The Washington men had to crawl back home, but they had had a taste of New York and were determined to open a way for themselves there. According to Charters and Kunstadt, Snowden, who married an excellent Washington pianist, Gertie Wells, and did not want to stray too far, got them a job in Atlantic City at a place called the Music Box. They named themselves the Washington Black Sox Orchestra, a name obviously meant to get attention, as some members of the Chicago Black Sox baseball team had been involved in a notorious game-throwing scheme in the 1919 World Series. The band probably consisted of Duke, Snowden, Greer, Hardwick, and Whetsol. The importance of the Atlantic City job was that it helped to shape the band and establish Snowden as at least titular leader.

Back in Washington they ran into Fats Waller, who was working with a touring band backing Clarence Robinson, a vaudevillian, in a burlesque show. He told them that he was bored with the job, that the musicians were going to quit when they reached New York in a week or so, and that perhaps the Washington men could have the jobs. When he returned to New York, however, Waller decided to stay with Robinson, but some of the other musicians quit, and Waller wired Greer and Hardwick to come up. Not long after they went, a second wire came saying that Waller had quit after all and that there was a job for Duke. Ellington got a train, assuming that a job awaited him, and spent the money J.E. had given him on a parlor car and a big dinner in the diner. He arrived broke, only to discover that the job was not going to materialize.

The Washington men were now back where they had been on the first trip. But this time they had some luck. Singing at an important black cabaret called Barron's Exclusive Club was a handsome woman named Ada Smith, who would in a few years become famous as Bricktop, the proprietor of a celebrated Paris nightclub. Smith occasionally played the Oriental Gardens at Ninth and R in Washington, one of the places where the young Washington sports hung out. She had met Duke and some of the others on these trips, and she liked them—once again, no doubt, middle-class manners paid off. When she realized they were stranded in New York, she per-

suaded Barron to let his band go and hire the Washingtonians instead. It
was the break they needed. Barron's was, indeed, as exclusive as it billed itself. According to Bricktop, in her autobiography, only light-skinned blacks
were welcome; men had to wear jackets and ties and women long dresses:
"It was the Harlem spot."[20]

The pay was thirty dollars a week, not high for those flush times, but
they might make an additional twenty dollars in tips each night. Wealthy
people, whom the band referred to as Mr. Gunions, probably because they
had not merely millions or billions but "gunions" of dollars, would change
a twenty-dollar bill into half dollars and fling them onto the floor when
they wanted to show their appreciation of the music. Duke said, "At that
time there were no other organized bands in Harlem. We were only five,
but we had arrangements on everything and it was what we've now named
under-conversation music, kind of soft and gut-bucket."[21] Duke was undoubtedly exaggerating the extent to which the music was arranged. With
only two horns, the "arrangement" would have been a simple routine in
which the two horns occasionally played in harmony and the melody was
passed around the band. Sonny Greer said, "Duke wasn't writing so much
but he would take the popular tunes and twist them and Toby was doubling on C-melody and baritone so we could sound like a big band, soft
and beautiful."[22] In any case, it was clearly not a jamming jazz band but
was playing quiet background music, mostly recent popular songs to match
the elegant tone Barron Wilkins wanted for his club. These young men, we
remember, were mainly out of the black middle class. They had been raised
to comport themselves well at all times, and they had by now come to recognize that being studiously well dressed and well behaved was important
if they were to get certain kinds of work. Ellington took this lesson to
heart. Throughout his life, when he was at home, off-duty so to speak, he
could slop around the house in carpet slippers and a sweater with holes in
it; when he appeared in public, though, he always dressed in something
both elegant and striking. He clung to that almost ritualized tony manner
of speech that he had acquired from J.E. This was in part due to his character, his sense of himself as aristocracy; but it was also contrived, something he had learned was helpful in business.

Meeting the right people was important, then, and among those whom
Duke and the others met was Maceo Pinkard, a black who would write an
endless list of important popular songs, including "Sweet Georgia Brown"
and "Them There Eyes." Pinkard had set himself up in the music publishing business. It was becoming the practice for music publishers to arrange
to have their songs recorded in order to publicize them, and in late July of
1923 Pinkard used the Washingtonians to cut some of his songs for Victor.[23] This was the first Ellington recording, but it was never issued. A cou-

ple of months later Pinkard arranged another session, but this record was not issued either.

The stay at Barron's was exceedingly important to the Washingtonians. The place was not just another Harlem spot. It was frequented by black intellectuals as well as by sports, gamblers, and show business people; and it was seen by these blacks, who felt themselves to be carriers of the spirit of the new age, as a kind of private club where ideas could be exchanged. Its importance is indicated by the fact that, when Barron Wilkins was murdered by a drug addict in midsummer of 1924, a consortium of important Harlemites, which included the pianist Eubie Blake, was put together to reopen it. "It was a great crowd of 'Bohemians' who stormed the place on opening night. Many of the downtown friends of the old place who have not been in Harlem since its closing were on hand for the opening," J. A. Jackson reported.[24] The "downtown friends" were white intellectuals and thrill seekers who had discovered the place somewhat earlier. Barron's would be, for a time, the magnet that first drew whites to Harlem, but when Ellington and his friends were working there it had a largely black clientele. Among them were local celebrities and community leaders, and many of them undoubtedly came to know and like this group of well-mannered youngsters from Washington, a city known to have an elegant and sophisticated black social set.

Duke Ellington now began making himself a citizen of New York. Although he would travel almost continually for the rest of his life, henceforward he would consider New York his home. He always kept at least one apartment there, ran his business from there, and eventually died there. For Duke, especially in the early years, New York had a glamour that existed nowhere else. It was a magical city where anything was possible, where nobody ever went to bed, where governors, senators, and princes of finance mingled with pimps, gamblers, and racket bosses in the nightclubs that feasted off them. Duke was proud to be a part of it. Over the years he would compose many tributes to the city: "I'm Slappin' Seventh Avenue with the Sole of My Shoe," "San Juan Hill," "Main Stem," "Sugar Hill Penthouse," and at least nine pieces with the word "Harlem" in the title, including a whole suite depicting the area. At the very end of his life, when the glamour of the city had grown somewhat torn and fretful, he wrote,

> New York is a dream of a song, a feeling of aliveness, a rush and flow of vitality that pulses like the giant heartbeat of humanity. The whole world revolves around New York, especially my world. Very little happens anywhere unless someone in New York presses a button!
>
> New York is its people, and its people are *the city*. Among its crowds, along its streets, and in its high-piled buildings can be found every

mood, sight, and sound, every custom, thought, and tradition, every color, flavor, religion and culture of the entire earth.[25]

Ellington was like a lot of people who are drawn to New York by tales of its glamour, wealth, power, and sophistication and who, long after they have become wealthy and glamorous themselves, go on feeling proud to be part of it.

For Duke Ellington, in 1923, New York was primarily Harlem. The area had not yet become the tourist draw for whites it would be in a few years, and the tone was still set by blacks. Harlem had been created by real estate developers around the turn of the century in the countryside north of New York City as a quiet enclave for well-to-do white New Yorkers who wished to live apart from the noise and tumult of the great city. A speculative boom in real estate ballooned and burst. In order to save their skins, the real estate speculators began subdividing the handsome houses and renting them to blacks. By 1920 Harlem—smaller in area than it is today—had become primarily a black neighborhood. It was not a slum, although it would be by 1930. It had sunlight, wide streets, and good housing, and was drawing to it black intellectuals, artists, entertainers, entrepreneurs, and ordinary people who wanted to live better than they could elsewhere.

But Harlem was not just a place; it was an attitude, a spirit, as well. The new age, we remember, called for people to be more emotional, open, and expressive. Blacks were seen as already being that, not only by whites but also by black intellectuals. W. E. B. DuBois, perhaps the most influential black thinker America has ever seen, had concluded, as early as 1897, that black and white souls were different. Compared with materialistic whites, blacks were a "specially spiritual people—given especially to music, to colors and language."[26] As a consequence, they could lead whites into the new spirit. At the time when Ellington came to Harlem, black artists, writers, and thinkers were beginning to believe they were at the cutting edge of the new spirit, and there was developing among them an intellectual and artistic ferment that came to be called the Harlem Renaissance.

Duke Ellington was not an intellectual, and he never commented very much on the work of such people as Countee Cullen, Langston Hughes, and others who were part of the Harlem Renaissance or on the spirit it engendered. But living in the midst of it as he did, and working at Barron's among the bright young people of the time, he appears to have soaked up a good deal of its zeitgeist. Ellington, as we shall see in more detail, generally preferred to ignore racial problems. But he was proud of his heritage—proud of being a Negro, as the term was then. Later on he would claim that he was writing not jazz but Negro music, and eventually he would compose a great many serious pieces celebrating his heritage—*Black,*

Brown, and Beige, *The Harlem Suite*, *The Liberian Suite*, *Creole Rhapsody*, *Three Black Kings*, and others. He had, of course, been raised to feel this racial pride, but it was certainly reinforced by the feeling of the black intellectuals of the Harlem Renaissance that blacks ought not to become imitation whites but should cultivate their own, more open and expressive heritage.

4

The Move Downtown

Duke Ellington's involvement with the Harlem Renaissance was peripheral: Ellington was not equipped to enter into intellectual discussions, and, as he always did when he was out of his own water, he kept his mouth shut. He was, anyway, far more interested in what was going on musically around New York.

Action for black musicians had originally been in the old Tenderloin sector in the West Forties and then moved up to the San Juan Hill area, about where Lincoln Center is now. As Harlem became the center for blacks, the music moved up there. Willie "the Lion" Smith, James P. Johnson, Fats Waller, and other pianists were working around the area in small cellar clubs, in the main, and there were various kinds of musical shows at the Lincoln and Lafayette theaters. Ellington took a particular liking to a club run by a man named Mexico, who had acquired the name because he had fought in the Mexican Revolution—on which side is not clear. Mexico's was a cellar club that featured cutting contests among the black musicians attempting to play the new, hot music. Duke said,

> My favorite of all the cuttin' contests were the nights Mexico had the tuba players fighting each other. The joint was small and it had a hard turn as you walked in downstairs. The cats who weren't actually playing all stood out on the sidewalk with their big tubas. It was too dangerous to fight your way through that hall and all those drunks with that big, valuable thing in their arms.[1]

Many of these clubs operated after hours, and Duke spent a lot of time going around to them trying to find out what was going on and learning what he could.

43

Once established at Barron's, Duke brought Edna to New York. Mercer remained for the moment in Washington, to be looked after by his grandparents. Somewhat later, he would come up and spend summers with Duke and Edna. They were living in rented rooms. Because of the high rents in Harlem, almost everybody took in boarders, and most musicians like Ellington lived in spare bedrooms of once-lavish apartments. Duke and Edna stayed in several such places, but the most important was a room rented to him at 2067 Seventh Avenue by Leonard Harper.

Harper was an important figure in New York's black show business. He and his wife, Osceola Blanks, had formed the vaudeville team of Harper and Blanks and had "made a distinct place for themselves in the cabaret field of amusements."[2] Harper quickly went on to choreograph shows and then to produce them for major nightclubs with white audiences, like the Hollywood, the Plantation, and Connie's Inn. Ellington was obviously making a point of meeting people who could be helpful, which Harper proved to be. While the Washingtonians were still at the Barron's, Harper was asked to put together a show that would be called "Harper's Dixie Revue" for a Times Square cabaret named the Hollywood Inn, located at Forty-ninth Street and Broadway.[3] He needed a band, and he chose the Washingtonians. In the first week in September 1923, the Washingtonians moved downtown from Harlem to the heart of New York's entertainment district.

The Hollywood was located in a basement room with a ceiling so low that it was not possible to play a string bass on the bandstand. The place has been described by Willie "the Lion" Smith:

> It was another basement joint like the clubs uptown and the bandstand was under the sidewalk in a corner. The bandsmen had to walk up three stone steps to get on the stand. Their dressing rooms were like "the Black Hole of Calcutta." . . . The stand there at the [Hollywood] only held six men and Duke had to play piano and direct from the dance floor. If you worked up on the deck long enough you wound up with hunched shoulders for good because the stand was about five-and-a-half feet from the glass grill up in the sidewalk.[4]

The club was owned by gangsters and run by a man named Leo Bernstein. According to Sonny Greer, the gangsters loved the song "My Buddy." He would sing it for Bernstein when he was drunk, and "he would cry and want to give the cash register away."[5] The club ran from about eleven o'clock at night until seven in the morning, and there were shows at midnight and two in the morning. The entertainment was not lavish—there was hardly room for anything more than a modest show—but the club had a small chorus line and singers and dancers, including Johnny Hudgins, one of the premier jazz dancers of the period, who would be termed "a great artist" by no less a critic than Edmund Wilson, writing in the New Republic. There was also a corps of B-girls, who doubled as prostitutes.

One important fact about the Hollywood was that, because of its hours and location, it attracted a lot of musicians and show people who were working in the theaters and clubs around Broadway. Bix Beiderbecke, who was playing with the Wolverines on Broadway in 1924, came in; Tommy Dorsey, who was free-lancing around New York, came in; the musicians from the nationally famous bands like the Vincent Lopez orchestra, the California Ramblers, and the Paul Whiteman orchestra came in. The Whiteman orchestra worked frequently at the Palais Royale, an elegant club virtually next door, and Whiteman, already famous, was often in the club, buying drinks and generally throwing money around.

Apparently, there was also a certain amount of racial mixing, for, it appears that here, as at the Winter Garden, black entertainers felt free to come in: Fats Waller, Sidney Bechet, and Willie Smith visited the club from time to time.

The Hollywood Inn was the quintessential New York hot spot of the day, well known to the sharps and sophisticates of the city, a place where big names mingled with gangsters, hustlers, and the lowlife in general. The entertainment was not noticeably polite; there was noise, drinking, and prostitutes, and nearly anything went. The customers at the Hollywood were not naive or prissy. They came determined to have a good time, and they spent money. "The money was flying," Sonny Greer said.[6]

Snowden, Whetsol, Greer, Hardwick, and Ellington had been a team now for perhaps a year and had developed a rather dulcet style of playing that was moving them ahead. But in the four years that the Washingtonians spent at the Hollywood, with a considerable amount of time out for one reason or another, the whole constitution of the band—personnel, music, and management—shifted dramatically: when the Washingtonians left the club for good in the fall of 1927, it was Duke Ellington's band playing Duke Ellington's music.

It is difficult to trace the course of this important shift, which would have such major consequences for American music. Ellington was always very cagey in describing what happened. Many of the principals died long before the history of the band was written, and others had reasons for telling their own versions of the story. In any case, the first change, a critical one, was the replacement of Arthur Whetsol by James Wesley "Bubber" Miley on trumpet. Whetsol had always seen music as secondary to his ambition to become a doctor. That fall he decided to return to Washington to study medicine at Howard University, and a replacement was needed.

Bubber Miley was born in South Carolina but came to New York with his family as a boy. He grew up in the San Juan Hill area at a moment when it was an important black community where a lot of musical activity went on. Statistics developed by Herbert G. Gutman for the area at that period show a disproportionately large number of blacks working as "actors and musicians."[7] Miley's father played guitar, so Bubber gravitated to music naturally. He gigged around New York and then, in 1921, went on the road with Mamie Smith. In the preceding year Smith had made a record called "Crazy Blues," which had become a surprise hit and started the blues boom. She was in the process of growing rich and emerging as one of the stars of black show business. That she chose Miley for her backup group suggests that he was already a fairly accomplished trumpet player.

Miley replaced a man named Johnny Dunn, who was then the most celebrated black trumpet player around New York among those attempting to play the new, hot music. We must remember that these New York musicians were getting their understanding of jazz largely at second hand—as much through the playing of white bands like Whiteman's, the Original Dixieland Jazz Band, and its imitators, especially the Original Memphis Five, which was recording for the black market as Ladd's Black Aces, as through the New Orleans groups that were playing mainly in Chicago and on the West Coast. Dunn was a showman. He played a trumpet designed like a coaching horn to be some five feet in length, and he specialized in "freak" effects. Dunn has been seen as primarily a specialist with the plunger, or "wah-wah," mute, which is generally simply the rubber cup from the end of a plumber's plunger, although many other objects have been used, among them ashtrays, glasses, and the player's free hand. However, for the most part, Dunn played open horn using the plunger only occasionally. At other times he half-valved—that is, played a note or two with the valve depressed only partway to produce a nasal whine, and from time to time he growled on a note, an effect produced by a sort of gargling action deep in the throat.

How much of this Miley took from Dunn and how much he got from other sources is an open question. In particular, Miley had been very impressed by King Oliver, a plunger specialist, at the time the best of the New Orleans jazz cornetists, aside from his protégé, Louis Armstrong. Possibly in the summer of 1922, Miley heard Oliver in Chicago, presumably at a rough, black dance hall called Lincoln Gardens, where Oliver was playing a long engagement. Garvin Bushell, a clarinetist who was with Miley, has said,

It was the first time I'd heard New Orleans jazz to any advantage and I studied them every night for the entire week we were in town. I was very much impressed with their blues and their sound. The trumpets and clarinets in the East had a better "legitimate" quality, but their sound touched you more. It was less cultivated but more expressive of how people felt. Bubber and I sat there with our mouths open.[8]

By the fall of 1923, when the Washingtonians were starting at the Hollywood, Oliver's band had cut a number of records, which we can assume Miley made a point of hearing. It is probable, then, that Miley got his plunger style more from Oliver than from Dunn. More important, although he may already have gotten some sense of what jazz rhythm was all about from other sources, the likelihood is, once again, that he learned a good deal sitting at the fount for that week in Chicago. Johnny Dunn, whatever his virtues, never really developed much of a feel for jazz rhythm. That was something Miley must have found elsewhere. He may, however, have gotten from Dunn the trick of growling from the throat, which was not an Oliver trademark. However he acquired these techniques, he proceeded to combine them to produce an effect that was new and very personal and that would have considerable influence on the jazz playing of his time. This is the critical point: Miley growled a great deal of the time when he was working the plunger mute, which the other two did not, and the result was a much hotter and fiercer fire than either of them produced.

According to Sonny Greer, the Washingtonians first heard Miley at a cellar club in Harlem, where they had gone to hear Willie "the Lion" Smith. They would presumably have known something about him anyway, as he had been traveling with the famous Mamie Smith. He was a slim, round-faced young man with visible gold fillings in his teeth. "He was completely uninhibited," said Toby Hardwick, who was reasonably uninhibited himself. "Nothing at all for him to stop in the middle of a chorus remembering some nonsense, double up in hysterics, nothing coming out of his horn but wind."[9] Louis Metcalf, a trumpeter who was with the band later, said that Bubber "was a wonderful guy, a very happy guy."[10] He was, needless to say, another one of those bad boys the band was filling up with, a heavy drinker and a playboy.

Precisely why the Washingtonians selected Miley is hard to know. He was playing a very hot style that had little in common with the rather polished music they were playing—or attempting to play. That may perhaps have been exactly the point: by 1923 it was clear enough that hot jazz was growing rapidly in popularity and that they ought to get somebody who could play it in the band. A year later, impelled by the same motive, Fletcher Henderson would bring Louis Armstrong into his band, principally to play jazz solos. Tom Thibeau, a white piano player from Chicago, said, "After I got out of school I went on the road with a band—a ten-piece band. We were playing vaudeville houses. We ended up in New York. This was in 1924. And we played the Palace for two weeks. And the reason we did was because we were so different from any other bands around."[11] The trumpeter Doc Cheatham said, "New York was the worst place in the world for jazz in those days. Chicago was the greatest town because of all the Creole and New Orleans musicians who settled there."[12] The New York musicians were beginning to realize they were running behind, and the Washingtonians may have reached for Miley to fill the gap.

Miley, we should keep in mind, had learned what jazz was all about from the New Orleanians, and it was something that Ellington never forgot, because, as he gradually turned the band into his own, he continued to look for players from New Orleans or ones who had been influenced by them.

Miley opened with the band on September 1. Two more additions to the band were John Anderson, who played trumpet and trombone, and Roland Smith, who played saxophone and bassoon, according to a notice in the *New York Clipper*.[13] Little is known about either Anderson or Smith. It is possible that they were brought in because they could read, which the others did very poorly, and could carry the band through the show music they had to play, but that is only conjecture. In any case, neither lasted long with the band.

Miley was the important one, and the Washingtonians were quick to sense what he could do for them. Not only did they find his music exciting themselves, but they saw how effective it was with the gangsters and sports and show business people who came into the Hollywood. The hot style was exactly what these sophisticated people, always on the lookout for something novel, wanted. They decided, then, rather than to mold Miley to their ways, to mold themselves to his. Ellington later said, "Our band changed its character when Bubber came in. He used to growl all night long, playing gutbucket on his horn. That was when we decided to forget all about the sweet music."[14] Bubber Miley thus became the centerpiece of the band. Mercer Ellington said, "The band was motivated around him and everything depended on his being in it, not only because of his solo role but, because of the phrases he knew and because of what his knowledge contributed in the background."[15] Mercer meant by this that Miley not merely contributed the important solos but also came up with figures and whole melody lines that Ellington and the others would add to arrangements or even develop into compositions. It is not too much to say that Miley made the Washingtonians: he was a major factor in creating the style that would make the group famous, and night after night he stirred up audiences so that people would walk out later remembering the band as much as the singers and dancers.

Ellington's role with the Washingtonians during this whole period—from the engagement in Atlantic City through the stay at Barron's and, finally, the first year or so at the Hollywood—is problematic. Snowden was still the ostensible leader. He had signed the contract with the Hollywood management, and for the next few months the group would be listed in the trade press as "Washingtonians, Elmer Snowden, director," or something similar. But Ellington was the pianist in the band, and they would have counted on him to work out harmonies and chord changes on new tunes they were interested in, and he was probably still "twisting" popular tunes around. As always, the arrangements were being worked out by the band together. Duke was not announcing tunes; there was a master of ceremonies at the Hollywood who did that, and, besides, Duke was a long way from being the confident spokesman for the band he would become. Whether he, Snowden, or somebody else was picking tunes and setting tempos we do not know.

Ellington was, however, beginning to write songs. At that period the biggest money in the music business was being made by the composers and publishers of songs, some of whom were becoming rich, primarily through the sales of sheet music. Records were seen only as adjunctive; for the publishers and composers they were a way of publicizing songs in order to generate sheet music sales; for the musicians they meant a few easy dollars to stick in their pockets, and a little boost to the ego. The real money was in song writing, and everybody who had a rudimentary knowledge of music and enough brass was trying to get rich in Tin Pan Alley. It was inevitable that Ellington would try.

In his memoirs he said, "During my first few months in New York, I found out that anybody was eligible to take songs into the music publishers on Broadway. So I joined the parade and teamed up with Joe Trent, a nice guy who was familiar with the routines of the publishing world. He liked my music and he was a good lyricist, so he took my hand and guided me around Broadway." Trent and Ellington very quickly sold a song called "Blind Man's Buff" and a year later two or three more. The Washingtonians eventually recorded some of the songs.

Ellington and Trent continued to work together, sold another song or two, and then, a year or so later, were asked to write a show that was eventually called *Chocolate Kiddies*. According to Duke,[16] Trent one day came around to see him and told him that they had a commission to write a show but that it had to be done that night. The promoter was Jack Robbins, who went on to build one of the biggest music publishing houses in New York, Robbins Music. Trent asked for five hundred dollars in advance, and Robbins pawned his wife's engagement ring to raise the money. Ellington and Trent sat down that night and wrote a show. They played it for Robbins the next morning. Robbins liked it and put it into rehearsal. He never managed to get it staged in New York, but in May of 1925 he took the show to Germany, using Sam Wooding's band. The show opened at the Admiral Palast in Berlin and toured all over Europe and as far as the Soviet Union, where it was billed as a "Negro Operetta."

That, at least, is Duke's story. How much of it is true is unclear. *Chocolate Kiddies* with Sam Wooding did indeed leave New York in May 1925 to make a successful tour of Europe, but what, if anything, Ellington had to do with this show is open to question. I have found no evidence that any of his songs were actually used.

In any case, during these early years Ellington was turning out occasional tunes, some of which the band recorded. They are all pretty bad, but no worse than much of the spillage that was pouring out of Tin Pan Alley. One of these songs, "Rainy Nights," is built around a device that Ellington would use endlessly throughout his working career, so much so that it almost became his private property—a move from the tonic chord to the flat sixth (sometimes interpreted as the Neapolitan sixth of the V chord).

In November, Harper began rehearsing a new show for the Hollywood. The Washingtonians' contract ran to March 1, 1924, and the band would play for the new show. At about the same time there was another important change in personnel. The trombonist John Anderson either quit or was let go and was replaced by Charlie Irvis. Irvis was a friend of Bubber Miley's and a better jazz musician than Anderson. Bubber probably persuaded the other men to make the change. However, Irvis had already appeared on some records and was known around New York.

Irvis was, or at least became, a growl specialist. There are reports—including one from Ellington—that Irvis had learned to growl independently of Miley. Duke said that Irvis had some sort of mute that was supposed to make the trombone sound like the saxophone. He dropped the mute one time, and it broke, but he continued to use the remaining portion of it and in this way developed his particular sound. My opinion, based on the slim evidence of a few early records, is that Irvis learned how to growl from Miley. He had, said Duke, "a great big fat sound at the bottom of the trombone—melodic, masculine, full of tremendous authority."[17] Later, according to Greer, he used a tomato can for a mute, "with the bottom smashed in like a cone."[18]

A month or so after Irvis joined the Washingtonians, a far more significant change took place. The story of how Elmer Snowden left the band and Duke was appointed leader has been told in several ways. Duke, typically, always slid away from the question diplomatically. Essentially, however, Snowden was accused of keeping more than his rightful share of the band's pay. Tom Whaley, a Boston pianist who came to New York later and was eventually copyist and musical factotum for Duke, recalled, "So Sonny, you know how Sonny talks, says [to Leo Bernstein], 'Man, when you going to give us a raise?' And the man said, 'I just raised.' He had raised Elmer, give Elmer the raise, and Elmer didn't give it the guys, so they fired Elmer and Sonny was supposed to take the job. Sonny said, 'No, I don't want the job, give it to Duke.' "[19]

Whaley's information was not firsthand, but other reports agree with the general shape of the story. It was an old situation. Big-name musicians, such as Whiteman, would charge for the band whatever they could get and pay the musicians whatever they felt they had to. However, in more ordinary bands it has always been understood that the employer is paying so much per man, plus something extra for the leader. It is a constant temptation for a leader to collect more for the job than he tells the musicians and to pocket the difference. King Oliver was reported to have done exactly that with the members of his famous Creole Jazz Band; when he was caught at it, the famous band broke up in anger. It would not have been surprising to find Snowden unable to resist the temptation.

In any case, the *Clipper* for February 22, 1924, contains two contradictory notices. The first says, "The Washingtonians, under Elmer Snowden's direction, have renewed their contract at the Hollywood, N.Y., for six months more." (Presumably the contract ran from September 1 to March 1.) The second notice is an advertisement paid for by the band that quotes an earlier review by the *Clipper*'s band reporter, Abel Green: "This colored band is plenty torrid and includes a trumpet player who never need doff his chapeau to any cornetist in the business. . . . Duke Ellington leads from the piano." The personnel is given as Ellington, Miley, Irvis, Hardwick, Greer, and George Francis, banjo and singer. Obviously, the Hollywood's management had given the *Clipper* the story of the new contract; but the signing had brought out into the open the question of salaries, so the band took the advertisement to make that new leadership clear.

Snowden ended his musical career in some bitterness. For a time, during the 1920s, he continued to lead bands around New York with considerable success. After leaving the Washingtonians, he organized a band for the Nest, a Harlem black-and-tan club, which included Jimmy Harrison, Walter Johnson, and Rex Stewart, all to become major figures in jazz. He was back at the newly reopened Barron's that summer and at various places thereafter. In the early 1930s he had a band in a club at 142 West Houston, in Greenwich Village, called the Hot Feet Club, which was an attempt to bring a Harlem club with black entertainment downtown. Snowden had in this band, at one time or another, such important jazz musicians

as Sid Catlett, Dicky Wells, Fats Waller, Roy Eldridge, Al Sears, Way-
man Carver, and the footloose Toby Hardwick.[20] Not long afterward,
though, Snowden fell into a feud with the musicians' union local 802 in
New York, and he was banned from the area. He worked in Philadelphia
for some time thereafter, but he never recovered his place in music, and
later, bypassed by changes in musical fashions, he slid out of sight. Not surprisingly, he was bitter at the enormous success of the band he had originally put together. But, of course, had Snowden remained leader, the
band's history would have been very different.

The job of "leader" of the Washingtonians was little more than nominal. Or, rather, it was whatever anyone wanted to make of it, as is frequently true in such situations. The others probably settled on Ellington
because they admired his manner and respected his authoritative bearing
and because he was more reliable than most of the rest and could be
counted on to tend to such business as needed to be done.

How Ellington viewed the position is hard to know. He could not, at
this stage, really hire and fire: decisions on personnel were still being made
by the band collectively. In fact, some of the men wanted the band to
incorporate, as other bands had done, so that the cooperative nature of
the group would be put on a legal basis. Had this been done, the history of
American music might also have been different, for decisions would have
been made by majority vote, as they were in cooperative bands like Casa
Loma and the Bob Crosby band. But it was not, and now we must look
at another aspect of Ellington's character that was critical to the way his
music was produced.

The Ellington band was always, especially in its heyday, notorious for
its lack of discipline. The men turned up late almost on principle, were
drunk on the stand, frequently rowdy. Year after year, Ellington turned
a blind eye to this behavior on the theory that a disciplined band would
not have the looseness and life that he wanted in the music. As a consequence, it has been widely believed that Ellington was simply an easygoing
fellow who let things fall out as they would.

Nothing could be further from the truth. Duke Ellington was by nature
a man who wanted to dominate in all situations and was generally able to
manage things so that he did. He was careful to make it appear that he
was unconcerned about the chaos that sometimes swirled around him, but
he was always far more in control of the situation than it appeared. Clark
Terry, a trumpet player who was with the band for a long period during
the latter days, said, "For all the seeming looseness of direction, Duke
really runs things and, it seems to me, that his main goal as a leader is
to mold a man so fully into the Ellington way of playing that he finds it
hard to pull away."[21] Mercer Ellington said, "Pop liked to argue and to

win arguments, even if he had to adopt a stand he didn't believe in. This was part of his pleasure in manipulating people."[22] Stanley Dance, who knew Ellington well, said, "He was shrewd. He was very experienced . . . and he was very good at summing up people's characters. . . . He thoroughly enjoyed manipulating people. . . ."[23] Duke's nephew, Michael James, who also traveled with him for a period, said, "The main thing that stands out would be his ability to be in control at all times. He was always in control of his situation."[24] His grandson, Edward Ellington, said, "My grandfather was really a conductor . . . he didn't conduct his orchestra solely. He conducted a lot of people—mainly his family."[25] Toby Hardwick said, "He likes to manipulate. It's a little quirk all his own. He thinks no one has the slightest idea about this. He likes to manipulate people around him and gets the biggest kick when he wins."[26] Russell Procope, another of his long-term musicians, said, "He rules with an iron hand in a mink glove."[27] And Duke Ellington himself said the same. After his death, Mercer found a note in the litter around him in the hospital: "No problem. I'm easy to please. I just want to have everybody in the palm of my hand."[28]

This aspect of Ellington's character, this need to dominate everywhere, was not so pronounced early in his career as it would become later. As a young man, Ellington could hardly command the authority he had as a famous musician later on. But the instinct to rule was surely there; and we are forced to believe that, once the band had been turned over to him, Duke would have begun the process of subtly making it his. He would not, certainly, have attempted to assert an authority based on the rather flimsy leadership he had been given. It would have been done quietly, adroitly, so that the men, without quite knowing how it happened, found that he was setting the direction for the band. And, within two or three years, it was no longer the Washingtonians but the Duke Ellington orchestra.

5

Duke Takes Over

If Ellington was beginning to mold the band to his wishes, he was still not yet ready to control the music. Greer said, "He never thought about writing compositions in the [Hollywood Inn]. We just took stocks and changed them around and made them a little different. . . . We take them songs, popular songs, and make them different."[1] In those days, with so much poor musicianship in hundreds of dance bands staffed by young amateurs, publishers found it necessary to supply leaders with "stock" arrangements of their songs if they were to get them played. Frequently, such bands would "doctor" the stocks to give them a little individuality, by adding introductions, codas, solos, counterfigures, and sometimes whole new choruses. The Washingtonians were following this practice, and it is probable that Ellington, as pianist, was making a good many suggestions for changes to the stocks. It was a first step toward composing.

A band in an important location like the Hollywood would have stocks pressed on them by "song pluggers" whose job was precisely to get band-leaders, especially those with airtime, to play their songs. And by about 1924 the Washingtonians were being broadcast frequently over WHN, a New York station. At that juncture the large networks of radios were only beginning to come into existence; radio was mainly local, although some very powerful stations could be heard over long distances. But radio and the bands were already entering into the symbiotic relationship character-istic of the next two decades. The bands provided radio with an almost endless source of free programming, while radio gave the bands critically important exposure to the general public.

The broadcasts from the Hollywood, or the Kentucky Club, as it would shortly be renamed, were apparently arranged by an aggressive young radio announcer named Ted Husing, who would become a major celebrity in a few years. Husing was a fan of the band, and he persuaded WHN and perhaps WMCA to "put a wire" into the Kentucky Club, from where the band broadcast from time to time. It was only a harbinger of greater things, however, for radio—and Husing—would become crucial to Ellington a few years later.

Sometime around the beginning of April, the Hollywood suffered a fire, which reportedly did $10,000 worth of damage, a substantial sum in those days.[2] This was not merely bad luck. In the days before air-conditioning, a cellar club like the Hollywood became intolerable during a New York summer. Such clubs usually closed from Memorial Day to Labor Day, and, from the viewpoint of the owners, it made good sense to torch the place, so that they could not only collect insurance but also get out of their contracts with their employees. The club had three or four such fires during the time the Washingtonians were there; it reached the point where Leo Bernstein would thoughtfully suggest that the musicians take their instruments home on the night in question.

The Washingtonians were out of work again, and it appeared they might be out of work for some time, because Leonard Harper was now putting together an "elaborate colored revue"[3] with a score written by the great stride pianist James P. Johnson, who would also conduct the orchestra. They were rescued by the Shribman brothers, Charlie and Sy. The Shribmans were enterprising young men from Salem, in the Boston area, who started as newsboys and shoeshine boys. They began booking bands as teenagers and opened a club called College Inn, which they quickly parlayed into a chain, including a billiard saloon and a bowling alley. In the summer of 1924 they opened a ballroom called the Charleshurst, in Salem Willows, a park; eventually, they had control of many of the ballrooms in New England.

The Shribmans liked dance music, and in their careers as ballroom operators they were always known for their fair dealings with musicians. They probably had heard the Ellington band at the Hollywood and, when they discovered that the group was out of work, booked them into Salem Willows for the summer. They would continue to book the Ellington band summer after summer when the New York clubs were closed, and so they became an important source of revenue for Ellington. Duke was always grateful for the Shribmans' support. He said, many years later, that Charlie Shribman "was one of the first people . . . to see the potential in the band."[4]

The James P. Johnson show, in any case, did not last; by October the Washingtonians were back in the club, now called the Kentucky Club.

They also made the first of what would prove to be thousands of records in Ellington's career, which would run for almost fifty years. Seven songs were cut, some of them by Ellington. None of them is of much musical value. I will discuss the records from this period later. They show a very rough band only beginning to grasp the essence of jazz, still playing a version of the syncopated music that black dance bands had been playing for a decade. The phrasing is stiff and jerky; the rhythm clops along like a milk horse. Sonny Greer sings a couple of these numbers in a high, nasal whine, which owed a good deal to Al Jolson. Duke plays acceptable piano, obviously derived from the stride players he had been listening to. There was little that could be called arrangement. The band depends on Toby Hardwick to carry the melody, with either Irvis or Miley, or both, playing awkward figures, undoubtedly of their own invention, behind him. For the rest, the other men would solo in turn as much as necessary to fill out the tune, and then Toby would restate the melody to a conclusion. This was an unsophisticated band playing rough dance music not nearly up to the level of the music of the Fletcher Henderson band, beginning to establish itself as the preeminent black band in New York, and a substantial distance below the music of the top white bands, like Paul Whiteman's, which was putting out slick, carefully arranged dance music that had as much jazz feeling as the Washingtonians had at this stage in their development. They were, in any case, no worse than hundreds of similar bands playing in clubs and making records in the big cities of America at this time.

There were at this time two major changes in personnel. The first of these brought Freddy Guy in on banjo. Guy would stay with the band for almost twenty-five years. He was born in Georgia, but, like many blacks of the period, he migrated north with his family, so Freddy was raised in New York. He was intelligent and, among the hell-raisers that dominated the orchestra, a beacon of sanity and good behavior. He was serious and "was always giving us advice," according to Duke,[5] but Ellington respected him for his behavior, because he was one of the few members of the band he would bring into his home and allow to associate with his family: "Out of the whole aggregation, whole band, Freddy was the sensible one," Barney Bigard said. "He didn't have no wild traits like the musicians, like us. . . . Nice looking guy, a ladies' man."[6]

The most important addition to the band at this time was the great New Orleans jazz pioneer Sidney Bechet, who started as a clarinetist but is primarily known for his work on soprano saxophone. Bechet had grown up in the heartland of jazz, absorbing the blues and the new, hot music through his skin from the time he was a little boy. As a teenager, he worked in the rough honky-tonks of the tough, black Storyville section of

New Orleans, where Louis Armstrong also apprenticed, saturating himself with the blues that the prostitutes at the honky-tonks wanted for the slow drags they used to entice customers.

Bechet was, however, something of a loner, constantly on the move, a prickly personality with an abrasive ego that created friction wherever he went. A fellow New Orleanian, Barney Bigard, said, "[Bechet] can't get along with nobody. He's got a temper."[7] As a consequence of his prickliness and his wandering ways, which took him to Europe for long stays, he did not develop a reputation with the general public until he became something of a folk hero during the New Orleans revival of the 1940s and beyond. He was, though, a man of strong and noble passions and a master jazz musician who, with Armstrong and Jelly Roll Morton, was among the first to truly swing. He never learned to read a note, but he could play the piano, as well as other instruments, and composed some excellent tunes. He liked to play phrases that were musically complete, and, to an extent, he worked out a lot of his solos in advance. Despite this planning, or perhaps because of it, his work was aboil with ideas and ferocious authority. He claimed he had a brief affair with Bessie Smith, and one can only wonder what these two passionate, barely controlled jazz masters talked about in their private moments. Sidney Bechet was the classic New Orleans jazz player, all his life producing music that epitomized that style.

Ellington had heard Bechet first in Washington, presumably at the Howard, in some sort of black vaudeville show—Bechet toured with many such shows playing hot specialties. On this occasion he played "I'm Coming, Virginia." Duke said later, "[It was] the greatest thing I've ever heard in my life. I never heard anything like it. It knocked me out."[8] Ellington was always somewhat chary of praising his musicians, ostensibly because it might cause them to ask for more money, but he was unstinting in his praise of Bechet and responded strongly to Bechet's playing. The explanation for this is simple enough. In 1924 not many musicians outside of New Orleans could really play jazz; musicians from elewhere were still struggling to learn the secret of it. Bechet was, unquestionably, the best jazz musician Ellington had heard to that point—he could not have heard Armstrong until the trumpeter came to New York to play with the Fletcher Henderson band in the fall of 1924.

Precisely how Bechet came to join the Washingtonians is not clear. However, he had been working at the Kentucky Club with the show James P. Johnson had written and been fired by Johnson, undoubtedly for some kind of fractiousness; presumably the Washingtonians simply swept him up, probably as they were leaving for the summer stint at Salem Willows. Sonny Greer offered this version of the encounter: "Sidney Bechet came in one night and pulled out his soprano. Right away he, Bubber, and

Charlie Irvis got to jamming against each other. It was wonderful. So then we hired him and he played with the Washingtonians, clarinet and soprano."[9] However it happened, Bechet had a substantial impact on the Washingtonians, especially in leading them out of the rhythmic woods they were lost in and into the broad pastures of jazz. Ellington left no doubt of his feelings:

> Bechet. The greatest of all the originators, Bechet, symbol of jazz. . . . He had a wonderful clarinet tone—all wood, a sound you don't hear anymore. The New Orleans guys absorbed something down there along with the Albert system. I consider Bechet the foundation. His things were all soul, all from the inside. It was very, very difficult to find anyone who could really keep up with him. He'd get something organized in his mind while someone else was playing and then he'd play one or two choruses—or more—that would be just too much.[10]

Elsewhere Ellington said,

> Bubber Miley and Bechet used to have a cutting contest nightly, and that was a kick. They would play five or six choruses at a time, and while one was playing the other would be backstage taking a nip. They were two very colorful gladiators. Often, when Bechet was blowing, he would say, "I'm going to call Goola this time!" Goola was his dog, a big German shepherd. Goola wasn't always there, but he was calling him anyway with a kind of throaty growl.
>   *Call* was very important in that kind of music. Today, the music has grown up and become quite scholastic, but this was *au naturel*, close to the primitive, where people send messages in what they play, calling somebody, or making facts and emotions known. Painting a picture, or having a story to go with what you were going to play, was of vital importance in those days. The audience didn't know anything about it, but the cats in the band did.[11]

Step by step, the Washingtonians, like so many jazz players of the period, were absorbing the influence of the New Orleans players. First had been Miley, who had sat at the feet of King Oliver. Then it was Bechet, with his engulfing sense of swing. After him would come a host of players who were either New Orleanians, like Barney Bigard and Wellman Braud, or had taken New Orleanians for models, like Johnny Hodges, Cootie Williams, Rex Stewart, and others. With the model of the New Orleans players before them, the Washingtonians, in the years at the Kentucky Club, were becoming a jazz band. It did not happen overnight—a feeling for jazz rhythm always takes time to develop. But the process was under way, and Bechet was a critical force behind it.

How long Bechet was with the band and exactly when is difficult to know. It was probably mainly through the summer of 1924, for Bechet was not on any of the records the band made that fall, as he would have been had he stayed. Barney Bigard said, "Maybe Duke would have kept Sidney in the band but he was always too hard to handle."[12] Bechet himself said that he left because of feuds with Bubber Miley and Charlie Irvis, but, since those two got along with everybody else, we have to suppose that Bechet's touchy ego was the problem and that he was not fired, but quit.

For the next two years the Washingtonians would be in and out of the Kentucky Club erratically, as it suited the whims of the gangsters, and the by now traditional springtime fires. There are reports of the band playing at various other clubs in the city from time to time—the Plantation, the Cameo, the Flamingo—but these reports are hard to confirm. It is clear, however, the Washingtonians did not have much control over where and when they worked; the gangsters were rapidly gaining substantial control of the city's nightlife, and it was difficult to get out from under their knuckles. The Fletcher Henderson band—of which in 1926 a band magazine called *Orchestra World* said, "There is no better dance orchestra than Fletcher's, white or colored"[13]—had grown so prominent that it was able to stay clear of the gangsters, but the Washingtonians were not yet that well known. (By contrast, Sonny Greer said later, "I keep hearing how bad the gangsters were. All I can say is that I wish I were still working for them. Their word was all you needed."[14])

The Washingtonians were, however, getting better known. For one thing, by 1927 they had been broadcasting regularly from the Kentucky Club for two or three years and were developing an audience. Furthermore, they were beginning to be mentioned in the trade press. Abel Green was keeping track of them in his *New York Clipper* columns; *Orchestra World* had taken to including them in its regular listing of America's best bands; and there were occasional mentions elsewhere. The most important story about them was a long piece in the *New York Tribune* that discussed the development of the group, one of the first pieces of jazz history ever written. "Musicians from every corner of New York would flock to the Hollywood Inn and sit until daylight," the article said, referring to the period of a few years earlier. It went on to point to "the remarkable rise of a musical organization that, within the past two months, has set the entire New England states dance crazy."[15] And it billed Duke as "owner, leader, and pianist" of the group.

There were by now further changes in personnel. Sometime in the spring or summer of 1925, Henry "Bass" Edwards was added on tuba. Edwards, who grew up in Georgia, was a well-schooled musician who had worked in Tim Brymn's celebrated 350th Artillery band during World War I, and had gone on to work in New York with top black bands, including the legendary Charlie Johnson band, with which he was playing when he came to the Kentucky Club. Edwards could reportedly play four octaves, a considerable feat on the tuba. He was, essentially, too good for the rough-and-ready Washingtonians, and he went to another band in the spring of 1926. He was replaced by Mack Shaw, who, according to Ellington, had had his face broken up by gangsters and occasionally as he played would spit out a piece of bone that had come loose: "He had a whole lot of loose bones in his face and he'd just put them together again and keep blowing."[16] Finally, in the middle of 1927, Wellman Braud, who would be the band's bassist until 1935, replaced Shaw. Braud played string bass as well as tuba, and his use of the bass, which was beginning to replace the tuba entirely in jazz bands, helped make the rhythm section swing a little more. Braud (a Creole name, pronounced "bro") was a New Orleanian who had worked with many of the pioneer jazz players there and in Chicago. He could not read, but he had a fine ear and, thanks to his New Orleans background, knew how the new, hot music ought to be played.

A far more significant addition was the trombonist Joe Nanton, almost always called Tricky Sam, for his plunger and growl effects. Nanton's parents had been born in the West Indies, and because of this he was seen as being a little different by the other band members. "He was an original in every way," said Ray Nance, who was in the band much later.[17] He had a high voice and could be comical but was basically somewhat shy. He was one of the band's heavy drinkers. He was a friend of Charlie Irvis; when he replaced Irvis on trombone, he also replaced Irvis as Bubber Miley's running mate. According to Duke, Tricky had been using mutes before, but most of what he knew about the plunger style he learned from Miley. Instead of manipulating the plunger mute over the open bell, he first placed a small "pixie" trumpet mute deep inside the bell and worked the plunger over that. This system eventually came to be widespread, not merely because of what it did to the sound but also because it made it a lot easier to keep the instrument in tune while opening and closing the plunger. For technical reasons, having to do with the principle of the closed-end pipe, brass instruments tend to go flat when the mute is introduced into the bell, forcing the player to retune or compensate with the lip. A plunger mute that is regularly opening and closing the bell requires constant adjustment of the lips to compensate for the steady alterations of pitch. However, with a small mute placed under the plunger, the "pipe" is already closed in a consistent fashion, and the effect on pitch of the plunger's movements is reduced.

Miley and Irvis had already formed a team of growlers, but Nanton was to make the method a specialty, employing it in his solos almost to the exclusion of open playing. As the so-called jungle sound became the band's trademark, Nanton's voice, more than any other, became its identifying sound. When you heard Nanton, you never had any doubt what band you were listening to, and, after Nanton died in 1946, Duke always found men who could come close to the Nanton sound. But none of them ever really duplicated it exactly. Nanton was, as Nance said, an original in every way.

A more temporary arrival, if useful for the moment, was the trumpeter Louis Metcalf, who was born in 1905 and grew up in St. Louis. Metcalf worked on the Streckfus riverboats, which at that time had a St. Louis and a New Orleans band on each boat. He had thus had at least some experience of New Orleans jazz quite early in his career. He toured with a popular show, Jimmy Cooper's Black and White Revue, for a number of years and eventually landed in New York. He was by then a thorough professional, a good reader who could "execute"—that is, play difficult passages that might elude some of the more homespun players who filled the ranks of jazz then. He worked in a club with Bechet, Hodges, Willie "the Lion" Smith, and Tom Benford, all topnotch players, and got some exposure to the New Orleans sound. By the mid-1920s he was in demand around New York, especially for recordings; according to Leonard Kunstadt, he may have appeared over the decade on some two hundred sides not listed in discographies.

Metcalf came into the orchestra in the fall of 1926, in part because of his ability to read the stock arrangements that were a staple of the band's repertory and in part as protection against Miley's unreliability. Metcalf stayed with the band into the spring of 1928 and left when Arthur Whetsol returned. Whether Metcalf was pushed out or quit is not known. He was considered something of a prima donna by the other men, but he probably could have made a good deal more money free-lancing than playing with what was by now the Duke Ellington orchestra. In any case, he looked back on the experience with fondness. It was "wonderful" working for Duke, he said. "I learned how to lead a band from Duke."[18]

Another man who did not last long with the band, for reasons we shall learn, was Rudy Jackson. A Chicagoan, Jackson had worked with King Oliver and had picked up some of the New Orleans feeling that Duke so admired. He toured with various shows and joined the Ellington orchestra in June 1927. Jackson was, like Metcalf, a competent professional, and it is clear that Duke was at this point attempting to beef up the band with good professionals who could read and play jazz if necessary. Jackson has never been considered a major jazz improviser, but at the time he was regarded as one of the top black professional saxophone players in dance music.

Jackson was probably taken on to fill out the band for the customary tour of New England for Charlie Shribman. By 1927 a solid saxophone section was coming to be seen as the heart, almost the sine qua non, of a modern dance band. Stock arrangements were generally worked out so they could be played by almost any combination of instruments, in very small groups if necessary; but they inevitably sounded far better when played by a band with a saxophone choir at its center. Until this point the Washingtonians had rarely had more than two saxophones and frequently worked with only one. But, from the summer of 1927 on, the band would always carry three or more saxophones.

The third saxophonist was a man who would stay with Ellington without a break until Duke died, some forty-seven years later. He was Harry Carney, a Bostonian. Carney's father was interested in music, at least to the extent of singing spirituals around the house, and Carney studied piano for a while as a boy. He was eventually attracted to the clarinet, which he played in a marching band. Finally, at about fourteen, he took up the alto saxophone. He lived just down the street from Johnny Hodges, a few years older than Carney, who would come into the Ellington band not long after Carney did. He and Hodges listened to records and practiced together, along with a third friend, Charlie Holmes, who would become one of the premier alto saxophonists of the Swing Era. Hodges was heavily under the influence of Bechet, and Carney picked up some of the Bechet influence indirectly from Johnny. Once again, the pervasive New Orleans style would creep into the band.

Like many of the Boston men, Carney was eager to visit New York. He made the trip, picked up a few gigs at the Savoy, and then, through Hodges's intercession, got a job at a place called the Bamboo Inn. This club burned down a few months later, and Duke, then getting ready for the New England trip, offered Carney a job to bring the saxophone section to three. Carney was basically an alto saxophonist who doubled on clarinet, but Rudy Jackson was the hot clarinet soloist and Toby Hardwick played alto. Carney took up the baritone saxophone, eventually becoming the leading jazz player on the instrument. He continued to play clarinet from time to time and, eventually, bass clarinet as well. But the baritone was his main instrument. With it, he anchored the saxophone section through most of the life of the band, providing a good deal of its swing. Never a highly imaginative soloist, he was nonetheless a hard swinger, influenced by the tenor saxophonist Coleman Hawkins and by the bass saxophonist Adrian Rollini, in 1927 one of the best saxophonists in jazz.

Not only was Carney a fine and reliable musician, but he was a reliable person as well. Quiet, rather low-key, he became a resource for Duke. In the latter days, Carney would start the band going for the first set, until Duke made his entrance, and direct it from his chair. He also became Duke's driver, taking Duke from one job to the next, so as to free Duke's mind, during the long nighttime rides, to work on music. (Ellington, who was considered a good, if reckless, driver, had apparently either given up his driver's license or had it taken away at some point. He always left the driving to somebody else but prided himself on his ability to "navigate" anywhere.)

The band, by the end of the Kentucky Club stay, had changed a good deal. But, of all the changes, the most important was an association with a dapper little music publisher named Irving Mills.

6

Enter Irving Mills

In the Victorian Age, when the entertainment industry was still relatively small, show business professionals were viewed by the majority of Americans as only a notch above hustlers, gamblers, pimps, and prostitutes. Decent people did not associate with singers, dancers, or actors; indeed, a good many of them would not even patronize the vaudeville theaters where show people worked.

It is not hard to understand how this attitude developed. Show people did not really appear to work; they traveled in groups of mixed sex, which no doubt encouraged immorality; and a good deal of what they offered the public verged on the sexual. In the nineteenth century entertainers were, to an extent, ostracized from the rest of society, and this is one reason why they were more receptive to racial mixing than other segments of the population: mixing with blacks could not lower them very much, because they were already fairly low down.

Black entertainers, of course, were lower down than whites. As the entertainment industry began to burgeon in the years after 1900, this fact proved to be troublesome, because many of the whites who were coming into places of power in music publishing, the movies, and the theater, were loath to lower themselves by negotiating as equals with the black entertainers they were almost forced to employ to meet public demand. It was one thing to invite into your office a well-known and well-mannered black bandleader like James Reese Europe; it was quite another to have a lot of rough black jazz musicians and song-and-dance men trooping through all day long.

For blacks the problem was to get a hearing with the people who ran the vaudeville circuits, the theater chains, the big music publishing houses.

They found the solution in yet another group of Americans who lived fairly far down the social scale: the Jews, most of them from recently immigrated families. We have forgotten that, in the 1920s and 1930s Jews were segregated from American life to about the extent that blacks were in, say, the 1950s and 1960s. They could not live in many areas, certain careers were not open to them, and a fairly large percentage of other Americans would not have them for friends or even invite them into their homes. Arnold Shaw, a music business historian who spent a good part of his life working in the field, wrote,

> The '40s were still a time when even bright Jews could not easily find a place in the WASP world of communications—advertising, book publishing, journalism, broadcasting, and even higher education. In motion pictures they could make it as administrative and creative people, but not too readily as actors. (John Garfield was the exception.) The music business, however, was as wide open for Jews as it was for blacks.[1]

If it was difficult for Jews to get into the upper reaches of the communications industry in the 1940s, it was a good deal harder in the 1920s. But Jews could act as intermediaries between black entertainers and the heads of the show business world; indeed, a considerable number of Jews would in time become those heads, as music publishers, presidents of movie companies, managers of theater chains. For Jews, black show business was an open opportunity; blacks needed white managers, and anybody willing to fill that need might do very well for himself. As it turned out, some of them did exceedingly well for themselves.

Blacks may have resented having to turn their careers over to Jewish managers, and some of them did; but most of them recognized that white management was essential to them, and they were to a degree grateful to them for providing it. Louis Armstrong turned his professional life over to Joe Glaser, playing whatever jobs Glaser told him to play, letting Glaser hire and fire his bandmen, and taking, without complaint, whatever sums of money Glaser chose to give him. Glaser built himself a show business empire on Louis Armstrong, but Louis accepted it all with equanimity because Glaser had made him rich and famous, something he could never have done for himself. Other black bandsmen from the Glaser stable felt more or less the same. Andy Kirk, a successful black bandleader of the Swing Era, spoke highly of Glaser: "If he made you a promise, that was it."[2] Resentment against Jewish entrepreneurs eventually blossomed, and by the 1960s black entertainers were battling to get greater control of their careers. But in the early days blacks, who saw walls around them everywhere, tended to feel grateful for what these Jewish business sharps could do for them.

Thus, during the 1920s and 1930s, a group of Jews began to take charge of black show business. Frank Shiffman ran the Apollo Theatre in Harlem; Joe Glaser eventually had Billie Holiday and Ellington as well as Armstrong under contract; Florenz Ziegfeld was employing Will Vodery as his musical director and many black stars in his show; Moe Gale and associates owned the Savoy Ballroom; Jack and Bert Goldberg produced a series of black musicals, including *Shuffle Along, How Come* and *Seven-Eleven,* employing, among others, Sidney Bechet. As early as 1925 J. A. Jackson in his *Billboard* column commented about how "our group and the Jewish theatrical managers are so frequently allied."[3]

Whatever anyone felt about it, it was a fact of life that black entertainers had to have white management. Louis Armstrong and Duke Ellington got it, and they became rich and famous; the more prickly Jelly Roll Morton and King Oliver did not, and they died penniless and virtually forgotten. The equation was as simple as that.

The Washingtonians came into the rough world of New York show business with no management except what they could provide for themselves, and they found themselves at the mercy of the gangsters who ran the Kentucky Club. Sonny Greer may have appreciated the fact that they were as good as their word, but it must have been obvious to at least some of the others that the band would not go anywhere as long as it was in thrall to the gangsters. Whether it occurred to any of them to seek out a white manager we do not know. Ellington was an ambitious man and undoubtedly was at least trying to find ways to rise, but he was not a man who would easily put himself under the guidance of somebody else, and it is impossible to guess what he thought. But, fortunately for him, the right man turned up at the right time and the right place.

Born around 1894, Irving Mills grew up to be a small but tough, aggressive, and dapper kid who saw opportunities in the rapidly growing music business. He became a singer of popular songs—not a bad one, in terms of the level of the times. He started as a song demonstrator, singing popular tunes in five-and-ten-cent stores to customers, so they could decide whether or not to buy the music. From there he became a song plugger for Lew Leslie, an important producer of Broadway shows, traveling around to the clubs and ballrooms urging bandleaders to play Leslie's songs. Then, in 1919, he and his brother Jack started Mills Music. Jack was boss of the operation. Their second song was "Mr. Gallagher and Mr. Shean," which went on to sell two million copies. They were off and running; by 1924 they were successful enough to need a larger staff and bigger quarters.[4]

In 1920 the blues boom broke with the startling success of Mamie Smith's "Crazy Blues." Irving Mills plunged in and began buying blues with both hands. His willingness to take almost anything became something of a joke among black musicians, who realized that they could always pick up fifty dollars by revamping an old blues and taking it in to Irving Mills. The interest in blues brought Mills into black show business. Publishers liked to sign up bandleaders as songwriters, on the theory that they would push their own songs, and Mills signed up a flock of black ones: Will Vodery, Tim Brymn, Lovie Austin, James P. Johnson, as well as some of the best black songwriters of the day. These included Shelton Brooks, who wrote "Darktown Strutters' Ball"; Henry Creamer, who wrote "Way Down Yonder in New Orleans"; and Spencer Williams, author of "I Ain't Got Nobody." Mills also had blacks on his office staff, among them Noble Sissle's brother Andrew and W. C. Handy's daughter Katherine.[5]

Like other publishers, Mills was eager to get records made of his songs in order to publicize them, and he was eventually able to arrange with a number of record companies to let him record anything he wanted, so long as he paid for the session. The companies did not necessarily issue what he recorded, and the scheme cost them nothing but a little studio time. For this purpose Mills needed bands, or at least a band. We can presume he wanted a black band, which supposedly would have a better feeling for the blues and, in any case, could be had cheaper than a white one.

Various sources have said that Mills first met Duke when he happened to come into the Kentucky Club. According to Mills himself, he was with Sime Silverman of *Variety* when he first came into the club, and was particularly struck by "Black and Tan Fantasy."[6] Ellington, for his part, said that he met Mills during his first six months in New York. Whatever the case, Duke accompanied Mills on a record made June 8, 1925, probably sometime before "Black and Tan Fantasy" was put together.

Mills decided that the Washingtonians were the sort of band he needed and that Duke Ellington was the sort of man he wanted to work with. Very quickly, a relationship bloomed between them. In general, Irving Mills has been treated badly by history. It is usually said that, like so many white managers of blacks, he rode to riches on the back of Duke Ellington and that when Ellington finally broke off the relationship Mills got what he deserved. To an extent this accepted view is correct: Mills earned a lot of money with Ellington, some of it unfairly. But there is a good deal more to it than that, for Irving Mills made Ellington famous, and Duke recognized this. For one thing, in 1925 Irving Mills was already a successful music publisher, on the road to big money with or without Duke Ellington. For another, at that time Duke recognized that he was a greenhorn, that he could learn a lot from Irving Mills, and that he needed a white manager to run interference for him through the jagged, broken field of show business. In a similar case, Louis Armstrong put blind trust in Joe Glaser, simply doing what he was told to do. Ellington and Mills appear to have been

coconspirators. Mills was just the sort of "carney man" who appealed to Ellington, and undoubtedly Duke was keen to learn the tricks and gimmicks
by which a show business reputation could be built.

On the other side, Mills, no matter how much he cheated Duke, especially by putting his own name on Ellington's songs, understood and respected him. He appears to have recognized very quickly that Duke Ellington was special. As Willie "the Lion" Smith said, "[Duke] was always a
good-looking, well-mannered fellow; one of those guys you see him, you
like him right away; warm, good-natured."[7] It was not just a question of
the good looks, the elegant speech, the tony clothes: a certain magnetism
in Ellington made you believe that he was going somewhere or at least, in
Mills's view, could be made to go somewhere with proper management.
Irving Mills was very smart about picking and choosing among the blacks
in the show business sea that he worked in. As we have seen, he drew to
him some of the best black songwriters of the day, and he would be quick
to sign up Cab Calloway, who was worth even more to him than Ellington,
when Calloway made his first little splash in New York.

One thing that Mills recognized early was Duke's imperious need always
to go first-class. Mills may even have been smart enough to realize that
style meant more to Duke than money and that if the band had Pullman
cars, the best uniforms, and a fancy stage setup, Ellington would be happy
and not fuss over the financial arrangements. It was, of course, an attitude
Duke had picked up from his father. Duke later on, in defense of Mills,
would again and again say something to the effect that he always saw to it
that he had the best of everything. Mills, he remarked, "always preserved
the dignity of my name, . . . and that is the most anybody can do for
anybody."[8]

However Mills may have manipulated Ellington, he was essential to his
success. Without Irving Mills, or someone like him, the Ellington music
would almost certainly have been much different, and perhaps not come
into existence at all. Mills was a music publisher and knew that the big
money would come from songs. As a consequence, he continually urged
Duke to write, got the songs recorded, and pushed them hard. Mills has
always been seen as a thief, because he invariably slapped his own name on
Ellington's songs, so that he not only took the ordinary publisher's profits
but shared in the royalties and gained an ASCAP rating as well. (ASCAP,
or the American Society of Composers and Publishers, licensed ballrooms,
concert halls, and, eventually, radio stations, to play its members' songs.
The money was then distributed to the publishers and composers under a
complex formula that, among other things, took into account seniority.
Members with a number of hits to their credit made a lot of money through
ASCAP.)

Yet, the fact that Mills had his name on Ellington's songs inevitably drove him to push them as hard as he could. Duke already had an inclination to write songs; he had turned out those first efforts with Joe Trent, which Mills would eventually record with the band. From 1923 to 1925, though, he wrote only six songs that we know about, a very small quantity at a time when songwriters frequently churned out several a week and sometimes several a day. Ellington later told the columnist Ralph Gleason, "Without a deadline I can't finish nothing."[9] He was not a man of great self-discipline, at least not in this respect; he would always do what was required, but not until it was required. Virtually all of his compositions, including almost all his greatest work—"Mood Indigo," "Creole Love Call," "Solitude," and many others—were put together at the last minute to meet a recording deadline, often right in the studio. If Ellington, like Louis Armstrong, had had a manager with no interest in the publishing side of the music business, he would certainly have recorded far more works by other people, and correspondingly fewer of his own. But the arrangement with Mills forced Ellington to create continually.

A lot of the men in the band did not really like Irving Mills, whom they saw as meddling in what had been a family. Louis Metcalf said, "[Mills] interfered with us so damn much. He kind of took a lot of spirit out of the band."[10] But most of the men grudgingly admitted that he was necessary. Sonny Greer said, "It was imperative that we have a man like that, a front man, because I don't think we could have done it alone without his guidance. When anything important pertaining to Ellington came up, he was there in person."[11] Mercer Ellington said, "If you wanted to get somewhere you had to make a deal with somebody to get your first tunes out. Irving was one of the first to demand that he get the same consideration as the big, white acts."[12]

Actually, Mills's habit of putting his name on Ellington's songs was not wholly thievery. Mills blandly said, "I wrote 'Sophisticated Lady' with him and 'Mood Indigo,' 'Solitude,' 'In a Sentimental Mood,' 'Azure.' . . . ."[13] In fact, he did contribute something to Ellington's compositions. For one thing, like any publisher, he often suggested to Duke the sorts of tunes he thought would sell. Mills said, "He followed instructions. He did what I wanted. . . . I want this kind of a tune or that kind of a tune."[14] He arranged for words to be put to Duke's songs, sometimes suggesting titles and themes. And he even made changes in the music itself. "Whatever they did, I thinned out. His music was always too heavy. . . . He overarranged. . . . I simplified most all the tunes."[15] This was undoubtedly true: Ellington was given to thick textures, which could become too complex for ordinary listeners. Metcalf said, "Mills always toned down the arrangements, changed them around."[16] Mills was certainly not entitled to

claim a portion of Ellington's royalties, as he did: publishers are supposed
to do the kinds of things for their songwriters that Mills did in respect to
Duke's tunes. But it must be said that he worked them over to make them
commercially acceptable, and he pushed them hard.

Duke, as he says, may have met Mills in 1923, but the business association between the two probably did not begin until 1925. Mills used Duke
as accompanist to his own vocal on a tune called "Everything Is Hotsy
Totsy Now" in June of that year. Then, probably sometime in early 1926,
he made a serious legal arrangement with Duke. They set up a corporation
in which each of them owned 45 percent, the remaining 10 percent being
in the hands of Sam Buzzell, a lawyer presumably associated with Mills.[17]
Ellington was president and Mills treasurer. The exact terms of the deal
have never come to light, but Barry Ulanov, in his 1946 biography of Ellington, says that Ellington, in exchange for what amounted to half of
himself, got pieces of some Mills properties. The primary effect of the deal
was to make Mills Ellington's partner in the band. It should be borne in
mind that the profits from running a dance band in those days were small
potatoes compared with what could be made in other parts of the music
business, especially the composing and publishing of songs. Mills's main
interest was not in the band's income, a lot of which would inevitably go
out for uniforms, publicity, bribes, and the first-class style that Duke required. What he wanted was hit songs, as well as a band with which to
promote them through records and radio broadcasts; the Ellington band
was for Mills primarily a machine for making hits.

There was, however, an important side effect to the deal. Before the legal arrangement was made, the band was called the Washingtonians, and
it was, effectively, a cooperative organization. Had Ellington attempted to
ride roughshod over the others, they could have fired him. Now, by a
sleight of hand, the band had become Ellington's. Mills was the one who
could get the recording contracts and find them jobs in the clubs, and
Mills was tied to Ellington, not to Sonny Greer or Toby Hardwick, neither
of whom was now essential to the band's success. If the players did not like
the new arrangement, they had no choice but to quit. That they did not
says a good deal about the respect and affection they felt for Ellington personally and no doubt also about Ellington's political skill. But it was now
Ellington's band. Records made in March 1926 were issued as being by the
Washingtonians; those made a month later were credited to Duke Ellington and his Washingtonians; by November the name was Duke Ellington
and his Kentucky Club Orchestra; and by February 1927 it was Duke Ellington and His Orchestra. The name "Washingtonians" remained in use
for several years, but only when Mills wanted to record the group outside

of its contract and needed a pseudonym. From now on, the bulk of the records would be under Duke's name.

Mills also markedly stepped up the pace at which the band was recording. There were three sessions in 1925, six in 1926, and thirteen in 1927. It has been reported that Mills signed Ellington to a Victor contract at this point, but that does not appear to have happened until later. He began getting the band dates with Gennett and Paramount, two labels trying to move into the record market among blacks.

Outsiders were brought into some of these recording sessions. At times this was to cover for the unreliable Bubber Miley; at times, simply to enlarge the orchestra and have on hand players who could read music and show the others how to play it. The April 1, 1926, session, for example, employed four brass and four reeds.

About half of these recordings are accompaniments for singers, presumably featuring Mills's tunes. The remainder are band numbers. The band had improved somewhat since the first recordings, but it was still far from being a finished professional group. Duke's piano roll of "Jig Walk," his own tune, is energetic, but much of the time he uses a simplified walking bass made up of quarter notes, instead of the more difficult stride bass, an example of the expedients he had taught himself in the old days down in Washington. The record is not helped by the inclusion of a mechanical snare drum at points.* On "Lucky Number Blues," Toby Hardwick shows some real blues feeling, with good tone and a little swing. But there is very little else good to be said about these records. The band numbers are uniformly bad. The tunes, many of them credited to Duke, are pedestrian and filled with clichés. The rhythm section clunks along like a wagon full of junk and the horns bumble and snort.

Among other things, it is apparent that nobody—Ellington or anybody else—was actually composing for the band. A substantial proportion of the numbers consist of jammed ensembles and strings of solos with perhaps some rudimentary stop-time support. "Choo Choo," for example, opens with an introduction worked out to suggest the sound of a train. The band jams a chorus, then Toby plays a chorus, with the horns jamming underneath him. Miley solos, Irvis solos, Miley and Hardwick make a stab at playing harmony, with mixed results, and the whole is concluded with a brief train coda. There is no sign of composition here. "Animal Crackers," an appalling novelty number named for a brand of crackers shaped like animals (the term may have had other connotations, according to the jazz authority John L. Fell), sounds like a stock that may or may not have been

---

* According to the Ellington specialist Jerry Valburn, recent research suggests that the pianist is not Duke.

doctored by the band members. The equally appalling "Li'l Farina," named for the black character in the "Our Gang" movie comedy series, is more jazzy and sounds like a simple head arrangement. Neither of them is of significant musical value.

At the Kentucky Club the band probably sounded more as it does on "Choo Choo" than on the latter two numbers. At the club it would have depended basically on jammed ensembles and solos, especially ones by Miley working the plunger mute. Presumably, they used some standard introductions and tags and background figures they had worked out, but these would have been simple to the point of crudeness. To this they added doctored stock arrangements. For example, "Trombone Blues," recorded in September 1925, was probably a stock, but it contains a sequence of harmonized breaks for two saxophones, which may have been added by the band, in imitation of the two-cornet breaks the famous Oliver Creole orchestra recorded two years earlier.

How much Ellington was composing for the band is moot. Such full arrangements as the band played, apart from stocks, were, almost certainly, written by others. For example, "Parlor Social Stomp," recorded in 1926, had Don Redman on saxophone. Redman was Fletcher Henderson's principal arranger, and he undoubtedly wrote this one and directed the recording session as well. Two substitute trumpet players were brought in to read the music.

In sum, the band that Duke Ellington gradually took over at the Kentucky Club was basically a rough, Dixieland band, no better and no worse than hundreds like it around the country that were trying to play the new, peppy dance music then in vogue. It was influenced both by the Original Dixieland Jazz Band, which had started the jazz boom some ten years earlier, and by King Oliver's Creole Jazz Band, which Miley and some of the others admired. Ellington was playing passable stride piano, given the limitations of his left hand. Miley was beginning to play good jazz but was still rhythmically stiff, and his growling at times fell into burlesque. The best musician in the band was Bass Edwards, but he is virtually inaudible on these records. It is surprising that so little use was made of him: he is given no solos on these cuts. In short, there is nothing in the music made by the Washingtonians at this stage to suggest even faintly what was to come in just a few months.

But there were major changes coming in the music business, changes which would have dramatic effects on Ellington's career. In about 1914, a drummer named Art Hickman took a band into San Francisco's prestigious St. Francis Hotel to play for dancing. Hickman's pianist was, or would soon be, Ferde Grofé, a trained musician, who had played viola with the Los Angeles Symphony Orchestra. At that time most dance bands, aside from the new-fangled jazz bands coming out of New Orleans, simply banged away at the melody, repeating it as many times as was called for to stretch the number out.

Grofé, possibly at the suggestion of Hickman, began to make arrangements for the group, which involved giving separate lines of music to the various instruments, in a kind of contrapuntal fashion. He—or Hickman—also decided to build this new style around a saxophone choir. He was no doubt motivated in part by the fact that saxophones were a novelty, vogue instruments only beginning to appear in dance bands. But there was also the fact that saxophones could play softer than groups of brasses and could therefore act as a string section in sedate locations like the St. Francis.

Grofé and Hickman thus created what was later termed the "first complete modern jazz combination" by Henry Osborne Osgood, a contemporary writer on jazz; Grofé, Osgood said, was the "father of modern jazz orchestration."

However, it was another man who would capitalize on Grofé's invention. Paul Whiteman was, like Grofé, a symphonically trained violist, whose father led the Denver Symphony Orchestra. Whiteman had led a Navy band during World War I and was intent on getting into the dance band business after he mustered out. He recognized the success that Hickman was having—Hickman was not only recording, but in 1920 and 1921 made visits to England—and he took over not only Hickman's style but his arranger Grofé as well. Whiteman's earliest records were enormous successes and by 1922, made him the leading figure in the dance band world. He then began publicizing his music as "symphonic jazz," which meant that it combined the new rhythms taken from black music with harmonic and melodic devices taken from classical music. In 1924, to make the point that jazz must be taken seriously, and to cleanse it of its associations with low dance halls and worse, he gave a legendary concert at New York's Aeolian Hall, at which he introduced a piece he had commissioned for the event, George Gershwin's "Rhapsody in Blue."

The Aeolian Hall concert made Gershwin's reputation and inflated Whiteman's even more. Through the midyears of the 1920s, a good deal of critical attention was paid to symphonic jazz, whose heroes were seen as Irving Berlin, Gershwin, Whiteman, and some others. The point was that this new, more intellectual music, purified of associations with bawdiness, should, and would, drive out the older, hotter, improvised Dixieland jazz. And in fact, it did exactly that: Dixieland, still being recorded prolifically in 1926, was finished, at least temporarily, by 1930. In its place stood symphonic jazz. It would not, however, be Paul Whiteman who was its major apostle: it would be Duke Ellington.

It is important for us to understand that Ellington, like other bandleaders, saw that the success of Whiteman meant the future of jazz was not the improvising Dixieland bands but the groups that played a more complex, arranged music. Whether musicians liked it or not, that was what the public wanted; and that was the way Ellington would be forced to go.

The Ellington men, in the Kentucky Club years, were a long way from being prepared to meet the challenge. They were playing a rough music because that is all they could play. They had, perforce, to find their own way. And they began to do collectively what Ellington had done individually in developing his piano style: discovering how to be effective within sharp limits. They were not learning what other young musicians were learning—skill at sight-reading and good technique on their instruments. They were, however, learning something that would prove to be more valuable: how to put together musical compositions of their own that would satisfy audiences.

7

The Cotton Club

By the mid-1920s the nature of show business in Harlem was rapidly changing. The theaters like the Lincoln and the Lafayette and the fancy cabarets like Barron's had been developed to supply the local black population with entertainment; and, while a few white bohemians would visit Barron's and one or two other clubs, the clientele in these places was mostly black.

But by the mid-1920s black entertainment was in vogue. The relationship of American whites to the minority of blacks among them has always been far more complex than simply that of master to servant, which it sometimes appeared to be to outsiders. White Americans have felt both attracted to and repelled by the blacks in their midst. Blacks have seemed, to many of them, coarse and uncivilized, and, even today, some whites believe that blacks are inherently criminal.

On the other hand, many Americans have been curious about blacks and black folkways and have been keen to get to know more about them. White slave owners frequently spent time out among the cabins watching blacks dance and sing, and the minstrel show, an important part of show business in the nineteenth century, was designed to exhibit black life on the plantations. Possibly of greater importance, although it has not really ever been studied, is the practice over perhaps two centuries among a good many whites—probably more than anyone has been aware of—of making undercover visits to black enclaves, especially to share in their amusements in honky-tonks, brothels, and wine barrel rooms. Until recent decades most American cities featured tenderloin areas where illicit sex, drugs, drink, and erotic entertainment were available. These areas usually had a black component: either they existed in or on the borders of black enclaves or they

75

included some black cabarets and brothels. According to Pops Foster, a pioneer New Orleans jazz musician, the honky-tonks of black Storyville "had two sides, one for whites the other for colored. The colored had so much fun on their side, dancing singing and guitar playing, that you couldn't get in for the whites."[1] In Chicago, it was the black and tans, in the Black Belt, which developed especially after Prohibition. At the Sunset Cafe, where Louis Armstrong first began to attract attention, "although the club was on the main stem of the Negro neighborhood, it drew whites as much as colored. Sometimes the audience was ninety percent white. Even the mixing of white girls and colored pimps seemed to be an attraction. People came in big parties from Chicago's Gold Coast to see these shows," said Earl Hines, who played there.[2] There were similar clubs in San Francisco's famous Barbary Coast, the Tenderloin district of New York, on Sixth Avenue south of Times Square, and elsewhere.

The black and tans featured black entertainers and black help and, although ostensibly designed for the black trade, were, in fact, also meant to draw whites with money to spend in search of an atmosphere less inhibited than they would find in their own saloons and cabarets. The institution of the "black and tan" played an important role in creating many of the dances and musical styles that eventually filtered up into the mainstream of the culture: ragtime, jazz, rhythm and blues, the trots, the Suzie-Q and Big Apple of the jitterbugs, and much else.

By the 1920s a combination of several forces was driving the black and tan out into the open. Prohibition had created the need for an array of clandestine drinking rooms, and many of them sprouted in black areas where it was understood that police enforcement would be lax. The spirit of the new age had made blacks fashionable among the bohemians who were, to a considerable extent, setting the tone for the 1920s: intellectuals and artists felt called upon to cultivate black friends. The success of the all-black 1921 Broadway musical *Shuffle Along* had markedly increased the demand for black entertainment among whites, most of whom believed that blacks had a natural gift for song, dance, and rough comedy. Carl Van Vechten, a highly regarded writer who had taken blacks for his subject, had a considerable success with a 1926 novel about Harlem called *Nigger Heaven*, which aroused interest in the area and in black life in general.

As a consequence of all these movements in the culture, the more daring bohemians began frequenting places like Barron's, striking up acquaintanceships with blacks, even taking black lovers. It quickly became apparent to entrepreneurs in the Harlem area that here was a need to be filled, so clubs began to open expressly to cater to whites from downtown. One of the first of these was Connie's Inn, founded by Connie and George Immerman, who had been running a delicatessen in Harlem that fronted for a bootleg liquor operation. Connie's Inn was segregated and offered black entertainment for white audiences. Other clubs, like Small's Paradise, the Nest, and Pod and Jerry's, had mixed audiences. Variety in May 1926 said, "Word-of-mouth plugging has made Small's an all-season playground. To see the 'high hats' [i.e., well-to-do whites] mingle with the native stepper [blacks] is nothing unusual. Where formerly the dance floor was either all white or all black, the races mix and the atmosphere permits for no class distinction." Other places were primarily black, but these, too, attracted a few of the more daring whites. The jazz writer George Hoefer said, "Only a small percentage of the visitors saw Basement Brownie's after-hour spa, Helen's Sex Circuses on 140th Street. . . ."[3] Variety pointed out, "There are one or two other 7th Avenue rendezvous which may be possessed of more native color but not considered very healthy as a general thing for the white trade."[4]

The Harlem clubs, then, were a mixed bag—some segregated, some mixed, some primarily for blacks. The change happened very fast: Barron's was still mainly a black club in 1923, but by 1925 or so, according to police estimates, there were eleven "white trade" clubs in Harlem. Many of these clubs had been opened by blacks, but, by the middle of the decade, the gangsters were pushing in and had taken control, although they might permit blacks to continue to manage the clubs. "In a very short time, the big-time mobsters were in control of the Cotton Club, Connie's and most of the other spots," said the nightclub columnist Robert Sylvester.[5] Police Commissioner Grover Whalen said flatly, "Gangdom is in control of the night clubs."[6]

Of all of them, the most famous was—and is—the Cotton Club, subject of a recent movie, a book, and innumerable magazine and newspaper stories. It was a centerpiece of the New York entertainment business for some fifteen years, a springboard to fame for dozens of dancers, singers, musicians, and songwriters, including Harold Arlen, Lena Horne, Dorothy Dandridge, Jimmy McHugh, Dorothy Fields, Cab Calloway, and Duke Ellington. According to George Hoefer, the building at the northeast corner of 142nd Street and Lenox Avenue that housed the Cotton Club was built in about 1918 as the Douglas Casino, which had a vaudeville theater on one floor and a dance hall and banquet room on another.[7] Customarily, there would be a basketball game before the dance. The Casino failed, and in 1920 the heavyweight champion Jack Johnson rented it and installed a supper club, which he called the Club de Luxe. Johnson "was not liked by the Harlem populace, partly because he insisted on making a spectacle of his white wife."[8] Once again the club failed, and in 1923 it was taken over by a syndicate of gangsters, led by Owney Madden.

Owney Madden was a character fit to build a movie around. He was small and soft-spoken, with a receding chin, China blue eyes, and a gentle manner. (According to Sonny Greer he talked like a girl.) He was not much of a drinker, disliked personal publicity, and was relatively well mannered. He was nonetheless a very hard man who could be cruel and was believed by the police to have killed several men before he was out of his teens. He fought to get a grip on New York's criminal gangs, and, though he spent a good deal of his youth in Sing Sing Prison, he managed to make himself "the hard and sensible boss of the New York underworld."[9] As such, he was "in many respects the most important man in New York."[10]

Madden had several partners in the club, although it is hardly possible to be sure of anything on that count. The two most important were Big Frenchy DeMange and Harry Block. DeMange was a bootlegger and former safecracker. He stood six feet two inches, weighed 240 pounds, and stared out at malcontents from under bushy eyebrows. Frenchy was around the club a lot as a kind of house gangster in order to give the place an air of naughtiness, but Block seems to have been the one who set policy. The club opened under this management in the fall of 1923. It could seat four or five hundred people. There was a small stage at one end, booths along the walls, and tables crammed around the small dance floor. False palm trees supplied a "jungle" atmosphere. The dinners ran to steak and lobster, and, of course, liquor was available. Block brought in Lew Leslie, a respected Broadway producer, to put together the shows. The formula was successful, but in 1925 the club was shut down for three months by liquor authorities. It reopened with Herman Stark, a bookkeeper and sedate family man who is said to have been a machine gunner in World War I, in charge, although Harry Block was still the boss behind Stark. Stark brought in the song-and-dance man Dan Healy in place of Lew Leslie to design the shows. The first ones were written by Jimmy McHugh and Dorothy Fields, who would write an extraordinary string of standards, including "I Can't Give You Anything but Love," "Diga Diga Doo," "Blue Again," and "On the Sunny Side of the Street," many of them for Cotton Club shows. But, according to Cab Calloway, Fields, whose forte was fairly sophisticated lyrics with a light touch, like the poignant lyric to "Blue Again," "wasn't funky enough to write the kinds of songs that would carry a Negro review of that type. The real down-to-earth Cotton Club shows, with double-entendre, nasty songs and the hurly-burly and bump-and-grind mixed with high-class swinging jazz, were produced by Harold Arlen and Ted Koehler beginning in 1930."[11]

The Cotton Club had at one time or another used the bands of Armand J. Piron, a New Orleans Creole, who had previously been at the Roseland Ballroom, and Happy Rhone, a popular Harlem leader. But by 1926 the band was the Missourians, led by Andy Preer. According to Dan Healy, "The chief ingredient was pace, pace, pace. The show was generally built around types: the band, an eccentric dancer, a comedian—whoever we had who was also a star. The show ran an hour and a half, sometimes two hours: we'd break it up with a good voice: Ada Ward, Ethel Waters. And we'd have a special singer who gave the customers the expected adult song in Harlem, a girl like Leitha Hill."[12] (Arlen wrote some of these adult songs, like "Pool Room Papa" and "My Military Man," but would not put his name on them.) On Sunday nights show business celebrities who turned up were expected to come onstage and do a turn.

The club was a great success, but then, in 1927, the young Andy Preer died suddenly, and the club apparently used his death as an excuse to get rid of the Missourians; the band was later taken over by Cab Calloway. The job was then offered to King Oliver, at the Savoy Ballroom, but Oliver, who had one of the best-known black bands, did not think the money was enough for a ten-piece orchestra. At this point Ellington's Washingtonians came up for consideration.

The story of how Ellington got the Cotton Club job has been told many times by many people in many different versions. Half a dozen people claim to have suggested Duke to Stark and Harry Block. One of these claimants is Jimmy McHugh, who appears to have worked for Mills as a staff writer and would certainly have known about the Ellington band; in any case, Ellington accepted McHugh's claim.[13]

In the fall of 1927 Duke was not working at the Kentucky Club and was taking whatever jobs he could get. At the moment the band was at Gibson's Standard Theatre, on South Street in Philadelphia, where Duke got a call to bring the band to New York to audition at the Cotton Club at noon. The band, however, was supposed to be built up to ten men; by the time Duke rounded up the extra musicians and got to the club, it was two or three in the afternoon. Fortunately for Duke, Harry Block arrived late himself, heard the band, liked it, and offered them the job. The pay was eight hundred dollars a week, a low figure even for those days, but the Cotton Club was an important location and, besides, promised to be more steady than the Kentucky Club had been. Duke and Mills jumped at the opportunity.

One problem remained: the band still had to fulfill a contract with the Standard Theatre. According to the frequently told story, somebody from the Madden group contacted a Philadelphia gangster named Boo Boo Hoff. Hoff sent Yankee Schwartz to see the theater manager. In a line that has become part of jazz folklore, Schwartz told the manager, "Be big. Or you'll be dead."[14] The manager was big and released Ellington from his contract.

That, in any case, is the story. The band opened on the night of Decem-

ber 4, 1927—today one of the most famous openings in jazz history but at
the time something less than a success. The musicians were poor sight readers; the underrehearsed band included two or three temporary musicians,
among them a violinist, Ellsworth Reynolds, who stayed with the band for
a month. Ned Williams, soon to be Ellington's publicist, heard the band
at that time: "I can't say I was too much impressed with the Ellington
crew on that visit. It definitely didn't have the form and polish that it acquired later on."[15]

Ellington's immediate concern was to stabilize the personnel and build
it up to the requisite ten. Operating as the band did on head arrangements
and not much on paper, a set group who could play the band's book from
memory was essential. Over the next two years Ellington would build
around a nucleus of Carney, Nanton, Greer, Braud, Guy, and himself a
formidable orchestra that would produce some of the finest jazz records
ever made, and make Duke rich and famous.

The first of the new men to come in was a New Orleans clarinet player
named Barney Bigard. He was born in 1906 to a typical black Creole family, which spoke French at home. Like many black Creoles, Bigard had a
number of musical relatives and grew up in an atmosphere full of music. It
was not, however, the blues and rough rags that were the heritage of mainstream blacks but "legitimate" music in the European tradition. Bigard
learned photoengraving and cigar rolling, an important occupation among
black Creoles, and studied clarinet on the side with the legendary New Orleans teacher Lorenzo Tio, Jr. "Lorenzo and his uncle taught me almost all
the rudiments of clarinet," Bigard recalled. "The whole family played clarinets—the great grandfather, the grandfather, an uncle, the nephew. . . .
The woody tone that Duke likes was a New Orleans specialty and it owed
a lot to the Tios and Alphonse Picou."[16] (The Tios were not black Creoles
but of Mexican descent.) Bigard also said that he "stole" a lot of licks from
Jimmie Noone, considered the finest of the New Orleans clarinet players.[17]

The New Orleans Creoles tended to play the older Albert system clarinet
rather than the Boehm, which has a somewhat different arrangement of
keys to make playing at faster tempos easier. There were reasons for staying
with the Albert, however. According to the clarinetist Bob Sparkman, who
has looked into the matter, the old Albert clarinets had a larger bore, as did
many wind instruments of the time, to provide them with greater tonal
weight, necessary for the outdoor playing that was so prevalent at the time.
Wind instruments with a larger bore are generally fuller and mellower in
the low register, at the expense of some brilliance higher up. These Albert
system Creoles took advantage of this fact to play long, fast passages at the
bottom of the horn, and Duke would make good use of Bigard's low-register
clarinet.

Bigard gigged around New Orleans as a teenager, playing for a while at the famous Tom Anderson's, a cabaret where a number of leading black jazz musicians played in the waning days of Storyville. In 1924 King Oliver summoned Bigard north. He worked with Oliver until 1927, when Oliver was having serious lip problems and was also beginning to have difficulties booking the band. He eventually landed with the Luis Russell band, then playing at the celebrated Harlem after-hours club the Nest, which had a mixed crowd:

> See, the Nest was a real after-hours place where all the show girls from the Cotton Club, where Duke Ellington was working, would come after work and bring their boy friends. They enjoyed themselves like mad and everyone spent plenty of money in that joint. People would come from the Broadway shows and practice what they called "slumming" at our place. They'd come down to the Nest and have a ball. . . . I remember people such as Fanny Brice, Bill "Bojangles" Robinson, Helen Morgan. . . . Sometimes we would stay so long I'd get home around noon or two maybe three o'clock in the afternoon.[18]

By the early winter of 1927 Ellington had become annoyed with Rudy Jackson. The chief problem was that at some point, shortly before the Cotton Club opening, Jackson had brought Ellington a tune he had "adapted" from a King Oliver tune called "Camp Meeting Blues." Ellington, in turn, "adapted" the tune from Rudy Jackson, put his own name on it, and recorded it as "Creole Love Call." Oliver sued, and, although he lost because his own copyright was defective, Ellington felt that he had been double-crossed by Jackson and decided to get rid of him. It is probably true that Duke, with his respect for the New Orleanians, had heard Bigard somewhere—Bigard played at the cutting contests at Mexico's—and liked his tone. So Duke sent Braud, as a fellow New Orleanian, around to talk to Bigard, although the two did not know each other. According to Bigard, Braud said, "You see, Duke has had this six-piece outfit on Broadway, but he has just landed this deal at the Cotton Club. The man there wants him to expand the band to ten pieces."[19] Braud told Bigard that the band was about to break into the big time and that it was a good opportunity for Bigard. After a second visit, Bigard agreed to go around to see Duke:

> I want you to join my band. . . . I don't know how long we're going to stay here but we are trying to build up a good band. If we can do it and the boss likes us then we can stay at this Cotton Club for a long time. We'll have a good job there.[20]

Bigard continued,

> I noticed he kept talking in the plural. . . . "Our band." "We can stay there," and I liked that from the start about him. He thought of a

band as a unit and I dug him. We talked for a half an hour or so and
he outlined his plans. He seemed to know what he was about to do and
he made sense all the way around. . . . It turned out to be a cheaper
salary than I was making at the Nest but the more the man talked, the
more I liked him. He was very ambitious, even then. . . . Just like he
was going to turn the music business upside down and you would be
part of it.[21]

Bigard joined about January 1928 and would stay with the band for fourteen years. He would bring in a number of important tunes, but his main
contribution was the "woody," somewhat hollow sound and his long, evenly
played runs, which would become an important part of Ellington's tone
palette and an identifying mark of the orchestra. Bigard was also fairly
levelheaded and not one of the heavy drinkers in the band. He was, however, strong-minded, and he once fell into such a feud with Johnny Hodges
that the two, who sat next to each other night after night, did not speak
for some time.

A second new arrival was a man even more important to the Ellington
sound—Johnny Hodges, who would go on to be one of the premier soloists
in jazz. Hodges was born in Boston in 1906 and given the name John Cor-
nelius, but he was known in the band as Rabbit. Conflicting stories about
the nickname have been told by himself and others. His own version was
that he was fast on his feet. His family wanted him to study the piano, but
he preferred the drums. "I beat up all the pots and pans in the kitchen. . . .
I liked the look of the saxophone and wound up with a soprano. I heard
so much about Sidney Bechet and my sister knew him when he was playing
in Boston at a burlesque house called Jimmy Cooper's Black and White
Show,"[22] a very successful show that grew out of the black entertainment
boom and featured white performers for one half of the evening and black
for the other half. J. A. Jackson reported that a few years earlier an integrated show like this would have been "totally impossible."[23]

After the show Hodges got up his nerve and went backstage, carrying his
soprano covered in a sleeve that had been cut off an old coat. Although
he had owned the instrument for only two days—he says—he played "My
Honey's Lovin' Arms" for Bechet. Bechet, in turn, showed him some things.

The Washingtonians were still spending their summers in New England,
especially at Salem Willows, and Hodges would go out to the dances to
hear the band. He said Ellington heard him at the Black and White Club,
presumably a black and tan, where he was playing alto saxophone for two
and a half dollars a night, and urged him to come to New York and join
the band. Hodges, who was shy, did not feel up to the challenge of New
York until 1925. At that time Sidney Bechet opened a club on 145th Street
in Harlem, called the Club Basha, and took Hodges in as his protégé.

Hodges stayed for several weeks, playing duets with his idol when he was there and playing solo when the footloose Bechet was absent. From 1925 on he moved back and forth between Boston and New York, playing with various of the better-known black bands. Duke continued to urge him to join him, but Hodges, probably still shy, refused. Then, in about May 1928, Toby Hardwick went through the windshield of a taxicab in an accident and cut his face badly.[24] This time Duke prevailed, and Hodges took the job, which would last, with an intermission in the 1950s, until his death in 1970. (It is possible that an accident was not the cause of Hardwick's departure but that he was fired for his unreliability.)

Hodges was seen by many to be a difficult personality, aloof, arrogant, and bristly. He appeared to be angry a good deal of the time, and Bigard, who feuded with him, said that it "looked like it hurted him to laugh."[25] He had a "kiss my ass" attitude, according to people who knew him. But Harry Carney said, "He was basically a shy person and people often misunderstood his shyness. Even after he got to play a lot of horn he wouldn't want to go out to the microphone but would prefer to take his solo sitting down."[26] He appears to have had a good and long-lasting marriage to a Cotton Club show girl named Cue. He was one of the worst readers in the band and continued to have difficulty with scores for most of his career. Bigard says that he and Carney frequently had to walk Hodges through new orchestrations in sax section rehearsals and that, when he wrote songs, he would play the melodies to the trombonist Juan Tizol, who came into the band not long after Hodges did, and have him write them down. It is always hard to explain why a consummate musician like Johnny Hodges finds reading so difficult. Bix Beiderbecke had the same difficulty. It is not a side effect of genius, for many brilliant jazz improvisers have been quick sight readers as well. It has to do, surely, with personality problems. Jimmy Hamilton, who played clarinet with the band much later, said of Hodges, "He could read but I think he'd just get scared."[27]

But if he could not read, he could do something far more important to a jazz band, and that was to swing. He was certainly the hardest swinger in the band, one of the most ferocious swingers in jazz. Furthermore, he played with the fluid grace of a hawk dipping and swooping through shining air. In his early stages he played with a rather busy, driving rush, but later on he tended more and more to use flowing glissandi so smoothly played they astonished other musicians. What really mattered, though, was the warm beauty of his tone and his swing. He was probably the finest alto saxophonist in jazz history before Charlie Parker, and in some aspects of his playing, especially in the undulating, sexual warmth of his sound, he was Parker's superior.

Hodges also, inevitably, played a good deal of soprano saxophone in the band. He was a master of this instrument, too, nearly the equal of his mentor, Sidney Bechet, and he played it with the same infectious, swooping swing that he brought to the alto. Unfortunately, he gave up the soprano in 1940. He said, "Duke had been writing a lot of arrangements with soprano on top and the responsibility of playing lead and then jumping up and playing solos, too, was a heavy one."[28]

It is interesting that Hodges at times sounded as if he were playing tenor sax instead of alto, as both Cootie Williams and Coleman Hawkins pointed out. Indeed, on "Cotton," made in 1935, he sounds so much like a tenor that we are tempted to think he was actually playing one. As it happens, on that day Ben Webster had been brought in to play the tenor parts; Barney Bigard's tenor saxophone would have been sitting unused in its stand, and it would have been wholly in character for Hodges to pick it up and play it just to show Webster that he was not the only tenor player in the band. But this is just supposition.

There can be no doubt that Hodges was heavily indebted to Bechet for both his approach to rhythm and his concept of a warm, rolling sound. Duke, by this time, was almost instinctively turning to the New Orleanians or to those who had learned from them. It was the woody Creole sound that Bigard got that attracted him, and, given his striking admiration for Bechet, it is little wonder he was so eager to get the New Orleanian's protégé into his band.

The saxophone section had been revamped, and now Duke would replace the trumpet section completely. First, in June 1928, Arthur Whetsol came in for Louis Metcalf. Whether Metcalf quit and Duke sought out Whetsol or whether Whetsol wanted to return and Duke used that as an excuse to get rid of Metcalf, we do not know. In any case, Metcalf went on to have a solid, if not celebrated, career in jazz and continued to lead small bands around New York when he was well into his sixties.

Next, Ellington hired a third trumpeter, Freddy Jenkins. He had used three trumpets before in recording sessions occasionally, but, from the Kentucky Club days, it had always been Miley and a second trumpeter with a smooth tone and reading skills who could play the pretty melodies any band must have in its books. There were grounds for adding a third trumpet, however. For technical reasons, a chord consists of three or more notes. Until this time Duke could voice the trombone with two trumpets to form a brass choir, to play off against the saxophone choir. But a better effect and more variety could obviously be achieved with the extra trumpet, for it would allow the trumpets to play as a unit and, with the trombone added, permit the playing of more complex four-note chords by the brass. As we shall see, by 1928 Ellington had become fascinated by dissonant harmonies, which nearly always demanded four voices.

Besides, Ellington's competitors in the band business were all carrying four or five brass, while Paul Whiteman had eight. By nature, Ellington writhed at running behind, and he would probably have added more musicians for this reason alone.

Freddy Jenkins was a short, feisty man who played left-handed, apparently because he was missing the tips of a couple of fingers on his right hand. He was a flashy dresser, and when he played he would stand with his head thrown back, his arms raised, one leg forward. The other men in the band were amused by this posturing and called him Posey as a consequence. By way of explanation, Posey once told an interviewer, "The correct standing posture for a right-handed player (of course I am left-handed myself) is to have the left foot forward, the chest well extended and the arms up. It is quite wrong to play with the arms down."[29] Jenkins, however, was a good reader, an "executioner" with a strong high register that Duke would put to work. He rarely played first and not many of the jazz solos. Cootie Williams said, "He had a peculiar style but he could play . . . very good section man."[30]

The third new man to come into the trumpet section would ultimately have as much effect on the shape of Ellington's music as any of the others added at this time. Cootie Williams was born in 1911 (according to his story; others give earlier dates) in Mobile, Alabama, a town some 150 miles from New Orleans. There were good train connections between the cities, and bands from the New Orleans area frequently played in Mobile. Cootie, who was christened Charles Melvin, thus grew up under the spell of the New Orleans style.

He was the third of four sons. His mother died in childbirth when Cootie was seven or eight, and he was thereafter raised by his father and an aunt. His father was by any measure a remarkable man. He was so big and strong that somebody wanted to train him to fight Jack Johnson for the heavyweight championship. Instead, Williams senior opened a gambling hall. The business was a success, but Williams spent most of the profits at the racetrack. He then went to Texas to work as a strikebreaker; blacks were frequently willing to be used for this purpose because they were barred from unions and therefore saw no reason to support them. Some time after he returned he gave up the fast life and became a minister.

The elder Williams respected music. Cootie got his nickname when, upon returning from a concert as a little boy, somebody asked what he had heard. "Cootie, cootie, cootie," he replied. The father insisted that all the boys study music. Cootie began at school on various instruments but, by the age of nine, was concentrating on the trumpet. Besides his school lessons he also "took" from a man named Charlie Lipscomb, who ran a cleaning and pressing shop and also played with the local concert band.

Lipscomb was a "legitimate" musician who disliked the new, hot music. He made Cootie work his way through the Arban book, which thousands of young brass players suffered through, even up to today, and this study gave him a foundation equaled by few of the early jazz players, especially by black ones, who frequently could not afford proper lessons.

Despite Lipscomb's warning, Cootie had become interested in jazz. The family owned a phonograph, and, by the time Cootie was a teenager, he was listening to the King Oliver band and especially to the Louis Armstrong Hot Fives just coming out, which would change the nature of jazz. He learned by heart a great many of Armstrong's phrases from these and other records and, fifty years later, would still quote them from time to time. He would also say that Armstrong was "the greatest trumpet player who ever lived." Cootie thus not only heard New Orleans musicians when they came through Mobile but even took as his model the greatest of them.

When he caught Cootie playing jazz, Lipscomb would give him a smack, but Cootie was undeterred. When the New Orleans bands paraded through town on wagons to advertise dances, Cootie would climb up and sit in with them. He played with the New Orleanian Edmond Hall, who would become one of the leading jazz clarinetists of the Swing Era, when he came through Mobile with the Pensacola Jazz Band.

Another band that came through during his boyhood was the Young family band, run by Lester Young's father. Cootie's father took him out to hear this band, and he went back the next night and sat in, aged eleven or twelve. He said later that he was very impressed with Lester, who played the same then as he did at his peak. Eventually, at fourteen or so, Cootie spent a summer with the Young band. He said he learned something about rhythm from Young, "because he was different from anybody [he] ever heard."[31] The band was not a jazz band but a show band with acts featuring a saxophone quintet, a common novelty of the time. Young's father was very strict with the boys and imposed a midnight curfew on them.

However, it was Ed Hall who got Cootie out of Mobile. Hall had left the Pensacola Jazz Band and was working with a group in Jacksonville, Florida, run by a pianist named Eagle Eye Shields. Hall recommended Cootie to Shields. As it happened, a gambling pal of Cootie's father lived in Jacksonville and could look after Cootie, so it was arranged for him to stay with the friend. The man was light-skinned enough to pass for white. According to Cootie, he used to gamble with big-time white gamblers, who killed him when they discovered he was black.

Cootie stayed with Shields for several years; then he and Hall switched to a band run by Alonzo Ross. The Ross band was playing a club called Della Robia. It broadcast occasionally, and in 1928 the broadcast was heard by somebody connected to the Rosemont Ballroom in Brooklyn. The Ross band was a cooperative group—the biggest black band in Florida. It was hired by Rosemont and came north for two weeks. When the job was over, they had nothing and returned to Florida. But Cootie and Ed Hall had been struck by the opportunities for musicians around New York and decided to stay. For a few weeks they hung around Brooklyn, living on soup at fifteen cents a bowl, and then somebody told them about Manhattan and a Harlem club called the Bandbox, which held regular cutting contests on the order of the ones held at Mexico's. Cootie went over on trumpet night. Somebody heard him and went out to get Chick Webb, who would have one of the best swing bands of the 1930s and was struggling for a foothold. Webb was so impressed by Williams that he took him home to live with him and hired him for thirty-five dollars a week, which was "big money" to Cootie. However, Webb had some trouble with the union, and Cootie was forced out. Early in 1929 he landed with the Fletcher Henderson orchestra, then at a peak of popularity. He stayed with Henderson for a few weeks, was briefly back with Webb, and returned to Henderson. He had been back only a short while when he got an offer from Duke.

Duke, as we have seen, always tolerated a good deal of irresponsible behavior on the part of his men, on the ground that these unbuttoned, "instinctive" players would produce a freer, more "natural" music. He even went to the point of marking "sloppy" on scores. Paradoxically, because of his Victorian upbringing and his need to maintain an aristocratic pose, Duke's own public posture was closer to that of the whites in his audience than to that of the supposedly less inhibited blacks who represented the intellectual ideal of the day.

But Bubber Miley carried things too far. After the job he would begin to tour Harlem, visiting women, dropping in on friends, seeing what was happening at other clubs. Often he would carouse around the clock until it was time for the next night's job. He would appear drunk and disheveled. His shirt would inevitably be filthy with spilled food and drink, and he would dust it with talcum powder he kept in his trumpet case for that purpose. He would be allowed to sleep between sets and in this way could get through the evening.

But many evenings he would not show up at all. Cootie said, "The reason why [Duke] fired Bubber Miley was every time some big shot come up to listen to the band, there wasn't no Bubber Miley and he had the whole band built around Bubber Miley."[32] Miley failed to show up for an important "Black and Tan Fantasy" recording session, and Jabbo Smith had to be substituted. (Ironically, Cootie had to fill in for Jabbo Smith for similar reasons at a James P. Johnson session a few months later; he remembered that the musicians had to call him Jabbo throughout the session to keep the recording director unaware of his substitution.) Finally, Bubber failed to turn up one night when an important booker had come to the Cotton Club to audition the band. They lost the job, and sometime early in 1929 Duke fired Bubber. What he said to him we do not know, but there can be no doubt that Bubber was fired and not, as has often been said, allowed to see that it was time to resign. And it was Johnny Hodges, who had played with Cootie briefly in the Chick Webb band, who said to Duke, "Why don't you get Cootie?"[33]

Why, precisely, Cootie made the change is not clear. Henderson's was the top black band in the country, and presumably he was paying more than Duke could. All Cootie said was, "Fletcher had the greatest band around but Duke's was coming up."[34] It turned out to be a wise decision, because the Henderson band would go through hard times for a year or so, and, by the time it was reorganized, the Ellington band was at the top.

For Duke, the loss of a musician was a severe problem because his own part of the band's book existed primarily in his head. The only way the replacement could learn his part was to study the records or hope somebody in the section would help him out. At times, many of the established men refused to help newcomers, out of simple nastiness. Typically, Ellington never told Cootie to take on the Miley role as a growl specialist. Duke never liked to give people direct instructions of this kind even when people asked for it. He would usually say something like "You'll find your way" or "Just do what feels right to you." It seems to have been a policy with him, possibly because he was, once again, afraid to spoil the instincts of the natural player. So for some months Cootie played open horn only, and Whetsol or Jenkins played the growl solos. "Night after night, I sat up there and nobody said a word. When Tricky Sam played, I laughed, because I thought it was funny. . . . But it dawned on me, finally, I thought, 'This man hired me to take Bubber's place.' "[35]

Cootie began at that point to listen carefully to Tricky Sam and practice with the plunger at home, and within four months he was using the plunger in the band. "I learned everything from [Tricky]. . . . I never heard Bubber play in person."[36] Cootie Williams proved to be an acquisition of enormous worth. He later worked for Benny Goodman, who, according to John Hammond, said, "Cootie Williams was, by far, the most versatile man that ever played in the section. He was a fast reader, had the biggest tone, and unlimited power. Nobody can play lead like Cootie and his solos are great."[37] Needless to say, Benny Goodman had some very fine trumpet players in his orchestra.

As a consequence, Cootie not only played endless major solos for Duke but also handled the lead when power was called for. In big bands, one man is rarely asked to play lead in a section and do the bulk of the solo work. In his solos he would always "try to tell the story of whatever you're playing." "Some people play on chord construction," Cootie explained. "I like to have a melody. I like to read the music down and see what the composer intended it to be."[38]

Cootie also wrote a lot of important tunes for the band, among them the hit "Do Nothing Till You Hear from Me." But his value was not just musical. In a band full of mischievous boys, Cootie did not drink, always "made time," as the musicians say, and conducted himself impeccably on the bandstand. Furthermore, he took it upon himself to say something to other musicians or simply glare at them when they were not giving the music proper attention. "I love music," he said, "and I don't like to see anyone mess music up. . . . They cursed me about sometimes. . . . But I don't care."[39]

It was inevitable that, sooner or later, Duke would add a second trombone, if for no other reason than to match Fletcher Henderson, who had been carrying two trombones for some time. The man he chose was a Puerto Rican named Juan Tizol, who was born in 1900. (Harry White, Duke's friend from Washington, may have preceded Tizol briefly.) His uncle Manuel Tizol was director of the San Juan Symphony Orchestra and of the municipal band, and he "was about the best musician in the country."[40] When Tizol was growing up, there was far less of the ragtime and the burgeoning hot music in Puerto Rico than there was in the United States, so he did not grow up absorbing it from the air around him as Americans had. Furthermore, Tizol came from a family that included other professional musicians besides Manuel, as well as lawyers and business people. Such a family would have looked down on the rough, improvised jazz music that was coming out of New Orleans.

His uncle Manuel specialized in the cello, trombone, and bassoon, all instruments that read the bass clef. Juan chose the trombone. Before the turn of the century, the slide trombone was a rarity; the valve trombone was the standard instrument, in part because it fingered the same as the whole family of brasses and, thus, made an easy double; in part because it was easier to manipulate in the close quarters of a marching band— especially on horseback, where bands sometimes were—than the slide trombone. The valve trombone, however, is harder to play in tune than the slide and is considered to have a thinner tone and has never been welcomed in symphony orchestras. However, the main reason why the slide came back into vogue in about 1900, after half a century or more of neglect, was its ability to play portamenti, or "slurs," for comical effect in rags and marches, like "Lazarus Trombone." It is not by chance that the slur became characteristic of the New Orleans "tailgate" style: these comical effects, played by the revivified slide trombone, were all the rage as jazz was developing.

Juan Tizol stayed with the valve, which could be played faster than the slide. (For the interest of Ellington specialists, I suspect that Tizol also, on rare occasions, played the baritone horn with Ellington. On the September 1929 "The Duke Steps Out," a French-horn player is listed, and the final note could have come from a French horn. It could also have come from a baritone horn, and it appears to me that on the February 11, 1932, "Creole Love Call," and the 1932 stereo version of the tune, Tizol plays baritone on the countermelody.)

Tizol played with the municipal orchestra as a teenager. He was brought to Washington with a group of other Puerto Rican musicians, who were recognized for their excellent musicianship, to play at the Howard Theatre, under the leadership of Marie Lucas. According to the story, a little Ellington group was playing at intermission from a box. Ellington and Tizol met, but it was years before they would work together. For the next several years Tizol gigged around the Washington and New York areas. He and his wife-to-be, Rose, opened a delicatessen in Washington. He worked with Arthur Whetsol in a small band doing one-nighters at a time when Whetsol was out of the Ellington band.

In 1929 Ellington had an opportunity to go into a Gershwin show called *Show Girl*. The band would have some fairly exacting music to read, provided by professional arrangers, and Duke, in somewhat of a panic, began to reach out for readers. Whetsol reminded him of Tizol, and he brought Tizol, who left Rose in charge of the delicatessen, to New York. The job with Duke ended when the Gershwin show was over; but then, in August or September of 1929, Duke asked Whetsol to call Tizol and offer him a job. Tizol accepted and would stay with the band for fifteen years, off and on.

Brought up as he was as a legitimate player in a culture with a minimum of hot music, Tizol never developed into an improvising jazz soloist. The many solos he played with the Ellington band are straight expositions of written melody in a relatively pure tone with flawless execution and the even dynamics typical of a symphony player. He became, in a sense, the Whetsol of the trombone section, an expositor of the pretty melodies Ellington liked. His style could hardly have contrasted more with that of Tricky Sam's, and he was thus another string to Ellington's bow.

But that was not the end of Tizol's usefulness to Duke. He was a highly skilled transposer who could read anybody's part; and because of this, and the speed the valves allowed him, Duke would sometimes put him in the saxophone section as a fourth voice. This skill at transposition also made him quick at "extracting" parts. Ellington never wrote out parts for musicians. Insofar as he committed anything to paper, it was always a very rough score in concert keys. Although he could have written out the parts in concert keys, he was not adept at it and, furthermore, did not want to bore himself with the task. He always hired others to do this work, and the first of them was Juan Tizol, whom he put to work copying parts almost from the moment he came into the band. At times Tizol would sit up all night taking pages from Duke as he wrote them. Because of his familiarity with the music and because of his musicianship, Tizol eventually became a sort of straw boss and would sometimes rehearse the band in Duke's absence.

With the arrival of Tizol, Ellington had finally put together the musical instrument with which he would create some of the finest jazz ever played and on which he could climb to fame. Over the next decade there would be one other major addition and a few other, less important changes. But this band, featuring Williams, Hodges, Bigard, Carney, Nanton, and Tizol, would remain intact for over ten years and would be the one that produced a substantial proportion of Ellington's greatest work.

8

Becoming Celebrated

Paradoxically, it is a lot easier to discover what Cootie Williams and Barney Bigard contributed to the creation of the Ellington music from this period than what Duke brought to it. Duke always liked to tell little anecdotes about how he wrote "Mood Indigo" while waiting for his mother to cook dinner or "Solitude" while standing up against the glass window of the recording studio—stories often demonstrably untrue—but he was never very explicit about his composing methods. In later years he would grandly announce that they "did this" at such and such a time, but he never provided much detail. It was always stories, and whatever he did offer implied a more rigorous and formal approach to composition than was actually the case.

Before playing the Cotton Club, Ellington had been content to be part of the glamour of New York and pointed his ambition toward becoming celebrated for writing hit songs. By 1927 the music business was changing somewhat. Hit songs were still the primary road to riches, but the new idea of the "name" band, led by a celebrated leader, had made it possible for dance band leaders to become rich and famous entirely on the strength of the kind of music they played—their "style," as it was said. Ellington could see Paul Whiteman's biography running as a three-part condensation in the *Saturday Evening Post* in 1926. He could see Fletcher Henderson broadcasting regularly and playing proms at Princeton and elsewhere. He could see other orchestras like Casa Loma becoming household words. It seems to me, then, that he began to concentrate his energies on making the Duke Ellington orchestra famous.

This meant that the band had to have an identifiable and consistent style that could be promoted through clever publicity. Although we have no hard evidence of it, we can imagine that he had long conversations with Mills about how this should be done. The gimmick they came up with was "jungle music." This was suggested by the fact that the Cotton Club was at one point using a lot of "jungle" skits as excuses to introduce erotic dances—shake dances and shimmies performed by the club's dancers, like Freddi Washington and Bessie Dudley, wearing little besides feathers and beads, supposedly to suggest jungle attire. Marshall Stearns, a highly regarded jazz historian, described one such skit in which a black aviator parachuted into the jungle, where he rescued a blonde "queen" of the natives, after which they performed an erotic dance.[1] (Examples of these dances appear in two early Ellington short films, *Bundle of Blues* and *Black and Tan Fantasy*.) Ellington said, "During one period at the Cotton Club, much attention was paid to acts with an African setting, and to accompany these we developed what was termed a 'jungle style' jazz."[2]

The basis for the whole thing was the belief of many white Americans that blacks were only a step removed from the jungle tribe with its "weird" rites and savage dances. To anybody with an understanding of African tribal society, to say nothing of black American culture, it was all ludicrous—indeed, as we have seen, shocking to Duke's family. Ellington, coming from a middle-class family that held itself above precisely those primitive passions that jungle music was supposed to express, might have felt that the whole thing was degrading. But he did not. He said, "As a student of Negro history I had, in any case, a natural inclination in this direction."[3] The jungle sound, he said, was primarily due to the use of plungers by Miley and Nanton. He continued, "This kind of theatrical experience, and the demands it made upon us, was both educative and enriching, and it brought about a further broadening of the music's scope."[4] The statement may seem self-serving, a rather tony way of looking on performances that verged on the pornographic, but there was intellectual support for it in the prevalent idea that blacks, less inhibited by the stultifying strictures of Western civilization, were closer to the emotional bone than whites and might show them how to get back into the woods.

In any case, Ellington and Mills seized on the idea of "jungle music." The band was already playing a perfervid, hot music suggestive to audiences of jungle frenzies in what was seen as the tigerlike growling of Miley and the primitive moaning of Joe Nanton, and Ellington set about cultivating the sound. Not all of the pieces would adhere to this formula, for the band had to support dancers and singers and play pop tunes for the customers to dance to. But a general line was set, and Ellington would henceforward create a lot of numbers supposed to suggest something of the frenzy of savage dances or the lugubrious moaning of blacks being transported to the Georgia rice fields in the hold of a slave ship.

We must see, then, that at this point, when Ellington was creating his first masterpieces, he was not thinking of them as compositions separate from his orchestra. Indeed, he would have been angry had anyone begun "stealing" his pieces. His main aim was to compose pieces that would make him a famous bandleader. "I don't think he really ever intended to be an arranger," Louis Metcalf said. "It was just something that . . . was put on him. He was given the job and he just went at it."[5] Even as late as 1929, according to Mercer, Ellington had been doing little real writing. He was composing not because he was driven by an inner flame, a vision of himself as a black Joyce who would forge in the smithy of his soul the music of his race, but because he wanted his band to succeed.

Once again, it is difficult to know exactly what Ellington was writing and how he was going about it. He was not, certainly, writing all the music for the Cotton Club shows or even the major portion of it. The songs were being written first by Jimmy McHugh and then by Harold Arlen, two men who would go on to become among America's finest songwriters. Neither needed advice from Ellington. Moreover, although Ellington created a certain amount of music for his singers and dancers in the show— "Rockin' in Rhythm" was put together expressly for dancers—many of the acts brought their own music, which the band would have to learn laboriously, often with Duke at the piano feeding out lines to the instrumentalists. Barney Bigard said, "Some of the acts brought in their own music but Duke wrote for a lot of them."[6]

How much music Duke wrote during this period, then, is hard to know, but he certainly wrote some. The band was recording regularly, and most of this music was created specifically for the recording dates. It also had to produce music for dancing and the radio broadcasts and some new music for the shows. Duke was being paid an extra fifty dollars a week to help Jimmy McHugh with arrangements, although that help may simply have been teaching the parts to the band.

Through all of his work, Ellington was developing his personal method of—we cannot say composing, but creating compositions. He would begin by bringing into the recording studio or rehearsal hall a few musical ideas— scraps of melodies, harmonies, and chord sequences usually clothed in the sound of particular instrumentalists in the band. On the spot he would sit down at the piano and quickly rough out a section—four, eight, sixteen bars. The band would play it; Duke would repeat it; the band would play it again until everybody got it. Years later, the pianist Jimmy Jones said, "What he does is like a chain reaction. Here's a section, here's a section and here's another and, in between, he begins putting the connecting links—the amazing thing about Ellington is that he can think so fast on the spot and create so quickly."[7] Along the way, members of the band would make suggestions. Cootie said, "Everyone in the band would pitch in and help write songs, everything that, almost, Duke did in those days."[8]

As a piece was developing, it would frequently be up to the men in the sections to work out the harmonies, usually from chords Duke would supply. When the trombonist Lawrence Brown came into the band a little later to make a third trombone, he was expected to manufacture for himself a third part to everything. "I had to compose my own parts . . . you just went along and whatever you heard was missing, that's where you were."[9] Ben Webster did the same when he joined the saxophone section ten years later.

Finally, the sections would rehearse by themselves to get the phrasing down. Jimmy Hamilton, another late arrival, said, "He just put the notes down. We would put that together."[10] Of course, Ellington, in the end, controlled the process. He would make changes as he saw fit, moving a solo from one man to another, changing the harmonies, switching sections around. A piece was never really finished but went on changing for as long as the band played it. This was relatively easy to do; since very little was on paper, it was simply a question of telling the men of the change. "We knew we could always take it after it was perfected by the whole band," Irving Mills said, "by taking it off the record and printing it."[11]

This rather helter-skelter method of composing did not lend itself to carefully thought-out pieces with developing themes, variations on material that has gone before, and other devices commonplace in musical compositions. But it had the advantage of tailoring the arrangements to the strong points of the group. An ordinary composer could not really write for this group successfully. It depended not merely on knowing in which part of the range Tricky Sam was most effective but on letting him develop the part as it suited him best. On the other side of it, Duke lacked the training to sit down at a piano and write a piece cold, although he would become better at it. This improvisatory method of composing was the only one that would work, given the skills and temperaments of both band and leader. And, of course, the more Ellington worked this way, the better his sidemen were able to function within the system, becoming increasingly skilled at working out voicings and finding supporting and answering themes for the melodic lines Duke brought them. It was a procedure that musicians unused to it would have trouble adapting to, as new men invariably did.

The system also depended on having at the head a man who was fully in control and had firm ideas about what he wanted pieces to sound like. Once again, we can see the importance of Ellington's character to the creation of his works. Without a liking for control and a subtle skill at manipulating people, he could not have composed as he did. Nor could he have worked this way had he lacked the confidence in his own judgment to decide instantly between this, that, or something else. A composer who fussed and agonized would have gotten nowhere using these tactics. Duke had an ability to trust his own taste: if it sounded right to him, he would use it; if it did not, he would not use it. Not all of us are blessed with that strength.

He had yet another trait that was artistically important. That was a need to succeed or, rather, the expectation that he should be admired as he had always been. An artist who does not care about being admired or even flouts admiration—there are such people—is not likely to produce works that people like. At this stage of his career, Ellington was fighting to be admired in the popular music business, not to create masterpieces, and he took the advice of Irving Mills, who, whatever else he may have lacked, had a thorough understanding of popular taste. Duke was writing for those people who were at the tables at the Cotton Club or who were listening to the music on their radios.

But creating the right kind of music was only half of it. Irving Mills had a keen sense of public relations, and he set about seeing to it that Ellington became better known. The first break came when one of the band's fans, Ted Husing, arranged for a national broadcast from the Cotton Club. When Duke opened there, it was broadcasting over the same local station, WHN, that had broadcast the Washingtonians from the Kentucky Club. By 1927, combines of radio stations were being put together to carry programs across the country—the forerunners of today's radio and television networks. These networks were brand-new in 1927, and Husing talked one of them, CBS, into putting a wire into the Cotton Club. Precisely when and how often the orchestra was on the air is hard to determine. At least two sources say that the band broadcast regularly at five or six in the evening for an hour, but others claim they heard the band late at night. It is probable that the broadcasting schedule changed from time to time, but the broadcasts were frequent and heard nationwide. Both Mills and Husing meddled in the broadcasts, and, possibly, so did Norman Brokenshire, who succeeded Husing and also became a famous announcer.

The broadcasts were critically important to establishing the Ellington band. During this period the Cotton Club was becoming the most famous nightclub in the country. As a consequence, the broadcasts got a lot of listeners. What could be more glamorous to a radio listener in Des Moines than to tune in to the Cotton Club, where show business celebrities, politicians, and famous columnists sat around with big-time gangsters and murderers? Eventually, Mills would put together a recording called "A Night at the Cotton Club," faked in studio, to capitalize on this interest.

At the beginning, once the band got the hang of doing the shows, it was all fun. Duke said, "At first I was happy. There were lots of pretty women and champagne and nice people and plenty of money."[12] The band played two shows, at 11:30 and 2:30, and between times it played for dancing and conversation. There was a master of ceremonies who made the announcements, so Ellington had nothing to do but direct the band. He was just as glad; at this stage of his life he was mike shy, and it was some time before he acquired the glib patter he became famous for. The big newspaper columnists like Walter Winchell and Louis Sobol were in the place constantly. Mayor Jimmy Walker came up; Bix Beiderbecke and some of the men from the Whiteman band came up drunk and sat in, and at the end of the evening Duke would play cards with Big Frenchy and some of the others. This was the height of the Wall Street boom, the heyday of the Jazz Age, and, for those in the thick of it, it was a golden time when it seemed that the money would never run out and the party would never stop.

The band was on the rise. "We started wearing tuxedos," Barney Bigard said, "but as we began to build up a band fund, we bought other uniforms. We built that fund up out of tips and added to it by fining each guy a dollar for every fifteen minutes late he came to rehearsal or band meeting."[13]

By 1929 the band had been at the Cotton Club for over a year, its name had become widely known, and Mills was pushing it into new arenas. For one thing, in the spring he arranged for it to work with a new show by Vincent Youmans, then called *Horse Shoes* but later to appear on Broadway as *Great Day*. The show, which Youmans was producing himself, was modeled on *Show Boat*, which had had an enormous critical and popular success not long before. The Youmans show was about river-boat gamblers and downtrodden blacks, and Youmans wanted a black orchestra for it. There was, however, some problem about the contract—it may have been that Mills smelled disaster, for there were rumors that all was not well with the show—and Ellington pulled out. Fletcher Henderson, with Louis Armstrong, got the job, and it nearly destroyed the Henderson band, for the white conductor began firing the Henderson men, one after another, and substituting whites, until the band was all white.

Mills still wanted to get the orchestra into a show, for the publicity value as much as for anything else. As it happened, Florenz Ziegfeld was preparing a new Gershwin musical called *Show Girl*, which would include "Liza" and "An American in Paris." Will Vodery, as usual, was acting as Ziegfeld's musical director, and it was almost certainly he who recommended the Ellington band to Ziegfeld. The band would have to read a score, and this was when Duke first brought Juan Tizol into the band.

The show was not one of Gershwin's best, and eventually some Vincent Youmans tunes were added to perk it up. However, it ran through the summer and into the fall.

Then, in March 1930, the Ellington band was teamed with Maurice Chevalier, the popular French ballad singer, who had had a successful appearance in New York the year before. Brooks Atkinson, who would become the country's premier theater reviewer, said, "Before M. Chevalier appears as the second half of the program, Duke Ellington, the djinn of din, and his colored Cotton Club Orchestra, devote an hour to elaborate devices for making noise."[14] Whatever Atkinson thought, the band's appearance was a success.

For the Chevalier show Ellington had to do his own talking, and he was thoroughly unnerved by the experience. He said, "I didn't know the first thing about how to M.C. and the thought of it had me half scared to death. Then, there we were on the stage and I opened my mouth and nothing came out."[15] Ellington always made a point of appearing confident, self-assured, and completely in control of things when in public, but, in fact, even late in life, radio and television interviews made him nervous. Helen Dance, who knew Ellington well, especially during the late 1930s and early 1940s, when she was producing a lot of his records, remembers when he did not have all the personality and confident approach that everybody came to know so well. She recalls once when he came out onto the stage, began to build up the singer he was about to introduce, and then forgot her name, and Sonny Greer had to feed it to him.[16] His cousin Juanita Middleton said that after an appearance on the important Edward R. Murrow show, Duke admitted that he had been nervous, adding that he was *always* nervous onstage when he first came out. Both Edmund Anderson and Barry Ulanov said the same.

It was typical of Ellington, however, that he recognized that he had to learn to handle the announcements if he was to get ahead, and he gradually developed the slightly ironic manner he became famous for. "He became more confident after a while," said Edmund Anderson.[17]

If radio was important to the building of celebrity, the movies were even more so. With the advent of sound films, at about the time Duke went into the Cotton Club, movie producers began scrambling about for material they could use. Inevitably, they fell back on music and began introducing band scenes into movies and even building whole films around musicians. Mills was quick to get Ellington into films. The first was *Black and Tan Fantasy*, a nineteen-minute short made by Dudley Murphy, more or less in tandem with another short featuring Bessie Smith. The films were shot in the New York area. Both had skimpy plots just elaborate enough to support the music. *Black and Tan Fantasy* concerns a dancer, played by Freddi Washington, who has a bad heart but performs anyway. She collapses and, on her deathbed, asks the band to play the title tune. (Arthur Whetsol plays the plunger portions made famous by Bubber Miley.)

The second movie from this period was a 1930 feature starring Amos 'n' Andy, two whites in blackface who had an enormous success on radio. The band played through the entire sound track but is seen in only one scene, in which it plays "Three Little Words" and an Ellington number, "Old Man Blues." According to David Chertok, an authority on jazz in films, Check and Double Check was "one of the worst movies ever made."[18] Among other things, the light-skinned Tizol and Bigard were blacked up so that the band would not appear integrated. But, Chertok said, "there is no question about the fact that films had a lot to do with [Duke's] national reputation."[19]

In addition, by the time of the Cotton Club stay, Ellington was beginning to receive newspaper and magazine attention. The first was the long piece in the New York Tribune in August 1927, even before the band opened at the Cotton Club, that praised the band extravagantly and referred to the old Hollywood Inn as "the most fashionable and exclusive night club" in New York, a statement that even the club's staunchest supporters would have trouble accepting. The band was also, by 1927, being mentioned occasionally by the trade press—Variety, Billboard, the New York Clipper, and Orchestra World, which in 1926 said that the band was supplying "high grade melody and rhythm" at the Kentucky Club.

The most important of the reports on the band were appearing in a periodical called the Phonograph Monthly Review, which was started in 1926 and died with the Depression. It was the first, and for a time the only, American periodical covering recorded music for the general public. Although its circulation was small—about fifteen thousand at its peak—it was relatively influential because it had the field to itself. The paper had a tiny staff, and most of the work of reviewing—indeed, at times, writing the whole paper—fell to an enthusiastic young man named Robert Donaldson Darrell, who had studied music at the New England Conservatory and would go on to become an important critic of classical music. The people on the paper were, Darrell said, "a screwball bunch of fanatics."[20]

Darrell probably can be called the first jazz critic. He was not, certainly, the first to write about the music seriously—there had been serious writing about jazz by Americans virtually from the moment it spread out from New Orleans a decade earlier. Nor was he, at first, very familiar with jazz. But he was the first to review jazz regularly with sensitivity and perception. He was fumbling in the dark a good deal of the time: he was simply opening the boxes of records that arrived in the office and playing them without too much idea of who was on them. But an astonishingly large percentage of his judgments stands up today.

He was primarily interested in classical music, but he began reviewing the popular records for the sake of completeness, and one day he was struck by a record by a group called the Washingtonians that he had never heard of before, playing a mournful tune with some strange, freak effects. This was "Black and Tan Fantasy." He said it deserved "first prize" among the dance records for the month and went on,

> In it the Washingtonians combine sonority and fine tonal qualities with some amazing eccentric instrumental effects. This record differs from similar ones by avoiding extremes, for while the "stunts" are exceptionally original and striking, they are performed musically, even artistically. A piece no one should miss! The snatch of the "Chopin Funeral March" at the end deserves special mention as a stroke of genius.[21]

(Actually, Darrell had reviewed "East St. Louis Toodle-Oo" the preceding month, calling it a "real winner," but he did not realize it was by the same band.)[22] Darrell then made a point of calling the record company to find out who the Washingtonians were, and he paid special attention to the band in succeeding issues. Four sides from Vocalion, among them another version of "East St. Louis Toodle-Oo," were "two of the finest jazz couplings perhaps ever released."[23] In January 1928, he said, "A new performance of 'Black and Tan Fantasy' by Duke Ellington eclipses even the startling Brunswick record of this remarkable piece," and went on to note, "There can't be too many disks of a work as original and inspired as this one."[24] And so it went: "Jubilee Stomp" had "a most arresting beginning and a development that sustains its first promise";[25] "Washington Wobble" and "Harlem River Quiver" had "all the throaty sonority and symphonic ingenuity which have made Ellington the most significant—if not the best known—figure in hot jazz";[26] "Doin' the Frog" had an "arresting beginning—a not uncommon feature of Ellington's arrangements, the first few bars of which are usually worth several complete pieces by less inspired directors."[27] Darrell continued to review Ellington in this fashion all through the Cotton Club period. His interest culminated in 1932 in a long piece on Duke for *Disques*, an American magazine, despite the title. The story was entitled "Black Beauty."[28] It was a serious and thoughtful analysis of Ellington's work, the first such to appear in print—and the first to make the comparison to Debussy and Delius that has usually been attributed to the English composer Constant Lambert. Darrell wanted to write a book about Ellington that would be both a biography and an analysis of Duke's music. He sent Ellington a copy of the *Disques* piece and arranged to interview Duke on one of his New England tours. (*Phono-graph Monthly Review* was published in Boston.)

Unfortunately, Ellington was typically evasive. "It was very, very unsatis-factory," Darrell recently said.

> He was very suspicious. I think I sent a copy, at least a typescript, of my piece. He wasn't as articulate then as he later became. Or he was very leery of me. . . . I was very, very discouraged. There was nothing there that I could get. . . . I was trying to get at how he went about things, what music had influenced him. I mean I was sure he'd listened to Ravel, Delius, and so on.[29]

My own supposition is that Ellington was completely thrown by Darrell's technical questions; he simply did not have the training to deal with them. Nor had he listened to Ravel, and it is doubtful that he even knew who Delius was. In the end, the book was not written, and that was, needless to say, an enormous loss to jazz history. But the Darrell reviews and the *Disques* piece had important consequences for Ellington. In England, dance band musicians, the editors of the *Melody Maker*, a paper started not long before the *Phonograph Monthly Review* began, and a few critics like Lambert were struggling to get information about the new, hot music, and they were reading Darrell's reviews.[30] They were also reading the *Disques* piece, which was eventually reprinted in London; ironically, the editor asked permission to alter it slightly because "some of the words used" might be "beyond the understanding" of his readership.[31] Darrell's enthusiasm for Ellington alerted them to the band. Eventually, the British jazz critics would claim Ellington as their own discovery, and it would be their praise, rather than Darrell's, that would convince him that he was not merely a bandleader but a real composer. The effect of Darrell's enthu-siasm would come later and at second hand, but it was felt nonetheless.

When Duke Ellington went into the Cotton Club in December 1927, he was known to New York sports and close followers of dance music as one of a number of black bandleaders; to the general public he was only a vague name and probably unknown to most. When he ended the Cotton Club stay in early 1931, he was well known, the leader of one of the most celebrated American dance bands and, moreover, someone intellectuals had come to consider a serious composer. In 1932 a poll of bands in a black newspaper, the *Pittsburgh Courier*, gave him first place among black bands, ahead of Fletcher Henderson, at last. Such was his renown that when, in 1931, President Herbert Hoover invited a group of black dignitaries to visit the White House, Ellington was among them. In 1932 the Australian-born composer Percy Grainger, in residence in the United States, arranged for Ellington to play a concert at Columbia and to lecture on music at

New York University: opportunities like those were not being offered to other jazz musicians. Over the next few years there would be major magazine pieces about him in the most prestigious American periodicals: *Time* and *Fortune*, among others. He was, in the early 1930s, already being seen as somebody special—not just one more bandleader, but somebody who was, somehow, more important than that.

Ellington's career, then, had changed markedly during the Cotton Club years; and so had his personal life. As we have seen, one of the things that had drawn Ellington to music in the first place was his taste for women. His sex life has been described in some detail in a book about him by Don George,[32] who later on would write lyrics for Ellington songs; but it is very difficult to sort out the truth. However, it is more probable that Duke was never strictly faithful to Edna. He was immensely attractive to women, for he was good-looking, tall, elegantly dressed, generous, given to making flowery compliments, and, eventually, celebrated. Even if he had little interest in women himself, he would have had a difficult time avoiding entanglements; and he had considerable interest in them. Moreover, he was not always scrupulous about whom he chose to interest himself in, and there are reports of his being involved with some of his musicians' women. Barney Bigard claimed, "He interfered in my sex life. I told him to cut it out," and threatened to give Duke a beating.[33] Bigard also claimed that Juan Tizol threatened to cut Ellington once for the same reason. And it is generally accepted that he had an affair with the wife of one of his trombone players.

How much Edna knew of these affairs is hard to say. She could not have been entirely ignorant of them. However, she may have also had her flings. Bigard insisted that she was seeing a man who was "quite a figure in the music world," adding, "That's all I'll say, and a real gentleman."[34] Who, in the end, accused whom of what we do not know, but there was a fight between them in which Edna slashed Duke's cheek with a knife or razor. Duke carried the scar to his grave, but, not surprisingly, he refused to talk about it.

In any case, by the end of the 1920s, there were growing problems between Duke and Edna. Duke had an affair with "a very beautiful and talented woman, an actress," which ended when the woman realized that Duke would never divorce Edna to marry her.[35] There was also a wealthy white "socialite" whose relatives were able to discourage the affair.[36] Finally, there was Mildred Dixon, a petite woman with long black hair, which she wore in a bun. Mildred was a dancer who opened at the Cotton Club with her partner, Henri Wesson, on the same night as the Ellington band. Mildred was well liked and diplomatic. Barney Bigard said, "Mildred is a cute little gal."[37] Fran Hunter said, "She was a great person. She understood his way of life and she accepted it. She was one of the women he truly loved."[38] In any event, probably in 1929, Duke broke with Edna. He took an apartment at 381 Edgecombe Avenue, in the fancy Sugar Hill area of Harlem, and moved Mildred Dixon in with him. They would live as man and wife for some ten years, although he would never marry her.

Duke and Edna remained on reasonably friendly terms. He never divorced her—this was, in part, a calculated policy that prevented him from marrying anyone else—and he provided for her for the rest of her life. According to Ruth, Edna "would come to the house and whatever she wanted he gave to her."[39] Edna herself said that she was jealous of the attention Duke was getting from the public—especially, no doubt, the female half of it—but years later she told an interviewer, "I love Ellington and I'm going to stick my neck out and say I don't think he hates me. I don't want a divorce and neither does he. We're proud of the way we get along. He has always provided for me through the years. . . . I was hurt, bad hurt when the breakup came but I have never been bitter."[40]

Then, in 1930, when the band was working in the Gershwin show *Show Girl*, Duke made another, quite interesting change in his personal life. For some time Mercer, Ruth, and other members of the family had been making visits to New York from Washington to see their by now famous relative, whose broadcasts they had been hearing at home. Now Duke decided that they should give up their Washington house altogether and move in with him. It was not an idea that would have occurred to every man in Duke's position. He was a celebrity, he was making money, he had a virtually unlimited supply of women available to him, and he liked the fast life. Why encumber himself with a mother who had Victorian ideas about sin and a kid sister who could not be exposed to the sort of life the Cotton Club epitomized?

Yet that is what he did. J.E. resisted at first. "I'm too young to stop working," he said.[41] He was only forty-nine years old; what would he do with himself? But Daisy had no doubts about the move; leaving J.E. behind in Washington to deal with the house, she brought Ruth and Mercer to New York, where Duke settled everyone, including Mildred, in the three-bedroom apartment on Edgecombe Avenue.

It was a curious thing to do. It was now impossible for Duke to entertain in his home most of his associates in show business; and it put Mildred in the position of being a daughter-in-law in what was, ostensibly, her home. But that was the way Duke wanted things, and Duke usually got what he wanted. Why did he do it?

For one thing, Duke was exactly what he appeared to be, a loyal and devoted son. He felt protective toward Ruth, he respected J.E. as a father should be respected, and he worshiped his mother. An interviewer who visited the apartment not long after the family moved in commented on "the unusually fine consideration that he shows for his mother, anticipating her slightest wish; attending to anything that might contribute to her happiness."[42] In return, Daisy gave Duke total acceptance. He could do no wrong in her eyes. She was a Victorian lady to the point that she would not, according to Ruth, even use birth control; yet she was able to close her eyes to the fact that her beloved son was associating with gangsters, pimps, prostitutes, and gamblers and was regularly being unfaithful to his common-law wife. It is a contradiction in Daisy's character that can be explained only if we understand that her devotion to her son went beyond the usual concern of a mother for her child. Duke, to her, was wonderful in everything he did, and it was not simply because of the "unusually fine consideration" he showed her—the furs, the flowers, the little courtesies—for she had felt that way ever since his childhood. "He had a kind of love affair going on all the time with his mother," Fran Hunter said.[43]

But there was more to it than that. At the core of Ellington's character were coupled two traits: a need to control, to dominate those around him, and an intense loyalty and protectiveness of these same people. He manipulated the men in his band, he had them do what he wanted them to do; but, at the same time, he was endlessly loyal to them. Jack Tracy, then a writer for *Down Beat*, once observed one of the saxophonists on the band lying on the bandstand while the band was playing, asleep from some combination of drugs or drink. But when he suggested to Duke that such behavior was harming the band's reputation, Duke became enraged and told Tracy some long fable about how the player had contracted malaria in the Pacific during the war and could not help himself.[44] Ellington simply would not accept criticism of "his" men.

It worked the same with the family. He was infinitely loyal and protective, but he wanted to dominate as well. Once an aunt of his visited him in New York and asked Duke for a drink. Duke gave her a glass of milk, saying, "I don't allow the women in my family to drink."[45] He moved the family to New York in part because he loved them all and wanted to give them the things that his new celebrity allowed him; but he also moved them in with him so he could control them. He became, in fact, the father in the family; he was able to do this because he controlled the money. He treated Ruth like a little princess—coddled, but protected. She said, "Edward wouldn't permit me to go anywhere at anytime."[46] He insisted that she come home directly from school and arranged for a car to take her to and fro.

His treatment of his son, Mercer, was even more confining. He saw him as a potential rival, and Mercer's hair was kept in braids for some time so that his father would tolerate his presence. After his father died, Mercer wrote a book about his relationship to his father that at times makes for painful reading. He wrote, "My father would never do anything overt or bad enough to really hurt but, if my foot slipped, he would let me go all the way down."[47] Elsewhere he said,

> In the final analysis, I don't think he wanted me to do anything. I think he thought that as long as I was devoted to him that was enough—he was capable of supporting me. He once said, "You have the children. I'll take care of them." It made me angry but, more than anything, it made me furtive. I started reading psychology books and my being versed in this subject put me in a peculiar relation to Ellington. I knew all the various ways you could trade on other men's weaknesses. But, if anything, it probably made matters worse between us. Before, he used to pull these little tricks and I'd be victim and the relationship would be good. But to rise up against him really made the old man mad. It became a cold war.[48]

Mercer undoubtedly exaggerated his father's competitiveness, but that was because so much of it was directed at him. It is all summed up, I think, in Duke's description of Mercer in *Music Is My Mistress*. The passage is brief and nowhere suggests the ordinary pride a father might take in a son's achievements. Instead, Mercer is praised for what he had done for Duke. The opening sentence is "My son, Mercer Ellington, is dedicated to maintaining the luster of his father's image."[49] Duke Ellington was a warm-hearted man who treated the people around him with loyalty and generosity; but there was a price that had to be paid.

9

The Ellington Style
Takes Shape

The records made by the Washingtonians in their first years of existence, like "Animal Crackers" and "Choo Choo," show a rough band dominated by the growling of Miley and Charlie Irvis, playing a music much like that produced by scores of incipient jazz bands around New York, except for what would be called the "jungle effect" provided by the growling brass. And then, suddenly the entire quality of the music changed, and it became recognizably what we think of today as Ellington music. In June 1926 the band cut the dismal "Animal Crackers" and "Li'l Farina." In November of that year it made its first major records: "East St. Louis Toodle-Oo" and "Birmingham Breakdown," two of Ellington's best-known numbers. These were not isolated examples; over the next four months the band would cut a series of important records, ending with the first version of "Black and Tan Fantasy," at the beginning of April 1927. There would be no return to the old way. Something new had arrived.

The differences between the old and the new modes are marked. For one thing, the old raggy rhythm has become a real jazz swing, with the putative eighth notes divided unequally and the lines hammered less directly on the beat. For another, the pieces are put together with much more imagination and intelligence, so that the music contains both surprises and logic. For a third, the musicians are more experienced and play better.

What happened? What caused this dramatic change in so short a time? So far as the movement out of rag rhythms into swing is concerned, it was a move made by young musicians everywhere. In particular, Louis Armstrong's sojourn with the Fletcher Henderson band from the fall of 1924 until the fall of the next year had shown the New York musicians what swing was all about. But Armstrong was not alone: the New Orleans rhythm was creeping into the consciousness of musicians through the recordings of the Oliver band, the New Orleans Rhythm Kings, and other orchestras and through the travels of these musicians and their imitators around the country. Swing was in the air. And for the Ellington men, there had also been the presence of Sidney Bechet.

For the Washingtonians, the significant change was the arrangement with Mills that gave Ellington real control of the orchestra. No doubt Mills wanted him to invent a musical style for the group, but, given Ellington's nature, he would have needed no urging to impose his own musical ideas on the band, in however subtle a fashion.

For some of those ideas, at least initially, he turned to the Fletcher Henderson orchestra. As early as the beginning of 1925, J. A. Jackson was claiming that the Henderson band was "the talk of the dancing folks of Broadway."[1] As a black columnist, Jackson might have been prejudiced, but he was supported in his view by Orchestra World, which said, "There is no better dance orchestra than Fletcher's, white or colored."[2] By this time the Henderson band was admired by musicians and by the dancing public of both races, and it is hardly surprising that Ellington would look to it for a model. He never made any secret of this fact. Decades later he said, "Fletcher was a big inspiration to me. His was the band I always wanted mine to sound like when I got ready to have a big band, and that's what we tried to achieve the first chance we had with that many musicians."[3] He spoke of this debt to Henderson many times.

Fletcher Henderson had studied classical piano for many years as a youth and knew something about how music was put together. His musical director at this period was Don Redman, who had had substantial conservatory training and could play a number of instruments. Between them they had devised a style of music, building on the Grofé-Whiteman model, which in turn owed something to Art Hickman and depended upon the complex interplay of soloists and sections of the orchestra. By 1926 Redman was chinking every empty hole in the music with breaks, call-and-answers, fills, and punctuation. In most Henderson arrangements of the time everything was constantly in motion. Redman was able to write these complicated pieces because he was a skilled arranger and because the Henderson men took pride in their ability to read anything, even in the unusual keys for dance bands that Redman frequently used.

What Ellington seems to have taken from Henderson in late 1926, when he discovered himself firmly in charge, was this system of punctuating, answering, supporting everything with something. As we shall see, he developed his skillful use of a rich tonal palette and of his unique harmonic system by himself; but his structural method was suggested to him by what the much-acclaimed Henderson band—and, to some extent, the Whiteman orchestra—was doing.

He may, as he suggested, have had this in mind for some time, and was now able to put it into practice because he and Mills had built the band up to ten pieces—at least for recordings—one fewer than Henderson had, so that he now had both three-piece brass and reed sections. Why the band was enlarged at this time is not known; it may simply have been the recognition that a larger band was more competitive.

But the crucial point is that sometime in the latter half of 1926 Ellington took over, once and for all, musical direction of the band. There is some suggestion that Ellington's taking command of the music was quite sudden. Louis Metcalf said that the men were surprised when Duke started making arrangements "overnight."[4] The sidemen continued to make suggestions, and Duke continued to take over melodic material that the musicians created. But from now on he would be the final arbiter of what went into a piece. As a result, from late 1926 on, the band had an identifiable musical personality—the personality that would mark it for decades. Moreover, this was not Fletcher Henderson's personality. Ellington's music of this period was less complex and busy than Henderson's, in part because neither Duke nor the sidemen had the skills that the Henderson men had. But his music seems to me more deeply felt; there is less flash, less showmanship, and more expression of genuine feeling.

Ellington's emergence as the true musical director of the group would certainly have forced him to learn a little more about the technicalities of composition—voice leading, structure, chord patterns, modulations, and the like. At some point during this period he began picking the brains of two distinguished black musicians, Will Marion Cook and Will Vodery. Both men were thoroughly schooled. Vodery, as we have seen, was Florenz Ziegfeld's musical director for decades and an important name in show business around New York; in his work with Ziegfeld, he necessarily had direction of many white singers and dancers, and this may have helped him to rise above segregation, to an extent. Ellington wrote that Vodery was a close friend of the great black comic Bert Williams:

> They were regularly seen together during the Ziegfeld period. Handsome, debonair, and always in gentlemanly attire, they were respected by everyone as they walked through the downtown streets. They patronized any place they chose in that Glitter Belt, even sometimes in company with those gorgeous Ziegfeld beauties, and there was no sweat, no color compromise![5]

Will Marion Cook, a graduate of Oberlin Conservatory, was said to have destroyed his violin when he realized that he would never be allowed to join a white symphony orchestra, although the story has been told in various ways. He thereafter concentrated on composing what he considered to be the music of his own people, a good deal of it those "syncopated songs" that were popular in America around the turn of the nineteenth century. He wrote the first important black musical, *Clorindy, or the Origin of the Cakewalk*, and many hit songs. Like Vodery, he was a figure of importance on the New York musical scene.

Precisely when Ellington began mining these two men for information is impossible to know, but I suggest that he may have been seeing at least one of them at this time. He said,

> Will [Cook] never wore a hat and when people asked him why he'd say because he didn't have the money to buy one. They'd give him five dollars and then he and I would get into a taxi and ride around Central Park and he'd give me lectures in music. I'd sing a melody in its simplest form and he'd stop me and say, "Reverse your figures." He was a brief but a strong influence. His language had to be pretty straight for me to know what he was talking about. Some of the things he used to tell me I never got a chance to use until years later, when I wrote the tone poem, "Black, Brown, and Beige."[6]

Cook was teaching Ellington some of the standard devices for melody writing taught at conservatories: play the melody backward, turn it upside down, and so forth. We shall see, ultimately, that Duke used the lessons well. Cook also told him, "You know you should go to the conservatory, but since you won't, I'll tell you. First you find the logical way, and when you find it, avoid it, and let your inner self break through and guide you. Don't try to be anybody else but yourself."[7]

It is unlikely that Duke needed such advice, for it was the essence of his character to break rules. In a famous scene in *Through the Looking Glass*, Alice gets into an argument with Humpty Dumpty over the huge egg's insistence that he can make a word mean anything he wants. "The question is," Humpty Dumpty says with a good deal of contempt, "which is to be master—that's all."

Duke Ellington had, I think, in respect to the standard rules of musical theory, the attitude of Humpty Dumpty: the question was, which was to be master, he or the rules. Stanley Dance said, "He liked to prove that the unorthodox would sound all right. You know, this is the truth. He always liked to do something which they said was wrong."[8] The musicians were frequently startled by what they saw on paper. One of Duke's copyists, Tom Whaley, said, "The first time I was copying his music I said, 'Duke, you got an E natural up there against an E flat.' He said, 'That's alright, put it down.' And, after you hear it, it sounds great."[9] Mercer said, "He didn't like the rules in anything. To discard a rule was a source of inspiration to him because he immediately saw the way to make it work in reverse."[10]

In the working out of his musical system, then, the first of Duke's rules was to break them. He was driven to this conclusion by temperament, not by any careful process of thought; and again we see how important character was to the shape of his work, because his contempt for the rules led him into certain practices that became characteristic of his work: the search for forms other than the eight- and sixteen-bar forms to which virtually all popular tunes were cut, the use of far more dissonance than was customary in dance bands of the time, the voicing together of unusual combinations of instruments. In truth, Ellington quite purposefully used the rules as inspiration: if he learned that you were not supposed to use parallel fifths, he would immediately find a way of using them; if he was told that major sevenths must always rise, he would write a tune in which the line descended from the major seventh. As we examine his music, we will, again and again, be able to explain many of his happiest effects by seeing them as opposed to some common rule of music theory.

But in truth, in most instances Ellington broke rules simply because he was unaware of them. He never, even long after he was writing extended and quite complex pieces, knew much about formal music theory. Nearly everything was pragmatic—done by ear. His method was to start with very basic material—one of the dozen or so standard chord sequences on which most popular music of the time was built, and one of the simplest patterns, such as the blues, or the standard sixteen or thirty-two bar AABA pop music form. He would then begin to elaborate on this, reshaping the form by adding or subtracting measures, and especially by tucking dissonant notes into chords in order to give them a particular quality he was looking for. Decisions as to what changes to make, what notes to add, were not based on theory; it was a matter of experimenting until he struck something he liked. I am certain that Duke would not usually have been able to analyze his own scores in the way that a more formally trained arranger would—that is, seeing this chord as an $E7\#5$, this one as a $B13$. This is precisely why a lot of his music is difficult to analyze: in altering a basic chord sequence, he might in the end change it to something quite different from what he started with. There is always a certain amount of ambiguity in Ellington's work; his habit of putting sevenths at the bottom, in Harry Carney's baritone, at times contributed to this. In analyzing Ellington's work, especially his harmonies, in my view it is closer to his own way of thinking to see them as alterations of simple material, rather than previously constructed building blocks set in a row.

Over the next few years after the November 1926 session, the band would record for seven different labels, using at least a dozen different names.

From 1929 through 1931 Victor seems to have had exclusive rights to the name "Duke Ellington," but Mills was recording the band for whomever he wanted, primarily to get more of his tunes on records, for other companies and under names dredged up by a sensibility closely in tune with the American delight in the comic darky: the Harlem Footwarmers, the Ten Blackberries, the Jungle Band, the Harlem Hot Chocolates, and others. At times, additional musicians were brought into the studio, especially to fill out the saxophone section in 1926 and 1927.

The tunes Ellington composed during the period after 1926 tended to fall into categories, many of them probably suggested by Irving Mills, who was quick to analyze popular taste in that way. There were slow "jungle" numbers, often in minor keys supposed to suggest spooky doings in the voodoo hut; "hot" horse race numbers worked out to back dancers or to feature instrumentalists playing flashy solos at high speed; and, inevitably, a lot of the blues that were then in vogue. It is important to remember that Ellington's music from this period was functional: it was meant to entertain, to serve certain purposes, to awaken certain responses in listeners. It was not cut to fit abstract rules and theories of art: if it did what it was supposed to do, that was enough, and, so far as Mills, Harry Block, or the record companies were concerned, it did not matter how Duke composed, so long as the music worked.

"East St. Louis Toodle-Oo," the first major work in the Ellington canon, was one of those "jungle" numbers, a composition that he would go on playing for fifty years and that would be, for a time, his theme. (The title is pronounced "toe-dul-oh," despite the spelling.) The first theme, a very simple saw-toothed line in C minor, has generally been credited to Bubber Miley. Bubber had a habit of singing words from advertising signs that happened to suggest music to him. As the story goes, there was a sign for a cleaner called Lewando that the band could see from train windows as they went from New York to Boston to begin their summer tours at Salem Willows. Bubber began singing, "Oh, lee-wan-do, oh lee-wan-do," and thus the theme was born.

The piece consists of three themes, in B-flat minor, A-flat, and E-flat. However, the second theme appears only once, as a kind of a bridge between sections of the first theme, making a standard thirty-two-bar AABA form; in the main, "East St. Louis Toodle-Oo" consists of alternations of B-flat minor and E-flat major themes. This E-flat major theme is a close variation of "I Wish I Could Shimmy Like My Sister Kate," which Louis Armstrong always insisted Armand J. Piron had stolen from him and made a lot of money from. It is, in any case, a trivial theme with, no doubt, a long history.

The number opens with an eight-bar introduction of the "leewando" theme alone, followed by Bubber Miley shouting and growling at his wildest and most intense. Tricky Sam solos on the second theme, the clarinet plays sixteen bars over the minor theme, there is a brass trio, a clarinet and soprano sax duet, and half a chorus by the full band, and then Miley plays an eight-bar coda on the minor theme to wind it up. It could hardly be more straightforward, and, in fact, although the reed duet has nice bits of melodic writing, possibly by Toby Hardwick, the whole thing hangs on Miley's plunger work over the minor theme.

The piece also includes a striking device that could prefigure much of what was to come: the "leewando" is voiced for saxophones and tuba, exactly the kind of novel combination of instruments Ellington would come up with, again and again. It also shows a principle that Ellington was developing, as he came more and more to command the band's music—that of playing his strongest cards. In Bass Edwards he had a superb tuba player, technically one of the finest musicians in jazz at the time. (I recently played "Immigration Blues" for some music students, in which Edwards plays a standard rhythm line; they all insisted that they were hearing a bowed string bass.) Ellington had Edwards, and here he put him to excellent use. The idea of voicing a tuba with saxophones would not have occurred to everybody, but, for precisely that reason, it occurred to Ellington.

A second version of the number, made for Columbia about a month later, is slightly different in that the reed duet is now a trio, and in which Miley is even more ferocious, if that is possible; other, substantially different versions, one of them called "Harlem Twist," were made somewhat later. By the time of the last of these, Bass Edwards had left. The theme is played by string bass and baritone sax, and it lacks the cold, smoky force of the first versions.

The point of "East St. Louis Toodle-Oo," besides Miley's intense playing, is the alternation, more or less, of the minor and major themes, the one fierce, hot, and dark, the other sunny and a little aimless. There is no logical development here, merely alternation, and the scheme was not well thought out, a little random even, with themes coming and going for no apparent purpose. What we do notice, however, is not only that the themes contrast in mode and quality but also that the sound of each section contrasts with the other. First, we have Miley growling into the plunger over deep chords anchored by the tuba. Then Nanton plays the cheerful second theme with the open horn. In turn come a clarinet on the minor theme, a brass trio in straight mutes, a clarinet and soprano sax duet, and, finally, to round the piece off, Miley once again growling over the minor theme. The casual organization of the themes is not very imaginative, but the use of the tone palette is. Ellington has, as early as this piece, settled upon a principle of composition that would be basic to him throughout his career: contrast. Everywhere in his work there is variety, change, movement. Nothing is static: at each step of the way something new appears. The variety, especially of sound, in Ellington's work was one of the traits that marked it off from the ordinary big-band sound developed by Grofé, Whiteman, Henderson, Redman, and others, in which choirs of reeds and brass answered one another endlessly. Already in 1926 Ellington was going beyond what the others were doing. With "East St. Louis Toodle-Oo" he has stopped being a mere songwriter: he is struggling to become a composer.

At the same session Ellington produced another tune with a couple of innovations. "Birmingham Breakdown" is an up-tempo swinger built, once again, on contrasting themes in C minor and A-flat major. The piece consists mainly of alternations of these themes, with some soloing and a jammed final ensemble. The second theme is twenty bars long, an unstandard length in popular music at a time when nearly everything but the blues was built on eight-bar segments. We should not make too much of this twenty-bar construction. It is not, for example, made up of two ten-bar sections, or four five-bar ones, or some more irregular combination. It is fundamentally two ordinary eight-bar segments, except that, instead of having the usual closing cadence at the end of sixteen bars, it remains open, and the last four bars are, more or less, repeated. The extra four bars are essentially a tag, a device Ellington hardly invented; significantly, when Toby Hardwick plays his solo, he limits it to sixteen bars without the tag, suggesting that the basic shape of the tune was sixteen measures. Nonetheless, it shows Ellington once again looking for novelty, a departure, a different way of doing things.

In the winter and spring of 1926–27 the band issued a total of twelve cuts. Not all of them are up to the level of "East St. Louis Toodle-Oo," but all of them contain something of interest. "Immigration Blues" is based on the standard blues form but with some chromatic chord movement in measures seven and eight, which is unusual for blues. It has a nice, if tiny, bit of melody and is again a unified piece of music in a quiet, somewhat pensive mood. "The Creeper" is a horse race piece built on "Tiger Rag," a number becoming standard for pieces of this kind: Ellington would make many similar ones. It includes a duet trumpet break taken directly from one played by Oliver and Armstrong on "Snake Rag." "New Orleans Lowdown" is somewhat noisy and jumbled but has a very nice, if small, piece of repeated melody beautifully played by Bass Edwards. On these last two numbers Ellington employs a device he would use again and again throughout his career. That was to turn the clarinet loose on the last eight measures or so to scream overhead in imitation of the red-hot final ensemble choruses of the New Orleans system. "Song of the Cotton Fields," written by Porter Grainger, who was in the Mills stable, has a lot of Miley's superb plunger work. "Down Our Alley Blues" has a quirky bit of melody built on an analogy to the blue notes.

Then, on April 7, 1927, Ellington recorded the piece that more than any other, was to give the band its first fame. "Black and Tan Fantasy" was again and again singled out by music critics and intellectuals in general, beginning with R. D. Darrell, as an example of what jazz could be. It was, to many of them, proof that jazz was art, and this was true not only in the United States but also in England, when the English intellectuals began to be excited by jazz two or three years later.

Why was it "Black and Tan Fantasy," rather than "East St. Louis Toodle-Oo," or something else, that took the fancy of the intellectuals? It opens with the playing of a simple but touching theme on a B-flat minor blues, probably worked out by Bubber Miley; it is my guess that it is a variation on one of many New Orleans funeral marches or dirges, which Miley may have gotten from Bechet, Oliver, or the others. It is played by Miley and Nanton in mutes accompanied by tuba, banjo, and sustained clarinet notes. Miley and Nanton appear to be using plungers over small mutes deep in the bells of their horns, but they are not opening and closing them to produce the characteristic wah-wah sound, nor are they growling. The effect is melancholy rather than fiery. This theme is followed by a very interesting and much more complex theme, played by Toby Hardwick on the alto saxophone. It jumps immediately from the B-flat minor of the preceding theme into G-flat major, an unusual sequence in popular music, although the reverse is more common; eventually, it lands in the key of B-flat major. Movements from the tonic to the minor sixth and back are scattered throughout Ellington's work, so much so that they became almost a personal signature. These are considered, in music theory, to be "distant" keys or chords, but the one can be built from the other simply by raising the fifth and lowering the third of the tonic chord half steps. Any imaginative piano student discovers the effect because it is visual, something that could be diagrammed. Ellington, we remember, had a strong visual sense, which he brought to his music, and I have no doubt that he stumbled upon the tonic–flat sixth relationship, which he was to make so much of, simply by looking down at his fingers as they played a C major chord and saying to himself, What if I spread these two fingers? We will soon see him thinking this way again.

The melody also employs interesting metric shifts in several places, especially in bars five, six, and seven and in the corresponding bars in the second half of the strain. Ragtime players had discovered that, if you repeat a figure made of three eighth or quarter notes over a 4/4 meter, you will have the effect of "cycling," in which the melodic accents move back each time the figure is repeated, so that the melody seems to be sliding backward. Whole tunes like "Fidgety Feet" and "Twelfth Street Rag" were built on the principle. The device was so widely used in jazz that Winthrop Sargeant, who was a musicologist but not an expert on jazz, mistakenly took it for one of the basic principles of the music. Ellington uses it here in the second theme to "Black and Tan Fantasy." It is a pretty melody as a whole, a bouquet of flowers, and contrasts in every way with the minor strain—in key, mood, and timbre.

The remainder of the piece is made up almost entirely of a string of solos on the blues in B-flat major: two choruses by Miley, tightly muted over tuba and banjo; a chorus by Duke unaccompanied; a chorus by Nanton; and, finally, another chorus by Miley accompanied by the band. The piece concludes with a brief snatch of the melody from Chopin's "Funeral March," played by Miley with the band. There are no drums, and the rhythm section is kept as light as possible.

What so excited the critics? For one thing, the touch of Chopin at the end, which Rob Darrell considered a "stroke of genius," suggested a greater musical sophistication than the Washingtonians possessed. I seriously doubt that any of them had ever heard the Chopin piece in its original form. The snatch of it used here was common parlance sung by schoolchildren in parody versions. However, the previous September, Jelly Roll Morton and King Oliver recorded versions of Morton's "Dead Man Blues," both of which included a brief theme from a very similar piece of music, "Flee As a Bird," which was often used as a dirge by New Orleans funeral bands: Morton opened his piece with the dirge; Oliver used it as a closer as Duke used the Chopin theme, and I have no doubt that Duke was inspired by the Morton tune. Morton eventually accused Ellington of stealing his stuff, and threatened to sue; it is likely he had in mind more than just "Black and Tan Fantasy." They remained on bad terms until Morton's death in 1941. Morton was one of the few people Duke ever publicly denigrated.

For a second, the "eccentric" growling and snorting by Nanton and Miley were, for listeners who had not been following the band, new and fresh. Plungers, growls, flutter-tonguing, animal imitations, and other stunts were not new, and people like Darrell and the British critics, whose experience of jazz, at this point, was limited, would have heard such efforts primarily as played by white musicians in big bands—for example, by Henry Busse with Paul Whiteman—who were imitating blacks like Oliver at a considerable distance. Darrell sensed the difference: unlike similar efforts by the imitators, the effects in the Ellington records are "performed musically, even artistically." This really was the essence of it: the more sensitive critics felt a sincerity, a genuineness, in the work of Miley and Nanton that was absent from the "stunts" of the players like Busse, the freak clarinetist Ted "Is Everybody Happy?" Lewis, and even such blacks as the clarinetist Woody Walder and Johnny Dunn.

"Black and Tan Fantasy" is a far from perfect work. We are given, at the beginning, two carefully worked out and nicely balanced themes, and are entitled to expect that something will be done with the contrast. Instead, the second theme is never heard from again, and we get a series of brass plunger solos, relieved only by a piano solo that strikes me as an irrelevancy. At the end, instead of at least some reference to the opening theme, we are given the bit of Chopin, which, however apposite, is plucked from the air. In my opinion, "East St. Louis Toddle-Oo," with its alternating themes and the rounding off at the end by a reference to the opening theme, is much better organized, although the soloing is poorer.

But the critics felt something in "Black and Tan Fantasy" that listeners still feel today: first, that sincerity which was lacking in the music of the popular dance bands they were more familiar with and, second, a consistency of tone and mood that suggested a unifying idea somewhere underneath it all—a sense that the piece as a whole was saying something with passion and conviction about human life. It sounded like a composition, which most popular music played by dance bands did not.

To be sure, it was partly a matter of luck that the critics lit upon this particular piece. Rob Darrell admitted that he was originally taken by its comic effects, and only after he had played it several times for the amusement of his friends did he begin to recognize the depth it possessed.[11] But, in time, people caught on. The importance of "Black and Tan Fantasy" to jazz history should not be underestimated, for this more than any other single record suggested to critics that jazz could be a serious business.

Actually, the band recorded the tune twice more in 1927—for Victor on October 26 and for Columbia on November 3 (two takes of the Columbia version are available). The October 26 version is taken at a faster tempo and uses the full rhythm section, which makes the performance clunky and spoils a good deal of the melancholy of the first version. Miley is wonderful, bobbing and weaving like a drunk in a barroom fistfight; on the whole, however, the piece has lost a good deal from the earlier version. Apparently, somebody realized this, because at the November 3 session, for Columbia, the band returned to the original tempo and confined Sonny Greer to playing occasional cymbal crashes, and it works much better. This was the session at which Jabbo Smith filled in for Bubber Miley. Smith had a superb high register and a fine tone and was highly regarded in the New York music world—certainly more admired than Miley as a general musician. But he lacked Miley's fire, and, although his solos are a good imitation of Miley's, they lack the drive of the original. To my mind, the first version of "Black and Tan Fantasy" remains the definitive one. But the public did not make much distinction from one version to the other. It became one of the band's most popular numbers and, as was noted above, the basis for a short film.

However, Ellington fans would probably pick another number as the greatest piece from this period. As we have seen, "Creole Love Call" developed out of King Oliver's "Camp Meeting Blues" and was brought to Duke by Rudy Jackson. The Oliver piece consists of two main themes, but the portion of it that Jackson passed along to Duke was the clarinet solo, played on the Oliver version by Jimmie Noone. "Camp Meeting Blues" has never been considered one of the major works in the Oliver canon, although the melodies are pleasant enough. Ellington turned the piece into one of the memorable works in the entire body of jazz, by reshaping the melody slightly, and thereby improving it substantially, and then by dressing it in novel tonal clothes.

The opening strain is played by a clarinet trio, a widely used instrumentation of the time. But each repeated phrase then ends on a note five beats long, which, at a slow tempo, cries out for a response. Oliver missed the opportunity, but Ellington seized it in a way that bowled over jazz fans of the day. Instead of doing the obvious thing and giving the open space to Miley, he brought into the studio a well-known singer of the time, Adelaide Hall, who had been in *Shuffle Along* and would later have an important show business career in Europe. He had Hall scat the answers to the clarinet melody in a rather singsongy guttural voice that was wholly novel and absolutely right. Once again, Ellington turned away from the obvious to reach out for the unexpected, and he made a jazz classic.

For the remainder of the record, as was now his practice, he clothed the music in contrasting timbres—a trumpet in the plunger; Rudy Jackson on clarinet playing the trombone theme from the Oliver record, with Duke playing felicitous little phrases underneath; a brass trio with the saxophones answering; a high clarinet trio, with brass answering; finally a return to the opening statement, with Hall, once again, scatting the response. The piece ends with a brief coda by Hall. There is a scattering of notes from the band and then one last one from Nanton, which is—lo and behold—a flat fifth, one more example of Ellington's penchant for breaking rules. According to standard theory, the flat—or, correctly, the diminished fifth, also called the tritone—is the most "wrong" note in the scale, to the extent that in an earlier day it was referred to as "the devil's interval." Given Ellington's temperament, once he knew that using the tritone was venturing into dangerous territory, he would have been driven to put it in someplace at the earliest opportunity, and here, as if to emphasize the point, he lets it stand alone and exposed. Yet it fits in so naturally that it has generally been missed by listeners.

"Creole Love Call" is a wholly satisfying piece of music. It could hardly be simpler, consisting as it does of two basic themes, one of which is played only once. Yet everything in it makes sense: there is just enough of everything. It is, furthermore, one of the most completely composed of Ellington's pieces to this time, for there is only one improvised solo, Hall's scatted responses aside. And, despite the fact that the themes were not original with Duke, this piece is stamped with the Ellington mark. The difference between "Creole Love Call" and "Camp Meeting Blues" is exactly why Duke Ellington is considered one of the major composers of the twentieth century and King Oliver is of interest mainly to jazz specialists.

In the year since the first recording of "East St. Louis Toodle-Oo," Duke had begun to find a method for himself—devices and ways of approaching music that he would turn to again and again and use with increasing confidence. He was, in particular, experimenting with harmonies more advanced than those being used by most dance bands. Ferde Grofé and Bill Challis, with the Paul Whiteman band, had been drawing on the theories of Debussy, Ravel, and Stravinsky, in particular, and were enriching the jazz language, but Ellington was inventing his devices. However, in both "New Orleans Lowdown" and "Awful Sad," Arthur Whetsol uses a whole-tone scale break. My guess is that Whetsol picked up this scale from Bix Beiderbecke, who knew some of the Ellington men and was using whole-tone scales himself in breaks. Ellington was thus at least aware of some of the innovations of the impressionists of the day.

In the spring of 1928 he produced a song called "Black Beauty," which shows some of his new trademarks. "Black Beauty" was intended as a portrait of Florence Mills, the first in a long series of musical portraits Duke would write over his lifetime. Pretty, petite, light-skinned, Florence Mills had jumped into stardom in Shuffle Along. She became a special pet of sophisticated New York whites, rode the wave to England, where she was rumored to have been involved with royalty, and returned triumphantly to New York, only to die suddenly of peritonitis in 1927. Her funeral was a great public ceremony attended by thousands, both black and white, and she was a natural subject for Duke, who was beginning to develop his interest in themes taken from black culture. Ellington recorded "Black Beauty" twice as band numbers, but it is best known in a solo piano version he made later. (There has been some confusion over the opening trumpet solo on the Brunswick version: in fact, Whetsol and Metcalf trade fours.) The piece consists of two strains, the first one an ordinary thirty-two-bar AABA form, the second a simpler sixteen-bar form employing a very common set of chord changes most familiar as "Sweet Georgia Brown." The second strain, in A-flat, is bouncy; the first, in B-flat, is much more pensive and is undergirded by harmonies which were quite sophisticated for the time, and still are not easy to analyze. It is my feeling, however, that Ellington developed the harmonic pattern out of a chord progression quite unusual in popular music, Bb/Faug/Fmin/G⁷. The movement from the F augmented to the F minor is unusual; the usual practice would have been to go from the F augmented to G minor or F major. I am convinced that, once again, we are seeing Ellington's visual sense at work. Beginning with a second-inversion B-flat, he would have been familiar with the very common practice of developing a chord sequence by letting the top note descend, chromatically, and adjusting the others as necessary to produce a smooth sequence, as in the pattern found, for instance, in "Blue Skies": Dmin/Faug/Fmaj.

And it occurred to Ellington to wonder what would happen if he held the F constant and moved the other two notes down by half steps. The result was the opening sequence of chords of "Black Beauty." It was not the usual way of going about things, and it grew out of Ellington's willingness to experiment, to try anything his imagination could conceive of.

It has been suggested by the late George Hoefer, an early jazz historian, that "Duke built 'Black Beauty' around a Bubber Miley melody."[12] That may be true, but the song shows a characteristic of Ellington's approach to melody that helped raise many of his songs above the ordinary hit song. The classic American popular song is built of one-, two-, and sometimes four-bar phrases repeated, usually with minor variations, frequently enough to make up an eight-bar segment, which is then itself repeated. Many of the most enduring standards are shaped by this formula, among them "Why Do I Love You?," "As Time Goes By," "Smoke Gets in Your Eyes," " 'S Wonderful," and almost all of Fats Waller's hits. Some famous tunes avoid this formula, like "Star Dust" and "White Christmas," but it is, nonetheless, by far the commonest pattern, the one that beginning songwriters almost automatically fall into.

Ellington would write in this pattern, too, as in "I'm Beginning to See the Light" and "Satin Doll," but more than most composers of popular songs, he tended to write more consecutive melodies, made up of quite different, even contrasting, phrases, producing more the effect of speech or dialogue. When well done, this system of writing inevitably produces a more interesting and melodically richer tune, although one perhaps correspondingly less acceptable to the ordinary ear. In "Black Beauty," we have an early example of Ellington's tendency to write consecutive, rather than repetitive, melody.

To back "Black Beauty," Duke cut another original piano solo called "Swampy River." Opening with a harsh, moody strain in F minor, it moves to a less intense strain in F major and then to an almost pastoral strain in A-flat major. There are brief interludes, and it is clear that Duke is attempting here to put together an organized piece of music, using both of the major keys related to the opening F minor.

In those two pieces Ellington was working in the ragtime tradition he had begun to learn back in Washington, when he memorized James P. Johnson's "Carolina Shout." We assume that, in its early stages in the saloons of St. Louis, New Orleans, and other places, ragtime was a rough, improvised music, but by the turn of the century it had become, especially in the hands of Scott Joplin, Artie Matthews, Joseph Lamb, and others, a formal, composed music based to a considerable extent on structures and devices developed in the early nineteenth century by European composers. The relatively complex rags of 1900 and thereafter frequently comprised several contrasting themes in different keys, repeated and/or alternated in a whole variety of forms. What, precisely, Ellington had learned about composing such rags from Johnson, Willie the Lion, and other stride pianists whom he got to know around New York is moot. But it is clear that Ellington's ideas about form, especially the use of alternating themes in related keys, was drawn from the formal rags and stride pieces he had learned about from them. The structure of these two pieces is not perfect: it is sometimes hard to discover why a given strain is placed where it is. Nonetheless, Ellington has come a long way from "Jig Walk."

Besides the piano solos and the jungle numbers, the band was turning out a good many fast swingers like "Jubilee Stomp," which has a good melodic line, and the slower "Take It Easy," which is effectively a sixteen-bar blues, with a number of interesting departures from the standard blues changes. Miley plays an exceptional solo on the Cameo-Pathé version (take one). Not all succeed: "Blue Bubbles" is a jumble, notable mainly for its solos, and "Washington Wobble" is ragged and very busy.

But the good numbers continued to come. Another of the jungle numbers that would have a long life was "The Mooch." Like many of the others, it features Bubber Miley in a minor mode with interludes in related major keys, in this case E-flat major and its tonic and relative minors. As had been pointed out by Harriet Milnes, who has studied the piece, it consists mainly of a series of duets, an unusual idea in popular music.[13] It opens on a chromatic scale, which winds slowly downward while Bubber growls and sniffs around it threateningly. There follow duets by Hodges and Miley and, in one version of the tune, a striking call-and-answer chorus between Lonnie Johnson, a popular blues guitarist, and Baby Cox, "a slim, beautiful, young girl" who worked in major black revues.[14] Cox scats in a remarkable growl style clearly drawn from Miley's work. "The Mooch" again shows the earmarks of Ellington's emerging method: the key shifts, the alternation of major and minor, the sharp contrasts in color as the music moves around the band.

The Ellington band, like other bands working clubs with elaborate revues, was expected to put on showy, "theatrical" pieces as part of the performance. It was taken for granted that bands would be seen as well as heard; the musicians would wear flashy uniforms, and some leaders, like Armstrong and Calloway, were always active, indeed, frenetic on stage—mugging and leaping around. Ellington always saw to it that Greer's elaborate drum set was prominently displayed on a riser behind the band, and he liked his soloists to come down front, where the mutes would easily be seen.

As part of the show, bands would put on spectacular hot numbers at tempos as fast as they could play. Frequently, these were built on the chords of "Tiger Rag," which were easy and changed infrequently, so the soloists would not have to worry about complex harmonies but could concentrate on flying around their horns. The Ellington band developed a number of these hot specialties. Typical is "Hot and Bothered," which it recorded in one version with Baby Cox growling a duet with Miley and a chorus by Lonnie Johnson. It has solos by various of the musicians, among them Bigard, who plays a classic New Orleans high-speed solo in the low register. There are also arranged choruses to show off the saxophones tearing through complex figures at high tempos. The piece has a lot of fire, but it is too fast for some of the musicians, and they stumble here and there. A second take was cut at a slower tempo.

Actually, when we look closely at many of the records the band made during this period, we are startled to see how little real composition was involved. Many of them are largely strings of solos with perhaps a single arranged chorus and bits and pieces of interludes, transitions, and lead-ups to solos here and there, many of which were suggested by members of the band. "Blues with a Feeling," for example, has only twelve bars that could be considered "composed" in any real sense; "Hottentot," a Fields-McHugh swinger, is almost entirely solos, except for one thirty-two-bar chorus that is clearly a head arrangement worked out by the band; "I Must Have That Man," another Fields-McHugh number written for a Cotton Club revue, is almost all solos; "Saturday Night Function," credited to Ellington and Bigard, was lifted almost whole from a spiritual and after the statement of the theme is a series of solos on the blues. (Duke was not the only one to take the easy way out; "I Must Have That Man" is a revamping of "I Can't Believe That You're in Love with Me," using identical chord changes.)

Some pieces are more thoroughly worked out, like "High Life," another of the "Tiger Rag" horse races, and "Diga Diga Doo," a Fields-McHugh tune, which has vocals by Irving Mills and Ozie Ware and a good deal of fancy writing. But more often than not, Ellington is content to let the soloists carry the burden. That is not to the bad, of course, for there is wonderful improvising on many of these records by Miley, Nanton, Bigard, Carney, and Hodges, who was rapidly developing into one of the major jazz soloists of his day. But it is nonetheless clear that Duke did not feel any great urgency to write any more music than he had to. He was still thinking of himself not as a composer but as a bandleader; he would be Fletcher Henderson rather than George Gershwin. As a result, a lot of the music was slapdash, depending especially on Bubber Miley to make the tunes work. But by the end of 1928 Duke's tolerance for Bubber's unreliability was wearing out. Duke was not a man for making carefully thought-out decisions. He avoided confronting hard choices as much as possible, and we can presume that he let the situation drag on for longer than 'he should have. Duke never said what he felt about it or even admitted that he had to fire Bubber, but it must have been painful for him. Bubber, more than anyone else—more than Mills or even Ellington himself—had established the Duke Ellington orchestra. Without Bubber the band would not have taken the turn it took when it went into the Hollywood in 1923; without Bubber it would not have drawn the attention it got; without Bubber it would not have been hired by Harry Block at the Cotton Club. Whenever there was a letdown, Duke could always count on Bubber to pick up the intensity, provided Bubber was there. On these records Bubber plays one wonderful solo after the next, not merely the famous ones on "East St. Louis Toodle-Oo" and "Black and Tan Fantasy," but on less well known ones like "Red Hot Band," "Take It Easy," and the call-and-answer choruses with Adelaide Hall and Baby Cox. In *Music Is My Mistress*, Duke wrote,

> Bubber Miley was from the body and soul of Soulsville. . . . Every note he played was soul filled with the pulse of compulsion. . . . Before he played his choruses, he would tell his story, and he always had a story for his music, such as: "This is an old man, tired from working in the field since sunup, coming up the road in the sunset on his way home to dinner. He's tired but strong, and humming in time with his broken gait—or vice versa." That was how he pictured "East St. Louis Toodle-oo."[15]

Bubber Miley was not a genius on the order of Louis Armstrong—or of Ellington, for that matter. Like many of the "eastern" players of the time, he was sometimes rhythmically awkward, landing flat-footed somewhere beside the beat. Nor had he Armstrong's enormous array of moods: Bubber was limited in his emotional range. Nonetheless, he was a marvelous jazz musician, and, although he did not invent the plunger system, he exploited it better than any other brass player in jazz, with the possible exception of his successor in the Ellington band, Cootie Williams. It was

Bubber, more than anyone else, who made the growl and plunger work a part of the vocabulary of jazz, and for that alone he would deserve a significant place in jazz history.

Poor Bubber did not long survive his departure from the Ellington band. For the next three years he free-lanced, playing with at least five different groups. Then, in 1931, Irving Mills backed him with his own band. But Bubber was already sick with tuberculosis, undoubtedly exacerbated by alcoholism, and in May 1932 he died.

10

On the Road

In the summer of 1930 the Ellington orchestra went out to the West Coast to make the Amos 'n' Andy movie *Check and Double Check*. That spring, Cab Calloway, then a relatively unknown singer who was fronting a band and heating up audiences with his frenzied and athletic delivery of songs, was working at a place called the Crazy Cat, in the Broadway area very close to where the old Kentucky Club had been. According to Calloway, one night four men in wide-brimmed hats and overcoats walked into the club and told Calloway, flatly, that he was going into the Cotton Club and that he should bring the band up the next afternoon to start rehearsals. Duke, they said, was going to California to tour and make a movie.

Calloway, needless to say, started rehearsals on schedule. He went on to make a home of the Cotton Club, being even more successful there than Ellington had been, with his good looks, good voice, and considerable showmanship. At about this time, Calloway signed with Mills, and it appears that, because of the nature of the agreement between Ellington and Mills, Duke actually had a piece of Calloway for a while.

Duke would return to the Cotton Club that fall and continue to play it from time to time, until it finally collapsed in 1940. But when his contract was up on February 4, 1931, the Cotton Club stay was really over, and Calloway became the favorite there. He said,

> Beginning that summer of 1930 Duke was on the road more and more. Things had really taken off for him and maybe the Cotton Club had become too confining. The club wanted mainly show music, pretty straight stuff. Duke was beginning to experiment with longer musical suites and more inventive things. He could do those in theatres and

concerts but, when people get out on the dance floor expecting to jit-
terbug, you really can't lay a "Mood Indigo" on them or some other
piece of mood music.[1]

Calloway may be right in suggesting that Ellington left the Cotton Club
in order to play more complex music, but certainly other motives were at
work. For one thing, the Cotton Club management may have decided
that it did not want Duke anymore. There is no evidence for it, but if
they had preferred Ellington to Calloway, Duke would obviously have
found it difficult to leave. In a similar situation occurring at almost the
same moment, Louis Armstrong had to slip out of Chicago in order to
avoid a conflict between rival gangs, both of whom wanted his services,
and, in part because of this problem, was unable to play extended engagements in both Chicago and New York for several years.

But it appears to me that Duke was ready to go. For one thing, he was
now a star. The primary factor in making him one, leaving aside the attrac-
tions of the music, were the national radio broadcasts for CBS, which were
almost daily for much of the time the band was at the Cotton Club. As
many of the broadcasts took place at five or six in the afternoon, New York
time (reports differ as to the actual hour), as well as late in the evening,
the broadcasts were available to virtually everybody in the United States
at one time or another. By 1930 radio had passed the novelty stage; to be
"on radio" was prestigious, and the mere fact that Ellington was being
heard nationwide made him important to listeners. These broadcasts,
coupled with the movies, especially *Check and Double Check*, made Ellington a name to millions of Americans.

As a consequence of this celebrity, he was seen by many as a spokesman
both for jazz and for his race. He was interviewed frequently by newspapers and magazines; there was a story in *Time* as early as 1933. There was
that visit to the White House, the lecture at New York University, the
poll victories. Especially interesting were the results of the running poll conducted by *Orchestra World*, a monthly magazine for dance band musicians
and their fans, which had begun publishing in 1925. The leading orchestras in this poll were invariably the white commercial bands, like those
of Whiteman and Rudy Vallee; but Ellington consistently ran in first or
second place, ahead of Whiteman, a clear indication of his standing among
jazz fans. (It is also interesting that, of those voted as top "players," such
important jazz musicians as Red Nichols, Louis Armstrong, Bubber Miley,
Steve Brown, Sonny Greer, King Oliver, and Ellington himself made the
top thirty, mixed in with strictly commercial players like Zez Confrey and
Ozzie Nelson.) In conjunction with this poll, in its May, 1931 issue, the
magazine said, "At the age of 32, Ellington is one of the few recognized

rulers in dance music, supreme in his field of the hot jungle tune . . . Ellington's meteoric rise to fame is a flowering of the trend toward negro
dance form so popular in America after the war." By 1932 the *Chicago Defender* could announce that Henderson was no longer in Ellington's class.[2]
Popular musicians had become celebrities in America, and Duke Ellington
was one of the most celebrated of all.

He could therefore tour, make movies, play prestigious locations, all
for a good deal more money than the thousand dollars a week I estimate
the Cotton Club was paying him.

Moreover, a lot of the old glamour of Harlem was beginning to look
stained and dirty around the cuffs. In the fall of 1929 a rival group to
the Madden syndicate put together a lavish nightclub modeled on the
Cotton Club, called the Plantation, which Cab Calloway was supposed to
open. Just before opening night the Madden gang broke up the place,
smashing the mirrors and throwing the elaborate bar out into the street.
In retaliation, the gangsters murdered Harry Block in the lobby of his
building. Block was the man who had hired Duke and, whatever his
morality, was a friend.

Not long afterwards, a pathological killer named "Mad Dog" Coll kid-
napped George Immerman of Connie's Inn, touching off a gang war with
the Madden people. Coll was eventually ambushed in a phone booth and
murdered. Violence was increasing, and, as the 1930s went on, customers
from downtown, who had previously found Harlem as safe as their own
homes, were being robbed. Robert Sylvester said, "The atmosphere in the
mid 1930s began to turn a little sour."[3] Eventually, a major race riot frightened off the whites for good, and the era of the big Harlem clubs abruptly
ended.

Things had not gotten this bad by 1931, but they were headed in that
direction. In fact, the Cotton Club glamour had always had dirt on its
cuffs. The show girls, in many of these clubs, were expected to make themselves available to big spenders from downtown. How much pressure was
put on them to do so at the Cotton Club is questionable, but there is no
doubt that many of the girls took advantage of the opportunity to make
a good night's pay for very little work after the show was over for the evening. Ellington was hardly a prude, but he said of this aspect of it,
"That part of Harlem was degrading and humiliating to both Negroes and
whites."[4]

Finally, it appears that by 1931, and probably a little earlier, Ellington
had begun to become more generally dissatisfied with his life, clearly less
interested in his music than he had been. Later on he called it "a bad
groove."[5] What the trouble was he never said, but it could well have been
the sort of letdown that often comes when a man has reached a major goal

and finds himself simply going through the motions thereafter. Ellington was a celebrity, the system for making the music was established, and there were no more challenges.

In any case, there were, after two years of stability, changes in personnel. The first of these was the arrival of Ivie Anderson as the band's principal vocalist. At the Cotton and Kentucky clubs, vocalists had always been part of the show, so the band had not needed one. On tour, Sonny Greer did whatever singing was called for. But when the band left the Cotton Club a vocalist was necessary. The first engagement was at the Oriental Theatre in Chicago, beginning on February 13, 1931. The producer wanted Duke to have a girl singer. It was suggested that he hire Mae Alix, a pretty, light-skinned singer who had a substantial reputation in Chicago among night-clubbers—she had appeared frequently with Louis Armstrong at the Sunset Cafe. But, according to Sonny Greer, Ellington thought that a very light-skinned girl, who might be taken for white, could cause problems. Another report said it was the Oriental Theatre people who were concerned. In any case, Duke turned to Ivie Anderson, who would stay with the band for ten years, until asthma forced her to retire.

Ivie was born in Gilroy, California, in 1905. She studied voice in her youth and began working in nightclubs as a teenager. She was in one of the touring versions of *Shuffle Along*, and, according to Linda Dahl's book on women in jazz, in 1928 she worked with the Anson Weeks orchestra, possibly the first black woman to sing with a white orchestra.[6] By 1930, when she was twenty-five, she had acquired a great deal of experience in show business and was working with Earl Hines at the Grand Terrace in Chicago.

Ellington's taste in vocalists was a little curious. Despite his liking for the natural, he preferred singers, male and female, who had big, trained voices to the self-taught jazz singers like Armstrong, Holiday, and Teagarden whose rough voices fit into the jazz context better than the more polished ones. This fondness for the trained voice is surprising because he had exactly the opposite taste in instrumentalists, seeking out the untutored Mileys, Bechets, and Nantons rather than players with better training. We must remember, however, that Ellington had come out of exactly this tradition of the trained voice, not that of the rough blues shouter of the South.

Ivie Anderson, however, was more of a jazz singer than most of the ones who came later; and, while she had her weaknesses, poor intonation being one of them, she could sing with jazz feeling. She quickly became popular with the band's fans. The English jazz writer Max Jones said that Ellington told him that even in the South "Ivie was popular . . . and guys would run after her. . . . Ivie used to kick white people's butts down south."[7] Ivie is reported to have been a poker shark, consistently taking money away from the other musicians on long train rides, and to have had a brief fling with Cootie Williams, who said that she projected better in person than she did on records.

A second new arrival was another trombonist. As we have seen in the case of the trumpets, the addition of a third voice would allow Ellington to compose for a trombone choir. The arrangement gave the whole band a great deal of flexibility, because Duke could now voice Tizol with the saxophones to make up a four-piece choir and still have five brass to voice together as well. But apparently these considerations were not the major factors in his hiring of Lawrence Brown. It was all done, as things in the Ellington band so frequently were, on a whim.

Lawrence Brown was a complicated man, wholly different from some of the puckish bad boys who graced the band. He was born in 1907 in Lawrence, Kansas. His father was a minister, his mother played the organ for the choir, and other members of the family were musical to one degree or another. The family moved frequently; by the time Brown was nine or ten, it was living in California, first Oakland and then Pasadena. Brown played a little tuba and violin but took up the trombone at about the age of twelve.

His father, like many religious blacks, was dead set against dance music. There has always been in the black community a strong current opposed to dance music and especially to the blues, which was seen explicitly as the devil's music. In many instances, children of blacks who had such feelings were disowned by their parents for going into secular music. Brown found himself in such a situation; in order to play or listen to local bands, he was forced to sneak out of the house through a window at night. He went to Pasadena College but continued to play popular music. Finally, his father told him either to give up his music or leave the house, so Brown left. He lived at a cousin's house and supported himself gigging at dime-a-dance halls and small clubs. Eventually, he landed a job with Paul Howard's Quality Serenaders, the house band at the most important cabaret in California, Sebastian's Cotton Club. It was located across the street from the MGM lot in Los Angeles and attracted movie stars, big spenders, and the usual assortment of criminals. Leadership of the band changed several times, but Brown remained with it. He was still there when Louis Armstrong came out to front it for an extended stay in 1930. Armstrong, Brown said later, "was the only man that ever made me enjoy coming to work."[8]

He had by this time developed considerable technical skill and played with a sound rich as chocolate and smooth as velvet. "I thought of my trombone as the violin of brass instruments," he said, "and I began to wonder why couldn't the trombone play the same type of music as the 'cello and I couldn't see why I had to still resort to that tailgate business. So I began to play melodies, using melodic type playing instead of the tailgate type."[9]

Brown was not the first trombonist to attempt to play legato instead of the rather heavy-handed marching-band style customary in concert orchestras or the staccato manner of the New Orleans bands. Virtuoso trombonists like the concert artist Arthur Pryor had for decades been playing in this fashion, and the jazz trombonists Jack Teagarden and especially Jimmy Harrison were creating a school of legato players at that moment. But legato trombone was still not common when Brown first began experimenting with it, and he became a specialist at playing slick melodies; at Sebastian's he was regularly featured on a sweet version of "Trees," a melody as sugary as the Joyce Kilmer poem that was put to it.

In 1932 Armstrong was once again at Sebastian's. On Easter Sunday his manager, a tough, hard-drinking, cigar-smoking, would-be gangster named Johnny Collins, ordered the musicians to come in for the taking of publicity photographs. Brown balked, both out of religious principle and simple orneriness. He either gave notice or was fired. Just at that moment, the Ellington band was at the Orpheum Theatre in Los Angeles. Irving Mills came into Sebastian's, heard Brown deliver "Trees," and was smitten. This was the Depression, when the music business was collapsing, and there was a theory going around—which turned out to be untrue—that Americans wanted sweet, dreamy music to help them take their minds off their troubles. Mills undoubtedly thought the addition of Brown would move the band toward sweeter music, and he told Duke to hire him. Brown went to see Ellington the next day. Duke said, "I never knew you. I never met you, never heard you. But Irving says get you, so that's that."[10] The idea that Mills had that much to say about how the Ellington band was run may be difficult to believe, but Brown told the story the same way to both Patricia Willard and Stanley Dance, who had long associations with the band and did not question the story. Duke had faith in Mills's instincts for what would succeed, a faith that Mills had again and again justified.

But the relationship got off to a bad start and remained abrasive. For one thing, the seventy dollars a week Mills offered was less than Brown was making at Sebastian's; furthermore, he was shocked to discover that the pay was prorated according to how many nights a week the band worked and that the musicians had to pay their own expenses on the road. Besides, Brown was the thirteenth member of the band (apparently Duke did not count Ivie Anderson), and he would not let Brown play until a fourteenth man was added. (However, Brown was recording with the band before the fourteenth man was added.)

But the offenses were not all on Duke's side. Brown was not only prickly and independent but also inclined to be morose. He claimed that he always got nervous when he had to play a solo in front of an audience: "I was never at ease and I've never been satisfied with anything I ever played. . . . Everything is alright until I have to solo and immediately the feeling of insecurity sets in. And I begin to become a little confused as to what I want to play and how I want one thing to follow another."[11] As a consequence, he frequently worked out his solos in advance to one degree or another, playing them over in his head while waiting his turn to solo.

Brown's moroseness was well known. Bigard said, "Lawrence was a nice guy, but always squawking on something. He was never satisfied with anything. Always going to quit in five years. Like I said he played great and I loved him but he was just grumpy."[12]

In particular, Brown was always "squawking on" Duke. He believed that the band ought to be a corporation, and he made more of an issue than the other men did of Duke's use of their melodic material without credit. He nearly left the band—or was fired—on several occasions. One of the worst dustups occurred when he told Duke, "I don't consider you a composer. You are a compiler."[13] Brown added that Duke's "ego boiled over."

A good many of Ellington's fans and the critics were disturbed by the addition of Lawrence Brown. It seemed to them that Brown's whole approach to the trombone was too slick and therefore was misplaced in the context of the more boisterous character of the band. John Hammond wrote, "I'm afraid that this brilliant musician is out of place in Duke's band. He is a soloist who doesn't respect the rudiments of orchestral playing. Constantly he pushes himself to the foreground."[14] And the English critic Spike Hughes said that Brown was "definitely out of place," for all his technical skill.[15]

But whatever the critics thought and however badly Brown and Ellington got along, Ellington, who had a taste for sweet sound, liked the way Brown played and always gave him considerable solo space. For one thing, Brown's rich, chocolaty style contrasted markedly with the rather pure, legitimate sound of Tizol's trombone and even more markedly with the plunger style of Nanton, adding to the variety Ellington had at his disposal. For another, Brown was not simply a sweet player. He could play fast and hot as well and often did. He would be with the band for a long time.

One final addition—the man who made the band fourteen and allowed Brown to play—was Toby Hardwick, returning in the spring of 1932, after an absence of some three years. Whether Hardwick had quit or whether Duke had used the automobile accident to push him out, because of his drinking and general irresponsibility, is moot. He worked in Atlantic City for a period and then, on a snap decision, took a ship to Paris. Here he went to work for the same Ada Smith who had gotten the Washingtonians that first job at Barron's—now Bricktop, the proprietor of a famous Parisian nightclub. He played some other casual gigs in Europe, returned to New York after a couple of years, and went into the Hot Feet Club, on Houston Street in Greenwich Village, which had a show modeled on the ones in Harlem with black entertainment for white audiences. The club had a lot of important jazz musicians in residence, including Fats Waller, and a naughty show. Between acts, a singing waiter, carrying a tin can, escorted a dancer from table to table caroling "Stick out your can, here comes the garbage man." If the tip that went into the can was sufficient the girl would oblige with a bump. Unfortunately, the owner tried to start a similar place in Chicago and was shot by mobsters, and the Hot Feet Club folded. It was apparently at this point that Toby asked Duke for his job back. Duke took him. His rule was not to forget but to forgive, and he forgave Toby this time. In any case, a few bands were beginning to carry four saxophones, and Duke may have wanted to get a jump on some of the others.

There would be further changes in personnel beginning in 1935, but relatively minor ones. This band would remain substantially the same for another eight years. It is, to my mind, the classic Ellington band. It produced a large proportion of the Ellington masterworks, and the sound of Nanton, Hodges, Williams, Brown, Carney, and Bigard is at the heart of Ellington's music. It has been argued, perhaps correctly, that the famous Victor band of the 1940s was the greatest of all Ellington bands; certainly, the Miley band of 1927–29 made some enduring masterpieces; and the bands of the 1950s and 1960s produced the long concert pieces for which Duke expected to be remembered. But this band of the 1930s was the one by which all the others are measured.

By 1931, when Ellington left the Cotton Club, the country was rolling down a steep slope into what was beginning to appear a bottomless depression. The music business was suffering. Several factors were hurting the nightclub business: the continuing efforts by federal authorities to enforce the Prohibition Act, which resulted in the shutting down, from time to time, of cabarets, even important ones; the drying up of the pool of big spenders who had been important in keeping the clubs going; and the sense, as newsreels brought pictures of families with six scrawny kids in battered automobiles leaving dust bowls for California, that going out to drink and dance was no longer charming and gay.

The record business was in even worse shape. At a time when many people were working for twenty-five cents an hour, seventy-five cents seemed a lot to pay for a record, especially in the face of free entertainment offered by radio. Sales of records, which had run to 150 million annually in the 1920s, dropped to 5 million in 1933.

But although the music business was hurt, it was not dead. If 40 percent of Harlem was on relief, a lot of people still had a little money to jingle in their pockets, and they continued to want music. The Duke Ellington orchestra was now acknowledged to be the leading black band in the country, and Ellington was seen as a figure of some importance—precisely for what, a lot of people might have been hard put to say, but he was clearly somebody more than just a bandleader.

Over the next two years the band would play a lot of theaters—for weeks, and split weeks, mainly. It spent a lot of time in California. The band was now traveling in two Pullman cars; Duke had a roomette to give him some privacy in which to compose. He had, by now, begun to separate himself from the men in the band to an extent, a separation that would continue to grow. At the beginning, when he was just the piano player in the band, he had always been "one of the boys," particularly with the old hands like Greer, Hardwick, and Whetsol, whom he had known as teenagers, when he was still getting by on three tunes played at different tempos.

But he had never been as close to the newer men, in part because, by the time the band went into the Cotton Club, he had a family and his own private life and was not running with the other horses through the wild life of Harlem. This was even more true after he brought J.E., Daisy, and the children to New York, especially because he would not introduce the less genteel men into his home. Ellington was, we remember, from the middle class, as were most of the Washingtonians he had run with as a youngster, and spoke good English and dressed with style. A lot of the newer men were from working-class families—Bigard, Williams, Hodges, Miley, and some of the others had come out of relatively rough backgrounds, spoke the English of the black ghetto, drank, gambled, swore, and lacked the elegant manners that Duke had learned from J.E. and his Daisy. Freddy Guy was apparently acceptable, and Toby Hardwick would have been, had he been better behaved; Nanton and Carney, too, had better backgrounds. But many of the others, despite his respect for their talents, and the warmth he felt for them, were not from Duke's social class.

In this respect Duke's behavior was no different from that of middle-class whites, who did not usually socialize, off the job, with the working people they were supervising in shops and factories. The traffic manager and the salesman, with their high school diplomas, might drink coffee with the warehousemen and truck drivers they worked with, but they did not bring them home for dinner. The Ellington sidemen, at various times and for various reasons, resented things in Duke, but they seem to have accepted with equanimity his right to set himself apart from them. He was not only their leader and, possibly, a man of genius, but also a member of a different social class. As Duke's celebrity increased, the gap widened. In these early years of the 1930s, Ellington was asked to meet the president, lecture at famous universities, and socialize with wealthy whites: the rest of them were not. In time, when they were not living in the Pullman, Ellington would sleep in good hotels, while the men scrambled for lodging in black boardinghouses. Because of his social status, Duke was able to slip through racial barriers a little sooner and a little more frequently than the others. According to Richard O. Boyer, who traveled with the band briefly in 1944, by that time Ellington was usually able to find white hotels that would take him in most cities, while the men usually could not. This, too, served to widen the gap between him and the musicians. Besides, there was always that natural reserve.

This does not mean, of course, that Duke was completely cut off from the others. He had old friends in the band, and he would always joke with them, sit around and tell stories. But the days when he would play cards with them or go out drinking with them after the job were going. He was moving into another world.

11

"Mood Indigo"

In the years between the departure of Miley and the first of Ellington's trips abroad, which would change his perception of himself, Ellington established himself as a celebrated musician. Yet, paradoxically, it was not as productive a period, musically, as some others. As we shall see, Ellington seemed to produce his best work in spates: "East St. Louis Toodle-Oo," "Black and Tan Fantasy," and "Birmingham Breakdown" in the winter of 1926–27; "Dear Old Southland," "Stompy Jones," "Daybreak Express," and "Solitude" in December 1933 and January 1934; "Ko-Ko," "Concerto for Cootie," and "Cotton Tail" within two months in 1940. There were sometimes long, fallow periods in between, where the masterpieces were spaced out; and this was one such period.

Duke was not, as we have seen, a man driven to compose. He needed something to stir him up: some person, some event, some inspiration from the outside. Otherwise, he would produce what was required of him, and nothing more. To be sure, his mind was often filled with music. He liked being on railroad trains because, he told an interviewer, "folks can't rush you until you get off."[1] On those long nights speeding through the countryside in the roomette or, later, in the car driven by Harry Carney, he would get ideas and make notes for things to use later. But the discipline required to pull together these snippets and pieces into a whole composition came hard to him. In this sense, he was "lazy." He liked things to go smoothly and easily, from the job to a meal to a woman. It was one thing to snatch bits of music out of sights seen from a train window, but writing a whole composition was hard work. And in this period he was not getting the challenge from the outside to charge him up to his highest level. He was, in fact, bored.

As a consequence he frequently took the easy way out and produced numbers like "Harlem Flat Blues," "That Rhythm Man," "Jungle Blues," and many more that consist mainly of one brief figure sandwiched between solos backed by simple chords by one section of the orchestra or another. The solos, played by Williams, Nanton, Hodges, Carney, Bigard, and the rest, are often exemplary and, sometimes, are superb pieces of jazz playing. But, taken as a whole, numbers like these can hardly be considered "compositions" in any real sense. Duke was clever, and he made these very minimal pieces succeed by keeping everything on the boil: sharply contrasting solos came and went, bits of melody bubbled to the surface and disappeared, and everything was in motion. But, the solos aside, such pieces exhibited more sleight of hand than musical thought.

For another, a number of these pieces appear to be stock arrangements doctored in spots by Ellington or other members of the orchestra. "Wang Wang Blues," "My Gal Is Good for Nothing but Love," and "March of the Hoodlums" fall into this category.

It is also my feeling that Juan Tizol was writing arrangements for the band. It is probable that, in the course of paying Tizol to extract the parts from compositions, Ellington also left it to him to voice the sections at times. From here it would have been only a step to making complete arrangements. Paul Eduard Miller, writing in *Down Beat* a few years later, stated flatly that Tizol was arranging for Duke, although it is possible that Miller confused arranging with extracting the parts.[2] In any case, "Maori," "Admiration" (which was written by Tizol), "Sweet Jazz o' Mine," and some others are not typical of Ellington's work; if Tizol did not arrange them, neither did Duke.

Finally, Ellington was under pressure from Mills and the record companies to turn out a lot of second-rate commercial work. Through the second half of 1930, for example, 65 percent of the records featured a vocalist of some kind brought in from the outside, in most cases, singing poor popular tunes like "What Good Am I Without You?" and "When a Black Man's Blue." With the best will in the world, it would have been difficult to make much of these things.

Yet, despite everything, in this period he produced some fine pieces and two or three very important ones. We also find a new mood coming into Ellington's work. In the past, if we leave aside the out-and-out commercial pieces, it tended to fall into two categories: the spooky jungle numbers and the sometimes frantic horse race pieces. Now we increasingly see in Ellington's work a third mode, drawn in pastels, in a range of mild melancholia running from nostalgia to deep sadness. This mode was highly personal to Duke, and in this period much of his best work was in it.

Irving Mills was recording Ellington with a number of companies, as was his habit, but the recording industry itself was undergoing a substantial change. The dozens of companies that had flourished during the glory days of the 1920s were rapidly going under and were being bought up cheaply by the larger companies, primarily Columbia and Victor. As a consequence, Ellington was, more and more, forced to record for the major labels.

It was characteristic that the band's appearance in the movie *Check and Double Check* inspired Ellington to create some of his better work in this period. This was one of the early band pictures, one of the first feature films to use a black orchestra and therefore a matter of prestige for Ellington. To capitalize on the film, Ellington put together a piece called "Double Check Stomp," although it does not appear in the film. The band cut the tune for three different companies between April and June. The first and third versions are quite similar, except that on the last one Duke has added a brass answer to the reeds in the main theme and Carney takes Hodges's solo. For the second version, an accordionist, Cornell Smelser, was added, apparently for no better reason than that he was in the studio to be featured in another of the band's tunes, "Accordion Joe."

I prefer the first, Victor version, which is the best recording of the three. Typically, Duke has made a great deal out of very little. The tune consists of a short introduction, which is also used as a coda, and a thirty-two-bar melody built, with variations, on a tiny fragment of melody two bars long, which opens and closes the record. Everything in between is a succession of solos with minimal accompaniment. What makes the record work are the ferociously hot solos by Williams in his Armstrong vein, Hodges, and Nanton, and the fact that the theme, however minimal, is attractive and is played by the band with great verve.

However, the movie itself contained two tunes that, from a compositional viewpoint, are far more interesting than "Double Check Stomp," for all of its wonderful solos. One of these was "Ring Dem Bells," which would remain part of the Ellington repertoire for years. According to Louis Metcalf, Sonny got a set of chimes, and Ellington, intrigued, sat down immediately to write something for them.[3] Sonny had no idea which notes were which and would mark the chimes with little slips of paper. One night pranksters in the band moved the pieces of paper around, and Sonny hit a series of excruciatingly wrong notes. Sonny was smiling so much about the prank that the house broke up.

"Ring Dem Bells" is built around a very simple melodic idea using a standard chord progression and depends for a lot of its effect on the steamy solos of Williams, Hodges, and the rest. Four cuts were made for Victor at two different sessions in Hollywood, and a fifth was made for OKeh in New York. All versions are quite similar except for some changes in soloing. The piece gets its interest from the ingenious use of call-and-answer, which makes the simple melody far more complex, rhythmically, than when it is standing alone. The call-and-answers are played at various times by bells and brass, Hodges and brass, Hodges and Cootie Williams's scatted vocal, bells and saxophones, and, finally, brass and Bigard. (The routine varies slightly from one take to the next.) Each little package of call-and-answer is theoretically two bars long, but in general the call begins two or three beats ahead of the downbeat, and the answer skips in correspondingly ahead, so that melodic line is set irregularly over the foursquare sixteen-measure structure of the tune.

Ellington, however, is careful not to overwork the device, and the call-and-answer segments are separated by straightforward solos. Here again Ellington supplies variety, for each of the solos is accompanied, sometimes quite subtly, in a different way. For example, on the first Victor take Bigard is accompanied only by banjo and bass; Carney, by banjo, bass, and piano. Behind Nanton, Ellington plays a single half and whole notes outlining the harmony. Bass and banjo accompany only the Hodges-Williams responses. Behind Cootie there are jittering saxophone riffs, and bass alone from the rhythm section. In almost all big jazz bands, the whole rhythm section plays virtually all of the time, except when bass or guitar is soloing. Ellington, however, had the imagination to break up the rhythm section in various ways to add variety, often subtle, as he does again and again.

In addition, the piece modulates from C major to E-flat major before Williams's solo, and the last two choruses contain some excellent writing for saxophone and brass sections.

Taken as a whole, "Ring Dem Bells" deserves the reputation it achieved. It is restlessly on the move, filled with contrast, shifting and changing both in bold foreground forms and in background details. The solos are of high quality—Williams again quotes from Armstrong—and the band is always swinging.

The second important piece from *Check and Double Check* is "Old Man Blues," one of Ellington's best-known works from this period. It was made for both Victor and Columbia in different versions; I discuss the Columbia version here. It is, to an extent, one of the train pieces that Ellington liked to write. It opens with a twenty-bar introduction in 2/4, which has the effect of a train standing at the station building up a head of steam. Suddenly the band opens out into 4/4 with the main theme, a standard thirty-two-bar popular song form with a very happy melody. Following the statement of the theme comes a series of solos by the main actors in the band, switching back and forth between bridge and the A theme. Then, towards the end, there is an eight-bar interlude in 2/4, and a repeat of the main theme, which gradually slows to a stop at the end as the train halts at the next station. Whether Ellington planned this as a train piece I do not know; it certainly has that effect. The piece is typical of Ellington's methods: a hot, uptempo swinger with lots of contrast, excellent soloing, and those surprising dips into 2/4 which suddenly suspend the motion briefly.

Another piece from this period that ought to be better known is "It's Glory." Of particular interest is the opening chorus, in which the saxophones play a melody counter, or complementary, to the main theme in the brass. As we have seen, the big-jazz-band style, originated by Art Hickman and Paul Whiteman and brought to maturity by Fletcher Henderson and his musical director, Don Redman, was built around the playing off of brass and reed sections against each other, with the trombones and trumpets sometimes, as the bands grew larger, being given separate roles. Customarily, while one section played the main theme, the other section either punctuated it with brisk, rhythmic riffs or answered in the gaps in the main line. This method of writing was, in part, dictated by the limited instrumentation of the dance bands, which did not have the great variety found in symphony orchestras, with their array of oboes, flutes, violas, and the rest.

Ellington, of course, employed this method of writing, which was hard to avoid. But he tended rather to write true countermelodies for the second section, especially for the saxophones, where the brass had the main theme. This use of countermelody is musically far more sophisticated than simple punctuation, essentially rhythmic in nature, and it is a main characteristic of Ellington's music that would culminate in the 1940 masterpiece "Ko-Ko." We see it displayed here in the first chorus of "It's Glory," where the saxophone line runs along almost continuously underneath the melody in the brass, complementing, supplementing, and supporting as it goes—never quite the same but never really opposed to it, either.

"It's Glory" also has fine solos by Hodges, who was at this time at the top of his form, and by Williams, who was not yet the fully expressive player he would be in a few years but who was beginning to play more thoughtful and organized solos. There is also an interesting voicing of Nanton's plunger trombone with the clarinet in the bridge of Hodges's solo. Altogether, "It's Glory" is one of those small gems that Ellington was then learning to facet and polish and that would become a major part of his work.

Certainly one of the best known of all of Ellington's compositions—and a particular favorite of mine—is "Rockin' in Rhythm." Once again the provenance of its various parts is hard to determine. Bigard claimed that he, Hodges, and Braud contributed to it, but it is generally believed that Harry Carney had a major role in shaping the main theme, and his name is on the tune, along with Ellington's. Cootie Williams said they were working at a Philadelphia theater with the comic song-and-dance man Pigmeat Markham, "And during rehearsals," he went on, "we had to get some music for him. And they started jiving around, and that's how 'Rockin' in Rhythm' came about. I think it was Harry Carney started playing or something."[4] George Hoefer said that the song-and-dance man in question was Snake Hips Tucker, who worked with Ellington frequently;[5] other sources report other comics. In any case, the number was an immediate success, and thereafter Duke would use it to back Bessie Dudley in one of her hot dance numbers in theaters.

Ellington recorded the number again and again. Initially, there were sessions for OKeh, Victor, and Melotone in the winter of 1930–31, all getting successively faster. The first two cuts are virtually identical, and there are minor changes in the third, Victor sessions, for which two takes are available.

The piece is simple in structure. Most of it is in C major, with an interlude in A minor. It opens with a chorus of the main theme by the saxophones, with brief trumpet answers (I am discussing the Melotone version). Cootie plays a worked-out solo, accompanied by a saxophone figure that parallels Cootie's line. It is worth saying something about this. Western music as a rule is either *monophonic*, that is, made up of a simple melody line, such as that sung in the shower; *homophonic*, that is, harmonized in the ordinary way; or *polyphonic*, that is, constructed of lines that are rhythmically different, as if two or more songs were being sung at the same time. There is a fourth system, rare in Western music, but common elsewhere, especially in African tribal music, called *heterophony*, in which the secondary voices sing variations of the melody, harmonized with it only approximately. That is to say, heterophony is somewhere between ordinary harmony and true polyphony.

It is not surprising, then, given the amount of heterophony in African music, that it found its way into jazz. We have always seen the early New Orleans bands as playing polyphonic music with a cornet lead topped by clarinet embellishments and supported by trombones providing links between the phrases, a system derived from the marches so popular at the time. And this, in fact, was the system that white Dixieland players used from the beginning. But in black bands the putative polyphony was actually a good deal closer to heterophony. Louis Armstrong, playing second cornet to King Oliver, played neither a harmony part to Oliver's melody nor a distinctly different line, but paralleled it in this heterophonic fashion.

Ellington, as we have seen, had little acquaintance with these earlier forms of black music, but a number of the other men in the band had more, including the New Orleanian Barney Bigard, and I suspect that he was responsible for the device here. In any case, it is very effective.

This solo is followed by a repeat of the main theme, and then Nanton plays a typical solo over a simplified version of the figure that supported the trumpet. The main theme is repeated once again, and it slows while a brief trumpet figure supplies a close.

It is all very simple: there is little recourse to the constant interplay of solos and sections that Ellington had acquired from Henderson. It depends almost entirely on the main theme for its strength, and it is a sign of Ellington's musical sense that he recognized how good the melody was, and so built the piece around it. It is not the standard thirty-two-bar form but is made up of three distinctly different motifs, which gain much of their interest from cross rhythms.

The first motif opens with three quarter notes, followed by a variation on itself. It is interesting that the quarter notes at the end of the second measure are played right on the beat, where an improvising jazz musician would almost by instinct have pushed them well behind the beat. But even years later, when no jazz arranger would possibly have written so many quarter notes flush on the beat, Ellington continued to play them this way, and it must be assumed that he preferred them this way.

This first motif is followed by an abrupt jump to a sawtooth figure whose accented notes fall on the second half of each beat, to produce a metric shift. This little arrangement of motifs is repeated to make up eight bars, and then we get a very simple figure composed of long notes by the saxes, with brief trumpet responses, repeated to make up eight measures. The third motif opens with a syncopated figure a measure long, which once again suggests cross rhythms, and is repeated to make up four bars. It now appears that this four-bar passage will be repeated, as similar ones were in the other two strains, but on the fourth beat of the second measure a brand-new figure suddenly appears; it descends rapidly for four measures, making this strain ten bars long, and the whole theme twenty-six measures.

It is all very cleverly done: the five or six little figures that make up the main theme are all simple, and at least two of them are the most obvious kind of clichés. Yet they are strung together in such a way as to create that sense of shimmering change that Ellington was mastering. The theme is filled with abrupt switches, but once we get over the first brief shock, we immediately see how appropriate the new line is.

In fact, the whole of "Rockin' in Rhythm" demonstrates Ellington's ability to make a great deal out of very little. Harriet Milnes, in her discussion of the piece, says, "The whole is greater than the sum of the parts. The form is nicely divided between solos and sections, although not symmetrically, and has enough repetition of material to lend cohesiveness, but not so much that the material becomes boring."[6]

I entirely agree. The brief minor interlude, which might seem at first an irrelevancy, is exactly the touch of bitter chocolate we need at this point to brighten the lighthearted, almost bubbling music that comes before and after. It does not hurt to think of Ellington not so much as a dramatist, as Beethoven was, or an architect, as was Bach, but as a planner of meals. This may seem an odd sort of metaphor, but in fact it is suitable. Duke Ellington was, if anything, a sensualist. He led a heady sex life, and he boasted many times of being a champion drinker (which was certainly not true). For a time he tried to keep up with drinkers like Fats Waller and Art Tatum;[7] it is a good thing he did not succeed, for alcohol killed Waller at thirty-nine and contributed to Tatum's death in his mid-forties. He loved rich food like steak, eggs, and, especially, ice cream. According to his sister, Ruth, he had a special silver serving spoon he used for eating ice cream and would buy four quarts at a time. He would even begin his meal with ice cream and proceed to the steak thereafter. He had, said Derek Jewell, a special dessert he would order composed of "chocolate cake, custard, ice cream, jelly, apple sauce, and whipped cream."[8]

Inevitably, by the time he was in his late thirties, he was fat, and he remained fat for some years. Over time, however, he reduced his drinking; and in 1955 he was ordered by his doctor to take off a lot of weight. By his sixties he had given up alcohol almost entirely, and stuck as much as possible to a diet of steak, black coffee, and grapefruit.

But asceticism was not his natural proclivity. His autobiography includes a whole chapter, some ten pages long, devoted to food and meals he remembered. Few autobiographies contain similar chapters. Thus, to think of Ellington approaching his music as a chef planning a meal is not as silly as it might sound. And we have him in "Rockin' in Rhythm" adding little treats and surprises, offering a bit of lemon sherbet to cleanse the palate after the beef bourguignon, sprinkling chopped nuts or mushrooms over the whole.

Another composition from this period that has always been highly regarded by Ellington's fans is "Echoes of the Jungle." It is a feature for Cootie Williams, and Gunther Schuller surmises that Williams wrote at least the main melody.[9] There is, however, a good deal more to it than Cootie's work, for it is filled with contrast—those sudden shifts of color that Ellington so liked. It opens with a simple theme for the brass section in plunger mutes, with Hodges playing interpolations. Within eight bars this gives way to a solo by Hodges, with the brass plungers now sinking behind him. In another eight bars Williams suddenly soars out into the open for sixteen bars and then dives back into the plunger mute for another sixteen. Hodges plays a brief, four-bar interlude over plunger brass ending on an unresolved ninth, and then an entirely new idea appears, a spooky theme by the low-register clarinet on a minor blues, with the guitar supplying shimmering fills. This is followed by a four-bar conversation between the tom-toms and plunger brass, again in a minor key. Nanton growls the minor blues again, and suddenly we return to the opening theme in major, with plunger brass and Hodges obbligato for eight bars. A clarinet trio then takes over the theme, with plunger brass beneath. But, much to our surprise, after four measures the clarinets move into minor, rising higher and higher into a coda, with the brass growling around below.

"Echoes of the Jungle" was written as one of those jungle pieces that the public had come to expect from Ellington, a functional number that turned out to be an important piece of twentieth-century music. What strikes us about it are the constant shifts and the inventiveness of the contrasting portions of the piece as they come along, one after another. Nothing is anticipated, nothing develops out of what went before; each turn in the road is a new adventure: the Hodges interlude does not forecast the surprising arrival of the spooky minor theme that follows; the sudden rise of the clarinets at the end into the minor comes completely without warning.

In a larger form this absence of structure, of parts relating to each other in some fashion, would be disturbing; when we come to some of Ellington's long concert pieces, we will sometimes wonder why the material was grouped together at all. But, in a short piece some three minutes long, it is not always necessary to relate all the parts to one another. Indeed, it can be a mistake to tie the parts of such a piece too carefully together, as it may make it predictable. In "Echoes of the Jungle" we are constantly gratified by surprise.

Jungle numbers like "Echoes of the Jungle" and hot swingers like "Ring Dem Bells," which had been central to the band's repertoire at the Cotton Club and critical to establishing its reputation, continued to make up a large part of any of the band's performances. But now the new, more pensive mood was beginning to come forward. Increasingly, Ellington was working in this mode, as with tunes like "Blue Mood," "Blue Tune," and "Clouds in My Heart." These tunes are characterized by a quieter, more pastel tone palette and by a greater reliance on section work and less on the hot plunger mutes, and the use of frequently quite dissonant harmonies. A composition of this type that has often been overlooked is "The Mystery Song." It was written to back a dance team, the Step Brothers, at the Cotton Club. It was probably intended to be one of those spooky jungle numbers, but it is in fact one of Ellington's pastels, filled with a quiet sadness. The main theme may have been suggested by the whole-tone scale, which had become a cliché in jazz writing by this time. In any case, it is rich with chromaticism and, as played first by muted brass, suggests a sense of the winding down of things. This theme is followed by a contrasting, cheerful and quite busy melody by the saxophones that seems light enough to float off the ground. Then the moody, muted theme is played again, this time by Carney, with Bigard supplying an improvised obbligato. Finally, the whole band plays a carefully composed and, again, very busy melody that is a variation on the main theme. To my mind, this last variation is the one mistake on the record, for it comes out of the school of symphonic jazz, being promoted especially by Paul Whiteman, with its devotion to pretentious devices like the quarter-note triplets found here, which are used everywhere in movie music for a hokey, dramatic effect but are rarely employed by an improvising jazz musician. This section lacks the conviction of the first piece and is an early symptom of Ellington's weakness for what he conceived to be "serious" music. Nonetheless, "The Mystery Song" largely succeeds, and it indicates that Ellington was gaining further confidence in his own skills as a composer.

One of the best of these pastels is "Blue Mood." It opens—after the introduction—with Bigard's low-register clarinet playing a moody and harmonically sophisticated melody, over chords played by muted brass. Some of these chords are extremely dissonant, but so cleverly does Ellington weave them together that we do not feel them as an astringent but as the shifting of clouds on a windy day. Then follows a second section, in which tightly muted trombones are answered by plunger trumpets. This segment is a standard thirty-two-bar form shrunk down to half size—that is to say, made up of 8 + 4 + 4 measures instead of the customary 16 + 8 + 8. The little four-bar bridge consists entirely of a long, slow descent by a muted trombone. Then the main theme returns, first played in a dulcet, legato fashion by the saxophones and then reiterated in a dramatic style by staccato brass, with cymbals crashing on second and fourth beats, a classic example of Ellington's penchant for contrast. That is all there is to the piece, but it offers a consistent mood of light melancholy, ending with a sudden burst of frustration at the unfairness of it all. It is yet one more illustration of Ellington's ability to make a great deal of very little by imaginative use of the tone palette and by deftly handled dissonance.

Of all the tunes that leap to mind when Duke Ellington's name is mentioned, the first would probably be "Mood Indigo." It seems to be almost quintessentially Ellington: the strange timbres, the muted palette, the dreamy, low-key mood. Yet, oddly enough, a good deal about the composition is atypical. Ellington tended to be a rather busy composer, employing a good deal of polyphony, rich and frequently dissonant harmonies, and a lot of contrast. "Mood Indigo" is almost stillness itself. It contains no polyphony. The harmonies are mainly simple, and there is minimal contrast between the parts. It shifts slowly, with the stealth of a sunset, and is suddenly gone.

Who actually wrote "Mood Indigo" is subject to question. Duke's story is that he needed a fourth number for a six-piece recording session Mills had scheduled and that he wrote the song while waiting for his dinner the night before. However, standard discographies show that the full band was in the studio and that "Mood Indigo" was the only small-group number recorded on that date.

Barney Bigard always claimed that he wrote most of the tune. Eventually, he sued Ellington, had his name put on it, and began to collect royalties.[10] He told his biographer Barry Martyn the first strain had been written by Lorenzo Tio, Jr., Bigard's old clarinet teacher from New Orleans, who had come to New York with a group of tunes he hoped to sell. Bigard "borrowed" this one: "I changed some of it around. For instance, the bridge on the second strain, and got something together that was really mostly my own but partly Tio's."[11] However, Al Rose, an authority on New Orleans jazz, says he heard the piece in its entirety played by the A. J. Piron orchestra before the Ellington version was made.

According to Ellington, the night after it was recorded, Ted Husing, as usual, asked for the night's tunes. They decided to do it and got a lot of mail as a result. Mills put a lyric to it, and it went on from there. Bigard said, "We didn't think anything of it and, all of a sudden, it began to get popular and that was that. I missed the boat for twenty-eight years on royalties. I didn't get a dime. It was all under Ellington's and Mills's names."[12] The tune was first issued as "Dreamy Blues," but Bigard insists that they always called it "Mood Indigo" and that the name change was made by the record company—as usual, without consulting anybody. Rose, however, says that "Dreamy Blues" was the title Piron used.

The tune was originally cut in three sessions for Brunswick, OKeh, and Victor from October to December 1930. The first two cuts were made with seven men and are virtually identical. The Victor session was made with a larger group, and subtle, but telling, changes were made in the arrangement. Most critics prefer the early cuts with the small band; the best, I think, is the OKeh version, simply because the recording balance is somewhat better.

The composition could hardly be simpler. There is no introduction and no coda, aside from a note or two picked out by Ellington as the piece ends. It opens with the famous trio of muted trumpet, muted trombone, and clarinet playing the first theme. This combination of instruments was daring and imaginative and yet so correct that it remains a wonder today. Making it yet bolder is the way Ellington has voiced the clarinet in the low register, where it would get the smokier sound that would blend best with the muted brass.

The melody of this theme is so minimal—seven notes over the first four bars at a slow tempo—that it can hardly be defined as a melody. It works because the chords are shaped by very small movements in the line of one or two instruments—for example, a shift of one half-step in the clarinet makes the chord change at the end of the first bar. It is all done in slow motion.

The first theme is followed by solos by Bigard and Whetsol on, or around, the second theme. Once again, it is atypical: in the best of Ellington's work, themes jump into distant keys, change timbre, mood. Here the two themes are similar—the same key, similar harmonies, related melodies.

One point of interest is that at various, somewhat different points during these solos, Wellman Braud plays a busy bass line, scattering little patches of eighth notes here and there. These quick little bass passages make a subtle contrast with the general stillness.

There is, then, a brief piano interlude that, characteristically, makes that favorite move of Ellington's into the flat sixth. Then we return to the opening chorus. That is all there is to it. But, like most great music, it leaves us with a sense of completion, a finality, a feeling that everything needed has been said. Duke Ellington played "Mood Indigo" countless thousands of times over his life and recorded it again and again, but never did he top these first versions made with three horns and a rhythm section. If ever less was more, it was here.

Important though "Mood Indigo" was, it was another work that proved to be critical in terms of Duke Ellington's future. This was *Creole Rhapsody*, the first of his "extended," or concert, pieces. Ellington hardly invented the idea of writing jazz pieces shaped like what I suppose still has to be called classical music. Some two decades earlier Scott Joplin had written a pair of ragtime operas—*A Guest of Honor*, now lost, and *Treemonisha*, which was finally produced in complete form in the 1970s. It was Paul Whiteman, however, who popularized "symphonic jazz." His father was a conductor, and he himself was classically trained. He had started thinking in terms of symphonic jazz very early in the 1920s. In 1924 he gave George Gershwin a commission to write such a piece for a famous concert he was giving at Aeolian Hall in New York. The Gershwin piece turned out to be *Rhapsody in Blue*, and the concert was a resounding success and was reviewed widely by the major music critics. In 1924, in answer to the Whiteman concert, a rival bandleader, Vincent Lopez, put on a concert at the Metropolitan Opera House using a forty-piece orchestra and played a piece called *The Evolution of the Blues* by W. C. Handy. In 1928 James P. Johnson produced a symphony called *Yamecraw* at Carnegie Hall, and Whiteman's arranger, Ferde Grofé, wrote a number of jazz concert pieces, the best known of which, *The Grand Canyon Suite*, contained the well-known melody "On the Trail." Bix Beiderbecke worked out a little piano suite of four pieces derived from the French impressionists, the best known of which was "In a Mist," which Beiderbecke played at Carnegie Hall as part of a piano trio in 1928. There were, in fact, numberless efforts during the 1920s to combine jazz and classical music.

The symphonic jazz movement was a significant cultural phenomenon in the United States during this period, reflecting the idea that jazz could be taken seriously if it was cast in more significant forms than the thirty-two-bar format of the popular song. In general, these symphonic jazz pieces tried to pour jazz rhythms, timbres, and typical jazz harmonies into sonata form, suites, tone poems, and the like. To establish its credentials as symphonic jazz, a piece therefore had to be longer than the three minutes of a jazz record and should avoid the thirty-two-bar AABA form. Strings, French horns, and double reeds helped give such pieces a symphonic air. But the employment of a form drawn from classical music was what really counted.

Ellington and Mills were thoroughly familiar with the whole concept of symphonic jazz. In 1931, when Ellington left the Cotton Club to open at the Oriental Theatre in Chicago, and would no longer have the radio wire, Mills began looking around for other ways to publicize the band. At some point during the Oriental engagement, so the story goes, Mills blandly told the press, "Tomorrow is a big day. We premiere a new long work—a rhapsody."[13] Ellington thereupon stayed up all night turning out the piece. Ellington was rather given to announcing that he had dashed off this or that of his classic numbers in a cab or in a record studio, as he did with "Mood Indigo." In fact, the first version of *Creole Rhapsody* was recorded in January when the orchestra was still in New York. Ellington, under the tutelage of Mills and Ned Williams, had by this time come to understand the uses of public relations, and I have a hunch—it can only be a hunch—that they had cooked up the whole thing for publicity. Ellington worked out the piece—a good deal of it in the studio no doubt—and the announcement of the "premiere" was held up until the records were released a few weeks later. However it came about, I am reasonably certain that *Creole Rhapsody* was conceived, at least in part, as a publicity stunt; but the ramifications were astonishing.

Two versions of *Creole Rhapsody* were cut in 1931, the first for Brunswick on January 20 and the second for Victor on June 11. Mills had been given a fairly free hand by the record companies to cut what he wanted, on the premise that his instincts were entirely commercial. It was stretching this privilege to record a serious work that took up two sides of a record, and the companies were not initially happy with the idea.

The first version was six minutes long; the second, expanded by the addition of a major new theme that did not appear in the first version at all and by various interludes, is over eight minutes long and had to be issued on a twelve-inch record. On the whole, the first version is more jazzlike in nature, but the second one, which Ellington was able to give more thought to, undoubtedly represented his view of how the piece should go, and this is the version I will discuss.

Taken as a whole, the piece is very chromatic for a jazz work of that time, both in the tendency of its chords frequently to move by half steps and in the use of a good many chromatic intervals in the harmonies themselves. It opens with a forceful, choppy theme in E-flat minor built around block chords shifting chromatically. Bigard's clarinet supplies "fills" or answers to the phrases of the theme. As the chords move back and forth, the string bass changes from playing on first and third beats to second and fourth, implying a metric shift; accents in the melody line through the sixth and seventh bars produce a shift of meter. The theme is typical of Ellington's writing—essentially quite simple but dressed in astringent harmonies, rhythmically interesting, and, to an extent, contrapuntal.

After a piano interlude to slow the tempo and change keys, there follow two solos on variant blues, then a return to the main theme, this time with Hodges supplying a countervoice. There is another interlude by the saxes and another return to the main theme for eight measures, and, once again, Ellington slows the tempo and prepares a modulation into A-flat major. Now comes the second theme, a slow, pretty, slightly plaintive thirty-two-bar melody built around a four-bar phrase featuring an unresolved major seventh, an interval that always tends to sound somewhat wistful. Breaking rules as ever, Ellington resolves the major seventh downward.

This new theme is played by Arthur Whetsol, to whom Ellington usually gave such plaintive themes, and it ends the first half of the piece—what was the first side of the record. The second side opens with the second theme, this time played by saxophones. There follows a piano interlude and then a curious segment in which Hodges leaps into a horse race tempo for a few bars. The second theme is then played out of tempo by the clarinet accompanied by piano; the main theme reappears briefly; there are snatches from trumpet and clarinet, another reference to the main theme, and then a return to the second theme, first by unison saxes and then by the full orchestra. The ending is abrupt, possibly because time was running out.

The critics of the time and most later ones have applauded *Creole Rhap-*

sody as one of the first successful efforts to play jazz in a larger and more complex form than the blues and pop tunes it had almost always been built on. They saw that the jazz suites of Gershwin, Grofé, and the others were not really jazz but symphonic music dressed up with a few jazz elements—syncopated melodies, buzz tones, and occasional jazz rhythms. *Creole Rhapsody*, despite some out-of-tempo sections, was clearly jazz.

But the critics have generally preferred the first, shorter and presumably more hastily put-together version. The English critic Charles Fox said, "Padded with out-of-tempo rhapsodizing, the logic of the original abruptly disappeared. Previously a strict, relentless tempo had defined the form of the work; now the slackening of tension destroyed its unity."[14] If Fox means that the first version hangs together better, I do not agree. As we shall see, one of Ellington's weaknesses in his longer pieces is the frequent introduction of interludes that are intended to act as connecting links but usually seem to serve no purpose and go nowhere. A second problem is that often in these pieces, thrown together in the studio, as they so often were, Ellington would introduce piano rambles improvised on the spot, to fill up the space. In adding the new theme to *Creole Rhapsody*, which is given as much prominence as the first theme, or even more, he was forced to cut other material to fit the length of two sides of a record, and what he cut out are some irrelevant piano passages and interludes. The alternation of the two themes, it seems to me, gives the second piece a unity lacking in the first one. In fact, the two versions of *Creole Rhapsody* are quite different pieces and perhaps ought to be treated as such.

Creole Rhapsody was critical to Ellington's career, for it was taken as proof, by those who saw in jazz a potential art form, that Ellington was a true composer. He would be the man who would lead jazz away from its dedication to the improvised solo into a more thoughtful and what was conceived of as a higher form, built on carefully structured pieces that maintained, as *Creole Rhapsody* was the first to do, the real jazz feeling. It was given the New York Schools of Music's annual award for 1932 as the best new piece by an American composer. Not all critics agreed: Rob Darrell, among others, thought that this and others of Ellington's extended pieces were "pretty good, but . . . didn't think they were masterpieces," and John Hammond would eventually accuse Ellington of giving in to the "bugaboo of art." But, for the most part, *Creole Rhapsody* was seen as confirmation of Ellington's emergence as a major composer. As Barry Ulanov put it in a nice phrase, Hammond and those in his camp "wanted jazz to flagellate their sense of propriety" and panned him when "Duke achieved any considerable mellifluousness in his music."[15]

The period between the departure of Miley from the band and the trip to Europe also produced two of Ellington's best-known songs. The first of these was "It Don't Mean a Thing If It Ain't Got That Swing." There is very little to the melody, very little to the words, beyond the title, which Cootie Williams insisted was a catch phrase of his. The popularity of the tune depended mainly on the catch phrase and the scatted vocal by Ivie Anderson, which made the record a hit for her.

A second important tune from this time was "Sophisticated Lady," which went on to become an enduring standard of the twentieth century. Who wrote the song is a matter of dispute. Ellington said that he had struggled over the tune for a month. The bridge, he said, was the problem. Barney Bigard said the tune was worked out by Lawrence Brown and Otto Hardwick.[16] Ulanov said it was "based on a theme by Toby Hardwick."[17] Brown claimed that he wrote the main theme and Hardwick the bridge.[18] Both Brown and Hardwick were featured on the original arrangement, and it continued to be a feature for Hardwick as long as he was with the band. On the basis of not much, I am inclined to believe Hardwick was primarily responsible for it.

The song is built on plaintive descending chromatics that do have something of the flavor of the decadent lady nursing her wounds in an expensive café. The bridge forms a sharp contrast: it is in a distant key, rises rather than descends, and is rather more diatonic than chromatic. Nonetheless, it maintains the air of subdued melancholy established by the first part. Alec Wilder, in his classic American Popular Song, spoke highly of the piece and said, "Its very ingenious return to A flat is a piece of linear wizardry and is enormously difficult to sing."[19] It certainly is: nine of the thirteen notes in the "turn-around," to use the jazzman's phrase, are different, producing a little piece of music that suggests atonality.

The original recorded version is almost entirely solos, with minimal backing from the sections, and is somewhat heavy-handed, with portentous brass stings and a showy introduction. A version made a little later is more fully scored, with orchestral playing replacing some of the solos, but the differences are not major. Eventually, Mills had Mitchell Parish, an excellent lyricist, put words to it, and it became a hit; but it continues to be played more than sung, a wonderful piece of mood music that needs no words beyond the title to set a whole scene.

A piece of curiosa from this period is worth mentioning. It has always been known that in February 1932 the Ellington orchestra recorded two sets of medleys of its hits, including "Creole Love Call" and "Black and Tan Fantasy," on a 33⅓ rpm record which contained almost twice as much music as the ordinary 78 rpm record. Experiments with longer-playing records had been going on for some time, but nobody had really followed them up. In 1932, with the record business in a shambles, some companies decided to offer longer-playing records in an effort to attract buyers. The Ellington medleys were among them.

But there was more to it than that. In 1984 two Ellington specialists, Steve Lasker and Brad Kay, compared what they thought might be two different takes of these medleys. They were startled to discover that the two records were identical. Yet there were subtle differences in the sound quality, and it occurred to Kay that what they had were the left and right channels of a stereo recording. After considerable effort they were able to synchronize the two records and subsequently issued the medleys in stereo.

Why these stereo records were made remains a mystery, as there existed no commercially available stereo players. Kay suggests that it might have been the accidental result of cutting two masters at once for safety reasons, but he suspects there may have been more to it. He says, "I can't chalk it all up to a gigantic act of serendipity; but then, how could this practice have been carried on for several years . . . with absolutely nothing to show for it until now?"[20]

Two things should be noted about these records. One is the inclusion of a very fast stride piano solo by Ellington, called "Lots o' Fingers," which shows that Ellington had developed a very competent right hand, although he is still using simple substitutes for the more difficult standard left-hand pattern. The second thing to be noted is how beautiful the band sounds magnified by stereo. The playing is not without flaws: there are intonation problems in spots and a couple of sloppy entrances, but the sound of the band is superb and forces us to realize that the records from the early days simply do not do justice to the band.

I have said that this period was not as productive as some others in Ellington's career, and yet, during it, he produced some of his best-known pieces, including "Ring Dem Bells," "Rockin' in Rhythm," "Old Man Blues," "Mood Indigo," and Creole Rhapsody. For most bands, this would have been a substantial achievement. But this was, we must remember, Duke Ellington, and for every "Mood Indigo" or "Old Man Blues" there were a dozen inconsequental cuts thrown together offhand to fill a need and many others not even written by Duke. It is, of course, absurd to demand that a composer working in a show business milieu, where there is always the pressure of time and often a sense that your work is ephemeral, always come up to a high level. My point is only that, as we shall see, Duke needed a prod, a sense that what he did would be appreciated, and that in the absence of one he could grow lax.

Ellington was quite candid about this. He told one writer, "Without a deadline, baby, I can't finish nothing." He liked to work out of a mood triggered by a sight, a sound, a memory. "Mood Indigo," for example, was "just a story about a little girl and a little boy. They are about eight and the girl loves the boy. They never speak of it, of course, but she just likes the way he wears his hat. Every day he comes to her house at a certain time and she sits in her window and waits. Then one day he doesn't come. 'Mood Indigo' just tells how she feels." "Warm Valley" grew out of the sight of some voluptuously curved mountains; "Happy Go Lucky Local," out of the image of a black fireman on a little engine who blew the whistle to his girl friends as he passed their houses. Almost all of Ellington's best work did not begin with a musical idea, but an image or a mood. Furthermore, such instructions as he gave the musicians were often couched in allegorical terms. He might tell Williams, "Coots, you come in on the second bar, in a subtle manner, growling softly like a hungry little lion cub that wants his dinner but can't find his mother."[21] He told Stanley Dance, "I don't believe in a lot of elaborate plans and preparations, either. Just pour it out as it comes, and then maybe do some reshaping afterwards."[22] A composer who writes out of mood so much of the time is not likely, then, to produce a lot of his best work when the mood is not on him.

12

The Trip to England

In nearly everything that has been written about Duke Ellington, the trip of his orchestra to England in the summer of 1933 is described as a critical point. There he discovered that he had a group of ardent admirers among musicians and critics, the chief ones being the composer Constant Lambert and young Spike Hughes, who played bass and dabbled in writing music. These people, Ellington found to his astonishment, saw him not merely as a successful bandleader but as a major American composer whose music had a value beyond providing entertainment for big-spending tourists at the Cotton Club. He went home from the trip, he said later, believing that "maybe our music does mean something."[1]

The extent to which Ellington was admired by the English and by Europeans in general has been somewhat exaggerated by many writers. As it happens, some of the most important writing about Ellington has been done by Englishmen, and their tendency to inflate English appreciation for him is understandable. It has long been taken for granted by jazz writers and musicians that there has always been greater sympathy and understanding for jazz abroad than in its homeland. The assumption is simply untrue. I have written at length on this subject elsewhere, and interested readers can find the details laid out for them there.[2] Briefly put, Europeans began to understand what jazz was all about in the late 1920s and early 1930s. Although by 1930 there were a handful of ardent and knowledgeable jazz fans in England, and more on the Continent a few years later, the actual audience for the music was tiny. It could be sold occasionally as a novelty, especially when played by blacks, who seemed even more exotic to Europeans than to northern American whites; but even a Duke Ellington or a Louis

Armstrong was not able to work more than irregularly in England or on the Continent.

But black entertainers had toured Europe successfully from time to time, and a few, like Ada Smith in Paris, had established themselves there. Since the time of World War I, when a substantial number of American blacks visited Europe, word had been drifting back that things were better there. These visiting performers tended to overestimate the tolerance of Europeans for other races, as the Ellington men would discover: the favor shown to well-known black entertainers was not necessarily extended to working-class Arabs, Indians, and blacks coming in from Africa, Asia, and the Caribbean, who were treated almost as much like second-class citizens as they were in the United States. Nonetheless, things were better for blacks in Europe. They were not lynched, and, although they could not usually expect to rise very far up the social ladder, they were not kept in a state of semiserfdom as they were in the American South and, to a lesser extent, in the North. This was especially so for entertainers: they could not get into every good hotel or restaurant in Europe, but they could get into some, and they could date whites, neither of which they could do in the United States. Because the black populations of European cities were far smaller than those in America, there was far less fear that opening the doors to a black singer or dancer would allow a flood of blacks to pour through the crack. For some years before 1933 it had been widely understood by black show people that Europe was a species of heaven, and many of them meant to go and see for themselves. One of these was Louis Armstrong, who in the summer of 1932 made a six-month visit to England, with a side excursion to Paris. The trip was not quite as successful as was later reported: the demand for Armstrong's music was not nearly so heavy as it was in the United States, and he was idle a good deal of the time. But he had basked in adulation from the jazz fans and musicians, had enjoyed himself a lot, and had been able to socialize more freely with whites than he could have in the United States. He came back to the United States eager to return to England in the near future.

Throughout their lives, Ellington and Armstrong maintained a distant but polite relationship. (They would record formally together only once, late in their lives.) When Armstrong arrived in New York in 1929 to begin his career as a popular entertainer, Ellington had established himself as the jazz king of Harlem and was rapidly overtaking Fletcher Henderson as leader of the most highly regarded black orchestra. Armstrong was reaching out for Ellington's audience. Moreover, many jazz fans and writers were saying that Armstrong, not Ellington, was the preeminent genius in jazz. None of this could have suited Ellington, nor could he have liked the idea that Armstrong had had a great European success.

Irving Mills was also aware of Armstrong's success abroad. To Mills, Europe was another market for music in its various forms: recorded, printed, live. On November 12, 1932, he sailed from New York to England in order to feel out the market there for his stable, especially Ellington and the Mills Brothers, whom he was now handling. Eventually Mills made an arrangement with the Jack Hylton organization to book Ellington for a brief visit. Hylton was England's most-admired dance band leader and had expanded his operation to form a large band-booking organization. He arranged for the Ellington band to play at the Palladium, regarded by many as the most prestigious variety theater in the Western world. Ellington would go into the Palladium on June 12, 1933, on a bill with the house's more usual acts.

Throughout the winter and spring the *Melody Maker* ran stories about the impending visit; by the time the band actually sailed, British dance band musicians and fans were wound up with expectation. The *Melody Maker*, moreover, arranged for Ellington to play a special concert for musicians at the Trocadero, a cinema house in London's Elephant and Castle that could hold four thousand people. It was the feeling of the paper's jazz critics that English musicians would want a bigger dose of Ellington than the Palladium would provide.

The band sailed from New York on the *Olympia* on June 2 to the accompaniment of a good deal of fanfare in the American press, orchestrated by Mills and Ellington's new publicist, Ned Williams, who would prove to be important to Duke's career. Williams had served his show business apprenticeship as press agent to nightclubs and had later worked for the Balaban and Katz theater chain. In this capacity he had met Mills and Ellington when the band played the Oriental Theatre in Chicago. The great success of the date had suggested to Mills that Williams might be a useful man to employ; when Williams lost the Balaban and Katz job, because of the deepening Depression, Mills hired him. Williams began by creating for Ellington the first advertising manual for a dance band and went on to arrange a good deal of publicity for Duke. He was, Duke said, "a natural wit and a bon vivant,"[3] and was described by Barry Ulanov as "a short, balding man who looked as if he sold something, something quite good, maybe. He always wore a flower in his lapel and waxed the ends of his mustache till they shone. He wore spats . . . and really loved Duke and his music and selling them both."[4]

The sailing was a typical Williams operation. The Mills Blue Ribbon Band played on deck, the newspapers sent reporters, and Paramount sent its newsreel camera. *Time* magazine used the occasion to run a piece on Ellington and the growing European interest in jazz. It would be years before the magazine gave another jazz musician such attention.

For the trip Ellington brought along not only the orchestra but also the dancer Bessie Dudley and the song-and-dance team of Bill Bailey and Derby Wilson. It is clear that he and Mills planned to put on a small-scale revue modeled on what had proved successful at the Cotton Club and in the theaters that Duke was then playing. As it turned out, a good many of the English musicians and critics expected something else.

Fanfare in the English press equaled that of the American press. Barry Ulanov has compiled a number of quotations from British papers that covered Duke's English trip. The *Evening Standard* called him a " 'hot gospeller' of crazy jazz music and Haarlem [sic] rhythm." The *Sunday Express* said, "This band, consisting of America's eighteen hottest rhythm boys, all of whom are Negroes, is considered, by experts, to be the finest hot-cha turnout west of Land's End." Another reporter said, "Ellington, you know, is no ordinary negro jazzist. His advance press agent describes him as 'well-educated and gentlemanly in his bearing.' " And he went on to quote Spike Hughes as saying, "Ellington and Walt Disney seem to be the only great men that America has produced without the help of the Jews," a statement that must have puzzled students of George Washington and Abraham Lincoln.[5]

The sea trip was uneventful but fun for nearly everybody but Ellington, who had a morbid fear of being shipwrecked and spent most of his nights sitting up drinking and playing cards. For a man so outwardly self-possessed, Ellington was subject to a considerable array of irrational fears and superstitions. He would not wear certain colors; he would not give or receive gifts of shoes, which suggested that the recipient would use them to walk away; he was afraid of drafts and kept the windows around him closed at all times; he was frightened of flying and refused to do it until the demands of travel forced him into planes; and he subjected himself to many similar taboos. Ellington was hardly the first person to be superstitious, but his collection of taboos make a richer array than most people possess. It is difficult to find an explanation for them.

In any case, the *Olympia* did not sink but docked at Southampton on Friday, June 9, at 12:30, where it was greeted by a crowd, including Jack Hylton and press photographers. The whole mob took the train up to London's Waterloo Station, where they were greeted by thirty-seven more photographers, according to the *Melody Maker's* count.[6] Unfortunately, among all the good cheer, it was suddenly discovered that no London hotel would take eighteen blacks. This was the first in a series of dents that the reputation, among the musicians, of European racial fairness would receive. Eventually Ellington was allowed into the prestigious Dorchester, and the other musicians were scattered around a number of small hotels and rooming houses. That evening, Hylton gave a reception for Ellington at his grand house in Mayfair, and at 9:00 P.M. Ellington was rushed to Broadcasting House for an interview.

The Palladium was basically a commercial variety house showing bills that included comics, standard song-and-dance men, and singers of sentimental ballads. Both Armstrong and the Ellington orchestra were fairly unusual, indeed exotic, acts for the house. Indeed, the preceding year, a reasonably large segment of the Palladium audience had found Armstrong, with his eye-popping antics, too exotic for their tastes and had walked out. It needs to be remembered that in 1933 the ordinary English citizen's idea of "jazz" was the standard band music of groups like Hylton's, which might feature an occasional improvised solo but which were mainly selling popular tunes in inoffensive musical garb; they had little or no experience of the stronger forms of jazz, like the pyrotechnics of Armstrong and the growling and yammering of Nanton and Williams.

The band opened on June 12, going on at eight o'clock, on a bill that started at six-thirty. The musicians were elegantly dressed in pearl gray suits; Duke wore a double-breasted lounge suit in pearl gray and a bright orange necktie. The program was typical of what Duke was giving American audiences. Bessie Dudley shimmied to "Rockin' in Rhythm"; Ivie Anderson sang the recent big hit "Stormy Weather" and the forgettable "Give Me a Man Like That"; the band roared through some of its up-tempo numbers like "Bugle Call Rag" and "Whispering Tiger," and it used "Some of These Days" and "Mood Indigo" for encores.[7]

The audiences were generally enthusiastic about the program, and attendance for the first week was just short of the Palladium record, but the *Melody Maker* critics were not happy. To them, the show had been a commercial shuck, in which Ellington had pandered to popular tastes. The paper's reviewer, presumably Spike Hughes, said,

> In the first place, there has been a lot of press publicity about Ellington as a sponsor of a new kind of music and all the lay critics, musical and otherwise, were waiting to hear it. Yet, "Mood Indigo" was what they got. What about "Blue Tune," "Blue Ramble," "Rose Room," "Creole Rhapsody" and the rest of those numbers Ellington has made peculiarly his own?

And he went on to complain that too much valuable time was given over to Ivie Anderson and the various dancers. It was hoped, Hughes said, that "the *Melody Maker* Concert will give an opportunity to the Duke to feature some of the quieter and more individual compositions of his which have not been, hitherto, played in London."[8]

Whatever Hughes thought, the general run of jazz fans was excited by the orchestra's presence in London. Musicians, particularly, were drawn to it, and they packed the Trocadero for the *Melody Maker* concert. The large theater was jammed with forty-two hundred people, who filled the air with "continuous cheering and clapping."[9] But Hughes, once again, was not entirely pleased. For the first half of the concert, apparently following Hughes's instructions, Ellington played some of his moodier and, perhaps, harmonically more sophisticated pieces. But he sensed, correctly or not, that his audience was not responding as warmly as he wanted, and after intermission he switched back to a more standard program. Hughes was annoyed. The expanded version of *Creole Rhapsody* was boring and meaningless, "Dinah" was noisy, "and Sonny Greer should not be allowed to sing," a judgment others had made before Hughes. Then, after intermission, "the rot set in."[10] Ellington brought out Lawrence Brown to play "Trees" and offered some popular tunes like "Some of These Days" and his own "Sophisticated Lady."

Spike Hughes was only twenty-one or twenty-two when he was castigating Ellington for his commercialism. It is clear that Hughes had a taste for Ellington's more introspective pastels. He would, not long afterward, come to New York and record a group of his own compositions in what he considered to be the Ellington manner with some American musicians; these pieces are mainly in the slightly melancholic vein of this part of Ellington's work. Anything else, Hughes seemed to feel, was commercial. Most critics today would agree that Lawrence Brown's playing of "Trees" and the shake dancing of Bessie Dudley were afflicted with commerce, but they would not necessarily agree that Ellington's fast swingers, like "Lightning" and "Dinah," which Hughes deplored, were also commercial.

But Hughes's was a minority opinion. Duke was mobbed on his exit, and people tore at his clothes and clung to the running board of his car as he was driven away.[11] The success of this concert persuaded the promoters to try another at the Trocadero, and this, too, was sold out. Once again, Hughes complained, "The mute brass passages of ["Ebony Rhapsody"] is not an occasion for the waving of hands and such"—Freddy Jenkins was apparently the offender—and he went on to chastise the audience for applauding the solos. But, again, most of the people in the audience were less stern in their views than Hughes and cheered the music enthusiastically.

Between times, Ellington, Mills, and the band, generally, were given a full-scale celebrity treatment. The papers ran articles about Ellington, some deploring him as a "Harlem Dionysus, drunk on bad bootleg liquor," others calling him "the first composer of uncommon merit, probably the first composer of real character to come out of America."[12] There were elaborate parties: Ellington and Mills threw a cocktail reception for Jack Hylton, and the band played at the Punch's Club for members of the British upper crust and were photographed there for the social pages of the papers.

Finally, there was a famous party given by Lord Beaverbrook at which the band drank with royalty and the Prince of Wales, later Edward VIII, sat in on the drums.

On Monday, July 24, the band left London for Holland, where it played a concert at Scheveningen. The audience was enthusiastic, although a few people stomped out angrily. It then went on to Paris, where it played concerts at the Salle Pleyel on July 22 and July 29 and a third one at the Casino de Deauville. Once again, there were parties, press reports, and flattering attention from the small but vociferous group of French jazz fans. Finally, weary and hung over, but full of good spirits, the entire group departed for New York.

The trip had not been an unalloyed success. Many of the bandsmen went home disillusioned about the degree of acceptance blacks had in Europe; there had been a hostile element in the press reports, probably mainly racial at base; and there had been the complaints of Spike Hughes and some others about the taint of commercialism in Ellington's programs.

But, taken as a whole, the experience had been an important one for Duke. Barry Ulanov quotes him as saying, "The main thing I got out of Europe was *spirit*; it lifted me out of a bad groove. That kind of thing gives you the courage to go on. If they think I'm *that* important, then maybe I have kinda said something, maybe our music does mean something."[13] In his two months in Europe, Ellington had attracted the attention of important people in the social system; he had received a great deal more press coverage than he would have gotten in a similar period in the United States; and, perhaps most important, he had been treated by musicians, the *Melody Maker* people, and critics like Constant Lambert as a major composer. Lambert would write in the *New Statesman*, "I know of nothing in Ravel so dextrous in treatment as the varied solos in the middle of the ebullient 'Hot and Bothered,' and nothing in Stravinsky more dynamic than the final section."[14] And it was this reception that finally convinced Ellington that he was—or could be—that genuine article, a real composer, with all that seemed to mean in terms of immediate prestige and future immortality. Again, Ellington's upbringing played a role in his reaction to all of this. Louis Armstrong, who had had a similar reception a year before, had been raised poor in a very tough ghetto where the majority of the people were illiterate. The concept of "art" as a special calling and the "artist" as a keeper of the flame was not part of his cultural baggage, and, when critics talked to him about his "artistry" and not "going commercial," he did not quite grasp what they were getting at.

But Duke Ellington had come from a middle-class home where the word "composer" almost automatically came attached to the word "great." He knew—or he thought he knew—what an artist was and, if that was what he was, he ought to live up to the role.

To a considerable extent, Ellington was deluding himself about his English reception. A good deal of the press excitement and popular furor depended on the band's novelty value: European promoters understood this and were not fighting to sign Ellington for a return engagement. Furthermore, the European audience for jazz was at this point pitifully small, probably numbering not more than a few thousand, a substantial proportion of them musicians. Moreover, the European musical establishment did not share Lambert's enthusiasm for Ellington's music and jazz in general: by and large, it looked down on it. The French intellectuals were generally scornful of it,[15] as Lambert himself had been a few years before.[16] Lambert, as a matter of fact, knew a lot less about jazz than he thought he did. Jim Godbolt noted in his history of British jazz, "Regarding jazz, Lambert's heart may have been in the right place, but his observations and strictures were as off-beam as any lay press hack. . . ."[17]

What remains puzzling about the episode is why Ellington had to wait for this European enthusiasm to see that his work meant something beyond the Cotton Club dance floor. The bohemians who visited Harlem had been telling him so for some time. He had been received at the White House, had lectured at colleges, and had been taken seriously as a composer by R. D. Darrell, Hammond, and others some years before the English trip. But it was the European interest, rather than the American, that impressed him, and he came home determined to write more serious music in the manner of *Creole Rhapsody*.

13

Duke Faces the
Swing Era

Duke Ellington came home from Europe charged up with a sense of his importance as an artist, a sense that his work mattered and that he ought to take it seriously. There followed one of those creative surges in Duke's life in which he wrote a number of important pieces in a few months. Within a year or so after the enthusiastic reception he had gotten in England, he turned out four or five of his best-known records, wrote two of his most enduring standards, and pulled together a piece of symphonic jazz that prefigured the extended works to come.

The first of the noteworthy cuts was made in September, about two months after his return. Constant Lambert was married to a Eurasian woman whose pronunciation of "Mood Indigo" turned it into something like "Rude Interlude," so Duke created a piece with that name.

The number does sound a bit like an interlude—a moment in which all activity is suspended—but it is the reverse of rude. It is a quiet, almost motionless, piece in which Duke has made a thing of shimmering beauty out of the simplest of materials. Atypically, there is very little soloing. Cootie Williams has eight bars in the plunger mute, and Louis Bacon, who was brought in for the recording session for reasons that are not clear, plays trumpet and scats a moody vocal in a deep bass voice. Aside from these and a few brief piano interludes, the piece is made entirely of a tiny, two-note phrase played by one or another section of the orchestra, with answers coming from another section. Harmonically, it is built on what feel like alternations of dominant and tonic but what are in fact so filled with suspensions, particularly of Ellington's beloved lowered sixth, that the harmony lacks the firm sense of purpose that dominant–tonic movement usually has. Instead, it drifts, so that the whole piece seems to float slowly into sight at one side of the field of vision and out the other. What movement it has is supplied by a generally rising line the tiny melody takes. It is a superb piece of shading, all muted colors, and shows Duke's absolute mastery of this kind of form.

Immediately after the band cut "Rude Interlude," it made "Dallas Doings," an up-tempo swinger, another carefully worked-out number that depended more on composition than on solos. It is built on three main themes, two of them quite simple, all of them in the call-and-answer pattern, which Duke dresses in different clothes and juxtaposes against one another. The more complex first theme, which is used both to open and to close the piece, employs a cross rhythm in the first four bars of the kind we have seen in Ellington's work before, in which a three-beat phrase is repeated to cycle over the underlying 4/4 meter. It is played by the saxes each time it appears, but the other two themes are moved around the orchestra. In the second theme, the answers are played first by duet trombone and trumpet in plunger mutes, later by open brass. The third theme is played once by the saxes, another time by trumpets in straight mutes. Typically, it is all change, all contrast, and the use of the first theme to open and close the piece supplies all the form necessary for a short piece of this kind. For once, however, this may have been a mistake, for this theme ends with a fanfare-like figure, which suggests things to come and works better as an introduction than as an ending.

In the next session, Ellington produced one number that depended almost entirely on composition and in which brief solos were subordinated to Ellington's musical goals. This was his famous "Daybreak Express," an uncanny musical re-creation of the sound of a train pulling out of a station and speeding through the night until it comes to a halt at dawn.

Ellington, as we have seen, was at this time frightened of planes and ships, but he loved trains and, through the 1930s and 1940s, spent thousands of hours on them, much of it in the roomette Mills saw to it that he had. Moreover, in the nineteenth century, and well into the twentieth, the railroad train had an almost mythic meaning for American blacks. The train had the power to take you away from misery—away from the cotton fields, away from the unfaithful lover, or, conversely, away from the cold city and back to the fondly remembered folks down home. It is not surprising that the hidden route out of the South, during slavery, was referred to as the "underground railroad."

Besides, thousands of blacks worked for the railroads as gravel tampers, track layers, baggage handlers, and, most particularly, Pullman porters. This last was a prestigious job among blacks, and the porters enjoyed dropping in front of envious friends the names of the big cities they had visited—"I just got back from Pittsburgh, Detroit, Cincinnati." The train seemed to have a special magic about it, and black music of the period is full of references to it: the train boogie was a staple in the repertoire of untutored black pianists, and the lyrics of the blues are about railroads almost as much as they are about the troubles of love.

Duke used train effects in several of his pieces, dating back to the execrable "Choo Choo," the first record issued by the Washingtonians, but "Daybreak Express" is the masterpiece of the genre. Barney Bigard told Stanley Dance,

> Well, when we were in the South we'd travel by train in two Pullmans and a baggage car. Duke would lie there resting and listening to the trains. Those Southern engineers could pull a whistle like nobody's business. He would hear how the train clattered over the crossings and he'd get up and listen to the engine. He'd listen as it pulled out of the station, huffing and puffing, and he'd start building from there. Then, for when it was really rolling, he'd put something there Bechet played into the song. He had the whistles down perfectly, too.[1]

The piece is, of course, program music, a showpiece, demonstrating Ellington's love for pure sound. Perhaps more than anything, this was what Ellington's music was all about. Form, architecture, did not particularly interest him; but he was enthralled by sound—those mutes, those voicings so tight they threatened to crack—and he had, by this time, made himself one of the great masters of it. We can hear this delight in pure sound in his extraordinary re-creation of the train whistle, made of a combination of tightly voiced clarinets and muted trumpets. We hear it in the brief growl Cootie emits just before the fast saxophone chorus to imitate the sound of the distant whistle as the train, now at full speed, hurtles through the night. We have no difficulty imagining Ellington, deep in the night in the middle of some southern landscape, listening to all those sounds and trying to figure out how he could replicate them with musical instruments.

The piece opens with a long introduction as the train begins to slide out of the station, gathering speed. Then comes Cootie's little distant whistle, which introduces one of those fast saxophone passages on "Tiger Rag" chord changes that Duke used so often, signaling that the train has now reached full speed. There follow two more high-speed choruses utilizing the whole band, built on the call-and-answer device, except that in this case Ellington has complicated the simple formula by supplying a sequence of three voices in place of the usual two—in the first chorus, a high trumpet note, followed by brass and then saxes; in the second, brass, saxes, and the trumpet high note, all filled with the sound of whistles and pounding wheels. This is, rhythmically, very complex music. The piece ends with a rather abrupt winding down as the train comes into the station and shudders to a stop. "Daybreak Express" is an Ellington classic, and it is hard to see how it could have been performed by any band other than the one Ellington shaped himself.

Not everything that Duke wrote in the period immediately after the England trip was as carefully thought through as "Daybreak Express." There were the usual commercial numbers, like "I'm Satisfied," an ordinary tune by Ellington fitted out with words by Mitchell Parish and sung by Ivie Anderson. There were the hasty pieces depending mostly on solo work to carry them, such as "Sump'n' 'bout Rhythm," featuring Freddy Jenkins. But there were more than the usual percentage of memorable pieces. "Delta Serenade" is a typical Ellington pastel with a pretty melody, featuring Bigard in the low register over muted brass. "Blue Feeling" is mainly a string of solos on the blues, but it has a very interesting eight-bar theme that appears three times dressed differently. The theme is made of three phrases of unequal length, which tend to begin and end at unexpected places over the eight-bar measures, and all three are quite different in nature, producing that sense of dialogue we get from consecutive melody, rather than the recycling of old news that repetitive songs give us.

"Stompy Jones" is yet another example of Ellington making a great deal out of a small piece of cloth. It begins with a series of solos over a very basic sixteen-measure chord pattern. Then we get five final choruses of riffs, mainly by the brass, all very simple but all felicitously put together to make the whole thing swing. One chorus consists entirely of a chord by the brass answered by a single "wah" from Nanton in the plunger mute. Nothing could be more primitive than this, but it works, and the piece romps and stomps along infectiously. "Porto Rican Chaos," later remade as "Moonlight Fiesta," is a piece with a Latin beat written by Juan Tizol and probably arranged by him, at least in part. The United States has seen successive vogues for dances imported from South America: the tango in the 1920s, the rhumba in the 1930s, the conga and the samba later. "Moonlight Fiesta," to use the better-known name, has a very pretty melody and enough complicated activity between sections to justify applying to it the term "chaos."

During this period the band also made a curious piece that went on to become one of its better-known works. "Ebony Rhapsody" was written by a team of film song writers, Sam Coslow and Arthur Johnson, for a scene from Murder at the Vanities, a film made in 1934. The scene opens on a small, string orchestra dressed in Hollywood's idea of eighteenth-century costume, complete with powdered wigs, playing one of Liszt's famous Hungarian Rhapsodies. The orchestra then dissolves into the Ellington band, in black tie, playing a swing version of the tune. Ultimately, the string orchestra reappears, and, in a bizarre ending, the musicians are machine-gunned from the audience. The tune was not, of course, Ellington's, and I suspect that the arrangement was written by a Hollywood arranger, but the piece was a successful novelty for Ellington.

From this period also come two of Ellington's best-known songs, "Solitude" and "In a Sentimental Mood." "Solitude," like so many other Ellington songs, was supposed to have been written in a rush to meet the demands of a recording date. Ellington said, "I was one number short and I wrote it in twenty minutes standing against the glass enclosure of RCA Victor's studio in Chicago."[2] In this case, the story is probably true; furthermore, according to Cootie Williams, the song was entirely Duke's. The key point to the song is the resolution at the beginning of a major seventh upward to the tonic. It is a haunting moment.

The first recording of "Solitude" shows some of the haste with which it was organized. It is a rather frail reading, with sloppy entrances, but I nonetheless prefer it to later versions. In particular, in this version, passages by the saxophone section gain color and strength by comments from Williams and Brown, whereas, in a version made several months later, they stand naked. The opening statement of the theme by muted trumpets and low-register clarinet, a by now familiar device, is appropriately subdued, in keeping with the haunting quality of the tune.

Irving Mills recognized immediately how fine a tune "Solitude" was and had lyrics put to it. The record became a big hit for Ellington, his most successful song to that time. It was recorded many times, sold hundreds of thousands of copies of sheet music, and went on to become one of the classic American songs of the twentieth century.

"In a Sentimental Mood" is another of the pieces that Duke had a story about. He was playing a party in Durham, North Carolina, where he acted as peacemaker between two girls who had been fighting, by "dedicating a new song to them."[3] However, the song features Otto Hardwick on soprano saxophone, and it is generally believed that he had a major role in its composition. We probably should take Ellington's story as pleasant embroidery. Still, the song has one of Duke's most obvious trademarks, a move into the flat sixth in the bridge. It is, as a whole, a very pretty song and became a considerable success. Curiously, Edmund Anderson once asked Duke what he considered a typical Negro piece among those he'd written, a reasonable enough question in view of Ellington's frequent insistence that he was writing Negro music. To Anderson's surprise, he gave "In a Sentimental Mood" as an example. "I protested a bit," Anderson recalled, "and I said I thought that was a very sophisticated white kind of song and people were usually surprised when they learned it was by him. 'Ah,' he said, 'that's because you don't know what it's like to be a negro.'"[4]

It is a very interesting answer because "In a Sentimental Mood" certainly has the feeling of sophisticated melancholy that we are more likely to associate with Cole Porter than, say, Fats Waller—the brittle lady at the bar with her cocktail and cigarette holder, so to speak. But we have seen Ellington in this mood of quiet melancholy many times before—witness "Mood Indigo" and "Rude Interlude," to mention only two. We need to keep in mind that to be black is primarily a matter of culture rather than genetics. Most cultures are divided into subcultures, and the black American culture, itself really a subculture, is divided into several "subsub-cultures." There has been a tendency among whites, especially the bohemians of the 1920s who were curious about the black subculture they really did not understand too well, to lump all blacks together as if their backgrounds were all the same. But Duke Ellington, as we know, had a background entirely different from that of, say, the blacks of the Mississippi Delta region who were singing the blues in rough juke joints. Ellington's understanding of what it was to be black was not the same as these sharecropping blues singers'. He had an emotional response to "In a Sentimental Mood"; he is a Negro, and, therefore, the tune must be a Negro song.

The productivity that followed the English enthusiasm for Ellington's work began to decline in vigor after a year or so, as frequently happened with Duke. For the next several years, the great works would not come so quickly. In part, this was due to a series of problems, some of them tragic, which would enter both Ellington's personal and his professional life.

Professionally, the Depression continued to trouble the music industry. Ellington had always refused to go south, but now Mills was pressing him to do so for economic reasons. It appears that, among other things, Ellington had lost some money as a consequence of the stock market crash of 1929, although I have been unable to find details. In any case, in the fall of 1933 Duke agreed to play a tour of the Interstate theater chain in Texas. It was the first such tour by a black band, and it broke records along the way. The next year he played some engagements in New Orleans, where there was a big turnout for Barney Bigard, a hometown boy who made good, and thereafter Duke would play the South routinely for the rest of his traveling career.

The racial problems that the band faced in the South were not as bad as Duke had feared they would be, but they were bad enough. The band members might have trouble getting cabs even in St. Louis; they might be ordered to take the service elevator in hotels to get up to the ballroom where they were playing; they would, inevitably, have trouble finding restaurants that served them. Once, in Henderson, Texas, a white woman sat down on the piano bench next to Duke. He called the road manager, Jack Boyd, and said, "Take this lady out of here." Boyd did so, but, as the band was packing, a big white man snatched Tricky Sam's trombone from the bandstand. "I'm gonna take this trombone with me," he told Duke, "and I don't care if you tell the police." Duke replied, "Well, if that's the way you feel about it, there's the trombone. If you want it take it." In response the man said, "No, it's all right. I don't want the trombone. All I wanted to see was how you was gonna act about it." This incident was reported by Juan Tizol, who claimed it was the worst episode of the southern tours.[5]

Duke Ellington's attitude toward racial problems was to ignore them as much as possible, an approach he tended to take to problems generally. To some extent this had grown out of his upbringing. Washington blacks were a little better integrated into white society than were blacks in most other places, especially those who worked in government, as J.E. eventually did, where they might have white coworkers. Furthermore, Daisy's father, as a police captain, must certainly have been dealing with a good many whites on a more or less equal basis. Ruth has insisted that the Ellington family was simply unaware of race. A white man with whom J.E. worked and who had become a friend used to visit their home, and Ruth would sit on his lap.

Duke was hardly as unconscious of racial matters as this suggests. But he chose to avoid the whole question; he did so, I believe, in part because of his ingrained sense that he would be lowering himself to do battle with the bigots. For example, according to Cork O'Keefe, in the early days Cab Calloway insisted on staying at a good hotel when he played Chicago, and, because O'Keefe had the right connections, he was able to arrange for him to stay at the Palmer House. But Ellington, rather than make an issue, would stay with friends.[6] It was part of the Ellington cool.

Ellington told one interviewer, "You have to try not to think about [Jim Crow] or you'll knock yourself out."[7] Mercer said that in the South

> someone was liable to call him George or something like that and he'd get very angry about it. But, by the same token, he also could be heard, in conversation, to admire the South for its frankness because, in the North, there was an equal feeling which was always underlined, and you never knew if you were or weren't in the presence of it.[8]

And Mercer wrote in his book,

> But as strong as his feelings were, Ellington recognized the persistent need for subtlety, for this was a touchy area open to all kinds of misrepresentations. . . . He firmly believed that blacks, in the United States, should look on themselves as Americans primarily and should try to straighten things out within the family before going outside. . . . He had a comprehensive library on black history and culture and had read a great deal.[9]

The net result, in any case, was that Ellington himself enjoyed far greater acceptance in white society than most blacks of his day; and he may well have thought that that was the best contribution he could make.

The Depression was now generally hurting the entertainment business, and expedients like the southern tours were becoming necessary. A second, more significant professional problem was the arrival of the swing band era, one of those sudden turns in musical fashion that have been typical of America in the twentieth century. The swing period would last from 1935 to 1946, more or less. It would elevate a number of hitherto obscure musicians into celebrity and riches, but it would not all work to Ellington's benefit.

The big band was hardly a new invention. As we have seen, the seeds for it were planted by Ferde Grofé, Art Hickman, and Paul Whiteman in the years between 1918 and 1922. By 1926 or so Ellington, Fletcher Henderson, arranger Bill Challis with the Jean Goldkette Orchestra, and some others, were devising a hotter version of Whiteman's symphonic jazz, using better rhythm sections, a good deal of jazz soloing, and the feeling of a jazz solo in the section work. By the end of the decade this version of big band music was beginning to overtake the politer kind. Even Whiteman recognized what was happening, and in 1927 he raided the Goldkette Orchestra for some of its best jazz soloists, including Bix Beiderbecke, and its chief arranger, Challis. Through the early years of the 1930s the hotter bands continued to climb in favor, especially with college students and younger people in general, although, because of dislocations to the music business due to the Depression, this was not immediately apparent.

The swing boom was triggered by the sudden rise to popularity of a band led by a young clarinetist named Benny Goodman, who made a name for himself as a free lance around New York but who wanted his own band. According to an oft-told story, in 1934 the band, essentially through the pulling of strings by John Hammond, who was a friend of Goodman's, got on a new radio show called "Let's Dance," which would feature, in turn, sweet, Latin, and hot bands. Goodman's was the hot band and appeared last, when it was assumed that sedate, older listeners would have gone to bed. The Goodman band was not a smash success, but it did well enough to be booked for a cross-country tour in 1935, which would end with a stay at the Palomar in Los Angeles. The tour was a disaster: dancers hated the hot music that Goodman played, and some even demanded their money back. The band members arrived in California utterly dispirited. They were thus astonished, when they showed up at the Palomar to begin the job, to find a line at the box office stretching around the block. They began the evening playing the sweet tunes audiences had been demanding throughout the tour. The audience was apathetic. Goodman then decided, as he said later, "the hell with it," if they were going to fail they might as well do it playing the music they liked. They broke out the hot numbers, many of them arrangements originally played by the Henderson band that Goodman had bought, and the next thing they knew the audience was alive and roaring.

What had happened, apparently, was that the "Let's Dance" show had gone on too late for young people in the East but had reached them in the West because of the time difference, and so the band had developed a significant following in California. The idea that the times called for sweet, romantic music proved to be incorrect. It appears there is always some demand among young people for a strongly rhythmic music. The death of the jazz boom after the 1929 crash had left a new cohort of young people without a music they could consider their own, and the Goodman band filled the void. The phenomenon would repeat itself some ten years later, when the sudden collapse of the swing bands would push younger listeners, in search of rhythmic music, into listening to "rhythm and blues" music intended for black audiences—with consequences for popular music that would be enormous.

After the huge success of the Goodman band, dozens, and then scores, of swing bands were formed to supply the young market with music. Within five years there were hundreds of such bands around the country attempting to make a mark. In the end, fifty or so became celebrated, and the leaders of perhaps a dozen—Goodman, Glenn Miller, Tommy and Jimmy Dorsey, and Woody Herman among them—became wealthy. "Swing" was a phenomenon written about regularly in the newspapers and magazines and dissected by professors in learned journals. The most famous leaders were treated like movie stars, their marriages and divorces being chronicled in the gossip columns. Several of the best known published ghosted autobiographies, and some had their life stories, usually badly distorted, made into movies.

People who were already leading bands in 1935 were like lazy swimmers suddenly being engulfed by a huge wave. It gave them a tremendous push forward, but it forced them to go in the direction it was going. The Casa Loma orchestra and the Dorseys, for example, managed to accommodate themselves to the wave and rose rapidly to fame. Fletcher Henderson, Ben Pollack, and some others could not adapt, and their bands foundered.

Duke Ellington was one of those who managed to adapt, but not without strain. The Ellington band was by 1935 one of the best known in the country, overshadowed only by two or three of the most popular white bands. It had already formed a distinctive style, one that did not quite fit the swing pattern, which had been based on the Fletcher Henderson orchestra's style. Ellington's music was more contrapuntal and less dependent on the interplay of brass and reed sections than the swing bands were. It employed more dissonance than were used by most swing bands, which stuck to blander harmonies. The Ellington band worked from a much richer tonal palette than most bands possessed; few of them made use of the eccentric or "freak" effects that were Ellington's stock in trade. Finally, while the swing bands all looked for original "hot" numbers they could be identified with, like Glenn Miller's "In the Mood" and Woody Herman's "Blues on Parade"—based on Rossini's *Stabat Mater*, incidentally—their repertoires included many of the hit tunes of the day. Ellington, on the other hand, played mainly originals, mixing in as few pop tunes as he thought he could get away with. Furthermore, Ellington was not shy about giving audiences his more difficult works, like "Ko-Ko" or "Diminuendo and Crescendo in Blue," as recordings from clubs and dances of the period indicate. The Ellington band was judged as a swing band, but it did not quite fit the model. It was offering the public a stronger and more sophisticated kind of music, and the public was not always sure it liked it. Ellington thus had a lot less to gain from the swing boom than other leaders did. He had already visited the White House, had his opinions quoted in the newspapers, appeared in movies, become internationally known. He did not really need a movement in popular music that would bring a lot of other bands forward.

Yet Ellington extracted some benefits from the swing boom. It was, after all, making the kind of music he played *the* popular music of the time, and giving musicians an acceptance as public figures that few of them had ever had. It was not all loss.

But the period also brought some real losses. In 1934 both Freddy Jenkins and Arthur Whetsol were forced out of the band by illness. The irrepressible Posey was suffering from tuberculosis, a disease that was then very difficult to cure, and particularly debilitating for a wind instrumentalist. Jenkins returned in 1937 for a brief period, then collapsed once again and left the band on the point of death. He survived, however, made a substantial recovery, and moved to Fort Worth, Texas, where he worked as a disc jockey, sold insurance, and eventually involved himself in local politics. Cootie Williams saw him there in 1962 and reported that he looked wonderful. Stanley Dance added that he had become "a deputy sheriff or something, and was wearing a Stetson and a gun" when Duke, Carney, and he last saw him.[10]

The Whetsol story had an unhappier ending. In 1935 Whetsol began to suffer from mental problems caused by a brain tumor. He was in and out of the band for the next year or so, but by October 1937 he was having periods when he was not lucid and had to retire. The disease advanced relentlessly, and he died in 1940. The loss of Whetsol was painful to Duke.

They had been together from the beginning, and Arthur had been part of Ellington's professional world for twenty years. Arthur Whetsol never achieved a great reputation as a jazz soloist, but Duke valued him highly for the purity of his tone and his beautiful handling of melody. He always considered Whetsol an important component of the band's sound; his illness was both a professional and a personal tragedy.

In any case, Ellington now needed replacements in his trumpet section. Once again, he reached out for a man who was both under the New Orleans influence and possessed a particular sound. This was Rex Stewart. He was born in Philadelphia in 1907 but spent most of his youth around Washington. His family was generally accomplished. His grandmother, who was half American Indian, played organ, wrote hymns, and had published a book of poems. Both his mother and father played a variety of musical instruments and sang semiprofessionally. Stewart was given music lessons of one kind or another from the time he was four years old, studying violin and piano. He joined a rough, juvenile band, in which he began playing brass instruments. Finally, he learned the cornet, which would continue to be his basic instrument even after most cornetists had gone over to the trumpet, following the example of Louis Armstrong.[11]

Stewart apprenticed with local bands, traveled with a musical revue when he was only fourteen, and eventually landed a job with the Musical Spillers, a fairly well known vaudeville group of the 1920s. By 1923 he was in the New York area, establishing himself as a professional, and in 1925 he joined Elmer Snowden, recently forced out of the Washingtonians. In 1926 he was asked to join the Fletcher Henderson band, then coming into musical maturity and considerable fame. He was taking over the chair of his musical idol, Louis Armstrong, and the pressure of succeeding the great man proved too much for him. He left Henderson on the excuse that his grandmother was sick, and disappeared. Eventually, Henderson found out what happened and, in 1932, brought Stewart back into the band. He was now a more confident player, and for the next several years, with occasional hiatuses, he was one of Henderson's star soloists.

By 1933 the Henderson band was having organizational problems, brought on mainly by the leader's almost pathological lack of self-assertiveness, and Stewart left and eventually landed in the Luis Russell band. He was playing with this group in Harlem when Duke reached out for him in December 1934, at a moment when both Jenkins and Whetsol were out, although Whetsol would return for a while.

By 1934 Stewart was a solid, experienced musician who could read and play with strength. He had been influenced over the years by various musicians, including Bubber Miley and Bix Beiderbecke, playing with diametrically opposed styles. But his primary influence was Louis Armstrong, whom he had heard in 1924 when Armstrong had come from Chicago to join the Henderson band as a jazz specialist. He said, in a statement that has often been quoted,

> Then Louis Armstrong hit town. I went mad with the rest of the town. I tried to walk like him, talk like him, eat like him, sleep like him. I even bought a pair of big policeman shoes like he used to wear and stood outside his apartment waiting for him to come out so I could look at him.[12]

Stewart was only seventeen at the time, while Armstrong was twenty-five or so, and the adulation was natural. In time Steward acquired a warm, full tone that owed something to Armstrong, but the overt influence of Armstrong appears far less often in his work than it does in that of Cootie Williams, who frequently quotes directly from Armstrong solos. According to the jazz writer Francis Thorne, who knew Stewart, he was, "essentially, modest, highly sensitive and, perhaps, even had a bit of an inferiority complex."[13] He was certainly intelligent. He was one of the very few jazz musicians of his time to write seriously about the music and contributed articles to a variety of publications, including *Down Beat* and the *Melody Maker*, some of which were later collected in the book *Jazz Masters of the Thirties*. In the Ellington orchestra he played his share of straightforward jazz solos, but he became particularly known for his "freak" effects—low-register growls, plunger work, and, especially, the use of the half-valve, where the valve is only somewhat depressed to produce a kind of nasal sound. Most trumpet players will half-valve occasionally for effect, but Stewart developed a manner of playing in which he would half-valve an entire solo. It gave Ellington a new sound to work with that was as distinctive as Nanton's growling.

By the beginning of 1935 Ellington needed yet another trumpet player. He took Charlie Allen, who was obscure even then, and forgotten now except by Ellington specialists. In the middle of 1935 Arthur Whetsol returned, and Allen left. Whetsol stayed for perhaps a year, but sometime in 1936 he left and was replaced by Wallace Jones. Jones would be with the band until 1944, but, with Cootie and Rex established as the band's trumpet stars, Jones was given little solo space. He, too, is better known to Ellington specialists than to ordinary jazz fans.

At almost the same moment when Ellington was rebuilding his trumpet section, he was also changing his basses. Precisely what happened is difficult to determine—witnesses differ. However, sometime early in 1935 Wellman Braud left the band. He was replaced by Billy Taylor, a well-regarded bassist who had worked with many of the best black bands around New York. Not long afterward, Duke added another bassist, Hayes

Alvis, who had been playing with the Mills Blue Ribbon Band. The idea of carrying two basses in a band was unique: I cannot think of another example of it. Why Duke wanted two is hard to discover. It is the opinion of Stanley Dance that it may have been mainly for the visual effect; we remember how conscious Duke was of putting on a show. Duke may also have decided that the rhythm section needed bolstering. Jazz rhythm is never easy to discuss, because it depends on extremely subtle details; deviations of a twentieth of a second can be critical. However, when the Washingtonians were starting out, the concept of jazz rhythm was badly understood by them, and the whole idea of the rhythm section was underdeveloped. Some of the greatest jazz of the time was made by odd rhythm sections: Armstrong's Hot Fives used banjo and piano and no drums. In the thinking of many the drummer was there for the dancers, not for the band. It has always been said that Sonny Greer was very good at working with show dancers, but he apparently never really understood the idea of driving the band. John Hammond said that Greer was a "melodic drummer" who played the tune "rather than with the drive the band needed."[14] The jazz composer Johnny Mandel said, "We used to say that nobody but Sonny Greer, who had strange time, could play with the band. We did not foresee how good it would sound when Sam Woodyard or Louis Bellson was with it."[15] I think Hammond is correct: my wholly subjective impression is that Greer was playing *along with* the band rather than supplying a foundation for it to work from. Gene Lees, a musician and former *Down Beat* editor, called Greer's time "slushy."[16]

Similarly, I do not think that Freddy Guy added very much. When the Washingtonians were starting up, the banjo was a popular instrument that all bands had to have; when Snowden was dropped, it was essential for the band to have another banjoist. When the guitar came back to replace the banjo around 1930 in order to produce a more sharply defined beat, Guy made the transition; by 1931 he was using both and by 1933 had dropped the banjo. He was in the band for mostly historical reasons, and, when he finally left, Duke did not replace him and continued without a guitar. For one thing, Guy tended to use much simpler harmonies than those Duke and the band were playing. Where Duke, for example, might play a C seventh chord with an A-flat tucked down inside it, Guy would be likely to leave the A-flat out. Guy, too, seems to me to be playing along with the band rather than supplying a rhythmic platform for the band to dance on. On top of it, there was a tendency for Ellington's basses, right up until the arrival of Jimmy Blanton in 1939, to play only on the first and third beats of the measure instead of on all four, as was increasingly being done in jazz in the 1930s. Ellington, in fact, was probably the strongest man in his own rhythm section. Duke, in my view, was a good jazz pianist but not a great one. However, he was seen by musicians who worked with him as an excellent band pianist. Oscar Pettiford, one of the major bassists in jazz history, said, "Duke's a very fine pianist, he's comfortable to play with, and that's very important. He has a good, steady beat."[17] Cootie Williams said, "Duke was the greatest piano player that I ever played with. . . . He could feel you. You know, how to back you up. . . . You were more comfortable playing with him, which I was, than any other piano player I ever played with."[18] Bigard said, "Duke himself would give us such great rhythmical backing at the piano. He knew how to feed somebody that's blowing a solo."[19] And Dizzy Gillespie said, "Duke is the best comper [i.e., accompanying pianist] in the world."[20] It is very difficult, I feel, to make judgments about rhythm players without playing with them. Testimony like this from people who worked with Duke is incontrovertible, especially when it comes from a bassist like Pettiford, who was listening closely to Duke all night long.

Ellington, then, was very conscious of what was going on in his rhythm section, and it may well be that he began carrying two bassists in the hope that they would give his rhythm section more drive. He would not fire Greer or Guy; his loyalty to his men, especially the old hands, was too great. So he would try this other expedient, and he carried both Taylor and Alvis until 1938, when Alvis left, for unknown reasons.

The changes in personnel that took place in the mid-1930s were hardly as drastic as the ones that had come at the Cotton Club, but change of any kind was not helpful in a band where so much depended upon having a fixed personnel not only familiar with the music but also able to help in creating it. Mercer said of the time that Lawrence Brown came into the band,

> Bringing a virtuoso like Lawrence into the band didn't present a problem within the trombone section because Tricky Sam and Tizol were so different as personalities and stylists. But, to the band as a whole, it meant one more "star" who had to be featured and, over the years, this was the cause of frictions, jealousies, resentments and cliques as the novelty of new talent squeezed, or threatened, the old.[21]

What had happened was that within the world of the dance band and its fans most of the men in the band had become recognized, and they had come to think of themselves as people of importance. Arthur Whetsol, Sonny Greer, and Toby Hardwick went back with Ellington to the Washington days, when Duke was merely a sideman like themselves; Tricky Sam, Braud, and Guy had played at the Kentucky Club and appeared on the first successful records; Hodges, Cootie, and Bigard had arrived early in the Cotton Club days, before the band had grown famous; and each group tended to resent newcomers, long after the newcomers had their own new-comers to resent. It was a problem that would plague Ellington for the rest of his band-leading career. It has to be said that he was part of the problem. He was perfectly well aware of the jealousies and resentments; however, instead of easing the new men in, letting them serve an apprenticeship as backbenchers before they were allowed to come forward, he tended, struck by the novelty as Mercer suggests, to give them solo space immediately: Rex Stewart played solos on six of the first seven records he cut with Ellington, getting more solo room than Cootie; Lawrence Brown began to solo with the band immediately (on records, at least) and, within three months or so, was the main trombone soloist with the band. It was not just the novelty, though, that caused Ellington to feature the new men; there was a certain element of manipulation in it, a mischievousness that was always a part of Ellington's character.

But Ellington could not carry this too far. Because of the problems the loss of a man caused, he could not easily fire the musicians and, therefore, had no stick to beat them with. As a consequence, they groused continually if they felt neglected, and, as a further consequence, Ellington had to see not only that the solo space was parceled out more or less evenly but that each man's specialties were played regularly at dances and theaters. This had two effects on the music. One was to make the jazz solo a more regular part of the music than it was in most other swing bands. The second was to fix the repertoire. Swing bands usually gave their audiences one or two of their old favorites, but most of the repertoire shifted continually to include the newest hit songs. Duke, however, had to return, again and again, to the old tunes in order to keep Hodges and Nanton and the rest of them content.

But, despite the grousing, Ellington always managed things so that the discontent never broke out into open rebellion. It was now clearly Ellington's band, as Toby Hardwick discovered on his return in 1932:

> When I rejoined the band it was just like I'd never left. Except this way, maybe. It wasn't our thing any longer. It had become Ellington's alone. This was inevitable, I guess. Ten years ago it was "We do it this way," and "We wrote that." Now, the "we" was royal. It seemed more inspiring, maybe more inspired, too, the other way but I guess it had to come to this. You love the guy right on. You have to admire him for all he's accomplished. You've got to be happy for him, he's that kind of guy. But in those early days, how we enjoyed what we did. We were privileged to make suggestions. If he liked it, if he didn't, he'd go along with it anyway. Every man in the band had freedom of expression. It was fun. . . . And then it was moreorless like family . . . even with the people who paid us. We never liked making a change. We shared

in everything, like in some of those numbers we wrote where two or three contributed a part. Of course, Duke wrote most of them, especially later on.[22]

But all the troubles with the orchestra were insignificant compared with another personal loss he would suffer during this period. Within a few weeks of his return from England, Dr. Thomas Amos, Mildred Dixon's doctor, who had become Duke's as well, examined his beloved mother for what seemed a minor complaint. What diagnosis Amos made is unknown, but Daisy was clearly sick. In early 1934 the doctor wanted to hospitalize her, but she refused to go, possibly out of the puritan's fear of being examined by a stranger. At any rate, by September 1934 it was plain that she had cancer and was probably fatally ill. She went home to Washington for treatment and was subsequently sent to Providence Hospital, a research center in Detroit. In late May 1935 the family gathered around her in the hospital. Duke spent the last three days of her life with his head on her pillow beside hers, and on May 27, 1935, she died.[23]

Ellington was devastated. His mother had been the center of his emotional life, the fixed pole to which he had been tethered. He had seen her as the endlessly loving, all-forgiving mother most people wish for and few get. He had chosen to live with her for a substantial portion of his adult life rather than live with a wife of his own in his own home. Indeed, he had replaced J.E. as her husband in many ways. He had become her provider, the bearer of expensive clothing and jewelry customarily brought to a woman by a lover. He was the sole source of her social status, the caretaker of her other child. Duke never lost his respect and his affection for his father, but he had become his father's employer and sometime before Daisy's death J.E. had taken to sleeping with Mercer. "He had a kind of love affair going on with his mother," Fran Hunter said.[24] "His world was built around his mother," Mercer added.[25]

This is no reason to think that there was anything "abnormal" in this relationship. In a sense, it might even be called "super normal," in that it would seem to some, as it did to Duke, ideal. But there is no question, either, that this mother-and-son relationship went beyond what is usual.

No wonder, then, that his life turned to dust. "The days after her death were the saddest and most morbid of his life," Mercer said.[26] Duke wept for days. He himself said, "I have no ambition left. When mother was alive I had something to fight for, I could say, 'I'll fight with anybody, against any kinda odds.' . . . Now what? I can see nothing. The bottom's out of everything."[27]

He expressed his grief in an expensive funeral. The service was conducted by the Reverend Walter H. Brooks of the Nineteenth Street Baptist Church in Washington. Duke ordered $2,000 worth of flowers and had her buried in Harmony Cemetery in an iron casket weighing half a ton, which would last indefinitely, and cost $3,500.[28] This, remember, was at the bottom of the Depression, when the majority of American families lived on less than $2,000 a year.

Not long after the death of Daisy, J.E. also began to feel the cold wind of failing health. In this case, the fault was primarily his own. Only fifty-six at the time of Daisy's death, J.E. had lived high for most of his adult life, eating, drinking and pursuing women as it suited him. He was, Fran Hunter said, "adorable. Duke was very much like his father. His father was witty, full of mischief. In those days, they lived just like anyone else. There was no maid, the father did all the cooking, kept the house immaculate, and where everyone had to go, he did all the driving. . . . He used to make the best biscuits."[29] Duke even took J.E. on tour from time to time. Once the bass player failed to make the job, and J.E. came out and faked for the evening, twirling the bass and showing off, while the band broke up with laughter.

During the years in Washington, J.E. had had a full-time job and moon-lighted, at times, at Washington parties, and his high living was, conse-quently, under some restraint. Once he moved to New York, he had no full-time occupation, aside from the make-work Duke gave him. He had plenty of money—Duke was infinitely generous with his family—and he began to drink too much. By the summer of 1937 he himself recognized that he needed to control his drinking, so he went off to the Catskill Mountains, presumably to breathe fresh air and drink milk. The cure failed, and that fall he entered Columbia Presbyterian Hospital in New York suf-fering from pleurisy. He died at the end of October and was buried in Harmony Cemetery in Washington, where his wife had been buried only two years earlier.

These deaths left a hole in Ellington's life. Not surprisingly, then, in about 1937, he formed a friendship with a man who would become more important to him than any one but members of his family. This was a doctor named Arthur C. Logan. His father, Warren Logan, had been on the faculty of Tuskegee Institute, an important college for blacks, and was for a time treasurer for the institute. Arthur was born on the campus in 1910. He came to New York at ten and attended the famous Ethical Cul-ture School, which was racially integrated. He graduated Phi Beta Kappa from Williams College in Massachusetts, a highly respected small college, where he was one of a tiny population of blacks. He went on to Columbia University's College of Physicians and Surgeons. He had thus been living in an integrated world from the age of ten—a world, moreover, that was placed well up the American social ladder. Relatively light-skinned, six feet two and a half inches, he had green eyes and wore a thin mustache. He was not merely intelligent and well-educated but also good-looking and personable, the sort of man marked for success from the start.

He had, moreover, a strong sense of duty, acquired from both his Tuskegee background and the Ethical Culture School. He belonged to all sorts of charitable and black advocacy groups, including Martin Luther King's Southern Christian Leadership Conference (he became King's personal doctor), and by the mid-1960s he was deeply involved in New York City's hospital system and was head of the city's poverty programs.

His wife, Marian Taylor, had sung in supper clubs at some point in her life, and it was probably through her that Duke met Logan. Eleven years younger than Duke, Logan was already becoming as renowned in his field as Duke was in music. Both men were handsome, charismatic, and used to success; they must have struck each other as two of a kind. They formed a deep friendship, certainly the deepest of any in Ellington's life. It seems clear, in retrospect, that Logan in some way filled the void left by the death of Duke's mother. Although he was the junior man and never had the public fame that Duke had, Ellington leaned on him. Later, when Duke was doing a lot of international travel, he would frantically wire Logan to come to him if he felt even a cold coming on, and Logan usually would come. Duke was, or at least became, something of a hypochondriac and always traveled with a doctor's bag filled with pills and lotions. It is not surprising, then, that when he picked somebody for support, he chose a doctor. In any case, from this time on Arthur Logan would be a central figure in Duke's life.

14

Concertos
and Small Groups

Given Duke's grief at the loss of his parents, as well as the illnesses of Whetsol and Jenkins, it is probably a good thing that the band was very busy in the years following the England trip. There were almost constant tours, with engagements at prestigious events like the Texas Centennial Exposition in 1936 at Dallas and a return to the Cotton Club in 1937, when the club moved from Harlem to Broadway in the aftermath of a race riot. There were more movies. One was a 1933 short called *Bundle of Blues*, which included "Rockin' in Rhythm" and Ivie Anderson singing "Stormy Weather," one of the great hits of the period. There were brief appearances in two Paramount Pictorial Magazines in 1933 and 1937. In 1934 there came out *Belle of the Nineties, Murder at the Vanities*, with the odd "Ebony Rhapsody" sequence, and, perhaps more consequential, a short called *Symphony in Black*. This was built around a tiny plot involving a black composer working on a serious piece of music. It included a number of older pieces, among them "Ducky Wucky" and "The Saddest Tale." But it also included "A Hymn of Sorrow," a lovely, quiet piece played mostly by Arthur Whetsol, which may have been the starting point for the "Come Sunday" section of *Black, Brown, and Beige*, one of Ellington's most successful extended pieces, composed almost a decade later. Three years later brought *The Hit Parade of 1937*, for which the band did some commercial, pop tunes.

There were magazine stories, the most important being an article in *Fortune* on the band's financial arrangements and, in 1938, a story in *Life*, rapidly becoming the most important magazine in the country, in which Ellington was named as one of the country's twenty "most prominent Ne-

178

groes." On Randall's Island in New York on May 29, 1938, there was a swing band festival, which included twenty-four swing bands.

Also in 1938 he was one of five American composers commissioned by Paul Whiteman to write suites on bell themes. Ellington's piece was called "Blue Belles of Harlem," using the pun as a chance to write on his favorite subject, women.

There were, finally, some changes in the recording arrangements with Irving Mills. For one thing, by the mid-1930s, recordings were overtaking sheet music as the most profitable aspect of the music business. Irving Mills, accordingly, wanted to get into it. He had a small stable of bands, and he owned what he claimed was "the world's largest collection of copyrighted tunes," for which he said he had turned down $750,000, offered by Twentieth Century-Fox.[1] If he owned a record company, all three hands could wash each other quite profitably, he assumed. Toward the end of 1936 he organized two labels, Master, which would sell for seventy-five cents a record, and, Variety, a low-priced line aimed at the jukebox market and, especially, the black market. The company began issuing records early in 1937.

He decided that he would put Ellington on the expensive Master label; but he needed product for Variety, the low-priced label. He could hardly allow Ellington to compete with himself at two prices; besides, he knew Ellington well enough to realize that Duke would not take kindly to appearing on a cut-rate label, especially if Cab Calloway were to be on the other one.

The answer to the problem was supplied by a young woman named Helen Oakley, the daughter of a wealthy Canadian family. She would, in time, marry the jazz writer Stanley Dance. She was living in Chicago in the mid-1930s, was a jazz fan, and knew Benny Goodman and his brother Freddy.

In 1935 it happened that Benny Goodman and the black jazz pianist Teddy Wilson fell into a casual jam session at a party, supported by a young amateur on the drums. Present at the party was John Hammond, who immediately urged Goodman to record as a trio with Wilson and his regular drummer, Gene Krupa. Everybody was aware that it was virtually impossible for blacks and whites to play in a racially mixed group, even in the record studios, although it occasionally happened; Hammond was motivated principally by a desire to dent the color barrier. In July 1935 the Benny Goodman Trio cut four sides. They were immediately successful and led to a whole series of Goodman trios, quartets, quintets, and sextets, which produced some of the finest small-band jazz of the period. When other swing band leaders saw Goodman's success, they formed small groups of their own—Woody Herman's Woodchoppers, Tommy Dorsey's Clam-

bake Seven, Bob Crosby's Bobcats, and more. These groups not only recorded but were usually brought down front for a portion of each evening
to play a hot jazz specialty or two.

In 1935, however, it was one thing to record a racially mixed group in
the relative privacy of a studio and quite another to present it in public. That happened late in 1935 when the Chicago Hot Club decided to
put on a Sunday afternoon concert at the Congress Hotel, featuring Benny
Goodman, who was playing there. According to John Hammond, it was
a wealthy jazz fan named Edwin "Squirrel" Ashcraft III who insisted that
the trio play.[2] But Stanley Dance says otherwise: "John Hammond always
gets the credit, but Helen sent the money to New York for [Teddy Wilson's] fare out and then had to persuade Benny to let him play in public."[3] Helen Oakley herself says, "I got Benny to introduce his trio publicly
in Chicago. And then I was helping Bob Crosby to form the Bobcats."[4]
Oakley was by this time working for the Mills organization, in charge of
the Variety label, and it was obvious to her that a small band, or bands,
could be drawn from the Ellington group, featuring the star soloists. She
broached the idea to Duke and Mills, and Duke in time agreed.

These small-band sides were a success from the start, and over the next
several years there would be dozens of them, most of them under the
nominal leadership of Rex Stewart, Barney Bigard, Cootie Williams, and
Johnny Hodges, presumed to be the best-known of Ellington's sidemen.
Although the putative leader of each group might provide tunes, Duke
was firmly in charge of the music, selecting the men for each date and
putting together the arrangements that were mostly minimal, in his usual
fashion in the studio.

These small-group records have turned out to be an important part of
Ellington's work. Jazz had begun in New Orleans as a semi-improvised
music played by small bands—frequently duets and trios, although somewhat larger bands were more common. The small band has been the primary one in jazz because more than three horns cannot usually improvise
successfully together. Although the big bands dominated popular music
during the years 1935–1945, small groups continued to play, record, and
work in certain clubs, and in retrospect we see that much of the important
jazz from this period was not made by the big bands but by small bands
utilizing, in the main, players from the big bands moonlighting for fun
and a little extra money. The small Ellington bands are among the best
examples of small-band jazz of this period.

Although Ellington was very busy during the years following the death
of his mother, a good deal of it was just going through the motions. His
spirit was so destroyed that his productivity fell sharply. Over the twelve
months after she died, he cut only sixteen sides. Two of these—"Isn't

Love the Strangest Thing" and "Love Is like a Cigarette"—are appallingly commercial numbers that do not sound to my ear as if they were arranged by Ellington. Two more—"Kissin' My Baby Goodnight" and "Oh Babe! Maybe Someday"—are not much better.

Nonetheless, during this dry period he did record one long piece and the first of an important series of concertos he composed for various of the star soloists. The extended piece was *Reminiscing in Tempo*, which he wrote in the weeks after his mother's death as a tribute to her. He said, "After my mother passed, there was really nothing, and my sparkling parade was, probably, at an end."[5] At the time, he was on a southern tour and spending many hours alone in the roomette in the Pullman car. "I found the mental isolation to reflect on the past. It was all caught up in the rhythm and motion of the train dashing through the South, and it gave me something to say that I could never have found words for."[6]

But there was more to it than that. Two years earlier, Duke had discovered a lot of English gentlemen crowding around to laud *Creole Rhapsody* and "Black and Tan Fantasy." But he had not yet written anything more to support the idea that he was a real composer of serious music. He now had, in a tribute to his mother, a subject worthy of serious music, and he set about writing something that would please the critics as well as honor his mother. He said, "I wrote it just for the [English critics]. That's partly the idea of the title."[7]

Fittingly, *Reminiscing in Tempo* is in a low-key, rather wistful mood and, like most of Ellington's forays into longer forms, has both virtues and defects. It was written in four segments of about three minutes each in order to fit on a pair of 78 records. It is built around two nicely contrasting themes, which appear and reappear, with some variation, painted in different tone colors—now unison saxophones, now trombones, now solo plunger trumpet, as was Ellington's customary method. The opening theme is one of his typical, plaintive little melodies, given first, as were many melodies of this kind, to Arthur Whetsol. The second theme is stronger and built around descending eighth notes with a good deal of chromatic coloring. Throughout, Duke uses a lot of thick-textured, chromatic harmonies with frequent shifts of key and a chord structure far more complex than was customary in popular music. Duke's control of the complicated harmonic pattern is by now sure-handed, and his mixing of sounds and his shifts are deft throughout.

But there are problems with *Reminiscing in Tempo*. For one thing, despite the usual contrasts of timbre, the piece lacks variety. The entire thing is played at one tempo and one dramatic level, something even a Beethoven would be wary of attempting for twelve minutes at a stretch. For another, it is not really a jazz piece. Less then 10 percent of it consists of improvised soloing, leaving aside several rambling piano interludes by Ellington. The strings of eighth notes of the second of the two main themes are played evenly, as they would have been by a symphony orchestra, a practice that is deadly to swing feeling.

Ellington, of course, would have said that it did not matter whether the piece fit anybody's definition of jazz, and quite rightly so. But this does force the critic to view it against other than jazz criteria. Jazz pieces are frequently based on quite routine forms: architecture is not an important concern of most jazz musicians. But more formal music is exactly that, and this piece never goes anywhere, but simply meanders hither and thither, almost entirely without direction. The only structure it has is provided by the steady reappearance of the two main themes. Between times, all seems to be transition—one transitional patch leading to another and another, leaving the listener to wonder what the point of it all is.

For example, in about the middle of part two we have a short, four-bar passage for winds that leads us into a brief improvisatory section by Hodges, which is followed by a short trombone solo, then a brief piano solo, then a sequence of rising chords in the brass, which brings us to a rambling piano solo to end the section. Each of these short passages sounds anticipatory, as if it were bringing us to some major statement; but the statement never comes.

The critics for whom Ellington wrote *Reminiscing in Tempo* did not like it. In England, Spike Hughes wrote that it was "a long, rambling monstrosity that is as dull as it is pretentious and meaningless."[8] Hammond said it "lacked the vitality which used to pervade [Ellington's] work."[9] And, according to Barry Ulanov, college swing fans got into debates over it that "rocked the college campuses," a statement that has to be taken as hyperbolic.[10]

The whole episode tells us something about Ellington's naïveté in respect to classical music. He did not know very much about it, and never would. At times, out of curiosity, people would play classical music for Duke. Edmund Anderson played him records of Delius, Ravel, and others who were supposed to have influenced him. "He was crazy about Stravinsky," Anderson said.[11] But it is clear that Ellington rarely listened to classical music on his own initiative. In fact, according to Stanley Dance, he did not listen to records of any kind very much, nor did he go out to hear other bands very often. What little Ellington knew about the techniques and practices of the classical composers he had gotten secondhand, through the tips and hints given to him by Will Marion Cook, Will Vodery, and, perhaps, a few others. Jim Haskins put it well when he said, "Vodery had assimilated the classical experience and translated it into successful comedy, pit-band style. It was much easier for Ellington to understand the harmonies and colorations of classical music in its translated form. . . ."12

But Vodery and Cook had not given Ellington a systematic course in composition, something that takes years of study to master in any case. They were showing him some relatively basic concepts that would help him solve the immediate problems of orchestration he faced in putting together music for the Cotton Club. Duke never really studied the schemes the nineteenth-century composers used to make a long piece hang together; and his naïveté lay in the fact that he did not realize there were things he did not know. What he needed, at this point, was a lot of good advice from somebody like Cook, who had been writing extended forms with unusual lengths and shifts of meter as early as *In Dahomey*, produced in 1903. But Duke was a proud man who did not like to seek help from anybody, and he went on reinventing the wheel—that is, struggling to solve problems that had already been solved.

The adverse comment on *Reminiscing in Tempo* was painful to Duke, who was more sensitive to criticism than people were generally aware, and he did not attempt another long piece of this kind for another eight years. But, whatever his failure with the long form, he remained a master of the three-minute piece enforced by the nature of the 78 rpm record. Not long after the unhappy debut of *Reminiscing in Tempo*, he wrote the first of what would be a long and wholly successful series of "concertos" for various of his star soloists. This was "Echoes of Harlem," originally called "Cootie's Concerto." In January 1936, probably, Williams came to Duke with what would prove to be the main theme for the piece. On January 20 the orchestra went into the recording studios in Chicago, and Ellington worked out the rest of the piece, no doubt in conjunction with Cootie and other members of the band as usual. The piece was recorded, and it may have been only then that it occurred to Ellington that they had written a concerto. Later on, Ellington and Bigard worked out a similar piece for clarinet, called "Barney's Concerto." Neither of these pieces was issued, but they were recorded again on February 27, 1936. It can be presumed that a good deal more work was done on them in the interim, much of it probably in the studio at the second recording date. These cuts of February 27 were issued as "Clarinet Lament" and "Echoes of Harlem," titles no doubt chosen by Mills as more salable than "concertos."

"Echoes of Harlem" is quite simply constructed, all of it cut into eight-bar segments, except one 4 + 10 bar segment in which Cootie plays over the band. Nor are there a lot of the shifts of key typical of Duke; the piece centers on A-flat and the relative minor, F minor. The ensemble writing is simple, for the most part little more than sequences of chords. "Echoes of Harlem" is largely a solo for Cootie Williams.

It opens with piano and bass doubling a moody ostinato in F minor typical of the supposedly eerie jungle sound the band made so such of. Cootie comes in after two bars with the plunger over the pixie mute, opening with a C bent halfway down to the B, and it is these bent notes, clashing as they do with the underlying chords, that give the minor portions of the piece much of their interest.

After sixteen measures, the band comes in for support, while Cootie continues in the same vein. This strain is fourteen measures in length and, at the end, begins to ease out of the minor into A-flat major. There is a sax interlude in A-flat that opens on an F minor chord, passes through D-flat and G-flat before slipping into a common chord sequence to finish up. Cootie now plays open trumpet over this major theme, a complete contrast to the plunger and bent notes of the minor theme. There is a brief recapitulation of the minor strain, with Cootie again using the plunger mute over the ostinato bass and piano.

There is really very little to "Echoes of Harlem." It is built on the contrast between the moody minor strain and the more optimistic open horn in a major key. It all hangs on the magnificent playing of Cootie Williams, especially in the minor strain; his mastery of the plunger is complete. The structure, however modest, is just right; it is exactly what we need, no more and no less. When we compare this wholly successful piece with *Reminiscing in Tempo*, we can see clearly that the requirement for writing this short form is entirely different from what is called for in even the relatively short space of twelve minutes. Psychologically, it probably has something to do with how long the human memory is able to carry how much musical material. The shorter the form, the less we have to be reminded of what went before by recapitulation, variation, and the like. Throughout the section in major, the minor section continues to echo in our heads, so that the contrast remains before us. "Echoes of Harlem" has been beloved of Ellington fans for decades.

Nonetheless, from a standpoint of composition, "Clarinet Lament" is more subtle and interesting. This piece, like many of Duke's pieces, was an effort to capture the mood of a time and place, in this case, the melancholy of the New Orleans Creole, which, of course, Bigard was. How much Bigard contributed is hard to determine, but it was certainly something. "We sort of worked it out together," he said.[13]

It opens with a winding clarinet figure derived from a Sousa march. The phrase, in F, is repeated by trumpet, then trombone. There follows an eight-bar interlude by the brass that brings us to the key of E-flat. Bigard now plays a lovely blues chorus supported by beautifully voiced chords with a clarinet lead, saxophones, and, I think, Tizol's trombone. However, in order to give variety to the blues chords, which may go on unchanged for two or three measures at a stretch, Ellington has inserted additional chords so that they change each measure.

This chorus is followed by a two-bar interlude that brings us to a second strain, in A-flat. This is, in fact, "Basin Street Blues," complete with the standard breaks, intended to evoke the spirit of New Orleans—although Bigard avoids playing the melody. After sixteen measures, Ellington has written a bridge in a new key, but it then returns to the "Basin Street Blues" theme.

What follows next is a twelve-bar strain that manages, subtly and cleverly, to combine, or perhaps suggest, both previous strains. It is twelve bars in length, divided into three segments, precisely as blues would be, with clarinet answering a brief riff by the brass, which is repeated in each of the three segments of the ostensible blues. However, the brass riff in each of these segments is based on the opening chords to "Basin Street." Furthermore, although this strain is actually in the key of E-flat, as was the earlier blues strain, the brass riff uses the "Basin Street" chords in A-flat as before. The piece closes with a brief tag. In effect, then, Duke has very skillfully combined two themes and two keys. Here, for once, we get some development, some sense that what comes after has been suggested by what went before. "Clarinet Lament" is a very fine piece of construction and a wonderful evocation of what Ellington conceived to be the New Orleans mood.

From this period, also, comes one of the biggest hits Duke ever had, "Caravan," which became an enduring part of the band's repertoire and a standard tune still played today. It was written by Juan Tizol, who sold it outright to Irving Mills for twenty-five dollars. It is sometimes difficult to understand why Ellington's musicians continued to give away their melodies for such tiny sums long after they must have realized that Ellington and Mills were making huge amounts of money on some of them. Quite late in his career with the band, Johnny Hodges used to count imaginary money when the band began to play one of the tunes Duke had written out of a melodic idea of Hodges. Somehow they were unable to assert themselves in this respect or, perhaps, felt happy to grab whatever money was offered, on the chance that nothing would ever come of the idea, which was, of course, what usually happened. In this instance, after the tune became a big hit, Tizol asked Mills for a share in the royalties, and Mills relented.

Ellington did not like the bridge Tizol had written, provided one of his own, and worked out the arrangement, presumably in the studio, following his usual method. The main strain is a moody, minor theme supposed to suggest the exotic Middle East of the title. Greer plays an appropriately Eastern beat on tom-tom or temple blocks. The second theme moves suddenly into the tonic major to provide the contrast that Duke always searched for. It is really little more than some loose-knit figures running over a very standard bridge built on a circle of fourths.

Tizol's melody is a perfectly acceptable one, but it is the arrangement that makes the piece. In the first chorus, Duke supports the theme with a brief, repeated saxophone counterstatement and, at points, adds a few growls from the trumpet to enhance the spooky, exotic mood, displaying his ability to manage a number of voices at once. Thereafter, the melody is moved around the band in typical Ellington fashion, now played by Barney Bigard, now by Cootie Williams with the plunger, now by a tenor saxophone. In each case the solo voice is supported by a modest, unobtrusive countervoice—the clarinet by mute trumpets, the trumpet by saxophones, and so forth. In "Caravan," Ellington makes a great deal of a rather simple melody. It is classic Ellington, filled with change, movement, but all meshing so easily that the listener hardly notices the parts for the total effect. As we have seen, again and again, Ellington works best when he is using visual image or mood as a point of departure. "The memory of things gone is important to a jazz musician," he once said. "Things like old folks singing in the moonlight in the back yard on a hot night or something someone said long ago."[14] Mercer said, "He always wrote what he felt. I don't think he ever wrote in contrast to his mood. The only time he was off guard was in his music. The happy tunes were written during happy days and the sad things were written when he was feeling sad."[15] "Caravan" was written in just such a way out of a feeling Duke had gotten from a mental image of the Middle East, based, no doubt, more on movie clichés than on reality.

Juan Tizol was also responsible for a lovely tune called "Lost in Meditation," which was a successful number for the orchestra. It was originally recorded as "Have a Heart" at a bouncy tempo, featuring Williams doing some superb plunger work, but it became apparent that the melody was better suited to treatment as a ballad, so the band recorded it again, at a slow tempo and this time featuring Tizol's trombone, under the better-known title. Finally, it was fitted out with lyrics and recorded a third time, by Hodges with a small group and a vocalist named Mary McHugh, who had a pure, accurate voice and sang the song precisely as written, without any swing feeling. Hogdes clearly liked the tune, for he fondles it gently in the last two versions.

Juan Tizol had never really been given his due as a songwriter. He was not in a class with the masters, like Kern and Youmans, but he was far better than many of the tunesmiths knocking out tune after tune in search of a hit who grew like fungi in Tin Pan Alley. In addition to "Caravan" and "Lost in Meditation," Tizol claimed he wrote "Perdido," "Admiration," "Pyramid," "Bakiff," and several others, and there is no reason to doubt his word. "[Duke] took credit for everything I did," he said.[16]

Two numbers that would eventually have important consequences for Duke were "Diminuendo in Blue" and "Crescendo in Blue," companion pieces intended to be more serious than much of what the band played. They were issued as opposite sides of a record. The plan for the pieces is simple enough: "Diminuendo" opens in a fury and gradually subsides, ending on a fading piano solo; "Crescendo" opens with a simple figure in unison clarinets, unaccompanied, and gradually builds in both volume and texture to a climax, with the clarinet trio, which dominates the piece, rising higher and becoming more dissonant as it climbs. To my mind, the pieces are more effective played in reverse so that, together, they constitute a rising, then falling line, instead of a fall and a rise, on the grounds that it is easier to grasp a lot of motion if a piece begins with a little and adds to it. But, undoubtedly, it was precisely because beginning low and rising was the usual way that Ellington chose the opposite.

The piece—if we may speak of it as a unit—is based on the blues progression, in some cases divided by brief interludes, but at the outset it is so busy that it is difficult to make out the blues structure through the wildly waving palm branches and debris flying through the air. From the first bars, Ellington has three, and sometimes four, contending voices, none of them able to achieve dominance. It is a little like a battle royal, and the effect is of an explosion of sound. Gradually, the wildness subsides until, toward the end, we have two voices at a time—growl trumpet answering the reeds, baritone winding around trombones—and, finally, the piano, alone, fades into silence.

The "Crescendo" section opens with those unison clarinets in the low register, but by the second chorus we have both trombones and trumpets commenting. It builds from there until by the end we have the whole band flailing away at once. Oddly enough, the piece appears to be much faster than it actually is: about $d = 160$, not much above medium tempo.

To my mind, the "Crescendo" section is the more successful, in part because it is structured along the more usual system of growing, rather than lessening, tension and in part because it is tied together by the clarinets playing variations on a simple theme.

Another interesting piece from this period is "Braggin' in Brass," based generally on the "Tiger Rag" chord changes Ellington used so often. It opens with some introductory dissonant growling by Cootie, then moves into tightly muted trumpets playing complex figures at a breakneck tempo. The trombones follow, crackling eccentrically—the three of them taking turns playing one note at a time. (Gunther Schuller has pointed out that this passage resembles "hocket," a thirteenth- and fourteenth-century device in which the melody was shared by two alternating voices.)[17] In both cases, the brass execute difficult passages very well, indicating that the days of the rough-and-ready band of the Cotton Club are long gone. There are solos by Stewart, Brown, and Williams, the last owing a good deal to Louis Armstrong's comic hit "Laughing Looie." "Braggin' in Brass" was a major feature of the 1938 Cotton Club show.

A more important brass number for Ellington was "Boy Meets Horn," created, in the main, by Rex Stewart. According to Stewart, in 1938 the band laid off briefly while Ellington was in the hospital. (Duke had a hereditary disposition to hernia and had at least four operations for it during his lifetime, the first one when he was a teenager.) Stewart set aside his horn for a few days; when he picked it up again, the valves were sticking, as valves will when the instrument is not used regularly. He blew it, liked the sound he got with a valve stuck partway down, and began experimenting. He found that, with experience, he could create a whole tune with the "half-valved" notes. He called Duke at the hospital and played his tune over the phone for him. Duke said, "You're crazy." But Stewart was determined, so he visited Ellington in the hospital and played the tune for him, and in the end Duke agreed to work on it with him.

How much credence can be put in the tale is hard to know. Any young trumpet player quickly discovers the half-valve effect, and Stewart's idol, Louis Armstrong, was in fact using it to a wearying extent during this period. Furthermore, Stewart himself had used the half-valve before, for example, in "Tough Truckin' " and "Lazy Man's Shuffle." But previously the half-valve had been used by trumpet players to embellish a single note. "Boy Meets Horn" is the first example in which the device is used methodically through a whole melody. It became a specialty for Stewart and led him to look further for freak effects that became his basic style.

The tune was first recorded as "Twits and Twerps," but not issued under that name. It opens and closes with the half-valve melody Stewart had worked out at home. The sound is wry and dry, the notes stubby. In the middle there is a contrasting, soaring melody, which Stewart plays open. That is about all there is to it: the piece is a tour de force that depends on the novelty of the half-valve, but so successful was it that it preempted the field; few other trumpet players have done anything further with the device.

Another brass tour de force was "Tootin' through the Roof," made in 1939. It is a simple, riff tune based on a common chord pattern featuring a good deal of soloing. The point of it is a trumpet battle at the end between Cootie and Rex. First, they snarl at each other in brief, two-measure remarks. There is a snatch of triple-tonguing, and, finally, the trumpets join to spiral upward in harmony to a high note at the very end. It is bravura trumpet playing, displaying full tone and complete command of the upper register, an exciting and imaginative construction for brass.

An important component of Ellington's work during this period was the large number of small-band sides that he recorded beginning in December 1936—some seven dozen titles over the next two years alone. (Actually, Ellington had cut two sextet sides under his own name in 1935, "Tough Truckin'" and "Indigo Echoes.") Helen Oakley had especially wanted to record Johnny Hodges and Cootie Williams and suggested these names to Duke. Typically, he replied, "Yes, we'll do Barney and we'll do Rex,"[18] and the first two small-band sessions were by Rex Stewart and his Fifty-second Street Stompers and Barney Bigard and his Jazzopaters. In the end, however, it was Hodges who proved most popular; some of his records, like "Jeep's Blues," became jukebox hits and brought in a lot of money for Ellington.

The personnel for the groups remained fairly consistent throughout the period. For example, Bigard's group usually included Williams and Tizol; Stewart's had Lawrence Brown and Hodges; Williams's usually had Nanton and Hodges; and Harry Carney played on nearly all of them, along with the orchestra's rhythm section. It was all carefully arranged in order to parcel out the work equally among the men.

Eventually, Ellington loosened his control of the small-group recordings. When Billy Strayhorn, a young arranger who would become an important member of the Ellington staff, arrived, Duke tended to let him organize the music for many of the sessions and play piano on them. As always, the musicians themselves contributed a lot, frequently bringing in riffs and tunes they had written in order to get a share of the royalties. But the small-group recordings, however done, always had the distinctive Ellington flavor. This was not only because they employed the voices of the Ellington sidemen but also because these recordings were being directed by the same musical personality who ran the big band.

The quality of these small-group recordings is so consistently high that it is difficult to single out a few for comment. Very few of them are failures, although some of them offer ordinary popular tunes sung by vocalists brought in from the outside and suffer accordingly. On the other hand, given the limited instrumentation and the casual way they were put together, they inevitably betray a certain sameness.

One of the best known was the hit "Jeep's Blues," featuring Hodges, who was sometimes known as Jeep. It is built on a brief, plaintive blues theme, led by Hodges on soprano sax for the first four bars of the blues form, with the remaining eight left open for solos.

A particular favorite of mine is another Hodges feature, "Rendez-vous with Rhythm," primarily for the two Hodges solos, in which his mastery of dynamics is plainly evident. His line is constantly coming and going. This is frequently the result of the natural dynamics created through the tendency of wind instruments to become louder as they rise, but it is also there as moment-to-moment shifts in loudness, weight, and accent, which are made deliberately, though not very consciously.

"Clouds in My Heart" is a feature for Barney Bigard, its composer. The melody is a lovely one, and it is surprising that Mills did not have lyrics set to it. Bigard plays typically liquid clarinet, and there is an excellent chorus by Cootie Williams that uses a long quote from Louis Armstrong.

A Williams number is "Downtown Uproar," an infectious romp that includes comic trombone effects, a few shouts from the band, fine soloing, and lots of drive from the rhythm section.

The foregoing is only a brief sample of the riches in these small-band sides made during the 1935–39 period. On the strength of these alone, Ellington would have earned a place in jazz history.

The period also produced two of Ellington's most famous songs. "Prelude to a Kiss" is rich with the chromaticism that had begun to creep into Duke's music early and was by this time a striking characteristic of his work. In fact, it was the chromaticism, more than anything else, that gave the ordinary swing fans difficulty. Used to the triads, sevenths, sixths, and ninths given to them by ordinary dance bands, they found the half-steps and blocks of seconds that permeated Ellington's work of this period jarring. In "Prelude to a Kiss," however, the chromaticism is laid out obviously in a descending chromatic line that is the main motif for the piece, and it troubled them less. Alec Wilder spoke highly of the piece because the melody was "supported by very gratifying, satisfying harmonies."[19]

However, the descending chromatic line of the main part of the melody is predictable, and I find the second of Ellington's major tunes from this period more interesting. "I Let a Song Go Out of My Heart" was developed from an idea Hodges played on "Once in a While," which the band did not record.[20] Ellington worked it out for the Cotton Club show of 1938. Duke played the song over the radio every night for weeks, several other bands picked it up, and it became a hit. It deserved to be. We have here again a consecutive, rather than repetitive, song, made up of three successive contrasting phrases, which gives the feeling of dialogue. It is one of Ellington's best tunes.

There is a great deal of fine music from these years at the end of the 1930s, far more than I can possibly cover: "Cotton Club Stomp," a swinger with excellent work by Williams; "Way Low," a moody number with harmonies so thick they nearly resemble tone clusters; and perhaps two or three dozen more of real musical interest. Once Ellington had begun to recover from the death of his mother, it was a very fertile period. He ground

out, as he always would, a lot of commercial numbers without much enthusiasm and thought, but the amount of memorable music from this period is substantial. It is not always easy to discover the reasons for the ups
and downs of Ellington's productivity. But, for one thing, he had now
spent a decade actively creating music, and he knew a great deal more
about it in 1938 than he had known in 1928. Second, his orchestra was now
staffed with very competent and, in a number of cases, superb jazz musicians: Williams, Hodges, Brown, Stewart, Carney, and Bigard were musically mature, their styles fully developed, and they were capable of playing
brilliant jazz at a signal from their leader. Third, the band as a whole was
far more technically proficient than it had been at the beginning of the decade, now boasting good readers in all sections and several virtuosos scattered throughout. Finally, the swing band boom had been both a challenge
and a reward to Duke. Through the first half of the 1930s, he had been a
major force in popular music and perhaps something more than that. Now
he was surrounded by dozens of bands, many of them very proficient and a
few of them innovative, who were jostling for his place. If he was to keep
from falling behind, he would have to produce music with a special quality—and very frequently he did.

15

New Additions to
the Band

Sometime prior to the spring of 1939, Irving Mills booked the Ellington orchestra for a European tour. The band would play in Sweden, Belgium, France, Holland, and Denmark, but not in England. English musicians had for some time been exceedingly wary of American competition, dating back to the 1920s, with good reason. As early as 1922, Abel Green was reporting in the *Clipper*, "The view is taken . . . that the American jazz . . . has reached such a pinnacle of perfection" that musicians elsewhere could not compete.[1] The next year, Robert Emmett Curran, an American musician returning after four and a half years in Europe, maintained, "European musicians are absolutely unable to grasp the underlying principles of American dance music. . . ."[2] At the same time, Paul Specht had an order from London for sixty musicians. Needless to say, English musicians were up in arms as early as 1922; but it was not until the 1930s, when the American musicians were trying to keep British bands out of the United States, that they were able to get the government to bar invading American musicians. The Ellington orchestra would not play England again until the 1950s.

Exactly why Mills decided to book the band in Europe when the Continent was on the verge of war is hard to know. It sailed on the *Champlain* on March 23, 1939. The hold of the ship was filled with crates of bombers, and evidence of war was everywhere. Passing through Germany, the band members were unnerved by evidences of Hitler's dictatorship and were glad to get away.

But the trip was a resounding success. There were huge ovations at the concerts, a great fortieth-birthday party for Duke in Stockholm, radio interviews, uproar in the press, and endless gifts from fans, who filled his hotel room with flowers at the time of his birthday. It was 1933 all over again. Ellington came home filled with good spirits. "Europe is a very different world from this one," he said. "You can go anywhere and talk to anybody and do anything you like. It's hard to believe. When you've eaten hot dogs all your life and you're suddenly offered caviar it's hard to believe it's true."[3] Racism was, of course, far more prevalent in Europe than Ellington was aware; but there was a real difference in degree, and the men in the band felt it.

Duke was fired up with confirmed notions of his importance as a serious composer. In the two years or so after his return, he would create some of the best-known works of his entire career: "Ko-Ko," "Jack the Bear," "Main Stem," "Cotton Tail," "C-Jam Blues," "Harlem Airshaft," "Warm Valley," "In a Mellotone," and "Never No Lament," which became "Don't Get Around Much Anymore," as well as numbers written by Billy Strayhorn and Duke's son, Mercer, that were identified with him, like "Chelsea Bridge," "Take the A Train," and "Things Ain't What They Used to Be." It was one of Ellington's greatest creative flurries—many consider it *the* greatest—and it would bring him, by the mid-1940s, to a peak of both critical and public acclaim that he would not reach again until the years before his death, when he had become the "Grand Old Man of Jazz."

The sudden creative burst was without doubt the result of the tumultuous welcome he had received in Europe, but other factors were at work as well. For one thing, just before he left for Europe he ended his working relationship with Irving Mills. Precisely why Ellington chose to leave Mills at this point is not certain, for Ellington never commented on it. However, some things seem clear. According to a *Down Beat* report in January 1937, Mills and Ellington had adjusted their financial agreement, probably as a result of the switch from Columbia to Master.[4] Mills gave Ellington his share in Duke Ellington, Inc., which effectively gave Ellington full control of his orchestra, in exchange for which Ellington gave up his shares in the publishing company that controlled Ellington tunes. Ellington would continue to receive royalties for the songs—assuming Mills paid them—and his share of the ASCAP income. According to Mercer, the value of the two companies was approximately equal, and the trade a fair one, if you accept the idea that Mills should have owned half of Ellington in the first place.[5] As of 1937 the Mills organization would continue to publish Ellington's tunes, book the band, and record it for Master.

But by 1939 Ellington was ready to make the break complete. For one thing, Master and Variety, Mills's labels, had gone under, and the company was leasing its Ellington recordings to Columbia and its subsidiaries. Perhaps more important, Ellington had been under fire from the black press for allowing himself to remain under the control of whites. Porter

Roberts, writing in the black newspaper *Pittsburgh Courier*, said, "No Negro writer has written the lyrics for any of Duke Ellington's melodies since he has been under the Mills banner. What's the matter, Duke? House Rules?"[6] Adam Clayton Powell, Jr., a force in Harlem and later a U.S. Congressman, wrote,

> Duke Ellington is just a musical sharecropper. He has been a drawing account which has been startled [sic] to run around $300 per week. At the end of the year, when Massa Mills' cotton has been laid by, Duke is told that he owes them hundreds of thousands of dollars. . . . Musical sharecropping doesn't just sing right to this grandpappy's son. The Negro has sharecropped too long. . . . We don't want anymore paternalism on our job. We want a chance and a fair wage. And, we'll take care of the rest.[7]

Powell, of course, had no idea what sort of financial business went on between Ellington and Mills. By this time Ellington was, among other things, charging off against the business a whole array of personal expenses that would ordinarily have come out of his own income—meals, clothes, the expenses involved with the women he sometimes traveled with, and the like. With his concern for going first-class, he thought in terms not of cash income—he was totally uninterested in saving anything—but of being able to live as he liked, and in this fashion he took out of the band's income a great deal more than the three hundred dollars a week Powell alluded to. Nonetheless, there was enough truth in Powell's accusation to hurt, and it certainly had an effect on Duke.

Ellington was never really candid about the reasons for the break. Barry Ulanov suggests that it was "lack of attention" from Mills, who was now running a large organization and could not devote himself to Duke as he had in the past.[8] In his own book Duke said only, "We dissolved our business relationship agreeably. . . ."[9]

Ellington always wanted to be the dominant figure in any circumstance he found himself in. However, he had never been able to control Irving Mills as he had so many of the other people around him. If anyone was dominant in the relationship, it was Mills. Mills made changes in Duke's songs, simplifying them as he wished, apparently without consulting Duke, but with Duke's tacit agreement. As early as the Cotton Club days, he would step in at the last minute and change the radio program around. In general, Duke went along with whatever Mills wanted. "Mills would fix a deal and tell Duke and then Duke would tell the band," Barney Bigard said.[10] As we have seen, Mills said that Duke "followed instructions."[11]

It is too much to say that Duke was afraid of Mills, but he recognized that Mills knew the music business better than he did and that what Mills wanted usually worked out for the best. "He also felt that if he were in trouble he could always go to Irving Mills and to no one else," John Hammond said.[12] Duke, then, had reasons for allowing Irving Mills a certain authority over him. But by 1939 those reasons no longer existed. It was thus not so much a question of money, which had been, or could at least have been, worked out. What mattered was that Duke now felt able to step out on his own. He had, said Mercer, learned the business from Mills, and "he grew up."[13]

In mid-April, just before the European trip, he turned to the William Morris Agency for representation. The agency was big and prestigious. It had recently taken on a young man named Willard Alexander, who had successfully promoted Benny Goodman to his first fame at MCA (the Music Corporation of America) and was now brought into William Morris to build a band department. Ned Williams was also with William Morris at this point, and it was probably he who got Ellington to make the change. "Duke was very respectful of William Morris," Edmund Anderson said. "I think he was a little awed by him."[14] Unlike Irving Mills, who was interested in money and little else, Morris was aware of Duke's role as an artist and wanted Duke to be more socially conscious than he was.

At the same time, Ellington signed with Robbins, a music publishing firm. Not long afterward, in 1942, Morris assigned a young man named Cress Courtney to look after some of Ellington's business.

Courtney had a stepfather named Reggie Charles, who conducted Broadway shows and eventually brought a band into the Roosevelt Hotel to replace Guy Lombardo. Courtney was only a teenager at the time. He said, "Reggie is completely naive in worldly affairs, you know, and I guess I was a tough young kid. So I took over the management of the band."[15] MCA took over the band eventually, and Cress went on the road for them, then moved to William Morris.

In 1939, early in his days with William Morris, Ellington was working at a Balaban and Katz theater in Chicago's South Side. Duke was closing his show with slow pieces like "Warm Valley," and the theater owners wanted him to end with something "peppier." The office sent Courtney out to talk to Duke about it. Cress said, "And after I got through talking with him, he said to me, 'That's a beautiful tie.' And I said, 'That's the deal, huh?' And he said, 'Yeah.' And I said, 'OK, here's your tie. Now play your goddam fast music.' "[16]

Duke always liked smart, tough people—Irving Mills, for example—and he began asking for Courtney at the Morris office when he had a problem to straighten out. Eventually, Duke asked the office to let Courtney handle the band. Willard Alexander, head of the band department, was particularly interested in Count Basie, whom the agency also handled, but William

Morris, Jr., was eager to see Duke handled properly, so the change suited everyone. Courtney would be part of the band's management, off and on, for many years.

A consequence of the change in management was a switch of record companies. The contract with Columbia ran out at the end of 1939, and Duke left the company. A number of reasons have been given for his departure, but it was almost certainly due to personal differences between Duke and John Hammond, who was recording a lot of jazz for Columbia. Frank Driggs, a jazz writer who worked for Hammond at Columbia at one point, said, "I guess, probably, because he and John Hammond never got along is one of the compelling reasons why he went to Victor."[17]

John Hammond was not only an influential critic but a mover and shaker of the jazz world who used power and his money to promote musicians he was interested in. He was high-handed, an idealist, ever quick to sniff out deviations from purity, a good many of which he detected in Ellington's work. In particular, he disliked the extended pieces. As early as 1936 he said, "Once this was the greatest band in the country but the bogey of Showmanship and Art have crippled it."[18]

Moreover, Hammond was deeply involved in the fight for black rights— he had even persuaded his wealthy, but conservative, father to contribute to the Scottsboro legal defense fund. He felt that Ellington ought to have taken a public stand on racial matters. Hammond was as opinionated as he was courageous, and he had detailed what he saw as Ellington's shortcomings in print more than once.

Ellington had responded. In a 1939 piece in Down Beat, on jazz critics generally, he said,

> Perhaps due to the "fever of battle" Hammond's judgment may have become slightly warped and his enthusiasm and prejudices a little unwieldy to control. Whether or not that may be the case, it has become apparent that John has identified himself so strongly in certain directions [i.e., Count Basie] he no longer enjoys an impartial status that would entitle him to the role of critic.[19]

Hammond's judgment of Duke was not all wrong, but Ellington was certainly right in pointing out that an executive of a record company, busily recording his favorite musicians, could hardly qualify as an impartial critic: on at least one occasion, Hammond actually gave an ecstatic review to a record he had produced without informing his readers of his involvement. There was, I think, some justice on both sides in the fracas; in any case, it would have been difficult for the two men, both strong-minded, to work together. At the beginning of 1940 Duke went to Victor.

Finally, when Ellington's contract with Robbins Music ran out, at the end of 1942, Ellington established his own publishing company, Tempo Music, which he turned over to his sister, Ruth, to run.[20] Its function was mainly to publish Ellington's music, but it also published pieces by various outsiders, like Harry James and Randy Weston. The first pieces it published were "Take the A Train" and "Flamingo," neither of them by Duke. When Ellington died, the Tempo catalog contained about a thousand of his tunes, of which perhaps six or seven hundred have never been played.

Ruth Ellington's stewardship of Tempo Music has come under some criticism. She had no training in business in general and, although she inevitably had learned something about the music business, she had not learned as much as she might have, because of Duke's penchant for keeping her isolated from the outside world. "The whole motto of the family was, 'Don't tell Ruth anything,' " she said.[21] As a consequence, she grew up something of the classic poor little rich girl, especially after the move to New York into the household of her famous brother. "We were always taught that we were the best. . . . My father, for instance, always said that my mother was his queen and I was his princess. . . . He told me so much that I was his princess that by the time I was eighteen, I became a princess and I still feel that way today."[22] She added, "Edward wouldn't permit me to go anywhere at anytime."[23]

It was Duke's nature to be infinitely protective of women, and he was especially so of Ruth. After the illness and death of their parents, Duke became, in effect, her father. He was a stern one and kept her at home as much as he could manage. "He just thought I should be there, like a doll," she said.[24] When she finally, in her twenties, fell in love and wanted to marry, Duke protested. He gave her an apartment, a mink, a Cadillac, an allowance—all in an attempt to persuade her not to marry. "And, of course, I was too painfully shy . . . because I was frightened to tell him I was lonely."[25]

The man in question, Dan James, was a white intellectual with liberal views who was struggling to make a living as a writer. He had been born in England and reared in Canada. He had met the Ellingtons through his association with the black actor Canada Lee. There arose a small fuss in the press over the interracial marriage, but it quickly subsided. Ellington immediately took James into his extended family and set him to running Tempo with Ruth. Eventually, James published a successful book entitled Che, about the Cuban revolutionary. He then asked Ruth to live on his income; he wanted to be something more than another adjunct of Duke Ellington. But Ruth refused, and the marriage broke up. She had two sons with James, Michael and Stephen. She made a second, short-lived marriage to another white man and eventually married a black singer, McHenry Boatwright.

Ruth Ellington was not universally loved by Duke's large, unofficial family. Fran Hunter said, "When we were youngsters she could be very cold. She could cut somebody down in a minute."[26] Juan Tizol spoke scathingly of her and claimed that she never paid him what he was owed for his songs. "Ruth hates to pay her bills," said Rose Tizol.[27]

In particular, Ruth has been criticized for having what has been called a "complex" about whites. Her first two husbands were white, she wears a blond wig, and she has always associated with many whites. The criticism, at a time when Americans are struggling to eradicate racial walls, seems unfair. What is interesting about Ruth's attitude is how it reflects the Ellington feeling that they were as good as whites and better than most. Ruth simply felt that the barriers were not there.

The sweeping changes in Ellington's management after 1940 finally put him firmly in control of his own affairs, enabling him to take any direction he wanted. More important to his music were changes in personnel that took place over a period of a few months on either side of 1940. The first new arrival was Billy Strayhorn, who would become Ellington's assistant and not only do a great deal of composing for Ellington but at times rehearse the orchestra and play piano with it.

Strayhorn was born on November 29, 1915, in Dayton, Ohio. His parents were James Nathanial Strayhorn and Lillian Margo Young. One of his ancestors, named Job, had a distillery just after the Civil War; another was part American Indian; yet another had been Robert E. Lee's cook. James Strayhorn and Lillian Young met at college in North Carolina. Neither graduated, but Billy Strayhorn clearly came from a family that was socially a cut above that of the average black workingman.[28]

The family moved to Montclair, New Jersey, when Billy was still a child. At some point thereafter, Billy was sent down to Hillsborough, North Carolina, to live with his grandmother. He stayed there until she died, when he was ten. By this time his father had moved to Pittsburgh in order to work in a steel mill. Billy rejoined him there.

His mother had played piano in churches, and, as a child, Billy fooled around with the instrument. He did not study seriously, however, until he reached Pittsburgh. At Westinghouse High School he took courses in music appreciation and may have played in the school orchestra. In any case, he appears to have shown promise, and his father, who pushed his other sons into construction work, sent Billy to the Pittsburgh Musical Institute, where he studied theory and the standard classical repertory. Even in high school he was something of an intellectual and dandy. He read the New Yorker, an unusual taste for a boy of his time and place, and he developed a liking for clothes. He was small—only five feet three inches as an adult—

and somewhat unself-assertive; and it is clear that his homosexuality was already developing at this point in his life.

He was apparently popular in high school. He involved himself in high school theatricals. The success of his work for high school shows led him, upon graduation, to write a revue called *Fantastic Rhythm*, which he and some cronies mounted. Two of his pieces from this show, "My Little Brown Book" and "Something to Live For," were eventually recorded by Ellington.

To this point, he had never taken much interest in jazz. But in 1934, the year he graduated from Westinghouse, Strayhorn heard the Ellington orchestra, probably in the theater. "I was hooked," he said.[29] But, for the moment, he did little more composing. He organized a small trio called the Tophatters, which for a while broadcast regularly from a Pittsburgh radio station, and he supported himself mainly by working in a drugstore.

Then, in December 1938, probably at the urging of a friend named Billy Esch, who was arranging for the bandleader Ina Ray Hutton, Billy went to the Stanley Theatre in Pittsburgh to see Ellington and afterward ventured backstage to show him some of his work, especially "Lush Life." Ellington was particularly impressed by the lyric and told Billy to come and see him if he reached New York.

By this time Esch was teaching Strayhorn arranging. "I learned a good deal from him," Strayhorn said later.[30] In January 1939 Esch lent Billy train fare to travel to Montclair, New Jersey, where he could stay with his Aunt Julia. He went into New York to see Ellington. Conflicting versions of what happened next have been given, but Ellington very quickly found uses for Strayhorn. He had originally seen him as a potential lyricist, but within a few weeks he had put him to work doing arrangements for the small groups, especially the Hodges groups, for whom he did "Like a Ship in the Night" and "Savoy Strut," recorded in February and March 1939. In the spring Ellington left for the European trip. He told Mercer to keep an eye on Billy, and soon Billy was living in the Ellington home.

By this time he was directing many of the small-group sessions, although Ellington was undoubtedly exercising some sort of ultimate control. Leonard Feather reported in *Down Beat*, "Billy has written the scores for practically all those swell records by the Johnny Hodges and Cootie Williams groups."[31] From there he went on to turning out the commercial arrangements of popular songs that the band had to have in its repertoire. Very quickly he became Ellington's collaborator, a junior partner in what would, more and more, become a joint enterprise. Despite his unself-assertiveness, Strayhorn could be firm with the band when necessary, according to George Avakian, who was involved in many Ellington recording sessions. Over the years Duke came to rely on him increasingly as a musical factotum.

But it was more than just a working relationship. According to Mary Lou Williams, an excellent jazz pianist of the time who did arranging for the orchestra, Strayhorn "loved Duke. And everything he wrote he just gave to him. . . . He was nice enough to write a tune and give it to Duke."[32]

The affection was mutual. Toby Hardwick said, "Strayhorn's death was the one thing I know of that really touched Duke. . . . Neither money nor business was an issue between them, ever. Billy just wanted to be with Duke, that was all. It was love—a beautiful thing."[33]

According to his nephew and executor, Gregory Morris, had Billy been more aggressive, he might have developed a reputation as a composer of his own: "He was very low key . . . a very humble person. . . . He was happy in what he was doing and he didn't need all the money, all the lime-light."[34] Moreover, Billy was lazy. He joined a group of young intellectuals, black and white, which included Lennie Hayton and Lena Horne, and he was much more likely to enjoy himself than to write. Cootie Williams said, "Strayhorn was a young boy, you know. He wasn't no stay-in like Duke and sit at no piano all day and all night. . . . He wasn't going to do that. He used to like to party and ball."[35] As a consequence, he was often late with his scores. Stanley Dance said that they had to "kick his ass" to get the work from him.[36] This lack of drive, of push, was no doubt what made it possible for Strayhorn to contribute heavily to Ellington's material for no credit in return.

Strayhorn could easily have been resented by the older members of the orchestra, many of whom did not like taking orders from Ellington, much less from an inexperienced young composer in his twenties. But, to the contrary, they quickly grew fond of him—protective, even. They called him Strays, Weely, and, especially, Sweetpea, a baby in the Popeye comic strip usually seen crawling in a nightgown that stretched beyond his legs. Toby Hardwick told Stanley Dance, "You know how Billy was little and sweet and everyone was crazy about him. He'd stop and talk to this one, then he'd go over and talk to the next. I told Sonny, I said: 'If that ain't Swee' Pea, I hope somethin',' and Sonny fell out."[37]

It is impossible, at this time, to know precisely what Strayhorn contributed to Duke's music. It was, however, a great deal, not just directly in written music that he supplied but also in a broader influence he had in respect to musical direction and taste. Among other things, Strayhorn was interested in the French impressionist composers, and he consciously brought to Ellington's attention devices that people assumed Ellington had known about for years. For another, because he had more training than Ellington did, he was better able to judge from a score how the music would sound, and he was therefore more willing to compose entire pieces before bringing them to the band—with allowances made for his laziness. After his arrival, sessions in the studio were somewhat less haphazard than they had been. Barry Ulanov said, "Billy sits in the control room at all Ellington record sessions to give final okays or turn masters down. Duke respects his taste above all others and lives by it musically."[38] Duke usually took Strayhorn's advice, and Strayhorn, despite his shyness, was not afraid of telling Ellington that he did not like something. Charlie Barnet, a bandleader and great admirer of the Ellington sound, said, "I'm convinced that Billy contributed more than a little to the band. Most of the more complicated chord progressions were his and I think he was responsible for the more delicate voicings and arrangements."[39] Lawrence Brown said, "And he was right in most everything he did. He was the genius, the power behind the throne all of those later years. . . . [His music] was so much richer. I can tell in a minute anything that was Strayhorn's."[40] Jimmy Hamilton, a clarinetist who came into the band during this period, said, "We always liked to play Billy's music because you know he got some real beautiful harmonies. Man, we liked to play the things he used to bring. Everybody anxious to play Billy's music because he had such beautiful taste and harmony. . . . Duke would do some things and Strayhorn would do some. . . . They'd debate on certain things."[41] Joya Sherrill, a singer of this period, said, "If Billy said it was good or wasn't good, he respected Billy's opinion."[42]

We must discount a little for the resentments some of these people came to feel toward Duke; nonetheless, we must always assume that from the time of Strayhorn's arrival, or a little later, until his death in 1967, he played a role, great or small, in nearly everything Ellington wrote. Indeed, even from the grave he may have been contributing to the Ellington book: according to Lawrence Brown, Strayhorn left some uncompleted works that Duke finished and presented as his own.

However, there is a tendency to forget that by 1939 Duke was an established composer with an international reputation and Strayhorn an inexperienced young man. Ellington told Strayhorn only, "Observe," but there can be no doubt that Strayhorn studied the Ellington method and that he took more from Ellington than he gave. In the end, he molded his style to Ellington's so that the music of one flowed, seamlessly, into the music of the other. Ellington told this story:

> Our rapport was the closest. When I was writing my first sacred concert, I was in California and he was in a New York hospital. On the telephone, I told him . . . to write something. "Introduction, ending, quick transitions," I said. "The title is the first four words of the Bible— 'In the Beginning God.' " He had not heard my theme, but what he sent to California started on the same note as mine (F natural) and

ended on the same note as mine (A flat a tenth higher). Out of six notes representing the six syllables of the four words, only two notes were different.[43]

Billy Strayhorn was, however affable, self-effacing by nature. Duke Ellington was a man who would slyly squeeze advice out of people, but he was hardly the sort of person who would mold his style on anyone else's. We can be sure that, though Strayhorn influenced Ellington and, undoubtedly, added something to his style, and changed other things, the essence was always Ellington's.

A second arrival into the Ellington family was a young bassist named Jimmy Blanton. Not a great deal is known about Blanton, for he died before interviewers had a chance to get to him. He was born in Chattanooga, Tennessee, in October 1918. According to Mercer, he was as much an American Indian as a black.[44] His mother played piano and led a local band for many years. Blanton studied violin and theory with an uncle and doubled on piano and alto saxophone. He also did some arranging, although how much is uncertain. He had, in any case, a very sound grounding in music—a far better technical background than that of most jazz musicians of the period, who were self-tutored in the main and knew little theory.

Blanton began his professional career at the age of eight with a gig at a local store on violin. As a youth he presumably worked locally, probably with his mother. Then he went on to study music at Tennessee State College. There he switched to string bass (according to John Chilton, he played a three-string bass, an unusual instrument), working with the college band and other local groups. He was by now a first-rate bassist—the best in jazz, in fact, although hardly anybody knew it. He was working the riverboats around St. Louis with Fate Marable during the summer season at a time when Marable could hire the best local men.

In the summer of 1939, however, he was playing at the Coronado Hotel ballroom in St. Louis. Jimmy Blanton loved playing more than anything else, and he was always available for jam sessions at after-hours clubs, where a good bassist, willing to work for nothing, would be highly prized. One such club was operated by Jesse Johnson, a promoter and figure of consequence in the black community. Blanton was jamming here when Johnny Hodges came in. Hodges rushed out to get Strayhorn, and, once Strayhorn had heard Blanton, the two dashed out to Ellington's hotel and awakened him. Ellington came down to the club wearing an overcoat over his pajamas, and shortly afterward he asked Blanton to join his orchestra. (Or so goes the story, which has been told somewhat differently by various people.)

Ellington, of course, already had Billy Taylor playing bass. Taylor had previously shared the bass spot with Hayes Alvis and may not have been

Most young men do not autograph photos of themselves to their mothers, but Duke signed this one, "To the Dearest Mother in the World" From—Edward. (Frank Driggs Collection)

Above: This is the band that opened at the Cotton Club. *From left*: Duke, Joe Nanton, Greer, Miley, Harry Carney, Wellman Braud, Rudy Jackson, Fred Guy, Nelson Kincaid, Ellsworth Reynolds. Reynolds and Kincaid were only with the band briefly, and Jackson left after the dispute over "Creole Love Call." The rest were the nucleus of what would become the Cotton Club orchestra with which Ellington would rise to fame. (Frank Driggs Collection)

Top left: One of the early pick-up bands at the Poodle Dog Cafe in Washington, in about 1920. Sonny Greer is the drummer; Sterling Conaway, who would spend almost two decades in Europe, the banjo player. (Frank Driggs Collection)

Middle left: Jazz, in the early days, was in part a comic music played in vaudeville. On their first foray to New York some of the Washingtonians landed at the Lafayette Theatre in Harlem with Wilbur Sweatman, whose specialty was playing three clarinets at once. A rack of his instruments can be seen between him and the vocalist. Duke is at the piano, Greer on the drums, Hardwick playing the saxophone at far right. (Frank Driggs Collection)

Bottom left: The Kentucky Club band, but not at the club, 1923. *From left, standing*: Greer, Charlie Irvis, Elmer Snowden, Hardwick. *Seated*, a rare picture of Bubber Miley, and Duke. Greer had not yet collected the panoply of drums he would later have, mostly for the showy effect. (Phoebe Jacobs Collection)

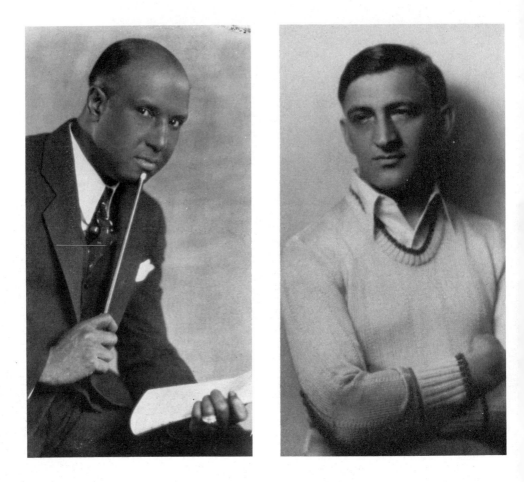

Some of the people who aided Duke in his career. *Above left*: A rare photo of Will Vodery, Flo Ziegfeld's musical director, who gave Ellington help in arranging. (Frank Driggs Collection) *Above right*: An even rarer picture of Charlie Shribman, New England dancehall king, who found summer work for Duke, and was well liked by musicians. (Courtesy of Herb Grey) *Right*: Duke with Irving Mills and Evie.

The Cotton Club was, in the 1920s and early thirties, the acme of glamor. The formula was top black talent, hot music, an exotic "jungle" atmosphere, and plenty of sex. *Above left*: Baby Cox, a fine dancer and singer who was featured on a few Ellington records for the period. The costume is supposed to suggest African tribal dress. *Left*: Freddi Washington, in the movie *Black and Tan Fantasy*, in a film version of the Cotton Club. Costume is again supposed to have an African effect. *Above*: Ethel Waters singing "Stormy Weather," one of the smash hits from the Cotton Club shows. Elaborate productions like this were typical. *Right*: Ringside seats along the dance floor. The famous Cotton Club murals are visible on wall behind. (All Frank Driggs Collection)

Some of the ingredients which went into the Ellington mix. *Top left*: The trombones: Tricky Sam, Juan Tizol, and Lawrence Brown. *Bottom left*: The saxophone section from the famous 1940s' band—Barney Bigard, Johnny Hodges, Ben Webster, Toby Hardwick, and Harry Carney. *Above*: The bass "section" of 1939 with Jimmy Blanton and Billy Taylor.

More ingredients. *Above*: Sonny Greer with the elaborate drum set he carried, which he used more for show than musical effect. (Frank Driggs Collection) *Right*: Two of Duke's most important trumpeters, Cootie Williams and Rex Stewart. *Below right*: Ivie Anderson in about 1940, not long before she was forced out of the band because of health problems.

Becoming famous. *Above left*: The band arrives in London for the visit during which Duke became convinced that he was, or could be, that noble object, a composer (from left): Dancer Bill Bailey, Tizol, Brown, English bandleader and promoter Jack Hylton, Nanton, (seated) Jenkins, Bigard, Ellington, Williams; (seated) Hardwick, Carney, Hodges; (half-hidden) Braud, Greer, Whetsol, dancer Derby Wilson, Ivie Anderson. *Below left*: Duke after a concert by the orchestra at New York University in the mid-1930s, surrounded by celebrated musical figures who had attended: (from left) Martin Bernstein of the N.Y.U. music faculty; Ralph Leopold, composer; Basil Cameron, conductor of the Seattle Symphony Orchestra; Percy Grainger, composer and director of the N.Y.U. music department, who arranged the event; and Wallingford Riegger, a very well known composer of the period. *Above*: Duke receiving one of his seemingly numberless honorary degrees, from Dr. Bernard Adams, president of Ripon College, in Ripon, Wisconsin. (All Frank Driggs Collection)

On the road. *Top left*: Duke and Ivie Anderson engaging in one of Ellington's favorite occupations, eating. *Bottom left*: Bigard and Hodges in one of the endless games of cards that killed time on the train journeys. *Below*: Mercer Ellington and Mike Douglas with the posthumous Ellington orchestra.

Overleaf: The face of a man who has seen everything and done most of it. (Frank Driggs Collection)

troubled by having to share it with a younger man. But Blanton was the best bass player in jazz, and Taylor found the comparison difficult. At times he switched to tuba, and, finally, in January 1940, when the band was playing at the Southland Cafe in Boston, he walked off the stand in the middle of a set and said, "I'm not going to stand up here next to that young boy playing all that bass and be embarrassed."[45]

This, however, was Ellington's story, and the fact that Taylor walked away in the middle of a set suggests there was more to it than that. Cootie Williams once said, "I don't think [Taylor] and Duke got on too well. . . . Billy was sort of independent."[46]

In the two years Blanton remained with the Ellington band, he revolutionized jazz bass playing. Before him, the bass had been seen as strictly a rhythm instrument whose function was to keep time and outline chord changes. Even the harmonic function was not essential, for most bands of the time contained a piano and/or guitar or banjo, which could state the harmonies more fully. The primary function of the bass was to supply a sharply percussive front edge to the ground beat. From the early days until well into the 1930s, basses almost invariably played on only the first and the third beats of a measure, to enforce the rocking back and forth swing that was subsequently called two-beat. Frequently, they played little more than tonics and dominants. By the early 1930s, however, some bass players were expressing all four beats of each measure. Walter Page, first with his own Blue Devils and later with the Bennie Moten band, which swallowed up the Blue Devils, is generally credited with having started this trend: the other members of the Blue Devils sometimes referred to him as Big Four. By the middle of the 1930s the four-beat style was becoming standard. Playing on all four beats of a measure gave the bassist a chance to play more notes of a given chord, and a system of walking up and down the three or four notes of the chord became standard procedure. Rarely, however, would they play any notes other than the ones in the chord.

Most of these early bass players had begun playing tuba or "brass bass" and had switched to string bass when the fashion turned against tubas around 1930. They thought of themselves, essentially, as "bass" players rather than "string" players. Jimmy Blanton, however, had begun as a string player, and he thought like one. Long before he knew much about the jazz bass, he knew something of violin pizzicato playing—that is to say, plucking rather than bowing the instrument. Music written for the plucked violin was not merely rhythmic or percussive but also melodic in the ordinary sense. Blanton thus brought to the bass the concept that a string instrument could play melodies plucked as well as bowed. This was hardly a startling insight, and the wonder is that it had not occurred to someone earlier. In any case, by the time Ellington heard Blanton, he was habitually playing melodies on the bass in his solos using not merely the quarter notes of the walking bass but also eighth notes, sixteenths, and the rest of it. He was using the bass, in other words, as a "horn." (Among other things, he was blessed with exceptionally long fingers.)

But it was not only in his solos that he brought a fuller, more varied approach to bass playing: he was also making changes in the way a bass worked in a rhythm section. Although he played on all four beats about half the time, he at times played only on first and third beats, at times only on second and fourth. At other times, he would abandon timekeeping altogether and phrase with the band. He did not simply walk up and down the chords, either, but selected notes judiciously to make musically intelligent connections between chords.

Besides, he had impeccable time and a full tone. According to Lawrence Brown, Blanton was recorded near the fingerboard, instead of lower down on the instrument; as a consequence, records do not give a true impression of his sound, which, Brown said, was similar to the sound Ray Brown got.[47]

The result of all this was that Blanton simply awed the other bass players. Milt Hinton, later to be an important bass player himself, said, "He shocked us all . . . he left us standing . . . he had those tremendously long fingers and he really knew his positions. Man, he was just amazing."[48] In addition, because Blanton wanted to do nothing so much as play bass, he practiced constantly, took lessons whenever he could as the band traveled across the country, and played in jam sessions as long as anyone else was willing to go on. There is at least speculation that exhaustion, caused by incessant playing, helped bring on the illness that was to kill him shortly.

Blanton's importance to jazz bass playing should not make us underrate Billy Taylor. He was a strong bass player with a good sound and excellent time, and he was considered one of the leading bass players in jazz of his day. Indeed, there are those who think he was superior to Blanton as a pure rhythm player. Cootie Williams said flatly, "I think Billy Taylor was about the best bass player [Duke] ever had. Not so much for solos but for carrying the band."[49] Stanley Dance has said the same. After Taylor left Ellington, he played with many of the most important musicians of the time, including Coleman Hawkins and Red Allen, and went on to work at both CBS and NBC studios, which demanded high standards of musicianship. But nobody in 1940 was going to top Blanton.

Yet a third addition to the Ellington band at this time, as important in his way as either Strayhorn or Blanton, was the tenor saxophonist Ben Webster. Through the early years of jazz the trumpet, or cornet, was the dominating instrument, and a disproportionate number of jazz heroes played it. Jazz "kings" were invariably trumpeters: Louis Armstrong, King Oliver, Bix Beiderbecke, and others. Most of the major saxophonists of the 1920s and 1930s played alto or C melody: Hodges, Benny Carter, Charlie Holmes, Jimmy Dorsey, Frankie Trumbauer. But by the early 1930s Coleman Hawkins, playing with Fletcher Henderson, was beginning to be seen as the finest of all saxophone players and one of the great jazz musicians of the time. As a consequence, the tenor saxophone began to be favored, and by the late 1930s it was being considered the major jazz instrument, the one that defined the music. Through the Swing Era every band had to have a good tenor saxophonist who would be prominently featured: Vido Musso or Georgie Auld with Benny Goodman, Tex Benecke and Al Klink with Glenn Miller, Lester Young and Herschel Evans with Count Basie, Bud Freeman with Tommy Dorsey, Joe Thomas with Jimmie Lunceford, and many more.

Ellington had never really had a first-class tenor saxophonist in his orchestra. In order to fit certain voicings, it was frequently necessary to have at least one tenor saxophone available, which was usually played by Barney Bigard. But tenor saxophone solos were relatively rare: record after record was made without one, which did not happen with other bands.

By the late 1930s, though, it must have been obvious to Ellington that the band ought to have a premier tenor saxophonist. He had brought Webster into the band briefly in the summers of 1935 and 1936, apparently because Bigard was taking vacations. Now, in 1939, he decided to hire him full-time.

Ben Webster was, in many respects, a difficult man—sweet and gentle when sober but constantly getting into brawls when he was drunk, which was frequently. He was nicknamed the Brute, and he claimed he had knocked Joe Louis down, which sounds unlikely. Once John Levy, another musician, was playing in a club when Webster came in "carrying that long, gold-topped cane he used to have, and he just swept it along the bar knocking off all the glasses onto the floor. And then I got down from the bandstand and took him by the arm and walked him out around the corner to another bar and sat there and told him he didn't have to act like that, how everybody really loved him. And it ended up with Ben sitting there crying."[50] And it is true that Webster, despite everything, was well liked by the men in the band, although they were at times a little unnerved by him.

He was born in Kansas City, Missouri, on March 27, 1909. He studied piano and violin as a child and became a good enough piano player to work in silent-movie houses, which would not, in any case, have required a very high level of musical skill. He began gigging around the Southwest with local bands as a teenager, mainly playing piano. In 1929 the Young family band, which Cootie Williams had worked with a few years earlier, came through Albuquerque, New Mexico, where Webster was working at the moment. According to his own story, he asked Billy Young for a job. Young agreed. Webster then said that he couldn't read. Young said that he would teach him. Then Webster said he didn't have an instrument. Young "cracked up," but he took Webster anyway and found him a saxophone, and for the next three or four months Webster practiced alongside Lester Young who would become, within six or seven years, one of the most influential musicians in jazz history.[51]

Webster learned his scales and how to read, up to a point (he was never a good reader), from Billy Young. He left after a short stay and gigged with a number of the better-known bands, becoming increasingly proficient, until, by the mid-1930s, he was recognized, by musicians at least, as a superior jazz player. On his own testimony, as a youngster he had listened carefully to Hilton Jefferson, who played with many of the leading bands of the time and has always been considered underrated by musicians.[52] He was next influenced by Coleman Hawkins, who became his primary model. Hawkins, who had somewhat more formal training in theory than most of his contemporaries in jazz, had developed a thick, rather busy and harmonically complex style that he delivered in a tone that grew smoother through the 1930s. His rhapsodic version of the ballad "One Hour," recorded in 1929, set a style for saxophone ballad playing that remained fashionable for several decades. Webster aped Hawkins's tone and approach, though not his harmonic complexity, so successfully that sometimes it is difficult to know which one of them we are listening to. Eventually, however, Webster began to search for his own way of playing and to shake off some of the Hawkins influence, although it remained evident in his playing for the rest of his career. He was particularly drawn to Johnny Hodges, who could produce a tenor sound at times. In an interview after Hodges's death, he said, "That's what I try to do, is play Johnny on tenor . . . so much feeling."[53]

Webster first heard Ellington in 1929 or 1930, probably via the Cotton Club broadcasts, and for years thereafter he wanted to join the band. "It was always my ambition," he remembered, "to play with the Duke. . . . Everytime I'd run across Duke I'd hit him for a job."[54] Webster was with Cab Calloway in 1935 and 1936 when he substituted for Bigard briefly; because Calloway was also in the Mills stable, Ellington could not raid him for talent. He told Webster that, should he ever be out of a job, he should come and see him. The Calloway band was celebrated, and Calloway not only paid well but was easy to work for. However, he featured himself on virtually every number, and there was little room for the soloists to stretch out in. Webster told Milt Hinton, the bassist with the band at the time, "Man, I don't get but about eight bars at the most as a solo and I am not using my instrument the way I want to in order to get some real feeling out of it."[55]

In 1937 he left Calloway, moved through several orchestras, and, finally, found himself out of work. He went to Chicago, where Ellington was playing and braced him for a job. This time Duke took him. *Down Beat* made it a front-page story.

The addition of Webster to the band gave Ellington a voice he had never had before—a strong, breathy tenor saxophone sound to balance the sinuous lighter voice of Jimmy Hodges. More than anything, the presence of Ben Webster marks off the 1940s "Victor" band from the ones that preceded it. Webster was already familiar with the Ellington book, but there was, of course, no part for a fifth saxophone, and he was warned by other members of the section to "stay off" their notes—jazz musicians frequently are very possessive about what they are playing. Webster had to find notes that would fit in with what was being played, and this by itself tended to thicken the chord structure of the section.

The celebrated 1940s band was now in place, and it immediately began to make the records on which its fame would be based: "Jack the Bear," "Ko-Ko," and "Concerto for Cootie" in March; "Cotton Tail" and "Never No Lament" in May; "Harlem Airshaft" and "Rumpus in Richmond" in July; "In a Mellotone" and "Warm Valley," to become the band's closing theme, in September.

The major changes to Duke's professional life that took place around 1939 were accompanied by a change in his personal life. In the spring of 1938 Ellington was in the new Cotton Club on Broadway when he was attracted to a chorus girl named Beatrice Ellis. She has been described as a "strikingly attractive, dark-haired woman"; "the most beautiful child-woman I ever saw"; "very, very lovely"; and "proud and petulant."[56] It has been reported that she had been involved with Joe Louis and Willie Bryant, a bandleader and Harlem man-about-town. Ellington was taken by her immediately, and they began an affair. In time, of course, Mildred Dixon found out. Mildred must have been aware that Duke had had other affairs, some more casual than others, but the relationship with Beatrice—or Evie, as she was generally known—was different. Late in 1938 she asked Duke about Evie, and early in 1939 Duke moved into an apartment at 935 St. Nicholas Avenue with Evie. Mildred handled the situation with grace. She moved back to Boston and by 1945 was working as an office manager for a music publishing firm.

Evie, it has generally been conceded, was difficult at times. The musicians in the band called her Thunderbird. Edmund Anderson said, "Evie was not an easy lady. She was kind of sullen, I would think, at times. . . . She was really a child when you got to know her."[57] But Mercer, in particular, liked her and became close to her: "I adored her. She was wonderful to me all through my life."[58]

Ellington's relationship with Evie was curious. Although she was widely believed to be Duke's wife and listed herself as Evie Ellington at the apartment, Duke never married her, claiming it would be too expensive to divorce Edna. They were apparently close, and Ellington was content to spend a good deal of time with her when he was in New York, slopping around the apartment in old clothes and tending to the pets Evie kept, apparently to ward off the loneliness she felt when Duke was out of town, which was most of the time. At first she was around the band a good deal, but gradually she became reclusive and eventually bitter that Duke never married her and was obviously seeing other women. But that would come later.

16

Black, Brown, and Beige

In 1940 Duke Ellington had a band filled with jazz virtuosos, some of whom had been with him for more than a decade and understood his working methods. He was, by now, no longer the unskilled and unsure musician who had constantly to dig basic information out of others but an experienced composer with a substantial body of work behind him, who was sure in his taste, his methods, and his goals.

Unfortunately, he would, just at this moment, find himself beset by a series of contretemps, and worse, which would make chaos of the music business all through the 1940s. There was, to begin with, the impending war. Already in 1940 the draft was taking musicians, and the first effects of shortages were being felt. In particular, over the next several years travel would become increasingly difficult.

More direct in its impact was a struggle between ASCAP (the American Society of Composers and Publishers) and the country's radio stations. ASCAP, which had been formed around the turn of the century, controlled a huge catalog of tunes, including the work of all the best songwriters and of a great many others besides. Most of the great music from Broadway shows and movies belonged to the ASCAP licensing system. Over the years the radio stations, which had built their programming around music, were brought into the licensing system.

By the late 1930s ASCAP had grown fat and cocky, and it decided to make a substantial increase in the radio fees. The radio stations chose this time to fight. They established a competing organization of their own, called Broadcast Music, Inc., or BMI, and set about collecting a catalog of songs that would allow the stations to operate without using any ASCAP songs. BMI hoped to find composers outside of ASCAP who could create a thousand new songs and, possibly, also to lure away from ASCAP some of the established publishers. Its quest for songs was greatly helped by the fact that the somewhat snobbish ASCAP had never been much interested in composers and publishers of blues, country and western, and the early rhythm and blues that would develop into rock and roll. BMI went after these people and, as a consequence, eventually had an inside track to both rock and country and western.[1]

BMI was activated by the broadcasters in February 1940. Its biggest attraction for composers was that it offered to pay a penny for each performance of a record. ASCAP had not then been charging the stations for the use of recorded performances. (This was before disc jockeys came to dominate radio; much music was live, played either by the stations' permanent studio orchestras or broadcast live from clubs and theaters.) This helped to lure some of the established publishers into BMI, and by mid-1940 the organization felt strong enough to force the issue: from then on, only BMI tunes would be played over the air.

For the big dance bands this was a serious problem. Many of their hits were ASCAP tunes, frequently including their theme songs, and they now could no longer play them on the location broadcasts that were so important in maintaining a band's following. But most of the swing bands ceaselessly churned over their repertoire to bring in the new songs, so that they could put together passable programs out of the BMI catalog, whose songs might then become hits.

Ellington, however, always depended for the core of his programs on his own tunes. Suddenly, he was unable to play on the air "Sophisticated Lady," "Mood Indigo," "I Let a Song Go Out of My Heart," "Creole Love Call," and the rest. He was forced to frantic expedients: as *Down Beat* put it, he was jamming "through four BMI tunes twice nightly on his Sherman Hotel airshots" in Chicago.[2]

The band was heading for the West Coast, and Duke, in desperation, wired Mercer and Billy Strayhorn to fly out, whereupon they sat down to write a whole new book for the band. "Ellington did nothing," Mercer said, ". . . It was a great day for both Strayhorn and I. . . . I mean it was a tremendous—like a gold era—about a year, year and half."[3] Out of this situation came some of the most enduring pieces in the Ellington canon: "Take the A Train," "Chelsea Bridge," "Moon Mist," "Things Ain't What They Used to Be," and others.

Fortunately for Duke, by early in 1941 it seemed clear that the BMI catalog would do for radio audiences. ASCAP was losing some $300,000 a month, and *Down Beat*, in its March 15, 1941, issue, announced, "It's all over but the shouting."[4]

During the stay on the West Coast in the years of the recording ban, a Hollywood songwriter named Sid Kuller conceived of the idea of putting on a Negro revue that would, for once, not employ the stereotypes around which black entertainment had always been built—erotic songs, skits of faithless lovers slashed by razors, jokes about watermelons and stolen chickens. According to one report, the idea was born at a jam session at Kuller's house at which a number of stars were present.

Kuller gathered around him some like-minded Hollywood talents and talked them into putting up some money, and they proceeded to put together a show, which they wrote and directed themselves, working out of an informal "collective" procedure to make decisions. It played at Hollywood's Mayan Theatre for three months. Dorothy Dandridge was the star, but Ellington's band played a major role; Duke contributed several tunes, and his vocalists, particularly Ivie Anderson, were featured. The show was built around the idea that Jim Crow and Uncle Tom were dead or at least dying and was fittingly entitled *Jump for Joy*. The title song contained lines like these:

> Don't you grieve, little Eve,
> All the hounds, I do believe
> Have been killed, ain't you thrilled,
> Jump for Joy.

Ivie Anderson sang "I Got It Bad and That Ain't Good," which went on to become a hit. The show also contained "Take the A Train," "Chocolate Shake," and "Rocks in My Bed," which was also a successful seller for Duke. The blues shouter Joe Turner was brought in after three weeks.

The show, which seemed to promise a great deal, lasted only three months and never played anywhere outside of Los Angeles, except for a three-week revival in 1958 in Miami. Why the show folded has never been made quite clear. There have been suggestions that it involved policy bickering in the collective and other suggestions that it was losing money and the backers got tired of sustaining it. However, at bottom, in 1941 the mass of Americans were simply not ready for a show of "social significance," as the phrase went, promoting the idea that blacks were as good as anybody else. It was the kind of show that could be done for special audiences, but it could not, and did not, work with the broader population.

In part because of works like *Jump for Joy*, there was a growing realization among jazz fans that the Ellington band was not just one more hot swing band. *Down Beat* had something to say about the band in virtually every issue. Ellington's successes and failures, even the comings and goings of his sidemen, were frequently front-page stories. Almost every issue carried a review of an Ellington record or public appearance, and most of them were ecstatic. "That Ellington is the most under-appreciated band in existence is no secret among musicians," said one story.[5] "Morning Glory" and "Jack the Bear" were "thrilling" and "perfect."[6] Regarding "Concerto for Cootie," the paper said, "Haul out the superlatives and grab a new needle."[7] "Ellington Hits All-Time New High on 'Cotton Tail' Disc," it trumpeted two weeks later.[8] The review went on to say, "Most consistent and invariably most thrilling band on records is Duke Ellington's . . . unbelievably high standard." Not every Ellington record received this sort of encomium. "Portrait of Bert Williams" and "Bojangles" were "not quite up to par."[9] "Plucked Again," the first of several duets by Ellington and Blanton, was "hardly hot jazz but darned interesting."[10] " 'Ko-Ko' sounds as if it were constructed in the studio and is mostly ensemble."[11] But, in general, the jazz critics found it a struggle to praise the band enough. Ted Toll, writing in Down Beat, said, "All the superlatives this reporter can dig up aren't sufficient to cover the significance of Ellington in modern jazz music." And he went on to quote the pianist Billy Kyle as saying, "Fifty years from now people will be marvelling at Ellington."[12] Making guesses about what works will be considered significant in fifty years is a risky business, but Kyle's prediction, obviously, was correct.

What was happening in 1940 was that a new generation of jazz fans, brought to the music by swing bands, was discovering Ellington. Many of these people, new fans, were too young to have been caught up in the excitement of the early discovery of "Black and Tan Fantasy" and "Creole Love Call." It was all new to them. In 1937 Down Beat started an annual poll of its readers to choose the leading swing musicians. In the 1938 poll Hodges won second place on alto, Ellington came in fifth as arranger, and others of the Ellington stars were named farther down the lists. The next year the band was ranked sixteenth as "sweet band" and sixth as "swing band." Ellington had moved into third place as arranger, and six of the sidemen were in the top twenty on their respective instruments. In the 1940 poll the orchestra came in second to Benny Goodman in the hot-band category. Hodges was ranked number one and Cootie, Bigard, Blanton, and Brown number three; and six others ran in the top ten on their instruments, meaning that two-thirds of the band was given high ratings, which never happened to any other band. In the years following, the Ellington orchestra was near the top in the swing band category year after year, beating out Benny Goodman for the number one position in 1942. Several of the sidemen were always near the top on their instruments, and Johnny Hodges would be named best jazz alto player in the country almost automatically, year after year.

Down Beat readers were somewhat more sophisticated about swing music than the mass audience, and more committed to their passions. The

Duke Ellington band was, probably, never the second- or even third-most-popular swing band in the country, as far as the ordinary fan was concerned. By 1938 or 1939, at least, the Goodman, Tommy Dorsey, and Glenn Miller bands would have been ahead of the Ellington orchestra in general popular acclaim. But Ellington was, during this period, up among the very most popular bands of the day, for the most part playing a much more complex music than the others. As live records from clubs and ballrooms show, Ellington used, as a matter of course, in his standard program, his most difficult works. For example, at a dance in Fargo, North Dakota, in November 1940, Ellington presented such complicated pieces, today considered among his finest works, as "Ko-Ko," "Harlem Airshaft," "Warm Valley," and "Clarinet Lament." This, mind you, was not New York or Los Angeles but Fargo, North Dakota. The point is that by 1940 jazz had moved into the center of American popular culture, and Ellington was one of the beneficiaries.

In the years following 1940 the Ellington band was on a crest. Duke grossed over a million dollars in 1940, not as much as, say, Glenn Miller, but still some indication that he was not laboring in obscurity. He was broadcasting every night; he was making movies; he was playing major locations, like the Hurricane Club on Broadway, where he "sat down" through the summer of 1943. This engagement was particularly important for him because it came during another of those dustups which were creating turmoil in the music business during the war years.

This time the battle was started by the musicians' union, led by James Caesar Petrillo, a tough and belligerent man who, paradoxically, refused to shake hands with people for fear of germs. He had risen through the ranks in Chicago at a time when the city was run by mobsters. Petrillo was primarily interested in getting some money from radio stations and jukebox operators, who were, as he saw it, using the work of the musicians without paying them. Petrillo felt—rightly, as it turned out—that mechanical entertainment would seriously cut into work for musicians and that there ought to be some compensation for it. His aim was to pull records off the radio and out of jukeboxes, but it quickly became clear that he would have to ban recording altogether to achieve that end. So, on August 1, 1942, the musicians were ordered to stay out of the recording studios.

The musicians were not entirely happy about this decision, but a good many of them at least recognized that it might be necessary. The record companies, needless to say, were more unhappy. They had a fair amount of unissued stock in their files, which they continued to put out, but by the fall they were beginning to suffer. Both sides held firm into the next year. In the summer of 1943, the Big Three—Victor, Columbia, Decca—taking advantage of the fact that vocalists were not in the musicians' union and, therefore not covered by the band, started recording singers like Bing Crosby, Dick Haymes, and others with choral backgrounds. This, however, was only a stopgap, and finally, in the fall of 1943, Decca, which did not have the large backlist Victor and Columbia had, surrendered. As it happened, Decca had an association with World Program Service, a transcription company that produced programs of music that local stations could buy and use as they needed. World was included in the settlement, and in November Ellington made a group of tunes for the company, a mixture of current pop hits and his standard repertoire. Some other small, independent labels signed with the union along the way, but Duke's own company, Victor, was determined to fight on and did not sign until the fall of 1944. For a period of almost eighteen months, the Ellington orchestra made no formal records aside from the World session. However, a great many broadcasts from clubs, especially the Hurricane in New York, have since been reissued, along with some concert material and music from films of various kinds. These records are not always technically of high quality, but there are enough of them to give us an idea of how the band was playing during the recording ban.

The stand at the Hurricane was of particular importance to the band. Ellington later told the critic John Wilson, "We were at the Hurricane in 1943 for six months and lost money. But we were on the air five or six times a week and, when we went back on the road, we could charge five to ten times as much as we could before that."[13] Mercer agreed that, through the Hurricane stay, Cress Courtney, who was now managing the band on a day-to-day basis, "doubled and tripled the money he made through one-nighters."[14] Almost as important was a long series of broadcasts sponsored by the Treasury Department to sell war bonds and featuring the Ellington orchestra. This radio exposure, at a time when no new records were coming out for disc jockeys to play, was crucial to maintaining—indeed increasing—the band's popularity. Over the next few years the band ran first or second in Down Beat polls as a swing band; and finally, in the poll of 1946, it was named winner in both swing and sweet band contests.

In fact, if we assume that the swing band era ran from 1935 through 1946, a case can be made that over the second half of the boom the Ellington band was, in the eyes of Down Beat readers at least, the leading band for the period. It ran first or second every year from 1941 through 1946; perhaps more significantly, when swing and sweet band votes were combined, it ran first from 1942 through 1946.

One result of this rise to celebrity was the appearance of a biography called Duke Ellington. It was written by Barry Ulanov, later a professor of English, and one of the best jazz writers of the day. The book is not without its flaws. It contains a good deal of invented dialogue, and some of the information has been controverted by later research. But it was serious in intent and a far better book than the run of celebrity "autobiographies" being ground out by professional writers for other swing band heroes, and it stands as the first important, full-dress biography in jazz.

Ellington's attitude toward the book was ambivalent. In his introduction, Ulanov said, "Duke Ellington was both flattered and flattering when he first heard I was working on this biography. About six months later, he had a second thought about it. 'Biographies, like statues, are for dead men, aren't they?,' he speculated."[15] Later in life, when Ellington was asked to write an autobiography, he always took the same tack: biographies were for dead men. I think, however, that the problem lay in Ellington's desire to keep his inner self private, his unwillingness to reveal too much of himself. Many years later, he wrote a preface to Stanley Dance's The World of Duke Ellington, a collection of interviews with Ellington and various of his musicians. He said, "Stanley is well informed about my activities and those of my associates. . . . However, I am sure he has not revealed more than he ought! He and his wife Helen are the kind of people it is good to have in your corner, the kind of people you don't mind knowing your secrets."[16] The Dances, of course, were close to Duke and quite rightly kept Ellington's confidences to themselves. Nevertheless, it is not customary to preface a book by saying that it will not be revealing. But so deeply ingrained was Ellington's wish to keep his inner self private that he assumed readers would agree with him.

The Ulanov book was published in 1946, the year in which Ellington's celebrity was peaking. But, in fact, by 1946 the Swing Era was over and the big dance bands were finished. At the end of that year, just as Ellington was savoring his triumph, eight major swing bands broke up. The problem was, in part, one of those changes in popular taste in music that have been characteristic of the music business in the United States in the twentieth century: the big bands had, through the Swing Era, increasingly featured their vocalists, to the point where many of them had become stars in their own right, in some cases more important to the band's success than was the leader. Many of these singers were breaking away from the bands and setting themselves up on their own with whatever support they needed for the occasion. From this time until rock groups began to dominate music, the vocalists were the stars.

But the major problem besetting the swing bands was financial. Competition for good players during the war had driven salaries up to unrealistic heights, and expenses generally had increased. The day was gone when musicians could be paid fifteen or twenty dollars a night and whole bands, especially black ones, hired for a few hundred dollars a week. Club owners could no longer afford to hire big bands; it was cheaper to present a name singer with a trio to back him up.

The big-band era waned rather than died. The innovative bands, led by Stan Kenton and Woody Herman, remained popular into the fifties, and Count Basie, after being reduced to a septet for a period, kept his band going until his death in 1985. But the only band that survived without a break was Duke Ellington's. And it was able to do so only because Duke could support the group with ASCAP fees and royalties from his songs.

In any case, by 1946 Ellington was less concerned with his general popularity than he might have been. His attention was now beginning to focus on his concert pieces, or "extended works," as they are usually called today. For the rest of his life he would see the band as being primarily in service of what he considered his serious music—the suites, tone poems, Sacred Concerts, and other longer pieces fashioned, however vaguely, after the works of nineteenth-century European masters. The band would produce money, and it would be the instrument that Ellington composed on; but it was there, in considerable measure, for the concert pieces.

The first of these major works was a long time coming. In 1933, during the first triumphant trip to England, Ellington had told an interviewer, Hannen Swaffer, that he was composing a suite in five movements telling the story of his people. Swaffer quotes Ellington as saying,

> I have gone back to the history of my race and tried to express it in rhythm. We used to have, in Africa, a "something" we have lost. One day we shall get it again. I am expressing in sound the old days in the jungle, the cruel journey across the sea and the despair of the landing. And then the days of slavery. I trace the growth of a new spiritual quality and then the days in Harlem and the cities of the States. Then I try to go forward a thousand years. I seek to express the future when, emancipated and transformed, the Negro takes his place, a free being, among the peoples of the world.[17]

How much of any of this came from Ellington, how much from Mills or Ned Williams, and how much Swaffer made up is moot. The tone is hardly Ellington's, and it was unlike him, given his natural reserve and concern for keeping his feelings private, to give out so elaborate a statement about a matter important to him. Nonetheless, there was clearly something to it. Ellington had made a point of doing some reading in black history, although probably not anything approaching an elaborate study, for which he hardly had the time. But the whole sense of black pride that had been instilled in him in his youth by his schoolteachers and his family would have driven him to find a way of expressing it in his music. He was certainly also aware that the history of his people would make a subject worthy of a major musical composition. It was a subject he would return to again and again.

But, regardless of what he told Swaffer, he had not started to compose anything; it was all rather vague in his mind and remained so for the time being. His next major work was *Reminiscing in Tempo*, dedicated to his mother.

But he had not forgotten the idea of writing something about his own people. In 1936 he wrote at least part of a score for a musical about a black woman named Ada Walker, who had made a fortune with a patented hair straightener and was famous around Harlem. Ellington had by this time made friends with a twenty-two-year-old stockbroker named Edmund Anderson, who had heard the Cotton Club broadcasts as an adolescent and had become enamored of the Ellington band. Duke showed Anderson the score. Anderson did not like it but was eager to get Duke to do something on a large scale. He suggested a Carnegie Hall concert, but when the idea was discussed with Mills, Mills backed away, apparently fearful of the bad publicity a failure would bring.[18] Then, in 1938 and 1939, John Hammond organized Carnegie Hall concerts featuring various blues and jazz artists. The first of these, the now-legendary Benny Goodman concert of January 1938, was a sellout and generated a great deal of publicity for Goodman. Mills wanted to hold an immediate press conference and announce a similar Ellington concert. This time Duke backed off. He must have been chagrined to realize that Mills's timidity had cost him the opportunity to be the first jazz musician to play a whole concert at the celebrated concert hall, and he certainly would not have wanted it to appear that he was going in there on Goodman's coattails. It must have hurt even more that the concert had featured some of his own musicians—Hodges, Williams, and Carney.

But the effect was to revive in Ellington's mind the idea of writing something about the Negro people, with a view toward a Carnegie Hall performance. The Goodman band had played mainly its standard repertoire at the concert; this would be something different. In the fall of 1940 *Down Beat* reported that Ellington was preparing a five-part piece based on the history of the Negro from Africa to the present, which was to be called *Boola*. He completed some music, part of which became his famous piece "Ko-Ko," and part of which eventually found its way into *Black, Brown, and Beige*. But he was still a long way from having anything to present.

By this time, however, the people around him—his friends and business associates—were encouraging him to get on with the work. In particular, by 1942 William Morris, Jr., who saw Ellington as potentially a major American composer, was urging him to write a long piece. Finally, sometime in the fall of that year, Ellington set about writing it. Billy Strayhorn had by then been with Ellington for nearly three years, but it is generally believed that he had very little to do with it.

Characteristically, Ellington threw the composition together in haphazard fashion. He started writing it during a theater engagement in Hartford, Connecticut, where the band was sharing a bill with a movie called The Cat Woman. As they traveled around the country that fall, he worked on it when he could, sometimes rehearsing it on the bandstand during a dance, a practice he would indulge in more and more. As the piece neared completion, the business people began shopping around for sponsors. They had difficulty finding one and finally were accepted by the Russian War Relief Committee. Ellington was still frantically trying to finish the piece up until the day of the concert—January 23, 1943.

From a publicity standpoint, the concert turned out to be a very splashy event. Eleanor Roosevelt and Leopold Stokowski both attended, along with a myriad of celebrities. Many of the major music reviewers appeared as well, and all of the jazz press was present.

The first half of the concert was devoted to some of the more complex pieces in Ellington's standard repertoire, including "Ko-Ko," various of his portraits, and some of the concertos. But it was Black, Brown, and Beige that the audience had come to hear—a major work by a black composer on black themes. The piece was, Ellington told them, "a tone parallel to the history of the American Negro." The first movement, "Black," was supposed to represent the early history of the Negro in the United States and included sections suggestive of work songs and spirituals. "Brown" celebrated various early American wars that blacks had fought in, and the last movement, "Beige," described the modern life of American blacks, especially their spiritual yearnings, their desire for education, and their patriotic contribution to the war then under way.

The audience was disappointed. The reviews were uniformly negative. Paul Bowles of the Herald Tribune said that it was "formless and meaningless—nothing emerged but a gaudy potpourri of tutti dance passages and solo virtuoso work . . . unprovoked modulations . . . recurrent cliches." Henry Simon at PM, a left-wing paper and sympathetic to Ellington, said, "The first movement all but falls to pieces." Abel Green of Variety, who had been writing about Ellington since the Kentucky Club days and who was also sympathetic to Ellington, called it "a bit self-conscious as these tone poems usually are."[19] Reviews from the rest of the papers said, more or less, the same thing; that is, whatever virtues Black, Brown, and Beige had were obscured by the patchwork nature of the piece, which appeared to critics to be made up of unrelated parts, generally going nowhere. Only the loyal jazz press felt that the piece had much merit. Mike Levin of *Down Beat* borrowed a recording that had been made at the concert—this was before the existence of tape, and concerts were not routinely recorded. He listened to the piece several times and concluded that it did have, after all, "form and continuity."[20] But Levin was almost alone. Most people, then and since, have found it difficult to relate the music to the historical parallel given by Duke and, in general, could not see what the "point" of the composition was.

Was *Black, Brown, and Beige* really as bad as all that? The first movement, "Black," contains two major themes, the work song and the spiritual, which, according to Ellington's introduction at the concert, are related. The work song is built around a brief but insistent theme that reappears a number of times and acts to unify the section: indeed, it is the main unifying element in the entire movement. Between the appearances of this theme are a variety of passages that seem to be little related either to the main theme or to each other. In fact, these passages, which make up a substantial proportion of the whole, tend to ramble. Few of them have distinctive melodies; rather, they seem to flow along like a hawk drifting in the air, pretty to watch for a while, but not going anywhere in particular.

The work song section of "Black" concludes with a long, superb passage for Joe Nanton's trombone. The virtue in it, however, is more the extraordinary vocal quality Tricky Sam produces than the melody, which, once again, is rather aimless.

Now the spiritual section is introduced with the sound of church bells. There follows another rather diffuse passage, which concludes with an interesting duet by Lawrence Brown and Ray Nance, who had come into the band in 1940, on violin, which is at least partially improvised. This gives way to what is unquestionably the high point of *Black, Brown, and Beige*— Johnny Hodges's tender, melting playing of "Come Sunday," a beautiful, slow melody that successfully suggests the quietude and repose of Sunday, devoted to church and rest. The tune itself is built on the standard thirty-two-bar AABA pop tune formula that Ellington by now had in his bones, and this may account for its success. It is, in any case, a very pretty song, which Ellington would play at concerts for the rest of his life, and it is made more beautiful by Johnny Hodges. By 1943 Hodges had developed a creamy sound and a skill at playing glissando that has never been matched, I think, by any other jazz saxophonist. He slips and slides through the melody, curling and weaving, like a line of dancers. It is virtually a cappella: the accompaniment is, for the most part, bowed bass, whispering reeds, and a touch of piano, here and there.

From this point on, "Black" goes back to its country ramble. There is a trumpet solo employing a movement up a diminished scale that has been used for suspense by every hack movie composer; then comes a brief recapitulation of the main theme, and a rather abrupt close.

Taken as a whole, the second movement, "Brown," is perhaps the most coherent. It opens with what Ellington called "a salute to the West Indian influence" in black culture. It is a typical and very good piece of writing for a swing band that expresses the "West Indian influence" primarily in the use of a vaguely Latin rhythm in the drum. This section is followed by one supposed to represent the feelings of blacks after the Emancipation Proclamation—joyous on the part of most blacks but with a strain of sadness as it was felt by elderly blacks who are wondering how they are to be supported in their old age now that the old system has been thrown down. The piece opens with a snatch of "Yankee Doodle" by the trombones, followed by a plaintive duet by alto and tenor saxophones. The remainder of the piece alternates between a jaunty little figure, played mainly by Rex Stewart with half-valves, and plunger trombone in duet. These two little units are tightly constructed and worked so well that, when Ellington played another concert at the end of the year, he used them as a sample of the entire tone poem.

The third section of this movement was described by Ellington at the concert as "mauve" and was somehow supposed to represent the Spanish-American War period, when the blues first appeared. The piece has more unity than much of the rest of Black, Brown, and Beige and was later taken out and used as a separate piece, called "The Blues Ain't Nothin' . . ." Here it is basically a vehicle for the singing of Betty Roche, who had recently come into the band, although it also contains a fine solo for Ben Webster and a brief, if unrelated, passage for trombones that sticks in the memory. The lyric opens thus: "The blues . . . the blues ain't . . . the blues ain't nothin' . . . the blues ain't nothin' but a cold, grey day, and all night long it stays that way. . . ." It includes lines like "The blues ain't nothin' but a ticket from your loved one to nowhere" and "Sighin' . . . sighin', feel most like dyin'." It closes by reversing the opening: "The blues ain't nothin' . . . the blues ain't . . . the blues. . . ."

Duke Ellington from time to time tried his hand at lyrics as well as various sorts of verse, prose poems, and aphorisms that he used on the Christmas cards he sent out by the thousands. I will have more to say about Ellington's efforts at writing later on; but this one is typical, based on cliché and verbal gimmickry and suggesting no true feeling.

The last movement of the tone parallel, "Beige," is the least satisfactory of the three, probably because it was done in the most haste. It is supposed to reflect the fact that the essence of black culture was not the world of big-time sports and the Harlem cabarets but family life, spirituality, and a desire for education. There was a movement in this direction but, just as the Negro was beginning to achieve "solidarity," by which Ellington apparently meant parity with whites, along came World War II, and "the Black, Brown and Beige were right in there for the red, white and blue."

"Beige" contains one pretty theme, which became known as "Sugar Hill Penthouse," but most of the rest of it is filled with a great deal of energetic running and leaping about to no particular purpose. Toward the end, there is an attempt at recapitulation: the "Sugar Hill Penthouse" and "Come Sunday" themes appear briefly. Strangely, the piece concludes without reference to the opening theme; instead, there is a long, bombastic passage that reminds me of nothing so much as Richard Rodgers's Victory at Sea. Then it ends. Undoubtedly, this part was put together at the last minute and barely rehearsed.

When we consider Black, Brown, and Beige as a whole, we are struck by the extent to which Ellington has abandoned the devices that brought him to Carnegie Hall. The whole work contains only three major solos: the Nanton solo on "Work Song," Hodges's beautiful playing of "Come Sunday," and Webster's somewhat wandering solo in "The Blues Ain't Nothin' . . ." Aside from Nanton's solo, there is relatively little of the growling, plunger work, and freak effects that had always been characteristic of Ellington's work. Nor do we have much of the familiar interplay of contrasting instruments. In fact, the bulk of the piece is devoted to large portions of the orchestra galloping along together. Clearly, Ellington did not set out simply to expand the sort of thing he had done with "Mood Indigo," "Creole Love Call," or "Rockin' in Rhythm." He tried, instead, to write something that seemed to him symphonic, using a lot of jazz rhythms and other jazz effects here and there. His model for this and subsequent extended works was not his own, shorter works but pieces like Rhapsody in Blue and the Grand Canyon Suite. The choice was unfortunate, for "Rockin' in Rhythm" and "Mood Indigo" are vastly superior to Rhapsody in Blue and the Grand Canyon Suite. I have seen this sort of thing happen, again and again: the writer of much-admired children's books abandons his method when he sets out to write an adult novel and tries to imitate Henry James; the successful advertising illustrator paints in a wholly different style when he does what he considers serious work.

Part of the problem lay in Ellington's belief that the literary parallel would hold the music together. It was a problem that would dog all of his extended pieces; he did not realize that a musical piece had to hold itself together in musical terms, separate from the program it was hitched to. Making matters worse, the literary parallel itself had no real forward thrust but comprised episodes related only because they involved black people.

A work of art that is essentially a design in time, as a symphony, a novel, a narrative poem, must seem to be going somewhere. A goal must be implied from the outset, and each episode, as we pass through it, must give us the sense that it is another step on a route to what we hope will be not merely a surprise but a new view of the countryside we have been traversing. We want to be able to come out at the end on a height from which we can look back, finally, and see the whole. *Black, Brown, and Beige* fails to give us that sense. We are constantly being led into byways that peter out in the underbrush, down culs de sac, from which, in some irritation, we must back out.

An artist can get away with momentary loss of momentum if he provides us with flashes and bangs and sprays of color. This was something that Ellington had always done in his shorter pieces, but in *Black, Brown, and Beige* he did not do enough of it to conceal the inadequacies of the form. And the critics told him so. As we have seen in the case of *Reminiscing in Tempo*, Ellington was far more sensitive to criticism of this kind then he let anyone know. Ruth said that after the unfavorable reception given to *Black, Brown, and Beige* he "sort of withdrew and was very quiet."[21]

But Ellington did not give up on *Black, Brown, and Beige*. He played it again a week or so later at a similar concert at Symphony Hall in Boston. He played excerpts from it at another Carnegie Hall concert in December 1943. By the time he got around to recording it, in December 1944, he had boiled it down to the eighteen minutes he could get on two twelve-inch 78 rpm recordings. This version was made up of "Work Song," "Come Sunday," and "The Blues Ain't Nothin' . . ."; and "The West Indian Influence," "The Emancipation Celebration," and "Sugar Hill Penthouse," now presented simply as "Three Dances." He played this truncated version at Carnegie Hall in 1944. Over the years, he continued to tinker with it, performing various portions of it at one concert or another. As late as 1958, he recorded a new version, with Mahalia Jackson singing, among other things, "Come Sunday."

To my mind, the 1944 version that was formally issued on records is by far the best, because most of the rambling part has been cut. The set pieces like "Come Sunday" and "The Emancipation Celebration" are as good as most of Ellington's pieces, except for the superlative ones. They are very good Ellington, and they deserve to be heard on their own as unrelated pieces. *Black, Brown, and Beige*, as originally presented, thus contained a lot of fine music. The problem was, and would continue to be, form.

Whatever the critical reception, the concert had been a huge success, financially and in terms of the publicity it generated. It grossed $7,000, of which $5,000 went to the Russian War Relief. Furthermore, despite the critical reception, it served to enhance Ellington's reputation as a major American artist. It is one of the curiosities of twentieth-century America that art does not have to be very good to establish its creator as a person of distinction. It is only necessary that it be art. The country is awash with painters, composers, novelists, and poets whose work few people find interesting, and which is not well reviewed, but who nonetheless have a significant reputation as persons of importance. This would now happen to Ellington. *Black, Brown, and Beige* was badly reviewed, was disliked by many of the people who heard it, and, except for one or two small sections, never developed an appreciable number of admirers. But it had been performed at Carnegie Hall; it had been reviewed by proper music critics; it was therefore art, and Ellington was therefore an artist. And that is how he would be seen, henceforward, by himself as well as by others.

It was now well over a decade since *Creole Rhapsody* had suggested to him and others that he might be a serious composer, but he was finally ready to proceed. For the next several years there would be annual Carnegie Hall concerts, each offering at least one new, extended piece. After 1948, new pieces appeared more sporadically, sometimes written for concerts, sometimes for television specials, sometimes for festivals and other events.

None of the premieres for later pieces were attended by the fanfare that accompanied the playing of *Black, Brown, and Beige* at Carnegie Hall. They were generally well attended, and audiences were sometimes pleased, but there was never any great upwelling of enthusiasm. Critics tended to be polite but little more. Ross Parmenter of the *New York Times* said of *Such Sweet Thunder*, "Altogether, the pieces were thoroughly winning for none went on too long and each sketch had sympathy as well as humor."[22] The anonymous reviewer of *The Tattooed Bride* for the same paper simply referred to "new compositions of interest."[23] Ellington seems to have been able to ignore the critics, and he went on producing these extended works regularly. They were, after *Black, Brown, and Beige*, his major interest.

By the mid-1940s Duke Ellington had reached a peak of celebrity, both as a popular entertainer and as an artist. His band was winning polls and attracting large audiences. His concert pieces were being played at Carnegie Hall. Unhappily, at the very moment that the edifice was rising to completion, the foundations were cracking, for the great Ellington orchestra, on which all of this had been built, was falling apart.

17

The Early 1940s
Recordings

Many, if not most, Duke Ellington specialists consider the band of the early 1940s, when Ellington was recording for Victor, the musical high point of his career. Not all agree: Stanley Dance, for example, thinks that it has been overrated in comparison with the 1930s band, with its stable personnel for so many years, in part because "the superiority of Victor's recording virtually gave the band a new dimension, at least compared with the cameolike sound of the masterpieces on Brunswick."[1] But his is a minority opinion.

Can the case be sustained? The so-called great period was in fact surprisingly brief. Ellington was with Victor from 1940 until 1946. However, most of the treasured items come from the first years of this period. The recording ban, major personnel changes, an increasingly commercial bent, for which Duke blamed Victor executives, and Duke's growing interest in his extended pieces—all worked against the creation of the jazz-based three-minute compositions that had been at the heart of his work heretofore. By the mid-1940s the band was recording strings of execrable pop tunes. Many of them were written by Ellington in search of a hit, like "I Didn't Know about You" and "Don't You Know I Care?" and were sung by Al Hibbler and Herb Jeffries in booming, pontifical voices, and by Joya Sherrill, who is less offensive but otherwise just an ordinary band singer, no better and no worse than many others around. Good pieces, like "Transblucency" and "Just Squeeze Me," both from a 1946 session, came from this later period, but they were getting farther and farther apart.

The recording ban no doubt deprived us of some Ellington masterworks. In the last session before the recording hiatus, the band cut one of Ellington's finest compositions, "Main Stem," and it is not likely that he would have dried up instantly thereafter. However, the number of great works we have lost is probably limited, because of the personnel changes and other factors that were affecting the music.

Furthermore, Victor gradually lost interest in recording the small groups. This may have been due to wartime shortages of shellac, which required the record companies to make hard choices about what they recorded. The consequence was that, because Duke was under contract to Victor but the sidemen were not, other record companies began to issue "Dukeless" small-group sessions. But they were not nearly as abundant as the early sets and generally not up to their level, nor could they have been without Duke to supervise the music.

Of roughly 175 cuts made during the Victor period, I estimate, 40 are significant and a good many others contain moments of fine music. For a band that had to produce a steady flow of popular music to fill public demand, much of it turned out hastily in the studio, that is a tolerable batting average, if not what we might have wanted. The period produced standards like "Perdido" and "Take the A Train"; a dozen Ellington classics like "Ko-Ko," "Cotton Tail," and "Concerto for Cootie"; three tunes that would, at one time or another, be Ellington themes—"Warm Valley," "Things Ain't What They Used to Be," and the aforementioned "A Train," as musicians invariably term it; and a score of others that would be on most "best of Duke Ellington" lists: "Chelsea Bridge," "Main Stem," "In a Mellotone," "Never No Lament," among them.

It is hardly possible for me to discuss in any detail here more than a handful of records. My choices, obviously, are somewhat arbitrary, and readers will no doubt have additions and deletions they would make. But certain ones are inevitable. The first of these is "Ko-Ko."

I have not been able to discover what the term meant. Charlie Parker used it as a title for what many consider to be his greatest record, too, a long improvisation on the chords to "Cherokee." Ellington said that "Ko-Ko" was supposed to be the description of Congo Square in New Orleans, "where jazz was born." (Congo Square was an open place situated about where Louis Armstrong Park is now, where, in the nineteenth century, blacks held Sunday dances to drum music that is presumed to have been close to African tribal music. Jazz was not born in Congo Square, which suggests that Ellington's understanding of the history of the music was as sketchy as most people's at the time.) The piece was meant to have been a part of the history of the Negro people that eventually emerged as *Black, Brown, and Beige* and that at one point was called *Boola*.

It was recorded on March 6, 1940. There were two takes, but, because there is little soloing, they are, for practical purposes, identical. There is also a faster version from the famous Fargo broadcast that December.

In structure, "Ko-Ko" is a twelve-bar blues in E-flat minor with an eight-bar introduction that is recapitulated at the close, as a four measure coda. The only jazz solo is two choruses by Nanton in the plunger mute, but so closely does he adhere to a pattern that it is likely that Duke gave him rather specific instructions about what he wanted.

Harmonically, "Ko-Ko" is an exercise in organ, or pedal, point, generally called "pedal" by musicians today. The term derives from the organists' old practice of holding down continuously one of the pedals that produce certain notes to create a drone over which the harmonies shift. Sometimes a lead weight was placed on a key instead. A pedal tone is usually taken to mean a low note, but it can correctly mean any note held continuously while the chords shift around it.

In Ellington's "Ko-Ko" the introduction and five of the seven choruses are built around pedal tones: a low E-flat by the baritone sax in the introduction; an E-flat two octaves higher by Tizol in the first chorus; an A-flat by unison saxes in the second and third choruses; a B-flat by unison saxes in the fourth chorus; and an F by the trumpets in the fifth chorus. The pedals are not held continuously, as, strictly speaking, they should be; instead, they are reiterated. But the effect is the same, the notes becoming more or less dissonant as the harmonies shift around them.

Harmonically, in any case, the piece is extremely dissonant, especially in the last two choruses, and the pedal tones, which themselves depart farther and farther from the basic harmony, provide a landmark for the ear.

Structurally, the piece is built by layering, that is, by stacking up simple figures, usually played by separate sections of the orchestra. Curtis Bahn, a music student who has made a careful study of the piece and has provided me with a transcription of it, points out that this layering "makes the harmonies used increasingly complex; however the complexity is unfolded linearly and each successive layer remains audible and accessible."[2] In general, the number of voices speaking at once increases as the piece goes on. The introduction has the pedal voice answered only by trombones, and the first chorus consists of Tizol's pedal E-flat against a reed figure. By the second chorus, the pedal is punctuated by a short riff figure by plunger brass and Nanton wailing at his best, also in the plunger. The fourth chorus has plunger trumpets punctuating the pedal note while Ellington smashes out eccentric and very dissonant piano figures underneath it all. In the fifth chorus, there are four voices—a pedal F by the trumpets, two separate saxophone figures, and punctuation by plunger trombones. The sixth chorus is a call-and-answer passage between orchestra and bass, but the orchestral call consists of four different voices, so that we hear a momentary babble that begins and ends suddenly as the bass appears and reappears, and sounds as if we were opening and closing a door on a cocktail party. There is no pedal point in this chorus or in the seventh. But here the chords are so dissonant that a pedal would hardly have been noticed.

Described thus, "Ko-Ko" sounds very complicated, and in the hands of a lesser musician the harmonic and structural complexity could have turned the piece into a writhing mass as confused as the Laocoon. But it is not. Ellington has made of it a coherent and biting piece of music. For one thing, virtually all of the figures are kept short and to the point, repeated frequently and well balanced against each other. We are able to follow without difficulty the role each is playing. For another, despite the dissonances— a pedal F against the E-flat minor chord, for example—the piece never drifts into atonality. The tonality is always clear, and even listeners with limited musical skills are able to follow the pattern of the blues.

From the point of view of timbres, or tone color, "Ko-Ko" is a good deal more monochromatic than most of Ellington's best pieces. Nowhere do the sweet sinuosities of Hodges or the airy flights of Bigard suddenly arise out of an orchestral mass. Trombones predominate; the plunger is in frequent use. The saxophones are subordinate, employed mainly to supply the pedal notes. It is black with, now and then, flashes of lightning.

But technical analysis does not explain why a work is a classic in a given form. There is in "Ko-Ko" an intense, almost satanic, drive. The intensity itself is frightening. Carney's baritone threatens us right from the introduction, and the pedal notes, with their refusal to shift to match the harmonies, are pitiless. "Ko-Ko" reminds me of nothing so much as Goya's famous flying witches careening half mad over a desolate landscape. This is Ellington at his best—the creator of a mood sustained without flaw for three minutes.

A week later Ellington went back into the studio to record a second classic, "Concerto for Cootie." The number has been discussed in extravagant terms by many writers, among them the French composer André Hodeir, who called it "a masterpiece." He said, "It displays an economy of means that is a sign of real classicism."[3] Cootie, it is generally agreed, contributed at least one of the themes and a good deal else to it.

The piece consists of two main themes. The first one of these is a simple, chromatic theme in F, played muted for the most part in a narrow, somewhat subdued emotional compass. The second theme is for open horn, strong and flamboyant, a shout or cry flung to the winds. It runs for sixteen bars, after which the original theme returns to close out the piece.

However, this broad structure, with its strongly contrasting themes, is filled with curious details. To begin with, the first theme appears at a casual listening to be in an ordinary, foursquare AABA pop form. In fact, in its first appearance it is actually seven bars in length, if we include the pickup bar. Ellington then adds three bars of orchestral response, a strong contrast with the subdued trumpet solo. When the section is repeated, it is still ten measures long, but this time Ellington has repeated the fourth measure of the trumpet melody and rewritten the orchestral answer to shorten it a measure, so that it all still adds up to ten bars. There is no reason for this change. It is an eccentricity that adds a fillip to the section.

Williams uses substantially different sonorities each time he plays this first theme. The first time he uses a plunger over a pixie mute and employs an extreme terminal vibrato. The second time he either holds the plunger fixed partway open or has actually changed to another mute, possibly a cup mute; perhaps some of the orchestral interludes were written to allow Cootie to change mutes.

After these two ten-bar segments of the opening theme comes what would be a bridge in a pop tune—a contrasting eight measures in which Cootie growls into the plunger. Finally, the main theme returns, but this time it is followed by just two bars of an orchestral answer and then a four-bar modulation to D-flat—that move into the flat sixth which Ellington loved to make.

The second theme is played open and gives us a sense of liberation after the confined quality of the first one. Structurally, it is a simple eight-bar melody, repeated, but as it begins on the second beat of the measure, it suggests a countermeter. Cootie plays it somewhat differently each time.

The open section is followed by a two-measure orchestral interlude to allow Cootie time to replace the mute, and then the first theme reappears. This time, however, after five bars Ellington cuts it off abruptly and moves into an eleven-measure coda, the only instance I know of in jazz where sixteen bars are so divided.

Hodeir does not hesitate to use the word "genius" in respect to "Concerto for Cootie"; although that is too much Gallic tempestuousness for me, it is certainly a remarkable work. Its form is excellent, with the contrasting elements well balanced; and yet it is filled with surprises—the sudden repeated bar in the second appearance of the main theme, the breaking off of the same theme at the end of the fifth bar in order to elaborate on the material in a more leisurely way, the contrasting keys and timbres. Ellington has, in this work, demonstrated complete mastery of the three-minute form.

It is interesting to compare "Concerto for Cootie" with the earlier "Echoes of the Jungle," which was clearly a precursor to the later number. There we are also given contrasting growl and open themes by Williams. In that case the open solo, which is somewhat similar to the one in "Concerto," comes first and the growl chorus afterward, and there is not that sense of opening out, of liberation, that we feel when the open solo is reached in the later piece. The problem of form, which troubled Ellington all through his career, is here solved.

Six weeks later, on May 4, the band again went into the studio and, in rapid succession, cut two of Ellington's most famous recordings, "Cotton Tail" and "Never No Lament," which would be turned into the popular hit "Don't Get Around Much Anymore." Jazz is more emotion than design. On some days the players are just more charged up by the music than on others, and we should thus not be surprised to find several good pieces coming out of a single recording session: December 13, 1927, when Louis Armstrong cut "Hotter than That" and "Savoy Blues"; September 15, 1932, when Sidney Bechet made "Sweetie Dear" and "Maple Leaf Rag"; November 26, 1945, when Charlie Parker made "Ko-Ko," "Now's the Time," and "Billie's Bounce." This session was another such time.

"Cotton Tail," the first tune of the day, is, at first hearing, a hard-swinging riff tune based on the thirty-two-bar pop music form. And it is all of that. The band tears through it with a great roar of triumph, and the soloists play with fire and drive. But on closer listening we discover that it is a good deal more than just another hot big-band swinger. The piece is a variation of George Gershwin's standard "I Got Rhythm," which jazz musicians have been improvising on since the 1930s. Scraps of the Gershwin melody surface from time to time, especially in Ben Webster's long solo, and the song is even reflected, vaguely, in the melody, in so far as the opening figures of both melodies emphasize the ninth. However, the Gershwin melody is an obvious one, built on a diatonic scale. Ellington's is more complicated, beginning on the ninth and incorporating a flat fifth, two examples of Ellington's penchant for rule breaking.

In fact, there is a good deal of rule breaking throughout. The piece begins abruptly, without any warning, on the first note of the tune, which falls after the downbeat, so we hear a fraction of a bass note before the tune leaps at us. It is therefore a moment before the meter establishes itself, and we are temporarily displaced. The theme is played for eight bars and repeated; then Cootie Williams growls over the bridge. We expect the normal recapitulation of the opening eight-bar theme; but Ellington is in a mood to break rules, so instead he gives us a wholly different theme, only four bars long, which, again, reflects the Gershwin melody.

Now Ben Webster plays two full choruses on the "Rhythm" changes, producing what is certainly his best-known solo and, probably, the most famous tenor saxophone solo in the entire history of the Ellington band. It exhibits all of Webster's strengths—his rich, full, slightly dusky tone, his power, his heedless forward motion. He is, at times, incoherent, but this is a powerful chorus, one of the memorable solos in jazz.

Following Webster is a chorus divided among the brass as a whole and solos by Harry Carney and Ellington. Then comes one of the high points of the record, one of those wonderful, sinuous saxophone choruses that Ellington had long since mastered. Then the brass returns, and the record ends with a recapitulation of the opening theme. That is all there is to it: one strong, interesting theme, a long solo and three short ones, and some straightforward writing for the sections—and half a dozen surprises. But all of it fits; there is nothing extraneous.

Immediately after making "Cotton Tail," the band cut "Never No Lament." Again, simplicity tells. The familiar six-note melody, a very plain descending diatonic line, was something, apparently, that Hodges used to warm up on. It is only four beats long, which left a substantial amount of space to be filled in each two-measure repetition, and Duke seized the opportunity to turn Hodges's little line into an exercise in countermelodies and answering refrains. Muted brass are complemented by saxes, a single-note piano line is undergirded by Lawrence Brown's trombone, Hodges's creamy playing of the melody is answered by the full orchestra, and unison saxophones play a beautiful counterfigure to Cootie's growl in the plunger. Color shifts constantly, reds are juxtaposed against blacks, greens against brown. It is all clean, sparkling, bright, and gay as a circus. Undoubtedly, Ellington brought almost nothing to the recording session but Hodges's little melody. The whole thing was constructed on the spot, and so sure, on this day, was Ellington's sense of form that he turned a fragment of melody—hardly more than a piece of a scale—into a jazz classic. It is a stunning example of Ellington's musical intelligence and once again shows us that he was at his best with the simplest materials.

"Harlem Airshaft," made on July 22, 1940, was, like so many of Ellington's compositions, triggered by a sensory experience, a physical memory, in this case the sounds and smells that drift down an airshaft into a Harlem tenement building. The tenements of New York, built in the first decades of the twentieth century, were constructed as close together as possible to exploit expensive land. In order to bring a measure of light and air into them, laws required that an enclosed space resembling a mineshaft, which might run five or ten feet in each direction, be left between each two buildings. The windows that opened on this shaft allowed tenants to look into the apartments across, which were almost within touching distance in many cases. Frequently, clotheslines were strung in the shaft from window to window. People across the shaft from each other might become neighborly, and housewives could lean out of their kitchen windows and gossip or even borrow cups of sugar and lumps of butter. Sounds and smells carried easily up and down the shaft, and, inevitably, everybody on the shaft knew who was eating liver and onions and which couples were fighting. Duke said,

> You get the full essence of Harlem in an airshaft. You hear fights, you smell dinner, you hear people making love. . . . You hear the janitor's dogs. . . . A wonderful thing, is that smell. . . . One guy is cooking dried fish and rice and another guy's got a great big turkey.[4]

Ellington's musical pictures were not always successful, especially where he attempts long and complicated descriptions. But when he confines himself to one simple image he frequently produces magic, as with "Daybreak Express." "Harlem Airshaft" is one of the most successful ones, and it adds to the music to understand what it is about. The activity in an airshaft is disorderly, a mélange, and this is what Ellington has constructed. The structure of the piece could hardly be more basic. After a twelve-measure introduction the remainder is built of eight-measure units, grouped, as in any popular song, in AABA fashion. The chords are of the simplest kind, and the bridge section is one of the standard "Sears, Roebuck" bridges. However, this simple structure, as is often the case in Ellington's work, undergirds a much more complicated musical skin.

The introduction signals what is to come. It is made of three quite disparate musical fragments, which, as they succeed each other abruptly, shift the mood exactly as in an airshaft when at one moment we smell the fish and at the next the roast turkey. The main body of the piece continues to mix and match contrasting, frequently jarring elements: muted brass playing a bugle figure against creamy unison saxophones; Nanton growling over the saxophones; trombones with Barney Bigard's clarinet flying over them. Particularly felicitous are episodes in the second chorus. In the previous chorus the bridge was played by Nanton growling over long chords by the saxophones. The second chorus opens with similar long chords, while the rhythm drops out to give the effect of the "break" so common in early jazz. We expect something similar to what went before, but this time, after four bars, Cootie, open horn, dives in as the rhythm section takes up. Then, as he begins to get up momentum, the saxophones suddenly take another break; and so it alternates through the bulk of the thirty-two bars.

The piece ends with a rousing chorus in which the airshaft is filled with flying objects: saxophone and brass all go hell-for-leather as Bigard screams overhead, as he had done so often for Duke in the 1930s. "Harlem Airshaft" works as program music in a way that others of Duke's pieces do not. In fact, the abrupt shifts in it would seem merely disruptive without an understanding of Duke's intention.

"Warm Valley," which Ellington would use as a closing theme, was also sparked by a memory. Duke said,

> While driving along the south shore of the Columbia River, east of Portland, Oregon, we had a good view of the mountains on the north

shore. They had the most voluptuous contours, and to me they looked like a lot of women reclining up there. "Warm Valley" came directly from that experience.[5]

The valley of the title, of course, was not the one between the hills along the Columbia River, and the whole song was intentionally erotic. It is built of descending chromatics, beginning on the major seventh, which wind slowly downward through a sequence of chords, many of them extended seventh chords which gives a peaceful, languorous effect, suggesting the sleepy aftermath of lovemaking in a warm, summer sun. Much of it was played by Hodges in his seamless purr. The music seems to drift like a cloud sliding across a summer sky over that peaceful valley. It is classic Ellington, the evocation of a specific mood.

In New York City the subways are denoted by letters and numbers according to the routes they take. The A train has for decades been the express that runs into Harlem from downtown Manhattan and elsewhere in the city. It remains an important part of the lives of thousands of Harlem residents and is surely the only subway line, anywhere, that has had a popular song named after it. Billy Strayhorn wrote "Take the A Train," but, as ever, there remains the question of how much of it he wrote and how much of the work is Ellington's.

If the work is entirely Strayhorn's, it is powerful evidence of the extent to which he absorbed Ellington's methods in two years with the band. Here are the interplay of two or three sections, the contrasts of timbre, the close intervals in the harmonies, the love of chromatics that runs all through Ellington's work. Here, too, is the simple construction that provided Ellington with the framework for most of his successes. The tune is set in the thirty-two-bar pop song form that was, by this time, second nature to working jazz musicians. The melody is simple enough. It gets its distinction from its primary movement, a chromatic one (in C) of G–G♯–A; and from a good deal of chromatic chord movement which, however, is arranged so that a C can be played throughout the A sections. The popular song of the first half of the twentieth century was heavily indebted to the circle of fifths for its chord structures, a system that had been developed by the European masters of the seventeenth century, almost forced on them by the rules against parallel fifths and octaves. In classical music these strictures had long since been overthrown, but they were still observed in American popular music. So far as jazz was concerned, Coleman Hawkins had begun experimenting with chromatic internal movement in the 1930s. In 1939 he made a record of "Body and Soul," which became a minor hit. Hawkins turned the tune into an exercise in chromatic chord movement, and the device had become fashionable among jazz musicians. It was still, however, sufficiently rare to sound novel in 1941.

The piece begins with Ellington's famous piano introduction, which suggests the chromatics to come. The main line is played by saxes in unison, with both trombones and trumpets in straight mutes playing contrapuntal figures in support. There are thus three voices working at once, but so deftly are the supporting voices handled that it all seems perfectly natural. The trombones play under the bridge, and, for the last eight bars, open trombones are voiced with tightly mute trumpets, an unusual combination that nonetheless works. One of Ellington's great strengths was handling contrapuntal play of this kind; if Strayhorn worked this out, he had learned his lesson from the master.

There follows a solo by Ray Nance, who had recently replaced Cootie Williams, in the straight mute, supported by subtle and discreet saxophone figures. Nance's solo is very well constructed, and it became famous, almost a part of the tune, which other trumpet players felt obliged to refer to. It made Nance's reputation.

After the solo there is a four-measure interlude by the trombones, which takes the piece from C to E-flat—most musicians are unaware of this modulation and invariably play the piece in C. Nance, open horn, now trades fours with the saxophones playing a rising figure on a diatonic scale, which has also become traditional with the piece. Over the bridge, Nance is again supported by a complex mix of trombones and saxophones. There follows the basic eight-measure melody, repeated three times, diminishing in volume, ending abruptly with a tiny tag. Again, simplicity tells: an interesting melody, ingenious counterpoint, and a good solo, played with a nice, relaxed swing by a band that knew what it was doing, add up to a jazz classic. The tune became an important standard, and the record was a hit.

The choice of a Strayhorn tune for this recording session was dictated by the necessities of the recording ban. At the same session the band also cut a Mercer Ellington tune, "Blue Serge," a moody tune that exploits the relationship between E-flat major and C minor. This tune also shows all the earmarks of Ellington's work. It opens with a clarinet trio, a device popular in the 1920s but, by 1940, unfashionable, except with Ellington. We have, as well, the thick harmonies, a clarinet lead with saxophones, and an attempt to create a specific mood. Mercer, too, was learning from the master.

Given that these two young men were working under Ellington's tutelage, it is possible that Duke contributed a good deal to Billy Strayhorn's best-known work, "Chelsea Bridge." Strayhorn took his inspiration, not from the bridge itself, which he had never seen, but from a Turner painting that actually depicted Battersea Bridge, a little farther west. The composition is once more based on the standard pop song form and structurally could not be simpler. Taken at a moderately slow tempo, two choruses fill the entire record. The lead is moved around the band in rather four-square fashion: sixteen bars of trombone, eight bars of tenor, sixteen bars for the saxophones, and so forth. (In a second recording, the routine is somewhat different.) Strayhorn plays piano.

The interest lies in the dense harmonies. There are a number of anticipations in the melody and frequent use of the flat fifth, the result of which is to suggest at a good many points the whole-tone scale, which Strayhorn had discovered through his interest in the impressionist composers and which Ellington was already familiar with. "Chelsea Bridge" is another of those pieces, which drift slowly rather than move purposefully, that Ellington liked.

On the same date when the band cut the first version of "Chelsea Bridge," it made the first of what would be a large number of versions of "C-Jam Blues." This was entitled "C Blues" and was cut by a small group under Bigard's ostensible leadership. It is a very nice, easy-handed version of the tune, with a rhythm section consisting of Blanton and Greer, and I prefer it to the somewhat heavier band versions that followed. The main theme is hardly a tune at all but a riff, and a simple one at that, using only two notes. It has an airy quality and has been played countless times at jam sessions as an excuse to play the blues. This first version has first-rate solos by Carney and Nance.

The first big-band version was cut a couple of months later. It opens with the simple melody played in single notes by Ellington, a minimal rendering of a minimal tune, showing that he not only understood the virtue of simplicity but also was not afraid of it. Most of the rest of the record offers a string of solos on the blues, each beginning with a break. These breaks are somewhat odd; customarily, when a solo begins with a break, the break occupies the first four bars of the structure. These breaks are separate and are all followed by a solo on a complete blues chorus. The record ends with the full band roaring out an elaboration on the theme.

On the same day when the band cut "C-Jam Blues," it recorded another tune that would become a classic and be recorded many times, Juan Tizol's "Perdido." The tune is yet another AABA thirty-two-bar song. The main theme is a riff that alternates dominant seventh and tonic chords. The "Sears, Roebuck" bridge has no real melody at all and is usually covered with an improvised solo. "Perdido" has been used as a vehicle for blowing even more than "C-Jam Blues" has. This first Ellington version consists mainly of solos, with the inevitable full-band uproar at the end.

Neither "C-Jam Blues" nor "Perdido" is an important piece of music—indeed, neither can really be classified as a "song," although both have brought in a lot of royalties over the years; but both were played cleanly and enthusiastically and became hits for Ellington. The lesson to be learned is that, in jazz, less is often more. These two recordings have outlasted a great many much more venturesome and complex pieces of that time by such musicians as Stan Kenton, Woody Herman, Boyd Raeburn, and Ellington himself. It is an inviolable rule of jazz: first you must swing. And these two minimal compositions swing.

"Main Stem," cut on June 26, 1942, just before the recording ban went into effect, swings at least as hard as the foregoing two. It is, however, less simple than it seems at first hearing. Ellington developed it by turning on its head a little figure that has been central to jazz and especially the blues from the beginning. The early blues employed not major or minor thirds or sevenths but "blue" thirds and sevenths, which lay somewhere in between major and minor—in the cracks between the keys of the piano, so to speak. These blue notes puzzled musicians who had not been raised on the blues; in any case, they could not be written down in ordinary notation. In casting about for approximations to them, musicians began substituting the minor third for the blue third and the sixth for the blue seventh. A jazz cliché then developed of dropping from the sixth to the minor third—from A to E-flat in the key of C.

The initial phrase—"remark" might be a better term—is this cliché, upside down, an upward leap from F to B, once again the "devil's interval" that Ellington delighted in using. There is no introduction: the composition starts abruptly on this upside-down figure played by the brass. The opening is so awkward—deliberately—that we feel we have come in at the middle of a conversation. The figure is only a measure long and is instantly answered by a related remark from the saxophones that is hardly any longer. These harsh, thrusting figures alternate like an argument over the twelve-bar structure of the blues. There follows a chorus made up of exchanges between saxophones and plunger trumpet by Rex Stewart that are dissonant, sardonic, harsh.

Next come five solos on the blues by various instrumentalists. Hodges, using his tenor sound, plays a beautiful solo consisting of three long, looping phrases flung over the three parts of the blues form. The supporting figures by the band mainly reiterate material from the opening section, which makes the solos seem part of the whole design rather than independent set pieces. However, under the first trumpet solo there is something new, a simple, syncopated figure by Carney, echoed by the trombones, one of those imaginative little items that are everywhere in Ellington's work.

So far, we have the blues. But, after Nanton's solo, Ellington abruptly switches to a new structure: a ten-bar interlude that makes the modulation from D to G, a solo by Webster, a repeat of the last four bars of the interlude, and a solo by Lawrence Brown. The band returns to D and the opening chorus to conclude. These last two solos feel, on a casual listening, like more solos on the blues; but they are not. In the first place, they are fourteen bars long, an unusual length for jazz solos. The chord sequence is quite simple, but unusual in jazz, and is worked out to produce an internal descending chromatic line, and it may have been the requirements of this line which enforced the fourteen-bar length. In any case, Ellington is once more disregarding the rules.

Throughout, we are repeatedly reminded of those two harsh opening figures: the argument continues. There is a hair-raising intensity to the piece as a whole. It is relentless: things are always leaping and charging unexpectedly from the underbrush. There are hardly half-a-dozen beats in the entire piece without activity. There is never a letup. To my mind, this is one of Ellington's finest works, a jazz masterpiece, a hard, slashing, sardonic, perhaps even evil number, which swings and swinges from the first note to the last.

There are many more fine records than this dozen or so from the famous 1940s band. There is "In a Mellotone," developed from changes of "Rose Room," which has wonderful conversations between Hodges and Cootie and the orchestra. There is "Transblucency," with a wordless vocal by Kay Davis harmonized with the clarinet in such a way that, at moments, it also sounds like a voice. Haunting and introspective, the tune is built on the most basic of all jazz numbers, a B-flat blues. There is Mercer Ellington's "Things Ain't What They Used to Be," one of the most famous pieces in the entire Ellington book. Oddly enough, the piece was not formally recorded by the big band for years: the first version, recorded in July 1941, was with a small Hodges group and was taken at a slower tempo than became usual. However, "Things Ain't What They Used to Be" entered the band's repertoire not long afterward.

Although Victor substantially reduced the number of small-group recordings made by Ellington, the company did not, at first, eliminate them altogether. A dozen sides were cut in November 1940 and another eight in the summer and fall of 1942. As usual, many of these contain fine jazz, especially in the solos. In particular, they show Johnny Hodges in exceedingly good form, especially in a July 1941 session that includes a typical Strayhorn piece called "Passion Flower," slow and lush, like great blossoms among the vines, which Hodges plays with his sinuous glissandi. This session also includes that first, slow version of "Things Ain't What They

Used to Be." Once again Hodges is at a peak. Yet another memorable cut from this session is "Goin' Out the Back Way," which shows Hodges's use of dynamic change throughout his line.

A 1940 session produced an oddity by Rex Stewart called "Menelik— the Lion of Judah." Menelik was an Ethiopian king and hero of his country, and in this piece by Stewart, using the pedal register of his instrument, roars like a lion. The arrangement of the piece is more complex than most of the small groups from this period, which were frequently minimal.

Like the earlier small groups, these all meet a high standard, and almost all of them contain first-rate solos. Some of them, like "C Blues," are hard swingers. But on the whole, because the arrangements are often so slight, sometimes little more than bits of melody, they are largely dependent on the solos for their interest.

What, then, do we conclude about the 1940s Ellington band? Was this really the greatest of all Ellington bands? It seems to me that nothing Ellington ever recorded was better than "Ko-Ko," "Main Stem," "Concerto for Cootie," "Cotton Tail," and one or two others from this period. Only the very best of his earlier pieces, like "Mood Indigo," and "Creole Love Call," can equal them. Both Ellington as a composer and the band as a unit were, for a brief period, at a peak. "Ko-Ko," "Cotton Tail," and "Concerto for Cootie" were all made in the spring of 1940; "Harlem Airshaft," "Don't Get Around Much Anymore," "In a Mellotone," and "Warm Valley" were made in the next three months—seven classics in six months. And, because of the recording ban starting in the summer of 1942, all of the masterpieces of the so-called 1940s band songs were actually made in two and a half years. When Duke returned to the studios in 1944, there was a substantial falling off in the music, which the critics recognized even then. Not only were Ellington's compositions much less interesting than what had come before, but the band itself was markedly inferior to the earlier groups. To a considerable extent, this drop in quality was the result of personnel changes that I will discuss in a moment. However, there were other factors. It seems to me that Duke was beginning to lose interest in the three-minute form. Many of his compositions in 1944 were execrable pop tunes, some of them with his own, appallingly bad lyrics, such as "Go Away Blues," which contains lines like "Go away blues, I don't want you around: go away blues, you bring me down." His interest was turning to the concert pieces that he was writing for the annual Carnegie Hall concerts and to the theater works like *Jump for Joy* and *The Beggar's Opera*. This, of course, was fair enough. Ellington may have felt that he had exploited the three-minute form as far as he was able, or wanted to. But it did mean that there would be no more "Ko-Ko"s and "Main Stems."

In sum, it seems fair to say that, for a brief period of six months, a year, perhaps two years, the Ellington band was at a peak that no other period quite matched; but, taken as a whole, the band of the 1940s cannot be held superior to that of the preceding decade.

18

The Old Hands Begin
to Depart

It is a rare artist who goes from triumph to triumph without here and there encountering slips and slides, and usually a final decline. Duke Ellington was no exception. Even at the moment when he was reaching a peak as a jazz artist, the great music machine he had built was falling apart.

The damage began with the departure of Cootie Williams. Sometime in the fall of 1940 Irving Goodman, Benny's brother, a trumpet player who helped Benny with the band's management, approached Cootie with an offer from Goodman, principally to play with the Goodman sextet. Cootie was torn: on the one hand he had an emotional stake in the Ellington band, which he had helped create, and he felt he owed Duke a certain loyalty; on the other hand Goodman was offering two hundred dollars a week, a substantial salary at the time, and more than Ellington could—or would, pay. Perhaps more important, Cootie wanted to play with the Goodman band. A good deal of the reason was Sonny Greer, whose irresponsibility Williams might have endured had Greer been a superior jazz drummer. He said, "But that Goodman band—I loved it. It had a beat and there was something there that I wanted to play with. When it comes to music, I forget about the world—everything else leaves me."[1] He liked the way Goodman played, and afterward he singled out Davey Tough, one of the finest drummers of the time, who would come into the band shortly after Cootie did, as having "terrific rhythm. . . . That was the main thing. The band had a terrific beat."[2]

Torn, Cootie told Duke about the offer. Duke must have been aghast, but he maintained his usual composure and urged Cootie to take the job. If Duke had asked him not to go, Cootie said later, he would have turned down Goodman's offer. But Duke no doubt did not want to compromise his royal bearing by appearing in any manner to beg, and he actually, on Cootie's request, negotiated the salary. He advised Cootie to work only with the sextet. "You'll get lost, sitting back there in the band," he said.[3] As ever, he was generous with his old hands.

Cootie's intention was to go with Goodman for a year and then return to Duke. Early in November he left. In the jazz world it was a little as if the pope had converted to Buddhism. A lot of the most ardent Ellington fans resented the wealth and celebrity Goodman had achieved playing what they considered to be an inferior brand of jazz, and they were outraged. *Down Beat* made it the lead story of its November 1 issue, all parties got a stream of angry letters, and the bandleader Raymond Scott wrote a tune called "When Cootie Left the Duke."

Cootie was happy with the change: "That was the most relaxed thing that I ever had in my life in music. . . . That year. . . . And that sextet used to romp. . . . I enjoyed it so much."[4] Cootie also played with the big band at times. Nonetheless, as he promised, he left Goodman after a year to return to Duke. But Ellington, for whatever complicated reasons, told Cootie that he was now a star and should have his own band, which would give him a chance to make a great deal of money. Cootie thereupon formed a band, which at times included people like Bud Powell and, briefly, Charlie Parker. Unfortunately, the band was not a success—according to John Hammond, because of "inept management and innumerable blunders."[5] Cootie started drinking, for a period at least. Eventually the band collapsed, and Cootie ended up playing with a small group, first as the house band at the Savoy and then picking up whatever he could get. It was a pitiable comedown for a man who had been, a decade earlier, at the top of the world of jazz.

When Cootie left, he suggested that Duke replace him with a high-note trumpet player named William "Cat" Anderson, then working for Lionel Hampton. Anderson would eventually come into the band, but for the moment Ellington made a different, rather surprising choice, a young, relatively unknown trumpet player named Ray Nance. Born in 1913 in Chicago, Nance started studying piano at six, the violin at nine. He went to Wendell Phillips, a black high school that had a famous music teacher, Major N. Clark Smith, who taught a number of important jazz musicians. Nance taught himself trumpet, began gigging around Chicago nightclubs, and then landed in Earl Hines's band, where he spent two years. By 1940 he was working in Joe Hughes's De Luxe Club in Chicago, as an all-around entertainer who sang, danced, and played trumpet and violin. Nance was only five feet four inches, but he was filled with energy and was as much a showman as a musician. With Duke, when he came forward to solo, he would strut to the front of the band, flipping his trumpet in the air. (After he began doing plunger work, he switched to cornet, because his arms were short.)

Ellington came upon Nance almost by accident. Shortly after Cootie left, the Ellington band went through Chicago on tour. Presumably, somebody suggested Nance to Duke, for he brought Strayhorn into the Club De Luxe to hear him, and took Nance with him when he left Chicago.

Why he made this choice is hard to understand. There were a number of better-known—indeed, better—trumpet players around who would have been delighted to join Ellington. Both Charlie Shavers, who was with John Kirby, and Paul Webster, with Lunceford, were suggested, and other, more experienced players like Bill Coleman and Joe Thomas were also available. In part it may have been a matter of price. Some of these men were earning more than Ellington wanted to pay, and Nance could be expected to jump at the chance to go with Duke without quibbling about salary. Second, Nance was an all-around showman, and Ellington had always tried to put on a good show. Third, Nance would be easier to mold than a more established player with a set style. Finally, Ray Nance was another one of those irrepressible naughty boys, like Sonny, Toby, and Bubber, whom Duke seemed to take pleasure in having around him. Among other things he was, or would become, a drug addict.

But the band's fans were not all pleased by the selection of Nance. The jazz entrepreneur Harry Lim told *Down Beat* readers, "Cootie's replacement is a kid that has a lot of showmanship . . . but who just doesn't meet the standard required by a band of Duke's calibre."[6] Nance simply was not in Cootie Williams's class as a jazz musician. He was a competent improviser, and his solo on "Take the A Train" became standard, but he did not make many other memorable solos with the band. Nonetheless, he was a useful addition, and Duke would, over many years, make use of his singing, dancing, and violin playing in various ways. His violin solo on Mercer's "Moon Mist," for example, is a fine sample of jazz playing on an instrument that has not often been successfully used in jazz. (Actually, the tune had been designed as a showcase for Ben Webster, but, according to Mercer, Webster was drunk and either missed the session or could not handle the task.)

The next loss was Jimmy Blanton. During the 1941 stay in Los Angeles, when the band was working in *Jump for Joy*, Blanton was rooming with Billy Strayhorn, who was closer to his age than many of the people in the band. One day he told Billy he was moving in with a girlfriend. In fact, he had seen a doctor and had discovered that he was suffering from tuberculosis. There was always hope that he would recover, but some reports indicate that he had at times collapsed from exhaustion from staying too late at jam sessions, and overwork could not have helped his condition. Ellington said,

> When he got very sick, and the whole thing came out and everybody knew what was going on, I tried to do something about it. I called doctor after doctor until I found out who the top people on TB were in Los Angeles. I made a date and took him down to the big city hospital, where there were three beautiful young, specialists. They all knew him; they were fans of his, and they talked about his music.
> "I'm getting ready to leave town," I said. "Will you take care of him?"
> "Yes, we will," they said. "Leave him right here. He'll just have to stay in the ward a couple of days or so until we can get him a room." A room at wherever it was they sent their people to for special care. He hadn't been there two days when some cat went down and said to him, "Why, the idea of Duke leaving you here in the ward!" He packed him up and took him out somewhere near Pasadena, I think it was. . . .
> When I got back to town, there he was, on his cot. They had nothing there, no X-rays or anything. "Well, you can't move him," they said, and he should have been moved a month before I got there. I took one look and knew he was gone.[7]

Blanton never returned to the band and died on July 30, 1942. His replacement was another surprise, an unknown bass player working with the obscure Wilbur Berranca trio at the Club Alabam, where some of Duke's men had jammed. His name was Junior Raglin, but so little known was he that *Down Beat* went on spelling it Raglund for several issues. No doubt everybody assumed that Raglin would be only a temporary replacement for Blanton. Raglin turned out to be a competent bass player. He worked in tandem with Blanton for a few nights to get the feel of the band, before Blanton went into the hospital. He went on working for Ellington off and on until his early death from alcoholism in 1955.

The next defector was Barney Bigard. He met the woman who would become his wife at the end of 1942. By 1942 the war was making travel for bands difficult. No longer was the Ellington group able to move comfortably around the country in Pullman cars; it was now a case of taking what could be gotten, which often meant that the musicians were jammed into a crowded bus or coach. Bigard had had, over the years, offers of other jobs, but he had been committed to Ellington and had never seriously considered them. Now problems of travel and a desire to be with his new wife made up his mind for him. "So when we got somewhere near California," Bigard said, "I made up my mind to give Duke my notice. When I told him I was leaving he just looked at me and didn't say a word. I have often wondered what he thought that night. . . . My notice terminated at the Trianon Ballroom, Los Angeles in June of 1942."[8]

Once again *Down Beat* made a big story of it. "I'm tired of travelling," it quoted Bigard as saying. " 'He's just leaving. That's all,' said Duke irritably, when asked for comment."[9]

Bigard's career in his post-Ellington period was happier than that of most of the men who left. He gigged mainly around California during the war. In 1947 he joined Louis Armstrong's new small band, the All-Stars, and stayed with it for five years, the only man to play important roles in the bands of these two great jazz musicians. He would leave Armstrong twice and return. He spent his later years playing with a variety of small bands, usually in the New Orleans or Dixieland format, a respected and honored figure in the world of jazz.

To replace Bigard, Ellington turned to Edmond Hall, a New Orleanian of Bigard's generation, considered by many to be an even greater clarinetist than Bigard, and one of the finest black jazz clarinet players of any period. Hall was working with Teddy Wilson and turned Duke down, possibly because of travel, money, or the fact that he had established a reputation in New York, thanks to long stands at Cafe Society, an important jazz club in Greenwich Village. (In retaliation, Wilson made an offer to Hodges.) Duke then hired another obscure musician, Chauncey Haughton, who had been playing with a band led by Ella Fitzgerald. Haughton never had an important career in jazz outside of his brief stay with Ellington, and he left after a year, when he was drafted into the army. His replacement was Jimmy Hamilton, who would have a long life with the band.

Hamilton was born in Dillon, South Carolina, but the family moved to Philadelphia when he was five, and he grew up there. His father was clarinetist with a town band, which played the standard repertory of marches, ragtime, and concert pieces. He started in his father's band on baritone horn at nine or ten, then went on to play trumpet and clarinet. At twelve he lost his father. He felt a duty, as the oldest child, to help out with the family expenses, and he became serious about his music. "If I'm gonna be in music," he said, "I gotta try to be as good as I can, so I put in the time. . . ."[10] Besides playing in church, he listened to the blues and took Louis Armstrong for his model.

Finally, barely out of his teens, he came to New York and began jamming where he could in the clubs. He met Charlie Parker and spent some time with him, but little of the Parker style rubbed off. Eventually, he got a job with a short-lived band led by the arranger Jimmy Mundy. When the Mundy band broke up, he was offered a job by Count Basie, but he preferred to stay in New York. Finally, he got a job with Teddy Wilson at

Cafe Society, working in a little trio that emulated the Goodman trio, in which Wilson had made his first public fame. After two years he was replaced by Edmond Hall. He said this was the doing of John Hammond: "He's one of the big shots in music, you know, where he could say, 'Well, yeah, he's all right, give him a break.' And you'd get a break. But if he didn't like you then you don't go nowhere."[11] How much credence should be put in the story is hard to know, but Hammond was particularly influential with Barney Josephson, the owner of Cafe Society, who was relatively new to jazz and often took Hammond's advice about musicians. If Hall had not replaced Hamilton at Cafe Society, he might have landed in the Ellington band and given it a considerably different sound. Hall played a gritty, driving style that contrasted sharply with Hamilton's smoother and more precise manner. He did not have the "woody" or liquid sound of Bigard, but Bigard had been trained in the Creole school of clarinet, which featured a relaxed, even system of playing, as against the rougher and hotter style of the New Orleans blacks from which Hall sprang. Hamilton's style was closer to Bigard's than Hall's was, and his arrival changed the band's sound less than Hall's would have. Hamilton came into the band for the Hurricane Club gig in 1943 and stayed with Ellington for twenty-six years, a tenure almost twice the length of Bigard's.

Then Ben Webster left. Precisely what happened is not known, but that there was clearly a lot of friction between Webster and Duke. Barney Bigard told Barry Martyn that Ellington was afraid of Webster: "He'd do a lot of things that we wouldn't dare do."[12] Duke may not have been exactly afraid of Webster, but, said Mercer, "nobody wanted to be in the band more than Ben. But there was a sort of conflict, a matter of chemistry where the two of them would get into arguments."[13] According to Mercer, they could not be in the same room without having an argument. Apparently, Duke, with his dislike of uproar and his need to dominate, found Webster's bellicosity too much to take. Something had to give, and in the end Duke seems to have told Ben that he could not take it anymore and that Ben would have to leave. The parting was no doubt sorrowful on Webster's part and probably was tinged with sadness for Duke, because Webster was exactly the sort of heedless, passionate player whom Duke liked best.

Webster went into the Three Deuces, a club on Fifty-second, or "Swing," Street. He continued to work in major locations, but by 1950 or so he, like many of the older players, had been washed aside by the bebop wave, and for a while he was unhappy and depressed. In 1964 he moved to Europe, where he found a devoted audience and spent most of the rest of his life. He made many records under his own name and others' in the years after Duke, and it is probable that his final reputation will rest on these, rather than the records he made in his relatively brief stay with the Ellington band. At his death Webster was considered one of the greatest tenor saxophonists in jazz of the swing period, at a level just below that of Coleman Hawkins and Lester Young. But it was his stint with Ellington that gave him his first major reputation, and certainly his best-known solos are the ones he made with the band—"Cotton Tail," "Just a-Sittin' and a-Rockin'," and the rest.

The next one to go was Juan Tizol. Sometime early in 1944 Tizol asked Duke to lend him $3,000 to pay off the mortgage on his house. Duke refused. Tizol threatened to quit, and word got around in the music business that he was available. He got an offer from Harry James for a good deal more money than Duke had been paying him and signed the contract. When Duke found out, he offered to buy back the contract and pay Tizol a better salary, but Tizol went to James anyway.[14]

That, at least, is Tizol's story. The defections of the others and the problems of wartime travel probably also entered into his decision. Duke replaced Tizol with Claude Jones, an excellent trombonist with a fast legato style who had worked with several of the best black bands, including Fletcher Henderson's. Jones was with Duke for four years.

Then Rex Stewart left. I have not been able to discover precisely what the problem was, but there were hard feelings about it later on. He left early in the summer of 1943 and was gone for four months before he returned. He stayed on for another two years, until December 1945, when he left for good. Stanley Dance says that some years later he ran into Stewart on the West Coast and suggested that they pay a call on Duke in his dressing room.[15] Stewart was at first reluctant, fearing that Duke would not want to see him. But Dance persuaded Stewart to make the visit, which proved cordial. Indeed, in Stewart's own account of the meeting, he said that sometime afterward Ellington asked him to rejoin the band.[16]

In 1946 two more of the old hands left. The first to go was Toby Hardwick. There had been, for some time, a certain amount of friction between Hardwick and Ellington, principally over Hardwick's drinking and his irresponsibility, and Duke had apparently fired Hardwick at least once before. The problem in 1946, however, was a woman with whom Toby had become involved. Duke disliked her intensely and told Toby so. The whole situation concerning Ellington and the musicians' girlfriends was often very troublesome. A good many of them had flings with Duke and went on to the lesser band members, which of itself must have caused certain wounds and jealousies. Sometimes Duke simply took a dislike to a woman and made his feelings clear. In any case, there were words, and in late May or early June 1946 Toby walked off the bandstand during a job in Washington, D.C., and out of the band.

His later life was not entirely happy. After those years washed in the glamour of the band business, he was reduced to working at menial jobs—as a shipping clerk at the Statler Hilton, as a busboy and a waiter—although he had apparently inherited a farm from his parents. He died in 1970, after a long illness in a nursing home.[17]

Toby Hardwick's replacement was Russell Procope, who would be one of the stalwarts of the band in the later years. He was born in 1908 of musical parents in the San Juan Hill area of New York. Bubber Miley lived nearby, and Procope went to school with Freddy Jenkins. He studied violin for eight years as a child, then switched to clarinet, using the Albert system, which he continued to play. "I wrestled with the clarinet for a year, but with no idea of jazz," he recalled, "because I had gone from long-hair music to military band music." He began working professionally as a teenager and eventually worked with Fletcher Henderson, Tiny Bradshaw, and Teddy Hill. His most important work before Ellington was with the small John Kirby band, which had considerable popularity during the 1930s and 1940s for crisply played, tight arrangements. With Ellington he became a mainstay of the saxophone section and did a good deal of soloing, mainly on alto saxophone, his principal instrument, but also on clarinet.

Two months after Toby left, Tricky Sam Nanton died. He had left the band late in 1945, apparently suffering from a stroke, but recovered enough to return. On July 21, 1946, he died in his hotel in San Francisco. "The fatal hemorrhage, which apparently came while Tricky Sam slept, ended the suffering that for long, frequent intervals during the past year had kept the great trombonist from his chair," the Down Beat obituary said.[18]

In a certain sense the loss of Tricky Sam was the most damaging of all. So many of Ellington's classic pieces, reaching from "East St. Louis Toodle-Oo" to "Ko-Ko," were dependent upon Nanton's plunger work for their effectiveness. Over the remainder of the life of the band, Ellington used several trombonists in Tricky Sam's spot, the best of whom were probably Tyree Glenn and Quentin Jackson, who I think came the closest to Nanton, but none of them were really able to get that haunting human sound that Nanton had made his own. Tricky Sam Nanton turned out to be irreplaceable.

The situation with the band's vocalists was even more chaotic than that with the instrumentalists. At the beginning of 1940 Ellington brought in a man who had made some reputation among blacks playing heroes in black western movies. His name was Herb Jeffries, and he was known as "the Bronze Buckaroo" in his movie publicity releases. Jeffries was not a jazz singer, but one of those vocalists with formal voices, trained to at least a degree, whom Ellington preferred. When he came into the band, he sang with a high, light tenor that had been in vogue in the 1920s but that had been replaced in fashion with the more masculine baritone voices of Bing Crosby and Ray Eberle. One day backstage between shows, Jeffries was doing imitations of other popular singers for the amusement of the musicians. When he got to Bing Crosby, Strayhorn and some of the others were instantly struck by the sound he got. "That's it," Strayhorn said. "Don't go any further. Just stay with Bing."[19] A comparison of an early Jeffries number with Ellington, "You, You Darling," an execrable song with a fine bit from Ben Webster, with "There Shall Be No Night," made a few months later, bears the story out. Jeffries does not sing particularly lower in the second number, but his voice is richer, mellower, and the resemblance to Crosby, "the old groaner," is clear. By the time of "Flamingo," which was a hit for Jeffries, he was singing in a distinctly deeper voice.

Jeffries was followed briefly by a now-forgotten singer, Jimmy Britton, and then by Al Hibbler, who had a long stay with the band. Hibbler was blind. He had auditioned for Duke as early as 1935, but he did not join the band then. He sang thereafter with a number of bands and was free-lancing around New York when Ellington decided to give him a second try. According to Hibbler, during the long stay at the Hurricane Club in 1943, he came in one night and sang, and the audience would not let him off until he had sung five or six tunes. Night after night Hibbler returned to the club, and Duke would call him up to sing. However, nothing was said about whether he had passed the audition. Finally, Hibbler approached Ellington and said, "Duke, I can't keep coming down here doing . . . this every night." Duke responded, "Go get your money, you've been in the band for two weeks."[20] Hibbler stayed with the band into 1951, for a period of eight and a half years, and became an established vocalist of the period.

Like Jeffries, Hibbler was not really a jazz singer. According to Leonard Feather, "much of Hibbler's popularity was achieved by the use of grotesque distortions, described by Duke Ellington as 'tonal pantomime' and valid more as entertainment than as jazz or pop singing."[21]

The male vocalists at least came one at a time. The females came in bunches. By 1942 Ivie Anderson was beginning to suffer badly from asthma, and it was clear that she could not be expected to do all, or much, of the singing. Sometime during that summer, when the band was in Chicago, Ivie and Billy Strayhorn went around the Chicago clubs looking for a replacement. They found Betty Roche, an experienced singer then in her thirties. Ellington hired her and began using her at army bases as the band went west. When they reached the West Coast, she called her parents. "I'm in Los Angeles singing with Duke," she told them. Her mother responded, "Betty, you're lying."[22] She stayed with the band for most of the 1940s until she got tired of traveling, left, and returned for a brief stay in the early 1950s.

At just about the same time Ellington also took on a pretty seventeen-year-old from Detroit named Joya Sherrill, whom he had first heard when she was fifteen. Joya's father had a master's degree in journalism from Northwestern University and was something of a figure among blacks in Detroit, where he was active in the fight for black rights. Joya was raised not to drink or smoke, and her middle-class parents refused to let her join the Ellington band. Eventually a deal was made by which Joya's mother traveled with the band as chaperon for her daughter, an odd arrangement to say the least. But she was young and inexperienced, and this stay lasted for only four months. Joya rejoined the band in 1944 and almost immediately had a hit with "I'm Beginning to See the Light."

But two singers were not enough. Eventually, Duke added a woman named Marie Ellington, no relation of his, who had a deep voice and in time married Nat "King" Cole, one of the most popular entertainers of the period. She actually did very little singing with the band and, frustrated, tried out for a Broadway show. This display of disloyalty angered Duke, and he fired her.

Yet one more singer was Kay Davis, another middle-class girl, whose father was a chiropractor in Bushnell, Illinois. She had formal vocal training, and although she was in the band for several years, Duke used her mainly on special occasions to sing concert pieces and occasional spirituals or to take the wordless obbligato part created by Adelaide Hall for "Creole Love Call." There were others who came and went: Wini Johnson, Rosita Davis, and Marie Bryant, who was with the band for *Jump for Joy*. At times Duke even had Joya Sherrill, Marie Ellington, and Kay Davis sing as a trio.

Of all the female singers with Ellington during the 1940s and 1950s, it is generally agreed that the best from the standpoint of jazz was Joya Sherrill. Kay Davis was essentially a recital singer; Betty Roche was a competent band singer but her stay with the band coincided with the recording ban, so it is hard to make a firm judgment about her work. The others were not with the band long enough to make a mark. Joya had a pleasant voice, her intonation was not bad, and, while no hard swinger, she had a semblance of feeling for jazz rhythms.

Ivie Anderson went back to Los Angeles in the summer of 1942, where she opened a chicken shack and was involved in other businesses. She continued to sing occasionally and even made a few records as late as 1946. Unhappily, she died in 1949, only in her forties.

By the mid-1940s, then, after so many years of stability, the band's personnel was in turmoil. Changes occurred monthly. People came, left, returned, left again. Between 1942 and 1949 Ellington recorded with fifteen different trumpet players, and there were others, among them Dizzy Gillespie for a brief period, who were not with the band long enough to record. Even Charlie Parker considered joining the band. He wanted $500 a week to support his drug habit, however, and Ellington is reported to have told him, "Bird, for that kind of dough I'd work for you."

The war was part of the problem. Some players were drafted out of the band, and those who escaped the draft were in demand and frequently could command good salaries without having to travel in the confusion of wartime. But it is also clear that the old esprit de corps was gone. Previously, the musicians had taken pride in being "Ellingtonians": not merely members of an important musical group but key players on a championship team, who were as much responsible as the coach for making the team famous. Now they saw themselves as working musicians, no doubt honored to be asked to join one of the greatest jazz bands of the time, but nonetheless hired hands who would leave when there was a better opportunity elsewhere.

The jazz press, and many jazz fans, felt that the band was collapsing—the roof leaking, the walls beginning to sag. In a 1944 review *Down Beat* said, "This is still the finest band in the country, make no mistake . . . ,"[23] the implication being that some people had begun to think that it no longer was. Two years later, in a review of a concert, the paper was saying, "It seemed almost as though Ellington had gone a shade stale, that the star instrumentalists were too obvious of their greatness, and a bit tired of it all. . . ."[24] By June of that year Bill Gottlieb was detailing the case against the band, citing too many ballads and too many changes of personnel as the major problems.

But no band could lose Cootie Williams, Joe Nanton, Ben Webster, Jimmy Blanton, Rex Stewart, and Barney Bigard without suffering for it. They were among the finest jazz musicians of their time, and they possessed the sort of individual voices that had been essential to the Ellington sound.

The whole question of individual sound is a crucial one in jazz. One of the most significant qualities of the great players who emerged in the 1920s and 1930s was the possession of a sound, an approach to the notes that was so personal that even relatively inexperienced listeners quickly learned to tell Beiderbecke from Armstrong, Goodman from Noone. It was not just a question of the player's melodic conception—that is to say, whether he was busy, spare, tended to play rising or descending figures, improvised "off the chord changes" or worked from the original melody, and the like. The identity marks of a given player's "style," as the fans frequently termed it, were more a number of subtle elements that listeners sensed rather than analyzed: the razor edge to the front of Armstrong's notes as opposed to the half-tongued attack of Max Kaminsky; the fast terminal vibrato of a Cootie Williams as opposed to the slower vibrato of Bobby Hackett; the coarse tone of Coleman Hawkins against the lighter, silkier sound of Lester Young.

This individualism had to do in part with the fact that most of these earlier players were self-taught. They somehow acquired an instrument and without much instruction began trying this or that, their aim being to reproduce a sound that appealed to them—something they took from an admired older player or invented themselves. But there was more to it than that: in the early period it was part of the jazzman's code to find his own voice. Benny Morton told Stanley Dance, "You accumulate from the people you hear, and express something of your own. Copying in those days was taboo. You could be *influenced*—but you didn't copy. It was a time of real musical individualism in jazz."[25] If you were to be a jazz musician, you were to "tell your own story," as many musicians said. You did not aim for a sound, a concept, or an approach that was traditional or established by others, as symphonic musicians did, but played what *felt* personal to you; you made a thing that you liked, that you wanted to make because it pleased you. It did not matter what others thought.

This aesthetic principle was central to jazz playing of the earlier period, and it produced the Bubber Mileys, the Tricky Sams, the Jack Teagardens, the Pee Wee Russells, the Red Allens, the King Olivers, and another few dozen who sparkle on the diadem of the first half of the history of jazz. Louis Armstrong and Charlie Parker were able to change the shape of the music because they produced styles of playing so individual that they cleared new paths as they went. By the 1940s this was changing. For one thing, the world of jazz was becoming filled with musicians who had had a measure of formal training. In most cases it was not much more than what any player learns in his high school marching band. But this training, which the young player would begin to acquire in his early teens, when he was still a half-formed personality himself, would aim at a "legitimate" style—a certain sound, a certain vibrato, a certain attack and decay, which would be the same for everybody, not merely under one teacher but under teachers everywhere who themselves had studied the legitimate way of playing music.

This tendency was reinforced by the dominance of the big bands during the 1930s and 1940s. The jobs and the prestige were in the big bands, and what the bands needed was a lot of players who could read quickly and blend themselves into their sections. These bands needed, of course, a few good jazz improvisers, but, for the young player trying to break in, an ability to handle the band's book, not an individual approach to improvising, was essential. And so, by the mid-1940s, when Ellington was looking around for replacements, he did not find out there a Bubber, a Tricky Sam, a Barney Bigard, men who may not have been good readers, nor able to produce a legitimate sound on their instruments, but who could do something more important—that is, to tell their own stories persuasively. Their replacements were people like the trumpeter Taft Jordan, the trombonist Sandy Williams, the saxophonist Skippy Williams, coming by the dozens. All of them were skilled readers, excellent musicians, and good jazz improvisers, but none of them was the fiery individualist the early men had been.

Yet, even taking into account wartime problems and the dearth of individualists, Ellington made some odd choices. For example, why choose Sandy Williams and the trombonists who followed him, like Tyree Glenn and Quentin Jackson, first-rate professionals, when he might have taken Dickie Wells or Benny Morton, both more important players who were gigging around New York at the time? Similarly, why choose Harold Baker and Taft Jordan when Bill Coleman, Charlie Shavers, and even Roy Eldridge were playing casual gigs during portions of the 1940s?

In particular, Ellington's choice of singers was not merely odd but, according to many fans, unfortunate. None of them were, in any sense, jazz singers, and Hibbler's pompous, booming baritone, which might have been acceptable in a concert hall, made even devoted Ellington fans wince at times.

So far as the singers are concerned, it is clear enough that Ellington had a taste for trained voices of the kind that, typically, were heard at the concerts put on by the black musical organizations that were so important a part of the social life of middle- and upper-class blacks while Ellington was growing up. To Ellington, rich, mellifluous basses and full-throated mezzo-soprano voices were "classy," and I think that even Duke's best friends would admit that he had a weakness for what appeared to him to have "class." The English critic Max Jones noted that Duke could, at times, be guilty of "affectation,"[26] and an English biographer, Derek Jewell, spoke of "that element of snobbism in his character."[27] Jones and Jewell were hardly alone in this view. It is my sense, then, that Duke was drawn to these trained voices, even though he must have realized that this was certainly not what the swing fans and his jazz following wanted.

But that still does not explain why he was choosing the Shelton Hemphills and Quentin Jacksons over much better, and better-known, jazz musicians. To be sure, price undoubtedly entered into it; some of the men he may have wanted might have cost too much. But there is no evidence that he even attempted to get any of these musicians.

It is particularly interesting that Ellington strongly resisted using white musicians until much later, when it became impossible to put together a big jazz band without using at least some whites. Mixed bands were not quite as taboo in America as many jazz writers have led us to believe. The first of the famous riverboat bands consisted of a duet of the black pianist Fate Marable and the white violinist Emil Flindt, who wrote the hit song "The Waltz You Saved for Me." Willie "the Lion" Smith reported having seen mixed bands on boats on the Hudson River when he was a boy in the first years of the twentieth century. Benny Goodman had begun using blacks in his trios and quartets as early as 1935, and by the early 1940s, several white swing bands were employing blacks, mainly jazz stars like Roy Eldridge, on a regular basis. Duke, in fact, was occasionally forced to use whites as hasty substitutes—for example, the white bassist Bob Haggart on a May 14, 1945, recording session after Junior Raglin was drafted. There were around, in this period, many white jazz musicians who were better than some of the blacks Ellington chose—more imaginative improvisers with strong personal styles. Lee Wiley and Peggy Lee were certainly better jazz singers than Joya Sherrill and Kay Davis; the trombonists Bill Harris, Jack Teagarden, and Lou McGarity were superior to Sandy Williams and Tyree Glenn; the trumpeters Bobby Hackett and Billy Butterfield outshone Shelton Hemphill and Francis Williams. And there were many more. Some of these musicians might not have been available, of course, and there was always the matter of money, but the white musicians, by and large, admired the Ellington band extravagantly, and many of them would have been honored to get a call from Duke, especially the younger ones like Zoot Sims, Stan Getz, and Sonny Berman. But the call never came, because Ellington did not want whites in his orchestra. It is reasonable to guess that, despite Duke's refusal to take a public stand on racial matters and despite his itch for meeting powerful and celebrated whites, he recognized that whites had generally, after all, treated his people brutally and even as late as 1945 showed little inclination to stop. Why should he do anything for white people when they had done nothing for blacks except use them as workhorses and cheat them as frequently as possible?

Furthermore, Duke liked molding musicians himself, which would explain why he might take an inexperienced player rather than one who had formed a fixed style.

Yet, none of these reasons for such choices of personnel seems entirely convincing. The main difficulty, I think, was once again a matter of character. Duke Ellington was simply not given to careful, long-range planning. He was essentially a tactician, not a strategist. He did not plan his compositions before he came into the studio but let himself be guided on the spot by his instincts. He did not plan his personal relationships but interacted with whomever happened to be there. He did not anticipate problems but waited until they thrust themselves on him and then dealt with them however he could. Mercer said, "Pop believed in peace and tranquility. He didn't like bringing situations to a head; he didn't like making decisions, absolutely direct changes or definite cuts."[28] Cress Courtney said, "Ellington was a great bird-in-the-hand guy. You know, he'd see cash, that was it. He didn't want to know about what went on the day after tomorrow."[29] Among other things, Courtney said, Ellington would take cash on the barrel head rather than make a percentage arrangement that might have been far more profitable. Again, there is the famous story of the time when some of Duke's associates went to a great deal of trouble to pull together a few of his scores—in itself, a difficult job—and had them bound in a leather presentation volume. After the little ceremony Ellington, much to the annoyance of the people involved, did not even bother to take the volume home. He was simply not interested in preserving the past for the future. For Ellington everything was now. He never saved money, did not write a will, did not make any attempt to bring order into his business affairs. Astonishingly, even though he saw his concert pieces as central to his life's work, he never bothered to put together definitive scores that might be played by other orchestras. After his death Andrew Homzy, a musician and Ellington specialist, had an opportunity to go through a trunk full of Ellington manuscripts in Ruth Ellington's possession. He found bits and scraps and pieces that simply defied being put into order. That, apparently, was all Ellington left, aside from the torn and yellowing scores, themselves scrappy, that Mercer was using with the orchestra—and, apparently, no safety copies existed for these, either. The baritone saxophonist Bill Perkins once had a chance to play with Ellington with a band put together for a television show. He reported, "I thought, boy, I'm going to get to play those marvelous Harry Carney parts. Well, the fact is, there were no Harry Carney parts—they were all kept in Harry's head. We were all disappointed, at first, because we had 'It Don't Mean a Thing' and there was no chart for it."[30] One other saxophonist once saw some Ellington arrangements and related that it was nothing but "goose eggs," that is, rows of whole notes as vague reminders to the original player of what he was supposed to play. With Ellington it was always now—this woman, this dish of pie and ice cream, this audience, this check, this orchestra, this piece of music.

So, rather than think through the critical question of the makeup of the band and whom, specifically, he should get to replace the departing veterans, he would wait for the crisis to arrive and then reach out blindly for whoever happened to stumble in his way in order to smooth the path in front of himself as quickly as possible. He chose Betty Roche because she was the first vaguely acceptable singer he came across when he needed to replace Ivie Anderson; he chose Ray Nance because he was the first acceptable trumpet player he heard when he had to replace Cootie; he chose Chauncey Haughton because he was the first acceptable clarinet player he could get when he needed to find somebody for Bigard. It was all done by chance and in haste, and we can only regret it. Imagine what a band Ellington would have presented if he had carefully rebuilt it with such players as Charlie Shavers, Bobby Hackett, Benny Morton, Jack Teagarden, Wardell Gray, Lee Wiley, and many others, black and white. But that was not Ellington's way, and in time the effects would show.

19

Decline and Fall

Over the ten years from 1946, when the Duke Ellington orchestra swept the *Down Beat* polls, to the Newport Festival of 1956, its reputation gradually, but steadily, declined both with the general public and with the ardent jazz fans. So far as the general public was concerned, the big bands were dead and singers like Eddie Fisher and Patti Page were the stars, who would soon find themselves overshadowed by the rock and rollers.

For the jazz fans a new wind was blowing. Bebop, carved into shape by Dizzy Gillespie, Charlie Parker, and a few others during the hiatus in recording, had struck the jazz world like a pie in the face when the ban was over. By 1945 Parker and Gillespie were known, if controversial, figures in jazz; by 1948 the new people were beginning to win awards in the polls; and by about 1950 bebop was established as the way jazz would go. The older players, some of them still in their thirties, suddenly found themselves out of date. No longer were the young jazz musicians and their fans running after Benny Goodman, Roy Eldridge, Coleman Hawkins; they were old hat. In the 1950s jazz would have a new set of heroes: Miles Davis, Dave Brubeck, Clifford Brown, Sonny Rollins, and, of course, Gillespie and Parker.

By the late 1940s, then, Ellington was, to critics and jazz fans alike, a relic. In 1949 *Down Beat* said bluntly, "Isn't it about time the Ellington orchestra was disbanded before what's left of a great reputation is completely dragged in the muck?" It was, the writer Mike Levin continued, "a sloppy, disinterested band," and Ellington himself was perhaps "dispirited, wondering if he was written out." And, he concluded, "Ellington has made no really good records in the past three years. . . ."[1] As if to point up

Levin's attitude, the same issue of the paper called his recent cut of "Singin' in the Rain" "one of the worst records Ellington has made in recent years."[2]

A month later the paper carried a defense of Ellington by Charlie Barnet, who had modeled his group on Ellington's. Significantly, Barnet did not attempt to deny Levin's charges. "Singin' in the Rain" is "dreadful," he admitted, and "Ellington sounds tired and dispirited a lot of the time these days."[3] But Barnet insisted that the decline was caused by hard times in the band business.

Down Beat was in the habit of cooking up controversies of this kind to promote sales, and, in any case, the paper would have inevitably taken a sterner view of Ellington's failings than a lot of fans. Nonetheless, its attitude was representative of what jazz fans and the music business, in general, felt. Ellington was on the way down. Not the least of the problems was that the money, which had always been there, was no longer flowing in so easily. Duke had from the beginning spent as he liked on the assumption that somehow the bills would get paid. He lived high and supported a large entourage, which at times included a barber and assorted factotums, as well as the musicians. Now band fees were falling, and by 1949 Ellington admitted, "Our band is operating at a loss now."[4] Fortunately for him, by this time his income from his songs, particularly his ASCAP money, based on the long success of standards like "Sophisticated Lady," "Solitude," and "Mood Indigo," was substantial, and he could use this money to subsidize the band. But the days of the Pullman cars were over: the band traveled by bus. And no longer could it attract the higher-priced players. In 1947 Taft Jordan and Wilbur DeParis left the band. According to Down Beat, "the Duke asked the men to take a salary cut. Instead, DeParis and Jordan checked out."[5]

The glory days were done. The party, which had gone on for twenty years, was over. The one thing that remained was the growing acceptance of Ellington as an important composer, based on the by now steady, if somewhat haphazard, production of concert pieces. It was certainly this reputation as an artist that encouraged Ellington to keep the band going, despite everything. He had still not trained himself to compose on paper. If he was to continue to turn out concert pieces, he needed the orchestra to work with. So he kept it going, at a financial cost he probably never calculated himself.

The situation was not aided by a series of changes in his recording arrangements. His Victor contract expired in November 1946. He was fed up with the company, which he did not think had promoted him hard enough and which was demanding a lot of commercial material as well. He decided, then, to see if he could get more control of his records than he had had.

He turned to a small company called Musicraft, which had been founded in 1937 to issue records exploring neglected areas that the majors found unprofitable, such as Negro spirituals, folk music, and works from the Renaissance. Duke apparently felt that Musicraft would let him record more of his serious work than Victor had been interested in; it also appears that he was given some stock in the company, presumably as an inducement to come to the company, which no doubt saw getting a major popular entertainer under contract as a coup. But Musicraft began having financial difficulties, which would lead to bankruptcy in 1949, and after a few months Duke left.

He then decided he ought to own his own record company outright. In collaboration with Arthur Logan and Mayo "Ink" Williams, a black record producer, he founded a company called Sunrise. It, too, foundered. Mercer remarked, "There were too many amateurs involved, too many committee-like decisions taken."[6]

Ellington then signed with his old company Columbia. Both John Hammond and Count Basie were gone from the label, and Ellington presumably felt better about it. But hardly had he signed than a second recording ban was imposed, which ran through 1948. As a consequence, Ellington made no formal records between December 1947 and April 1949, aside from a handful of transcriptions and some V-discs that were exempt from the band. But by 1952 Ellington was dissatisfied with Columbia. In the spring of 1953 Down Beat reported that Duke was leaving the company to go to Capitol. "Ellington's contract with Columbia did not expire. He asked for his release and got it," the paper noted. And it quoted Ellington as saying, "I signed with Capitol because this firm is doing an excellent job of presenting all its artists, particularly as it concerns exploitation."[7] Capitol, founded in the early 1940s by a group including the songwriter Johnny Mercer, had quickly made itself into an important record company by aggressively going after major entertainers and just as aggressively promoting them.

It seems to me that this restless shifting from company to company was caused not by the failure of the companies to promote Duke's records but by his unwillingness to admit that he was no longer at the front of the pack. Yes, the concerts of the extended pieces were always well attended, but his popular audience was dwindling, now composed mainly of the old fans and a smaller group of young people who wanted to dance and did not much care what the music was like, so long as it was danceable. By the mid-1950s, when Ellington was back at Columbia once more, his records were selling seven to ten thousand copies apiece. Sales of this magnitude suggest that the fault did not lie with the record companies.

By 1950, then, things were worse than ever. The personnel continued to turn over at an alarming rate. Changes occurred from month to month, and rarely did two successive recording sessions use the same band. Then, around March 1951, came a blow as devastating as the departure of Cootie Williams ten years before. In one swoop, Sonny Greer, Al Sears, Johnny Hodges, and Lawrence Brown left to work in a band led by Hodges. The departure of Greer was not surprising. His drinking continued to be a problem, and he was also beginning to suffer from a difficulty with his legs that made it hard for him to play, especially at fast tempos. By 1950 Ellington was carrying a second drummer, Butch Ballard, to fill in for Greer as necessary. On one European trip there had been a bad quarrel, which had led Ellington to fire Greer, but they had patched it up.

Brown, too, had for some time been telling people he wanted to leave. He was by nature a complainer and was always carping about one thing or another, especially his salary. He and Duke had quarreled intermittently. We remember his telling Duke "You're a compiler."[8] Again according to Brown, when Tricky Sam died, Duke asked him to play the plunger parts but would not pay anything extra for the work. "I did it for a while and pretty soon I rebelled," Brown recalled. "So he says, 'You're fired.' "[9] On this occasion Brown left the band. He returned shortly and in fact sometimes played the plunger parts.

Hodges, too, felt somewhat dissatisfied, especially because Duke was making a lot of money on tunes that Hodges felt he had, in the main, written. There were, then, a number of raw spots rubbing sore. It cannot have helped that the band was being seen as in a decline and that money was becoming a problem. Moreover, the players must have recognized that the band was increasingly becoming an adjunct to Ellington's other ambitions— especially the composition of the longer pieces. The musicians were no longer stars in a joint enterprise but hired hands who would do what they were told. Hodges, in particular, knew that he was considered by critics and fans one of the finest musicians jazz had ever seen, and he must have felt that he ought to be more than a badly paid sideman in somebody else's band. Possibly, neither he nor any of the others would actually have left; but sometime early in 1951 Norman Granz proposed that he back a band led by Hodges, containing whoever of the Ellington men would come along.

Granz was a jazz entrepreneur who was having an enormous financial success with a sort of traveling jam session that he called Jazz at the Philharmonic. Critics have always complained that JATP, as it came to be known, offered a good deal more crowd-pleasing honking and screaming from the horns than good jazz, but the musicians liked working for Granz because he paid them well and treated them with respect. According to Derek Jewell, Granz said,

Sure, I pulled Johnny and the others out of the band. I'd been very close to him ever since 1941 when *Jump for Joy* was in Los Angeles and I was doing my first jam sessions out there. I'd used him on jam sessions, and from time to time after the war I'd presented Duke's band in concerts. I felt Johnny was kept down in the band. I wanted to record him outside of the Ellington context, and that's why he and the others came out. Harry Carney almost came too, but he was afraid to quit. . . .[10]

Granz, of course, was well aware of the dissatisfaction that was roiling the band, and he had little difficulty persuading Hodges to leave. However shocked Duke's fans were by the departures of these men, who had spent a total of something like a hundred years with the band, they were not indentured servants, and it was perfectly reasonable for Hodges, especially, to want to set himself up in his own business.

As it worked out, the Hodges band was never more than marginally successful. It had one hit tune by Al Sears called "Castle Rock," and it worked fairly regularly for a time. But it folded after some four years, and Hodges returned to Ellington. Brown would also return to Ellington, but for a while he worked for the CBS studio orchestra and did some free-lancing around New York.

Sonny Greer did not last long with the Hodges band. It was given out that his wife was ill and that he did not want to travel, but his health and his irresponsibility were certainly the real reasons for his leaving. To many jazz fans Greer was a legend, a figure from the enchanted early days of jazz, and he was able to get work. In the 1970s he played as a duet with the pianist Brooks Kerr, then a very young man who made a specialty of playing Ellington's works. But, basically, he was supported by Ellington, who kept him on the payroll right along.

Amid all these defections Ellington maintained his composure, as he invariably did, but he must have been badly jolted. It was going to appear to many people that the ship was going down and the sailors were leaping for the lifeboats. In order to stabilize the band and repolish his reputation, he had to do something.

Precisely who approached whom is not known, but, within days after the departure of Hodges and the others, it was arranged that Tizol would leave Harry James and return to Ellington. Perhaps more important, Tizol, presumably acting at Duke's behest, persuaded James's alto soloist, Willie Smith, and his drummer, Louis Bellson, to come along with him. Inevitably, the switch was called the Great James Robbery in the jazz press.

Willie Smith had been, through the 1930s, a star soloist with the Jimmie Lunceford orchestra and was considered by many to be almost on a level with Hodges. Bellson, who would be the first white to have a prominent role in the Ellington band, had played with a number of the best-known bands, including those of Benny Goodman and Tommy Dorsey, and was considered one of the finest big-band drummers in the business—a fiery performer with a fine technique. The Great James Robbery was a real coup for Duke. It showed the jazz world that the old master could still command the best talent when he wanted and that he was not going to let the band slip any further.

As it happened, neither Smith nor Bellson stayed with Ellington for very long. Smith went off to greener pastures in the fall of 1952. Not long thereafter, Bellson fell in love with the singer Pearl Bailey and, after a whirlwind courtship, married her and left Ellington to work with his wife. But Bellson, in particular, had an important effect on the band. For one thing, he badly dented Sonny Greer's reputation, for it was clear that Bellson could drive the band in a manner Greer had never been able to achieve, and he left people wondering what the band might have sounded like ten and twenty years earlier if it had had a first-rate jazz drummer pushing it. Greer's playing was unfocused—"slushy," to use Gene Lees's term. That is, the beat was demarked not like a gunshot but in a series of splashes. Bellson, on the other hand, was firing a gun. The beat was stated precisely and forcefully. Bellson was clearly in command, whereas Greer was not. Even a relatively inexperienced jazz student should be able to tell the difference with a little concentration.

Despite the brief tenures of Bellson and Willie Smith, Ellington was gradually able to bring some stability to the personnel through the 1950s. There would always be changes, but by the middle of the decade he had put together a core group that would shift only slowly. The trumpeters Cat Anderson and Clark Terry and the trombonist Quentin Jackson, who was filling the Nanton role, remained with the band through the decade. The older hands Jimmy Hamilton, Harry Carney, and Russell Procope stayed longer. Hodges returned in 1955 and remained until his death.

Of particular importance was the addition, in 1950, of the tenor saxophonist Paul Gonsalves, who would also remain with the band until his death, only days before Ellington's. After Webster, Ellington had tried two or three tenor saxophonists before settling down with Al Sears, who was with the band from 1943 until 1951, with a few brief absences. Sears had never been considered an important jazz musician before his tenure with Ellington. He was forceful, producing a gutty tone, but he had none of the inventiveness of a Hawkins or a Young, nor the sheer swing of Webster. But Sears left to go with the newly formed Hodges band in 1951, and Gonsalves replaced him.

Paul Gonsalves came from Pawtucket, Rhode Island, a member of an ethnic group that is indigenous to that area of Rhode Island and Massachusetts and that has its roots in a racially mixed people from the Cape Verde Islands, off Portugal. He started playing guitar as a boy, took up saxophone later, and gradually worked his way up in the music business, eventually playing with Count Basie and the short-lived Dizzy Gillespie big band. He was influenced by Coleman Hawkins, as were most of the tenor saxophonists of his time, but his principal model was Ben Webster. He eventually learned all of the major solos that Webster played with Ellington. His tone could be thick and guttural, after the manner of Webster and Hawkins, but he generally used a smoother sound that lacked some of the character of his mentors' tones. And he did not have the inventive genius of Hawkins. But he was a hard-driving player who could lift a band, just what Ellington needed at a time when the critics were accusing the band of lacking spirit and enthusiasm. Gonsalves always had enthusiasm, and through the last twenty-five years of the band's existence he was one of its principal soloists.

Unfortunately, Gonsalves was one more of the naughty boys who had always infested the orchestra. He was a drinker, and endless stories have been told about his falling off his chair during a performance. Once, in Japan, he literally fell face down on the stage while he was playing a solo and had to be carried off by stagehands. It was not just alcohol: Gonsalves had a classic addictive personality; he became hooked on heroin and may have experimented with other drugs, including LSD. Typical of such people, he was, when sober, very shy. He reminded Fran Hunter of Stan Laurel. But like a lot of people in the Ellington band right from the beginning, Gonsalves managed to drink and play—most of the time, at least. He was not, in the overall view, one of the great saxophonists in jazz; but in 1951, while the critics were shooting at Ellington from behind every bush, he was just what Duke needed. And it was Paul Gonsalves more than anyone else who suddenly, at a stroke, turned everything around.

Before that happened, though, the band reached what a lot of fans considered a nadir. In 1955 Duke was hired to play the "Aquacades," a water show regularly produced on the outskirts of New York City, which featured water ballets, fireworks, and the like and had little to do with jazz. Some of the musicians, among them Paul Gonsalves, could not play the date because they did not have appropriate union cards; a string section was added, another pianist substituted for Duke a good deal of the time, and a professional conductor led the band for most of the evening. It was the final indignity, and many of the band's fans felt it was now finished. The general attitude in the music business was summed up by *Down Beat*'s description of the band in its annual band directory in its April 18, 1956, issue: "Suave, polished, and internationally-known, Ellington continues to draw well, particularly on college dates and one-nighter locations where people still come out to hear music as well as to dance to it. The sounds and the arrangements have varied little over the years, and the Ellington personality continues to win admirers." And this was the band that the same paper a decade before believed to be the finest one in jazz history.

But the band was not yet dead. In 1954 a young jazz fan named George Wein, who played piano and was running a small Boston jazz club called Storyville, cooked up the idea of putting on a major festival of jazz, similar to the festivals of classical music that had been put on for some time at places like Tanglewood, in the Berkshire Mountains, and Robin Hood Dell, outside of Philadelphia. His backers in the scheme were the wealthy Louis Lorillards, who owned a huge "cottage" at Newport, Rhode Island, a town that had in the nineteenth century become a summer colony for the extremely rich of Boston and New York. The first Newport Jazz Festival commanded a good deal of media attention and was a great success. Ellington would play the Newport Jazz Festival many times.

One of those invitations came in 1956. Duke opened the final Saturday night concert with a short set at about 8:30 and then gave way to a series of programs by modernists of the time: Bud Shank, who was associated with the so-called West Coast school of jazz; Jimmy Giuffre and Friedrich Gulda from Austria, who belonged to the avant-garde of the day. The playing was cool and intellectual and, while interesting, did not stir the crowd to great enthusiasm. The concert was supposed to close at midnight, more or less, but the Chico Hamilton group, which preceded Ellington, did not take the stage until 11:15. By this time the Ellington men were growing annoyed at having to sit around for three hours, and Ellington was wrathful. "What are we—the animal act, the acrobats?" he snarled, in reference to the vaudeville practice of using a lesser act to close the bill as the audience was preparing to depart.[11]

In this state of mind, then, the Ellington band took the stage at 11:45 to play a piece especially pulled together for the occasion, The Newport Jazz Festival Suite. It could not have improved Duke's spirit that people were starting to leave. Duke began by thanking the musicians for the work they had done on the piece and gave them a little pep talk. They played the suite to a solid, if not uproarious, response and followed with a couple of standard works. Then Ellington turned to the band and called for "Diminuendo and Crescendo in Blue."

A number of different versions of what happened next have been given. They had not played the arrangement, which had been originally recorded in 1937, very frequently. In fact, according to one story, Gonsalves, who would be featured on the piece, could not remember what he was supposed to do. He was told not to worry. "It's just a blues in B♭ [actually D-flat],"

Ellington said. "I'll bring you in and I'll take you out. That's all you have to do. Just get out there and blow your tail off. You've done it before."[12]

The idea was that Gonsalves would play a solo with the rhythm section between the two arranged segments of the piece. Duke kicked the band off. Out of the audience's sight but near the stage, where the band could see him, Count Basie's great drummer Jo Jones was beating time with a roll of newspaper. According to George Avakian, who was recording the concert for Columbia, "no one will ever know for sure, but perhaps the Ellington band might never have generated that terrific beat if it weren't for Jo Jones, who had played drums that night with Teddy Wilson."[13] Some members of the audience denied that Jones had any role.[14]

The audience response to the opening section was enthusiastic but nothing like what was to come. At its close, Ellington played a piano solo to allow Gonsalves time to come down front. Gonsalves started blowing over the rhythm section. Audience reaction began to build. By the sixth chorus there were shouts and handclaps; within a couple of more choruses the crowd noise had grown to a continuous roar, and a large part of the audience was standing. Avakian said,

> At about the seventh chorus the tension, which had been building both on stage and in the audience since Duke kicked off the piece, suddenly broke. A platinum-blonde girl, in a black dress, began dancing in one of the boxes . . . and, a moment later, somebody started in another part of the audience.[15]

Leonard Feather, who reviewed the concert for Down Beat, did not mention the platinum blonde but said,

> Here and there in the reduced, but still multitudinous crowd, a couple got up and started jitterbugging. Within minutes, the whole of Freebody Park was transformed as if struck by a thunderbolt. Photographers rushed madly to the scene of each gathering knot of onlookers while Gonsalves, Duke, and the whole band, inspired by the reaction they had started, put their all into the work. He kept on rolling for twenty-seven choruses. Hundreds of spectators climbed up on their chairs to see the action; the band built the magnificent arrangement to its perennial peak and the crowd, spent, sat limply wondering what could follow this.[16]

Avakian added, "Halfway through Paul's solo, it had become an enormous single, living organism, reacting in waves like huge ripples to the music played before it."[17]

At some point the promoter George Wein, fearful that the crowd was about to riot, asked Duke to stop the performance, but "once aboard the victory train with the crowd behind him, Duke wouldn't stop."[18] He called for two quieter tunes, "I Got It Bad" and "Jeep's Blues." That was still not enough, so Ray Nance did his special song and dance on "Tulip or Turnip," after which Wein once again asked Duke to stop. Duke responded by calling for "Skin Deep," another roaring number featuring the drummer Louis Bellson, and, finally, after something like ninety minutes on the stand, he quit.

What mattered most of all was the roughly six and a half minutes when Paul Gonsalves stood out front, blowing. Gonsalves was not one of the premier saxophonists in jazz, and this long solo was not a masterpiece of jazz improvisation. However, neither was it one of the screaming, frenetic solos that saxophonists used to whip up crowds at Jazz at the Philharmonic and similar concerts. It was solid jazz, blazing hot; and it says something exceedingly important about the music that, after a long evening of cerebration by the modernists, after the elaborate sculpture of Ellington's suite, four men went out and played the blues for six minutes and blew the joint away. This was an audience not of stoned-out hippies or beer-sodden bikers but of people drawn largely from the American middle class: college students, garage mechanics, doctors, housewives, and a sprinkling of the very wealthy of Newport, who happened to be jazz fans. They were shaken by the music, and those who were there would never forget it. Over the years there have been certain events in jazz that any fan would give an arm to have been present at: the Original Dixieland Jazz Band's opening at Reisenweber's; the first-ever jazz concert at the Chicago Coliseum in 1926, when the bands of King Oliver, Clarence Williams, and Bennie Moten and the Louis Armstrong Hot Five all played; the famous concert at Massey Hall, in Toronto, with Charlie Parker, Dizzy Gillespie, Charlie Mingus, Max Roach, and Bud Powell in 1953; Benny Goodman's opening at the Palomar, in Los Angeles, in 1935, which triggered the swing band boom. The midnight hour at Freebody Park, in Newport, on July 7, 1956, was another such moment.

Certainly, those who were there felt they had been part of a historic experience. Leonard Feather began his *Down Beat* story by saying, "The final night of the 1956 American Jazz Festival will not soon be forgotten by those who were smart enough to stay until the end. . . ."[19] Avakian wrote, "Within an hour, reporters and critics were buzzing about it. By the next morning, it was generally conceded to have been one of the most exciting performances any of them ever heard."[20] These were people who had heard a great deal of jazz in their lives. Rapidly, the word went out from Newport: Duke Ellington was back. And within weeks Ellington's picture was on the cover of *Time*. The record of the Newport concert sold in the hundreds of thousands and became Ellington's biggest seller.

This leaves the question of how valuable the music was in the long period from the end of the first recording ban to the 1956 Newport Jazz Festival. I will set aside for now the question of Ellington's extended pieces, which he considered the crux of his work from this time.

The period began well enough, despite the loss of Cootie and the others. "The Unbooted Character," based on a good riff, has long solos by Lawrence Brown and Jimmy Hamilton; it concludes with a conversation between Taft Jordan using a straight mute and Shorty Baker the plunger, a classic instance of Ellington's employment of contrasting tonal colors to excellent effect. "Gathering in a Clearing" was meant to suggest the groups of black slaves who would meet clandestinely in the evenings and on Sundays to learn to read from one among them who could, the theory being that salvation for blacks would come through education. The interesting main theme, which Al Sears claimed was his, is played by Hodges, and there is excellent plunger work by Cat Anderson. "Suddenly It Jumped" is a hard swinger that does indeed jump. It includes a fine solo by Taft Jordan and an ending filled with that contrapuntal disarray that Ellington so loved: the saxophones have one figure, the trombones another, and the trumpets a third, and first one and then two trumpets are turned loose to blow skyrockets in the upper register over the turmoil. It is exciting, driving stuff, in spirit resembling the all-out final choruses customary in the New Orleans or Dixieland style, from which Ellington drew so much.

Another piece from this period that the band continued to play was "Transblucency," subtitled "A Blue Fog You Can Almost See Through," a typical example of Ellington's use of a vision as a starting point. It consists of a theme adapted from Lawrence Brown's solo from "Blue Light" and is played by a band comprising Brown, Ellington, Oscar Pettiford on bass, Jimmy Hamilton, and one other reed. The main point, however, is the wordless vocal by Kay Davis, which she sings in duet with Hamilton. Patricia Willard, who was associated with the band at one stage, points out that Davis frequently sang ordinary vocals with the band on location, but, for reasons nobody understands, on records she was almost always confined to wordless vocal or concert pieces. It is too bad, because she had a good voice, a nice sense of time, and was a generally better all-around singer than many of the others Duke employed. "Transblucency" was first performed at the 1946 Carnegie Hall concert, where Duke sprang it on the musicians while they were onstage, something he liked doing from time to time.

"Magenta Haze" is another of those pieces that drift slowly from beginning to end, like "Warm Valley." The tune is built around a major seventh, as are many of Duke's pieces of this kind, and is a feature for Hodges, who solos for most of its length.

And there are more: "Primpin' for the Prom," which has some nicely voiced passages for saxophone; "Air Conditioned Jungle," which employs a lot of even eighth notes and is therefore a step removed from jazz but shows off Hamilton's virtuosity; "Brown Betty," with good plunger work by Nelson Williams, one of the trumpet players who passed through the orchestra. Another is the curious "Pretty and the Wolf," a recitation by Ellington of the story of an innocent girl who comes to the city but, instead of being fleeced by the wolf, skins him instead. The music was worked out by Jimmy Hamilton and is played by him. I do not have a high opinion of Ellington's literary abilities, but I find "Pretty and the Wolf" to be oddly effective, because it is a simple story, simply told—cute, of course, but unpretentious.

A curious footnote to this period was a tour made with the guitarist Django Reinhardt, at the time the most respected of European jazz musicians. It was Reinhardt's only visit to the United States, and the sole opportunity for many American jazz fans to hear him. The tour went through the Midwest through most of November, ending with concerts at Carnegie Hall. It was a success, but Django played as a soloist, with rhythm support, and many in the audiences were disappointed at not seeing the guitarist work with Ellington's famous soloists. Unhappily, no records were made of Reinhardt either with or without Ellington men, but recordings of concerts show Django in typical form, accompanied by one of the greatest bassists of the day, Oscar Pettiford, who was with Ellington at that moment.

In any case, despite the many excellent pieces put together by Ellington over this long period, they came farther and farther apart, mixed with an increasing number of shabby swingers and second-rate pop tunes: "Joog Joog," a terrible novelty dance number; "The Blues," an attempt to cash in on the burgeoning rhythm-and-blues market, with Jimmy Grissom singing over a shuffle beat; "Boogie Bop Blues," a misguided attempt to play big-band bop along the lines of the Gillespie band; and all those pop tunes, among them those that Ellington and John Latouche had written for *Beggar's Holiday*. Ellington's music for "Take Love Easy" and "Brown Penny" is pedestrian, and Latouche's lyrics are awful, to wit: "Take love easy, easy, easy; never let your feelings show / Make it breezy, breezy, breezy, easy come and easy go."

Ellington must be forgiven his attempts to find hit songs, which he needed to bring in the money necessary to make the whole machine go. Furthermore, nobody can be expected to turn out one masterpiece after another. Periods of letdown are inevitable in any artistic career.

Nonetheless, it seems to me that this was more than just a fallow period. For one thing, the orchestra as a whole simply does not have the vitality and vibrancy it had during earlier periods. In part, this had to do with the inevitable staleness that comes from playing the same kind of music— indeed, the same music—for years at a stretch. In part, it had to do with the replacement of too many of the great individual voices with accomplished but lesser people. In part, it had to do with the enlargement of the band, especially the brass section, with a consequent loss of lightness and ease. In part, it had to do with the dispiriting effect of changes in the American taste, changes that not only presented Ellington with serious and wearing financial problems but also edged him farther and farther out of the limelight and into the shadows. But beyond all, I think Ellington was making some bad artistic decisions. This point, however, I will hold for the moment.

20

The Last Band

The wave of enthusiasm for Ellington that followed the Newport success did not immediately ebb. "Duke Ellington and his orchestra, riding high since their triumph at the American Jazz festival, have been booked back into Birdland for two weeks, opening November 5th," *Down Beat* said.[1] Ellington was on the cover of the August 20 issue of *Time*, whose story said, in part, "The event last month marked not only the turning point of the concert, it confirmed a turning point in a career. . . . People turned back at the exits; snoozers woke up. All at once, a new excitement revived the dying evening. . . . One young woman broke loose from her escort and rioted solo around the field."[2]

Actually, there had been some feeling before the Newport concert that the Ellington band was reviving. Back in January *Time* had run a short piece entitled "The Duke Rides Again," which said that the band was practically "reborn" and credited a new drummer, Sam Woodyard, for infusing the band with some of the old spirit.[3] There had been a story in *Saturday Review* in May and one in the August issue of *Coronet*, which had been scheduled before the Newport concert. But it was the Newport concert that "confirmed," as *Time* put it, that the Ellington band was once again in the middle of the American mainstream.

This sudden success was a big financial help, but it did not solve all the problems. Ellington had signed with Columbia yet again shortly before the Newport concert and would work there with Irving Townsend, who was sympathetic to Ellington's serious ambitions and proved willing to let Duke record some of his extended pieces. But there were still difficulties. The big cabarets, where the band could sit down for weeks at a stretch, were disappearing, and so were the theaters, which had provided shorter respites. The band was now playing mostly one-nighters—college dances, special affairs, even wedding receptions. According to estimates made by *Time*, the Glaser office was finding about $500,000 to $700,000 worth of bookings a year for the band. The musicians were being paid from $300 to $600 a week, a substantial wage for the time, especially considering they were virtually guaranteed full employment. Ellington was supporting not only some eighteen or twenty musicians but bandboys, managers, public relations people, the barber, and an uncounted number of strays like Sonny Greer as well. According to Ruth, he had a chauffeur running all over New York delivering money to people with whom he had, or had had, some relationship. The annual bill for wages could not have been less than $500,000, and to that had to be added the cost of carting this huge organization all over the country and, eventually, the world, often by airplane. Ellington was forced to pour his ASCAP money, royalties from songs and records, into the orchestra, and he was always running one jump ahead of the bill collector. Stanley Dance one morning found Duke awake at eight o'clock, absurdly early for him, scratching out figures on a piece of paper. He explained to Dance, "I'm trying to see where we can get some money to pay the bus company."[4] The problem was not that there was no money coming in; one way or another he was unquestionably taking in a million dollars a year. It was just that he spent, as he always had, profligately.

But, on the whole, things were improving. For one thing, the personnel began to stabilize. There were still the usual comings and goings, but a lot fewer of them. In part, this was due to the return of some of the old hands. Hodges came back in 1955; Tizol and Lawrence Brown, in 1960. Tizol's stay was brief; he simply got disgusted with the music business and left. But Brown stayed until 1970, when he, too, got tired of it all. "I lost all feeling for music," he said. "I just don't care to play anything."[5]

Cootie Williams also returned. By the 1960s he had fallen on hard times. He had become musical director for an act and was not playing the trumpet very much. Mercer Ellington, who had become the band's road manager, was conscious of Cootie's situation and wanted him back, but he was aware that the rapprochement would have to be handled with discretion. "I knew that pride would prevent either one from approaching the other. For Cootie, it would have been like giving in and begging for his old job back."[6] Mercer engineered Cootie's return, getting him to sit in on a record date and then asking him to continue for the next engagement. "He kind of faded back into the outfit," Mercer said.[7]

The return of Williams, Hodges, and Brown restored some of the tone colors that had been central to Ellington's sound of the great days. Moreover, the saxophone section, consisting of Hodges, Hamilton, Carney, Gonsalves, and Procope, remained unchanged from 1955 until 1968, when Hamilton retired to live in the Virgin Islands and was replaced by Harold Ashby.

The trombone section, too, saw a period of stability starting in 1962, when it was made up of Brown and two younger men, Buster Cooper and Chuck Connors.

The worst problems were with the trumpet section, as they had frequently been. Between 1960 and Ellington's death, in 1974, twenty-two trumpet players worked in the band, in addition to a large number of temporary substitutes who came into the band for a date or two. Matters were worse than even this suggests, because many of those twenty-two shuffled in and out, leaving for vacations or over some real or fancied slight or were simply tired of the road—only to return when the problem faded and they needed a job.

The most important of the newcomers, it is generally believed, was the drummer Sam Woodyard. Born in 1925, Woodyard was primarily self-taught, as most of the older men had been. He had not had much big-band experience when Ellington brought him into the band. He was not a subtle drummer, nor did he have the technical skills that Bellson possessed; but he was steady, tended to play simple, driving figures, and worked hard at pushing the band. His presence made the band more forceful than it might have been with another drummer. Ellington thought him one of the best drummers the band had ever had, and some of the band's fans considered him important in improving the music during this period.

Along with such gains, there were always problems. Duke's bent for replacing naughty boys with other naughty boys kept the band filled with fractious personalities. In 1961, while the band was working one of the lucrative gambling casinos in Las Vegas, Ray Nance and Paul Gonsalves were arrested for possession of marijuana. At that time the offense was taken much more seriously than it is today. Gonsalves was let off on probation, but Nance claimed that the arrest was due to racism, made a fuss, and was given a jail sentence. As a consequence, the people who controlled the Las Vegas casinos blacklisted Duke, and the band did not play there for two years, until Cress Courtney got somebody to intercede with the powers there.[8]

Then, in 1964, the band manager, Al Celley, gave up a fight against failing eyesight and quit. Duke prevailed upon Mercer to come in as road manager and occasional trumpet player. Mercer was determined to be tough with the men. He wanted to clean out the worst of the drug users; he wanted the men to come onto the bandstand on time. He wanted, in general, to see that things ran in an orderly fashion: "I soon began to get into a psychological battle with the seniors in the band. Here I was in a position where I had to overlord people who had led me by the hand to the movies, who had taken me out to the circus, who had bought me candy apples or gone swimming with me."[9] Mercer had to fight not only the old hands but also Duke, who was always inclined to be lenient and put up with the antics of his schoolboys rather than make a fuss.

One of the biggest problems facing Mercer—and Duke—was another one of those switches in popular taste that have been characteristic of the United States. By the early 1960s rock and roll was pushing everything else aside, and by the last years of the decade it was dominating everywhere. New York City, which at times had had twenty-five jazz clubs at once, was down to six, and many writers were saying that jazz was finally dead.

A partial solution to the problem was an increasing demand for the band abroad. As I have said, the jazz audience in Europe before World War II was tiny and smaller than even that elsewhere outside of the United States. But by 1950 that audience, fueled by a boom in New Orleans, or "trad," music, was growing rapidly.

Ellington, in particular, was seen as more than just a jazz musician, and he had, moreover, performed in Europe before. Now his managers began scheduling long foreign tours regularly: Japan in 1964, North Africa in 1966, Latin America in 1968, Eastern Europe in 1969, both Russia and Latin America again in 1971. These tours not only increased his international fame but also raised his prestige in the United States, where they generated a lot of publicity. Mercer said,

> Despite problems and occasional setbacks, dates began to improve and the band to strengthen. . . . I remember Billy Shaw, the agent, telling me, in the old days, that when two promoters asked for you on the same night, it was time for the price to go up. We couldn't accept all the work coming our way now, so it was time for the price to go up, and it did and everything began to work out well again.[10]

But if there were gains, there were losses as well. The most serious of these was the death of Billy Strayhorn. Precisely when Strayhorn was diagnosed as having cancer, I have not been able to discover, but he went into the hospital to have his first operation for the disease about mid-September 1965. There was, at first, some expectation that he would conquer the disease, but he rapidly worsened and, in the spring of 1967, was back in the hospital with cancer of the esophagus, eating pulped food through a tube and receiving chemotherapy. Duke was in Reno when he died. He remembered,

> It was early in the morning of May 31, 1967, when my sister, Ruth, called, crying, and told me Billy Strayhorn had just passed in the night.

I . . . don't know what I said, but after I hung up the phone I started sniffling and whimpering, crying, banging my head up against the wall, and talking to myself about the virtues of Billy Strayhorn.[11]

Strayhorn's influence on Duke Ellington was incalculable, but it was considerable, both personally and artistically. Somebody told Derek Jewell, "I think Duke was a much simpler character before he met Strays. You could even say he was sweeter. But he was so much more *interesting* once Strays happened along. Duke picked up some of his fine language from elegant sentences Billy used."[12]

There is, undoubtedly, some truth in this, although how much is difficult to say. Billy Strayhorn had a taste for literature and the arts and, intellectually, at least, was broader than Duke. Ellington, we must remember, had never been a particularly assiduous student in school. He never showed any special bent for intellectuality. Those long nights on trains or after the job he spent not reading books but either being in company or working at the piano. Music was what interested him and, really, only his own music. It is somewhat surprising that he never made an effort to study the whole tradition of Western music, which he was so keen to emulate and on which his own work was so heavily based.

Strayhorn, on the other hand, although he had never gone to college, liked to be around people of some cultivation, read more deeply than Ellington, and, furthermore, being lazy by temperament, had time to devote to concerts and art exhibitions. There were many things he could teach Duke.

Musically, of course, his presence was everywhere. Ellington said,

Any time I was in the throes of debate with myself, harmonically or melodically, I would turn to Billy Strayhorn. We would talk, and then the world would come into focus. The steady hand of his good judgment pointed to the clear way that was most fitting for us. He was not, as he was often referred to by many, my alter ego. Billy Strayhorn was my right arm, my left arm, all the eyes in the back of my head, my brainwaves in his head, and his in mine.[13]

This statement does not really suggest the full extent of Ellington's debt to Strayhorn. Ellington would not, I think, ever have taken a piece of material from somebody and use it unchanged. It would not have fitted his temperament to do so, and, besides, he had his own ideas about things. But nearly everybody connected with the Ellington orchestra agrees that Strayhorn supplied a great deal of music that went out under Duke's name. How much and which portions would be exceedingly difficult to determine.

But Strayhorn's influence may not have been entirely salutary. Ellington always evinced a tendency—weakness, if you will—toward lushness, prettiness, at the expense of the masculine leanness and strength of his best work, the most "jazzlike" pieces. Strayhorn encouraged this tendency. We remember that he originally attracted Duke's attention with "Lush Life" and "Something to Live For," both rather moody and overripe songs. His best-known works, compositions like "Chelsea Bridge," "Snibor," and "Charpoy," are thick textured and dense and are dependent for effect on their heavy harmonies rather than on the sheer sounds of plungers and growls and low-register reeds that had been characteristic of Duke's work in the early days. To be sure, Strayhorn wrote some very nice swingers, such as "Rain Check" and, of course, "Take the A Train," but in the main he was exploring a tropical rain forest thick with patches of purple orchids and heavy bunches of breadfruit. Duke's work increasingly moved in this direction. It was a question, then, of Strayhorn's reinforcing a bent that was already there, and we wonder how Duke's music might have gone if he had teamed up with a musical taste that counterbalanced this tendency—a Fletcher Henderson or a Fats Waller, let us say. But, given Duke's middle-class background and his penchant for the high style, he was inevitably drawn to somebody like Billy Strayhorn.

In discussing the influence of Strayhorn on Ellington, we must not lose sight of the fact that the basic conception for the whole body of his work came directly from Duke's viscera. Strayhorn may have contributed, may have shaded and colored Duke's taste, but at bottom it was Ellington who formed the music, and it went on after Strayhorn died.

Then, on May 11, 1970, Ellington suffered another personal and professional blow of the severest kind when Johnny Hodges suddenly died. He had been suffering from heart trouble for some time. He was visiting a dentist in New York, fell ill, and went to the bathroom. When he did not return, somebody went looking for him and found him, dead.

Hodges, with the arrogance that masked his shyness and his displays of contempt, could be difficult. As Barney Bigard once said, "It looked like it hurted him to laugh."[14] But the warmth of his sound, which seemed to be pure feeling poured as blood from the heart, and his enormous swing had made him beloved not merely by millions of jazz fans but by Ellington and the men in the band. Russell Procope said that he heard the news on his car radio and was forced to pull off the road to vomit. When the question of getting someone to replace Hodges was raised with Duke, he said flatly, "Johnny is not replaceable." He added, "Because of this great loss our band will never sound the same."[15] He was gone; but few jazz musicians left a nobler heritage.

During this period one more woman, the last significant one, came into Duke's life. He had continued for some twenty-five years to live as man and wife with Evie. However, Evie had become more and more reclusive and somewhat embittered, and Ellington had usually taken Ruth as his consort at official occasions and award ceremonies. There had been any number of affairs, mostly of very brief duration, but some of them longer lasting.

The new woman was Fernanda de Castro Monte, whom everyone came to call "the Countess," although she certainly possessed no title. She met Duke in about 1960 during one of his stays in Las Vegas when she was singing there. She was no ordinary club singer but a cultivated woman who spoke a number of languages and was at home in most of the major cities of Europe. She was also a handsome woman of about forty and altogether the sort who would appeal to Duke—worldly and knowledgeable about art, wine, food, and clothing. She could not have fit his ideal better if he had invented her.

The Countess began to change his taste away from the down-home American food, like the ham and eggs and the ice cream he had always liked, to caviar and escargots. She got him to dress in a more cosmopolitan, casual style, and to give up the somewhat flamboyant clothes he had always worn. She made herself useful in translating for him on foreign tours, seeing to ordinary arrangements of travel and the like, and in general acting as a kind of executive secretary for him. Most of the people around Duke respected Fernanda and have spoken well of her. Duke continued to see Evie in the apartment they kept together, but the Countess had become the principal woman in his life.

By the later half of the 1960s, when Duke was approaching seventy, he had become something of a grand old man of American music. The steady outpouring of his concert pieces, in particular, had marked him as a composer, and perhaps an important one, and he was seen everywhere as a distinguished artist. He was now being showered with awards, honors, degrees—fifteen honorary degrees (most of them coming in 1967 or later), the Presidential Medal of Freedom in 1969, keys to cities, Grammys, tributes, poll awards, and more.

However, it was an award he failed to get that gained him the most publicity. In 1965 the music committee for the Pulitzer Prize concluded that no composition worthy of the prize had been uncovered. They decided then to give Ellington a special award for "the vitality and originality of his total production." Unfortunately, the overseers who had to give the final approval turned the recommendation down. There was a considerable furor in the press, almost all of it sympathetic to Ellington, who responded by saying, "Fate is being kind to me. Fate doesn't want me to be famous too young." Two of the committee members resigned—Robert Eyer and the noted Winthrop Sargeant, who had written one of the earliest significant books on jazz, in which he spoke with admiration of Ellington's "astonishingly durable . . . sensitive orchestrations."[16] There may have been perfectly good reasons for denying Ellington the award, but, if so, they never came out, and the whole tenor of the reporting on the misadventure was that Ellington was a musical genius and that a mistake had been made. In fact, Ellington got a good deal more publicity out of the set-to than he would have gotten had he actually received the award.

The prestige that was by now accruing to Ellington made him an obvious subject for a biography of some sort. The Ulanov book was by now outdated, and some other books on Duke had been devoted primarily to his music. For many years Sam Vaughan, an editor at Doubleday and a jazz fan, had been asking Duke to write his autobiography. In the end, however, it was Vaughan's boss, Nelson Doubleday, who persuaded Ellington to do the book, and he did so by offering an advance of $50,000—far too much for a book of that kind. Inevitably, Duke spent the advance long before he had written very much, but by the 1970s he was making notes on scraps of paper, even on paper napkins. These were turned over to Stanley Dance, who was faced with the task of turning a mulch of miscellaneous notes into a coherent book. Dance, fortunately, had known Ellington well for years and had the background that would enable him to fill in the gaps. But given Duke's almost instinctive penchant to keep the central portion of himself private, the book was bound to disappoint readers who expected insights into the workings of Ellington's mind.

In any case, after the bad years before the 1956 Newport concert, Ellington was once again famous, more famous than he had been even in the great days of the Cotton Club. What can we say of the music from this period? For one thing, the suites and other concert pieces were taking ever more of his time, and his production of purely jazz pieces was correspondingly reduced. Then, too, he was still running a popular dance band, and he was forced to play a lot of material by other people—big popular tunes like "Moon River," "Days of Wine and Roses," "Chim Chim Cheree," and even a Beatles tune, "I Want to Hold Your Hand." He was also still forced to search for hits to help support what had now become a small industry. And by the late 1960s, when rock dominated popular music, he was finding it hard to get record companies to record him at all. In 1968, for example, he made a cut of the Second Sacred Concert and a set of tunes for Fantasy in February; a set with bass and vocalists for Tetco in June; and the Latin American Suite for Fantasy in November. That was all the formal recording he did that year.

This does not mean, however, that Ellington was not recording. For one thing, many hundreds of hours of his work were being recorded officially and unofficially at concerts, dances, and club appearances. For another, Ellington had more and more adopted the practice of bringing the band into recording studios at his own expense. The primary reason for doing this was to work over pieces he was in the process of composing, especially the extended works. These were as much rehearsals and composing sessions as formal recording dates. It was a very expensive way of doing business, obviously, but it was the method Ellington had always used. As a consequence, there exist today hundreds of hours of tape from these studio sessions, mostly uncataloged, almost none of it edited, and most of it never played. Yale University, which has always taken an interest in Ellington and which has an Ellington archive, hoped to get this material, but Mercer Ellington donated it to Danish Radio because, he said, he could not get an American radio station to promise to perform it regularly. (Mercer is married to a Danish woman and spends much of his time in Copenhagen.)

Yet, despite everything, during this period Duke did manage to record a good deal of excellent music. Two good sets of music were made during a brief stay with a new company, Bethlehem, and, in particular, during a fertile stretch in the early 1960s when he was recording for Columbia and working with Irving Townsend, who was sympathetic to his ambitions.

He was also, at this time, being recorded with various guest artists and fellow stars, including Louis Armstrong, Coleman Hawkins, John Coltrane, and vocalists like Theresa Brewer. The set with Hawkins, made with a small group including Hodges and Lawrence Brown, is especially good. Among the numbers is another of Ellington's portraits, this one of Hawkins. The melody is very pretty, if somewhat derivative, and Hawkins plays it with a melting tenderness.

Another excellent showcase for a guest is a version of UMMG (Upper Manhattan Medical Group, an institution Arthur Logan was involved with), featuring Dizzy Gillespie. Dizzy is in excellent form, and it seems clear that even established jazz musicians like Gillespie and Hawkins felt challenged to do their best in front of Duke.

The Bethlehem sets consist mainly of standards, both by Duke and by others. Paul Gonsalves, for example, plays a touching version of "Laura" in a breathy tone that is closer to Ben Webster's than is usual with Gonsalves. The Bethlehem sessions also produced "Lonesome Lullaby," one of those slightly melancholy, drifting pieces that Ellington had been writing since the beginning of the 1930s. The melody could not be simpler, a spare eight-measure line, which at one point Ellington has played by two trumpets, with minimal accompaniment. At a time when big bands were using eight or even ten brass, the employment of a trumpet duet was refreshing. In "Lonesome Lullaby" Duke again shows us what can be done with simplicity.

Similar in mood is "Paris Blues," written for a 1961 movie about a musician. The melody line is frequently nothing more than whole notes. The piece is twelve bars in length, as in a standard blues, but the chords and harmonies in general are far more sophisticated and dense—a movement to the augmented dominant in the second bar, for example, hardly typical of the blues. The melody is basic, frequently nothing more than whole notes drifting past. It is a wonderfully evocative piece of music.

Of the records made during this period, one of the most highly regarded has always been *And His Mother Called Him Bill*, a group of Strayhorn tunes that Ellington cut three months after Billy's death. The set includes some of Strayhorn's best-known numbers, like "Rain Check" and "Day Dream," but perhaps one of the most moving of them, when we know the circumstances, is "Blood Count." It is the last piece Strayhorn wrote, as he lay dying of cancer. It is a feature for Hodges played at virtually a stand-still, with typical dense harmonies. At its center is a haunting little six-teenth-note figure, which, in view of what Strayhorn was facing, is heart-breaking; and Hodges plays it in a way that makes it so.

This later Ellington band was capable of producing excellent music but does not really stand up to the early groups. For one thing, the orchestra was forced to play many of the old favorites again and again to please the public, and it inevitably sounded tired at times. For another, by the mid-1960s some of these men were tired, sometimes ill, and bored. The endless travel, the missed meals, and, for some of them, the dependence on alcohol and drugs exacted a real price. These were not young men exhilarated by their first successes: by the end of the sixties many of them had reached retirement age.

Their ranks included, however, some master jazz musicians, and at its peak the band was a hard-driving jazz band that could stand up to any competition, as it did at the famous Newport concert. And Ellington was still capable, when he wanted to, of turning out wonderful little pieces like "Lonesome Lullaby," the portrait of Coleman Hawkins, and others. For many of the younger Ellington fans whom Duke acquired in these later years, this, and not the bands of "Black and Tan Fantasy" and "Ko-Ko," was the Duke Ellington band.

21

The Concert Pieces

Duke Ellington wrote approximately thirty-three extended pieces intended for concert performance rather than for a dance or cabaret show, depending on whether you count such items as the three arrangements of W. C. Handy tunes that Ellington thought of as a group and the so-called *Tonal Group*, consisting of "Rhapsoditti," "Fugueaditti," and "Jam-a-ditty"; brief, hastily pulled together items like *La Scala* and *Non-Violent Integration*; and his version of *The Nutcracker Suite*. He also wrote music for films, the number once again depending on whether you count movies like *Black and Tan Fantasy*, which did not contain much original music; and some theater pieces, including *Jump for Joy, Beggar's Opera, My People*, and *Pousse Cafe*. Most of this movie and show music took the form of pop songs or jazz pieces, but some of it, from movies like *Anatomy of a Murder* and *Paris Blues*, can be classified with what Duke considered his more serious work.

If we include the marginal items, the concert pieces constitute about sixteen hours of recorded music. Adding to this the more serious work from the movies and shows, we have a total of somewhere between twenty-five and thirty long-playing records. This is a respectable body of work for a composer, the equivalent, let us say, of two dozen symphonies or ten operas. However, it is only a fraction of the total of Ellington's work. It has been estimated by Erik Wiedemann, a Danish authority on the subject, that Ellington created about twelve hundred compositions, many of which were recorded in several, often quite different versions. At a very rough estimate, Ellington's finished compositions—if any of them were ever finished—amount to perhaps one hundred and fifty hours of music, of which the concert pieces make up about 15 percent.

The concert pieces share at least four different characteristics. First, they always include both purely jazz passages and elements drawn from elsewhere. Second, they invariably are meant to illustrate a mood, describe a place, depict literary or historical events, or make a statement of some kind or other. They are, in this sense, program music. Although the programs were important to Ellington, he was frequently not very careful in working them out, and we often find it hard to recognize in the music what it is supposed to be depicting. Third, as Jules Rowell says in his descriptive analysis of the bulk of the pieces, "Ellington's concert works are essentially outgrowths of 8-, 12-, and 16-bar blues patterns and song form (e.g., ABA, AABA, and ABAC). Development is achieved through expansion of basic formal cell units in elaborate settings for improvisation and by transitional elements. This is as true of Duke in 1931 as in 1972."[1] That is to say, Ellington was not inventing novel forms, nor was he employing the irregular structures, with melodies that ran on without looping back at regular intervals, that were characteristic of the composers of the late nineteenth and early twentieth centuries. The music generally grew out of the popular song form that was his stock-in-trade from the beginning. Fourth, the bulk of these pieces are not "through composed"; rather, they are "suites" made up of independent and often quite differing pieces, which have been organized for contrast rather than to form some kind of unified whole built on similar themes or common principles of some sort. Creole Rhapsody, Reminiscing in Tempo, and Black, Brown, and Beige were through composed, in that Duke attempted to tie them together by reiterated themes; but thereafter virtually all of Ellington's work in longer forms is unified primarily by the program it is set to.

A good many of these long pieces do not warrant extended discussion. Some of them, like Non-Violent Integration and La Scala, She Too Pretty to Be Blue, are short, scrappy pieces, cooked up by Ellington virtually in rehearsal, and cannot stand much scrutiny. Others, like Tonal Group and The Beautiful Indians, are really short jazz pieces that Ellington grouped on very slim musical grounds. I will discuss, therefore, only those that seem to me to have been given more thought and are better worked out.

Black, Brown, and Beige, we remember, was given bad reviews by the regular newspaper critics, who called it "a gaudy potpourri," "pretentious," and similar things. Ellington was very disturbed by the criticism, but he was determined to fight it off, and he immediately returned to the same theme, his own racial heritage. A black writer named Roi Ottley had recently published a book detailing the black's past in America, and his expectations of a better future, which he called New World a-Comin'. Within months of the premiere of Black, Brown, and Beige, Duke began to work on a new piece inspired by Ottley's vision. "I visualized this new world as a place in the distant future where there would be no war, no greed, no categorization, no nonbelievers, where love was unconditional, and no pronoun was good enough for God."[2] The piece was given its premiere on December 11, 1943, in Carnegie Hall. It was essentially a piano concerto, with Ellington improvising a certain amount of the piano part. The recording ban was on at the time, and the piece could not be issued. Later it was rescored for symphony orchestra and performed by the NBC Symphony and other orchestras. Ellington continued to play versions of the work throughout his career.

Unfortunately, the idea of a brave new world in the offing led Ellington into a good deal of portentous writing. Much of New World a-Comin' sounds as if it were movie music designed to accompany the covered wagons as they at last roll into the lush California valley where the brave pioneers will build their new lives, after the long trek westward. There are jazzlike sections with Latin rhythms; but the bulk of the piece has the manner of a Chopin piano concerto, without any of the substance. In New World a-Comin' Ellington had allowed himself to stray a long way from his musical home into a world he did not understand, and it shows.

In the piece that received its premiere a year later, also at Carnegie Hall, Ellington stayed closer to home, and the result was better. Called The Perfume Suite, it comprised four brief sections intended to "capture the character usually taken on by a woman who wears different . . . blends of perfume," as Ellington told his audience. The four sections—really individual pieces—are supposed to represent four moods: love, violence, naïveté, and sophistication. The "naive" section, as Jules Rowell has pointed out, is a reworking of "Pitter Panther Patter," a piano-bass duet Ellington had worked out with Jimmy Blanton, which, strangely enough, Ellington included in the same concert. The final, "sophisticated" section is a feature for Cat Anderson, similar to showy tours de force Harry James had done before, like "Concerto for Trumpet" and "The Flight of the Bumblebee." The opening section, representing love, which was written by Billy Strayhorn, is built on a very pretty melody very much in the Ellington manner. It could easily have been made into a successful popular tune and is well worth the rest of the suite.

The work written for Carnegie Hall in 1946 was The Deep South Suite. It has never been issued on records in its entirety, but various portions of it have appeared, and it is possible to put together most of it.

The Deep South Suite was intended to be a portrait of the South, although, as ever, it is difficult to relate the program to the music. It is divided into four movements. The first, which Duke called "Magnolias Dripping with Molasses," is made up of two parts. The first is slow and features Lawrence Brown for a good deal of its duration playing a very pretty melody. This rather charming picture of the South confused critics, who assumed that Duke viewed the South with a good deal of disdain. In fact, despite the virulent racism that existed there, Ellington had a sneaking fondness for the area, and his tone pictures of it are usually appreciative. It is therefore not surprising that the second section of this first movement is a rather happy big-band swinger. The main theme is distinctly related to a tune usually called "Ole Miss," the football song for the University of Mississippi, but which has appeared in various other guises, especially as "Show Me the Way to Go Home" and as Horace Silver's "The Preacher," which was meant to suggest the music of the sanctified church of the South.

The second movement of *The Deep South Suite* is called "Hearsay," the suggestion being that behind the happy face of the South presented in the opening movement there lies a darker heart, talked about only in whispers. The piece is intense and brooding. It opens with brief dramatic figures in muted brass, tom-toms, and the like. This leads to a slow, haunting melody played by the trumpeter Shorty Baker, which both begins and ends on emphatic major sevenths, hardly a usual procedure in popular music. The trumpet solo is followed by one of those diffuse patches that beset Ellington's longer pieces, but then the music turns back to the intense, brooding mood of the opening. The trumpet melody reappears, and the piece ends on a dramatic turn.

The third movement, called "There Was Nobody Looking," is a piano solo. The title was supposed to mean that, when the authorities are not paying attention, people from diverse backgrounds can get along well. It opens with a simple, rather cheerful melody with a ragtime feel, which gives way to a slower, more pensive passage that is little more than a scale, after which the opening part returns. It could hardly be simpler, but it has a charm.

The final movement of *The Deep South Suite* was called "Happy Go Lucky Local." It was supposed to tell the story, not of the powerful train of "Daybreak Express," but of a rusty little train running on a spur line through the rural South. The essence of the piece is a shuffle beat suggesting the "clickety-clack" of a little train. Characteristically, whistles and other train sounds are carefully worked out for the instruments, all a little rusty and squeaky, as befits a backcountry train. It is not a tour de force to equal "Daybreak Express," but it is comic and good fun. Ellington was always at his best when he was evoking a specific mood, event, or circumstance rather than a long, complex idea or series of episodes. "Happy Go Lucky Local" is direct and specific, and it works both as music and as storytelling.

Taken as a whole, *The Deep South Suite* is one of the most successful of Duke's extended pieces. Each of the four sections has a greater unity than he achieved in most of these works, and the four pieces contrast nicely in theme and mood. It is ironic that, of all his suites, this one was never properly recorded, while some less meritorious ones were given elaborate productions and issued in fancy packages with considerable fanfare.

Duke continued to play the "Happy Go Lucky Local" movement frequently as a separate piece, with the usual changes and modifications over time. In part, this was because the piece became a hit for somebody else. At about the time of the Carnegie Hall premiere, Ellington had a saxophonist named Jimmy Forrest in the band. A problem occurred, and Forrest was fired. The band had rehearsed "Happy Go Lucky Local" but had not yet played it in public, and Forrest in retaliation took the main theme out of the book, turned it into a song called "Night Train," and had a substantial hit. Or at least so Cress Courtney says.[3] The song had another minor role in music history when it was played by Forrest at the famous 1952 dance put on by the disc jockey Alan Freed that first brought rock and roll to public attention. In fact, the boogie-like main theme Ellington had written to imitate the sound of a train starting out of a station was very much in the manner of the rhythm and blues out of which rock and roll evolved.

But Ellington's weakness for grander things persisted. The temptation next manifested itself in *The Liberian Suite*, composed for a 1947 Carnegie Hall concert in celebration of the granting of universal manhood suffrage in Liberia, an African republic founded by former American slaves. It consists of an opening portion called "I Like the Sunrise" and five unrelated "dances." The opening part is banal, and fitted out with a jejune lyric sung by Al Hibbler at his fruity worst. One line goes, "Every evening I wish upon a star that that brand new tomorrow is not very far."

The five dances are somewhat better, and the last of them contains a nice touch for Tyree Glenn and one of the trumpets in plunger mutes. But these, too, are derivative: the third dance is played by Ray Nance on violin and sounds like any number of "Hungarian" dances.

The Tattooed Bride, performed at another Carnegie Hall concert in November 1948, is based on the story of a bridegroom who discovers on his wedding night that his bride has been tattooed, presumably on her rump, but little in the music suggests this—or any—story. There are fewer of the pompous devices found in so many of Ellington's extended pieces, nice patches of contrapuntal writing here and there, and excellent long solos by Lawrence Brown and Jimmy Hamilton. Taken as a whole, this is one of Ellington's better concert pieces from this period. It is lighthearted, as befits the story it is supposed to be telling, unassuming, and much more of a jazz piece than, say, New World a-Comin'. However, once again Ellington has eschewed the rich tone palette that he had relied on in his writing for twenty years: this piece could have been written by any one of a number of jazz composers of the time, many of whom were writing concert pieces of this sort but who were less able to get them performed than Ellington was.

The Harlem Suite, written in 1950, is, to my mind, one of the most frustrating works that Ellington ever produced. It was commissioned by the NBC Symphony Orchestra, then under the direction of Arturo Toscanini, as part of a series of portraits of New York. Duke wrote it on the Ile de France on his return from a European tour. I have not been able to discover that the NBC Symphony ever performed it, possibly because there was never a complete score for it, but Ellington recorded it in December 1951 and performed it subsequently.

The Harlem Suite is chock-a-block with wonderful moments: a Carney solo with bouncy clarinet punctuation, several interesting themes for trombone, nicely managed changes of tempo, a lovely contrapuntal hymn using clarinet, trombone, trumpet, and other instruments. Indeed, from minute to minute there is always something of interest.

On the other hand, it is a classical example of Ellington hoping that the literary program will hold the piece together. The description of Harlem opens with a trumpet pronouncing the word in a descending minor third. There follows a jaunt around Harlem on a Sunday in which no fewer than eighteen unrelated snapshots are presented in the space of fourteen minutes. Here lies the problem: no sooner has Ellington unfolded a nice bit of musical material than he drops it and shows us something else. Nothing is ever developed; and just as we are getting interested, he jerks the piece away and moves on to the next thing. In his liner notes to the 1951 recording, Stanley Dance called it a "continuous, kaleidoscopic piece of music";[4] that is all very well, but, unfortunately, kaleidoscopes hold the attention only briefly.

Nonetheless, The Harlem Suite seems more successful than many of Duke's extended pieces. Although it is frequently without strict tempo, it is mainly jazzlike in feeling. It does not have a great deal of soloing, but there is a lot of the contrapuntal writing at which Duke excelled; moreover, it is not marred by too many of the heavy-handed devices, drawn mainly from movie music, as I believe, that wounded other of Ellington's long pieces. Duke understood Harlem, loved it, and brought his feeling for it into this music. What is so frustrating is that had Duke simply known more about how this sort of thing should be done, he might well have made a masterpiece of it. Despite everything, though, it deserves a listening.

The Controversial Suite is a curious little piece that also had its premiere at Carnegie Hall in 1951. At the time, one of several feuds in the jazz world was between the modernists and the Dixielanders. The Dixieland movement had grown out of the revival of New Orleans jazz sponsored by early jazz critics and some musicians in 1939 and thereafter. It had become a serious movement, led by a cadre of musicians of Duke's generation, mostly white, around Eddie Condon in the East and Turk Murphy and Lu Watters on the West Coast. The modernist movement that Ellington was referring to was dominated by the elephantine Stan Kenton band, with its experimental music, forays into atonalism, and the like. This was also a white movement, and there is in Duke's send-up of both groups a certain amused attitude that these white styles were only imitations of the real thing.

The first half of the piece, which tackled Dixieland, was entitled "Before My Time," a statement of questionable accuracy. It opens with a parody of Dixieland that includes snatches of "Tin Roof Blues," breaks out into a big-band swinger that attempts to catch the flavor of Bob Crosby's big Dixieland band, and then returns to the small New Orleans format, with street drumming and suggestions of "Tiger Rag," a song Ellington himself had worked from often enough. The second half is mock Kenton and includes a lot of portentous stings and fanfares. Actually, these parodies are largely successful, good fun to listen to, if you are familiar with their subjects.

The Night Creature is a three-part work commissioned in 1955 for the Symphony of the Air, to be played by that orchestra and the Ellington band. As usual, Ellington has provided a program for the piece, this time three unrelated little tales involving bugs, monsters, and such, which emerge at night to dance and enjoy themselves. Insipidity and bombast alternate, the former coming out slightly ahead.

The Newport Jazz Festival Suite is much better. It was, like so many of these pieces, cooked up hastily: apparently, as the 1956 festival that would be so important to Ellington approached, George Wein asked Duke if he had something lying around that could be turned into a suite dedicated to the festival. Publicity, rather than art, was the generator. Ellington threw something together mostly in rehearsal at the festival. As he often did in such moments, he relied on long solos to carry the piece, providing enough ensemble work to tie the thing together and give it a semblance of a composition.

The work has three parts. The first and third are good swingers, with first-rate solos from Jimmy Hamilton, Clark Terry, and the man who would be the hero of the evening, Paul Gonsalves. The middle part is a blues in

D-flat, based on a four-note riff played in two or three variations, and is mainly solos. The whole thing could have been worked out in half an hour in rehearsal. It opens with a long clarinet solo, by Russell Procope, surprisingly. Procope played with a warm, liquid tone and used flurries of fast figures, derived from the Creole school of clarinet playing that had spawned Barney Bigard. Jimmy Hamilton had begun as a disciple of Benny Goodman, but over the years his sound had grown increasingly legitimate and his approach more precise. Procope's somewhat richer sound and more abandoned playing is a pleasant contrast.

The major piece for 1957 was a curious work called *A Drum Is a Woman*. It purported to tell the story of jazz in the tale of a Madame Zajj, who comes out of the jungle and eventually travels all over the world, as jazz did. Much of it is narrated by Duke. In fact, it has little to do with the history of jazz; it is mainly a series of erotic portraits of Madame Zajj as she dances in Congo Square, flies about in a flying saucer, and parades in the Mardi Gras. The music is, to put it charitably, pedestrian, and the text is embarrassing. The one point of interest is the section called "Rhumbop," one of the very few pieces of straightforward bebop in the Ellington canon.

One of the most highly publicized of Ellington's suites was *The Shakespearean Suite*, better known as *Such Sweet Thunder*. The band had appeared at the Shakespeare Festival in Stratford, Ontario, and afterward Duke and Strayhorn decided to write a series of portraits of Shakespeare's characters. According to Duke, the two of them sat down and read all thirty or so of Shakespeare's plays "quite thoroughly,"[5] a statement I view with a certain skepticism. It does not seem to me that Ellington managed to really capture much of the flavor of Shakespeare's thick-textured verse or the nature of his characters. Lady Macbeth, I would aver, does not have a little ragtime in her soul and is not reflected in the lighthearted piece called "Lady Mac." Nor do I think that Henry V is best represented by abrupt changes of tempo, which are supposed to suggest "the changes of pace and the map as a result of wars." Only two of the thirteen compositions that make up the work seem to me to be effective. "Up and Down, Up and Down" does have something of Puck's mischievousness, and "Half the Fun," a title derived from the advertising slogan "Getting There Is Half the Fun," captures the languorous sensuousness of a lavish barge trip down the Nile. The rest of it strikes me as a collection of self-indulgent fragments that are tied to Shakespeare by great leaps of logic and that show very little understanding of what the plays are actually about. I suspect that a good deal of the material in *Such Sweet Thunder* was already in existence and was attached to the characters in the best way Ellington and Strayhorn could find. The *New York Times*, in its brief review of the work, suggested that one of the virtues of the piece was that "none went on too long."[6] However, "Star Crossed Lovers," the piece about Romeo and Juliet is frequently played by jazz musicians.

The genesis of the *Queen's Suite* was an introduction to the queen of England that had occurred at an art festival held in Leeds, one of the grimy cities of England's industrial belt. The festival was organized by the earl of Harewood, who had a stately home in the neighborhood. His brother, Gerald Lascelles, well known for his interest in jazz, had suggested that Ellington should be included. The queen was present, as she frequently was at events of this kind, and Ellington had a brief chat with her as he passed through the reception line. The meeting meant a great deal to him. Ellington had always had a weakness for both celebrated people and women, and who could be more celebrated than a queen? He thereupon created this six-part suite and recorded it in February 1959. Only one copy was pressed, for presentation to the queen, and Duke specifically stipulated that no more would be made. After his death, however, it was issued in the ordinary way. Irving Townsend, who was Duke's record producer of the time, said that Ellington did not pay for the recording date himself, and as Ellington "never spoke of his death, there was no certainty what he intended when he was gone." Townsend added, "Ellington went about the composition of 'The Queen's Suite' with greater concentration than he displayed for any other music with which I was associated."[7]

Once again I believe that a certain amount of the music for *The Queen's Suite* was already in existence in one form or another when Duke started the work. All six pieces were inspired by nature—a mockingbird seen at sunset, northern lights, lightning bugs, the sound of frogs, and the like. Taken as a whole, *The Queen's Suite* is one of the best of these suites. The music is simple, often very pretty, and quite clever in spots. "Apes and Peacocks," inspired by a gift given to King Solomon by the queen of Sheba, is eccentric, opening with drums and cymbals, which do seem to suggest the jerky strutting of peacocks and the waddling gait of apes. "Sunset and the Mockingbird" is appropriately quiet, built on a simple melody played mostly by piano, with thoughtful support from various reeds. "The Single Petal of a Rose" is a slow, out-of-tempo piano solo in D-flat, accompanied in part by bowed bass. It is based on a very simple, almost pentatonic figure that implies B-flat minor. Billy Strayhorn was particularly fond of this little melody, and after his death Duke frequently played it at the end of an evening.

Another of Ellington's better-known suites was *Suite Thursday*, commissioned for the Monterey Jazz Festival of September 1960. It was based on a sentimental novel by John Steinbeck, and the suite is intended to suggest various aspects of the background and story. A good deal of it was written by Billy Strayhorn. It is supposed to be held together by a minor-sixth interval, which begins and ends the piece, but there seems little else to unify it. In my view, the work's most impressive number is "Schwiphti"—that is, "swifty." After an eccentric piano solo by Duke in the middle of the piece, there is a well-conceived passage for full band, with interpolations by growl trumpet and baritone saxophone. As a whole, "Schwipthi" is very active, with sections diving in upon each other, like football players going after a loose ball.

The Girls Suite was also first performed at the Monterey Jazz Festival in September 1961. It is, like the best of these suites, unpretentious. It consists of ten relatively brief pieces related primarily by the fact that each had a girl's name and by the general simplicity of the compositions. It is an odd mixture. Four of the pieces are built on tunes Duke knew as a youth, the barbershop quartet numbers like "Sweet Adeline" and "Juanita," with close harmonies that he undoubtedly heard his father's vocal group sing. Most of the others are dedicated to singers he knew: Mahalia Jackson, Dinah Washington, and Lena Horne, who was a very close friend of Billy Strayhorn. Some of the pieces work better than others: "Mahalia" has a nice, easy swing and good plunger work from Nance; "Juanita" has a duet for plunger trumpet and trombone using the old barbershop harmonies, which is a considerable harmonic departure from Ellington's highly dissonant practice, and the result is playful, even funny; "Clementine" ends with an interesting counterpoint duet by Hodges and Russell Procope on clarinet over plunger brass. A few other felicities are scattered through The Girls Suite, but most of the rest of it is pedestrian, the sort of thing any professional arranger would turn out quickly with no difficulty.

These earlier suites of Ellington's tend to be relatively short. The Controversial Suite, The Liberian Suite, The Perfume Suite, Suite Thursday, The Queen's Suite, The Newport Jazz Festival Suite, and others take up at most one side of a record, and many of them run less than ten minutes. However, in the later stages of his career Ellington began writing longer ones. The Latin American Suite, The Far East Suite, The Afro-Eurasian Eclipse, The New Orleans Suite, and The River, all written by 1966 or afterward, run to at least forty minutes each, and appear to have been designed to take up a full LP recording.

In general, this works against Ellington, for the simple reason that, the longer the composition, the more essential is some sort of architecture to let the listener know why a given part is where it is and what purpose it is serving in making the whole. No work of art can transcend its parts if there is no sense of destination. Each piece of it must seem to serve a purpose in a larger movement. No collection of short stories, however masterly, can equal a novel from the same hand, and these suites are short-story collections. Or worse: too many impressions of Brazil, a South American square, Argentina, the snow-capped mountains above Mexico City, coming along one after another, remind us of slides of somebody else's trip.

The Latin American Suite, for example, first performed in Mexico City in September 1968, is made up of seven pieces that, taken separately, are pleasant enough, if rather derivative and somewhat unimaginative. But they are all played to similar Latin rhythms, and nearly all are taken at a moderate dance rhythm. There is little soloing, and what there is goes mainly to Gonsalves and Ellington himself. Therefore everything depends upon the ensembles, and they tend to consist of short, simple riffs repeated a good many times at a stretch. There are, inevitably, happy moments—for example, a novel passage for trombones in "Brasilliance"—but lacking momentum, the suite suffers from sameness, a lack of contrast.

The Afro-Eurasian Eclipse, is equally damaged by a lack of purpose. It was dedicated to the proposition that "the whole world is going Oriental," but it is difficult to find the theme in the music, some parts of which are based on gospel; some are pseudo-rock, some vaguely Asian in character. Jules Rowell is charitable when he says, "Certainly in the recorded version of this suite Ellington assumed, at times, an insouciant attitude towards strict pursuit of the direction indicated by the title," and he quotes John McDonough's Down Beat review suggesting that the suite is "really not important Ellington."[8] By this time Duke had taken to putting four-letter shorthand titles on his pieces—in this case, "Gong," "Tang," "True," and the like; when the suite was issued after his death, nobody was able to figure out what he meant by them. This did not help matters.

The New Orleans Suite, commissioned by George Wein in 1970 for a performance at the New Orleans Jazz Festival, is similarly aimless. The suite was pulled together in haste while the band was at Al Hirt's jazz club, where it was playing prior to the festival. The pieces that make up the suite were supposed to reflect various aspects of New Orleans—Bourbon Street, the so-called second line of dancers who follow the parade bands, and such. Two of the pieces, I think, succeed. One is "Portrait of Mahalia Jackson," which evokes gospel-like sounds, with long organ chords supporting various soloists, and has a rather pastoral feel to it, thanks in part to the use of the flute. Perhaps the best of them is "Portrait of Wellman Braud," which is based on an interesting fast descending line with a 6/8 feel played by the brass and, at times, other instruments. Gradually, storms and cries, among them Cootie Williams's plunger trumpet, gather over the insistent bass line, and then the clouds break up, until the bass line is alone again. This sort of arch structure is hardly a complicated one, but at least it is a structure, which most of the other pieces do not have. Indeed, many of them, such as "Thanks for the Beautiful Land on the Delta," are played mostly in a single voice throughout, and those contrasts, which have been Duke's trademarks, are absent, leaving us in a monochromatic landscape, a risky thing when form also is lacking.

Les Trois Rois Noirs, it seems to me, hangs together somewhat better than some of the others. It has climaxes, dynamic shifts, and ups and downs in mood and is in general more varied. But too much of it sounds like movie music—bombastic and overdramatized.

Of these later works, the most successful, I think, is The Far East Suite, an opinion shared by other jazz writers. Ellington made tours of the Middle East and Japan in 1963 and 1964, but not until 1966 did he sit down to celebrate his experiences with a suite. Wisely, Ellington eschewed attempts to incorporate various kinds of Eastern music in the work, which on his own admission he had never studied and did not understand. The best pieces in the suite are simply Ellington music. "Isfahan," named for one of Iran's most beautiful and ancient cities, is in the main built around a slow, languorous melody played by Johnny Hodges in his sensuous fashion, as a whole akin to earlier compositions like "Warm Valley" and "Come Sunday." The melody would have made a wonderful song and has become a jazz standard. "Depk," one of those untranslatable four-letter titles, grew out of a dance Ellington saw performed somewhere on the trip. It is built on a very interesting melody played by various parts of the band; this melody rises and then at the peak suggests countermeter as it descends. In the last version it is harmonized, with Carney deep at the bottom and Hamilton up high, so far apart that they are virtually playing countermelodies, rather than harmonized lines.

Not all of The Far East Suite succeeds. At times Duke succumbed to the temptation to use exotic "oriental" effects. In "Amad" (the first four letters of "Damascus" reversed) he uses a melody based on minor chords with bent major sevenths to suggest the Orient, a stunt popular songwriters had used early in the century. But on the whole, there is more interesting music in The Far East Suite than in most of these late compositions.

It should be obvious to readers at this point that I do not regard these suites and other extended pieces highly. It will also be clear that I tend to prefer the more jazzlike portions of them, and it could be objected that Ellington did not pretend he was writing jazz and that they should not be judged as such. I would respond simply that Ellington knew a great deal about writing jazz, and not so much about writing other kinds of music, and that it is therefore not surprising that the jazz pieces work the best.

It would be one thing if I were a minority voice in respect to these pieces.

Unhappily, I am not. The jazz writers by and large found good things to say about many of the extended pieces and even hailed a few as masterpieces; and the lay press usually was polite about them. But I have not been able to find any major critic, trained in the kind of concert music that Ellington was trying to write, who had much good to say about them. Rob Darrell, who had been the first serious critic to promote Ellington, was generally disappointed by the long pieces. "They did not stick in my mind the way earlier things did. To me it was a letdown when these things came along."[9]

Basically, the professional critics simply ignored the long pieces. So did the public. Duke's friends, associates, and ardent fans would loyally turn up for the concerts and tell Duke how wonderful the music was, but the records never sold very well. Nor did his fans clamor for him to play favorite parts of these pieces at dances and concerts. Play them he did; but the requests for them were few. In sum, these long pieces have left both critics and Ellington's public unmoved. A time may come when another generation will see virtues in them that his contemporaries missed. However, I, for one, would be surprised.

22

The Sacred Concerts

For roughly the last decade of Duke Ellington's life, far and away the most important thing to him was his Sacred Concerts. Precisely how and when Ellington decided to dedicate the remainder of his work to the service of God—he saw himself as "God's messenger," he said—we do not know. Ellington was never a churchgoer. Keeping late hours and traveling as he did, he would have found it almost impossible to attend church more than occasionally. In any case, he does not seem to have made opportunities to go to church.

Nonetheless, there can be no questioning the sincerity of his religious feelings. He claimed to have read the Bible several times, and we have no reason to doubt his word: witnesses observed him with the Bible deep in the night after a gig. However, it is also clear that his religious feeling came on him in mid-life, or later. As a boy he was required to attend both the Kennedys' Nineteenth Street Baptist Church and the Ellingtons' John Wesley A.M.E. Zion. For a while he also went to Sunday school, and in between times his mother would talk to him about God and religion. He was thus raised to be familiar with Christian doctrine. But as he became a teenager and then a young man, his interests shifted from the sacred to the profane. There is certainly no hint of religion in anything he said or in his work from that earlier period.

At some point what he had learned in childhood returned to him, as it often does to people at middle age. By the mid 1950s his interest in religion had grown substantially. He said in his *Music Is My Mistress*:

> When I really settled down to read and to think about what I was read-
> ing in the Bible, I found many things that I had been feeling all my

life without quite understanding them. On becoming more acquainted
with the word of the Bible, I began to understand so much more of
what I had been taught, and of what I thought I had learned about life
and about the people in mine.[1]

Ellington's religious beliefs were, like his music, to some extent home
brewed, but basically they were typical of the time and place he had come
from: God is unknowable, love is central to his message, people ought to
be kind and caring and considerate of one another, forgiveness is one of
the greatest virtues, prayer is the way to God. He said,

> There have been times when I thought I had a glimpse of God.
> Sometimes, even when my eyes were closed, I saw. Then when I tried
> to set my eyes—closed or open—back to the same focus, I had no success,
> of course. The unprovable fact is that I believe I have had a glimpse of
> God many times. I believe because believing is believable, and no one
> can prove it unbelievable.[2]

Ellington had written a little religious music before the Sacred Concerts, in particular "Come Sunday," from *Black, Brown, and Beige,* and
various snatches of gospel music from other works. He might never have
written any more, for he always needed an assignment and a deadline to
force him to write. He got the assignment he needed from Dean C. J.
Bartlett and the Reverend John S. Yaryan of Grace Cathedral in San Francisco in 1965. The cathedral was completed and consecrated that year, and
a number of celebratory events were organized. Undoubtedly, a certain
element of public relations was involved in the selection of a jazz musician
to give a concert: Duke was news, and the idea of his presenting some sort
of jazzy religious music in a church would be even bigger news.

Ellington was delighted by the offer for a number of reasons. "Now I
can say openly what I have been saying to myself on my knees," he said.
But given Ellington's ambition to work in what he conceived to be more
prestigious forms—suites, tone poems, and the like—it seems likely that
he was much taken by the idea of emulating the great European composers whose oratorios, masses, and chorales are at the heart of Western
music. Because of his upbringing, hardly anything could have suited Ellington better than writing religious music.

He wrote, finally, three sets of religious pieces, known as the First, Second, and Third Sacred Concerts. The first two were performed many
times; characteristically, they varied somewhat from performance to performance. Each of them comprises approximately a dozen pieces, only very
loosely related in that all have religious content (in the last one, most also

have love for a subject). Probably about a third of the Sacred Concerts is jazz, the same sort of music the band would play in clubs and theaters, including jazz soloing. The rest is a mixture of recitative, choral singing, and vocal solos by people with trained voices who had no particular experience with jazz. The Sacred Concerts are, like many of Ellington's extended works, something of a mishmash, with little linkage between successive pieces. Some of the pieces are fifteen minutes long; some, three minutes. However, since the works are billed as concerts, it is not fair to expect the pieces to be related any more than the works at any concert.

The First Sacred Concert had its premiere at San Francisco's Grace Cathedral on September 16, 1965, but the record we have of it was made at a repeat concert, with somewhat different soloists, on December 26 at New York's Presbyterian Church on Fifth Avenue. The concert consists of ten pieces. Three of them utilize the "Come Sunday" theme, once sung by the gospel singer Esther Merrill in the gospel tradition, played by Hodges in the familiar version, and used at a quicker tempo as a background for the jazz dancer Bunny Briggs for the closing piece, "David Danced before the Lord with All His Might." There is another gospel piece by Merrill called "Tell Me It's the Truth," a pseudo-spiritual sung by a choir and the vocalist Jimmy McPhail, who sings in the trained voice Duke liked, a replication of music from New World a-Comin' and a jivy gospel version of the Lord's Prayer.

The main piece is a fifteen-minute loose structure called "In the Beginning God," which Duke obviously meant to be the primary piece in the concert, the one he had worked hardest on. It opens with a six-note theme to accompany the opening six syllables of the Bible, "In the beginning God . . ." The theme is played successively on piano, by Harry Carney, and on clarinet, possibly by Russell Procope. Brock Peters then recites words to the effect that in the beginning there were no headaches, no aspirin, no men trying to fill inside straights—a long list. Gonsalves next blows over gospel organ chords by the saxes; the choir recites the books of the Old Testament; Cat Anderson plays his usual high-note routine representing man's highest aspirations; Ellington plays piano fills while the choir recites the books of the New Testament at gathering speed; Bellson plays a solo emphasizing "the sounding brass" of the cymbals, his virtuosity again symbolizing man's aspirations; and, finally, the choir sings the main theme.

The piece opens well enough. The successive statements of the theme leading to a climactic revelation of the words for the theme provide a measure of the development that is frequently lacking in Ellington's extended pieces. The vocal continues as the band picks up an easy swing tempo and Peters goes on to recite the long list of modern foibles that did not exist at the beginning. Peters then concludes with a repeat of the six-note theme, with a leap into the upper register for a powerful last note. Taken as a whole, this section is put together well and forms a rounded unit, and although the recital of the long list of contemporary foibles is trite, it does not dangerously mar the piece.

But then the structure falls apart. The recitations of the books of the Bible are banal and suggestive of nothing; the Anderson and Bellson set pieces are irrelevant, except insofar as Anderson touches on the main theme; and the sudden return of the entire ensemble to the main theme for a brief statement at the end is inadequate. It is Ellington's old problem: How do you put together a long piece that is not just a string of episodes held together only by some sort of literary concept?

Of the remaining portions of the concert, the best received were the gospel songs, sung by Esther Merrill in a powerful voice and authentic gospel spirit, and the dancing of Bunny Briggs to the piece that closes the concert, a felicitous idea for which Ellington deserves full credit.

The First Sacred Concert has its ups and downs, but it contains many fine moments: Merrill's gospel singing, the dancing of Briggs to the fast version of "Come Sunday," Hodges's always lovely handling of the same theme. Even the main piece is an interesting failure, and with some editing and with a little more connective tissue it could have been turned into a first-rate composition.

The Second Sacred Concert, however, is, from an artistic viewpoint, an almost unmitigated disaster. It was first given on January 19, 1968, at the huge Cathedral of St. John the Divine, in New York City. Gary M. Jetter, a music student who has studied the work, concludes that it was "often trivial and stereotyped."[3] There are, I think, a couple of good moments: Alice Babs's singing of the fairly interesting melody of "TGTT," which stands for "Too Good to Title"; and the closing all-out swinger, which has good spots. For the rest, the music is empty when it is not obvious and banal when it is neither. Duke appears in this piece to be doing what beginners at any art form generally do: that is, try to create something that looks like a painting, reads like a novel, sounds like an opera, rather than attempting to make a felt statement about something. In this music—despite Ellington's strong religious convictions—nothing is felt. It is superficial, and because the concert is nearly twice as long as the other two Sacred Concerts—some eighty minutes—it appears to go on forever.

But the music's amateur quality is not the worst of it. Almost every item in the concert has words—spoken passages, recitatives, vocal solos, and offerings by no fewer than four choirs. The words are consistently embarrassing—puerile and filled with cute paradoxes and sophomoric insights:

> Does your anger run so rife
> That you'd like to use your knife?
> Don't do it! Cause you'll wind up in the clink.
> And after you've calmed down cool,
> You'll find that gossips talk the fool,
> And nothing's on the brink of what you think.

But enough. These lines would not be acceptable coming from a bright high school student. And they are not the worst examples, but typical of the concert as a whole—indeed, typical of Duke's writing in general. For most of his songwriting career Ellington depended upon professional lyricists whom Irving Mills or others supplied for his songs. Some of them, like Mitchell Parish, who put words to "Sophisticated Lady," Don George, who did "I'm Beginning to See the Light," and Johnny Mercer, who wrote "Satin Doll," were excellent lyricists. But by the 1950s Duke was writing a lot of his own lyrics, and they were uniformly bad. The fact must be faced that Duke Ellington was a dreadful writer. It is not merely that he employs false rhymes and lines that do not scan, or that he is addicted to the obvious and cute. The trouble runs much deeper—all the way to the bottom, in fact. There is nothing in the interviews he gave, in his book *Music Is My Mistress*, which was put into shape by Stanley Dance, and in lyrics such as these to suggest that Ellington was in any way the wise and ultimately sophisticated man he actually was. Worse, they are entirely empty of human feeling. There is no passion in them anywhere.

It is true, as I pointed out earlier, that Ellington got only the education that any lazy high school student of his time got. Besides, he attended a vocational high school, where he found less emphasis on the classics than the students at Dunbar had. Presumably, he was required to read little more than some Shakespeare, a little Milton, a little Shelley, a little Dickens. On his own, later in life, he seems not to have read much literature of any kind. Being unfamiliar with the best kind of writing is a handicap for a writer, because he is without a baseline against which to judge his own work. Ellington was not able to see how bad his stuff was, because he did not really know what good writing was. Nobody familiar with the opening lines to "Ode on a Grecian Urn" or "The Tyger" could have written,

> Freedom, Freedom, a perfect healing salve.
> Freedom, Freedom, it's what you've got to have.

I do not mean that Ellington is to be judged against Keats or Blake; I am saying only that, had he been more familiar with better work, he would not have permitted himself to be so bad in his own.

But I do not think that his lack of education was really the problem. Other jazz musicians with no more education than Ellington, like Danny Barker and Rex Stewart, wrote far better. The problem lay in Duke's unwillingness to expose himself, his need always to fend off intimate inquiry, his inability to really unbutton himself except with very few people on rare occasions. The English jazz writer Max Jones, who knew him off and on for many years, said, "He was a most mysterious man. . . . I never understood him. Never got to any sort of comfortable place with him."[4] Charlie Barnet, who fashioned his band's musical style around Ellington's, said, "He is a very complex man and I don't think anyone knew him really well, for no one could get past the front he always maintained."[5] John Hammond, who admittedly did not get along with Duke, said, "I never felt close to Duke as a person, and indeed, there were few who did. For all the up-front gregariousness—'We love you madly'—he was a very private person."[6] Nat Hentoff quoted a "veteran Ellington reed man" as saying, "He may be troubled but the public never knows it, and most of the time we don't either. Except for his sister, Ruth, I don't know anybody who really gets close to Duke. Sure, he kids around with us, but there's always a distance between him and everybody else. If you get too close to Duke, he'll make a joke or put on, and edge away."[7] Rob Darrell, who interviewed Duke in the early 1930s, said, "A nice looking guy, and very pleasant, but I just had the feeling that he put a wall between us."[8]

The point—the *whole* point—of writing is to let the world know what you are thinking and feeling. Duke's effort in writing was exactly the opposite: to avoid letting the world know what he was thinking and feeling. In his writing he could not, then, offer us what he knew about how the world worked, which was considerable, nor could he talk about the things he felt strongly about: his need for God, his triumphs, his failures, his regrets. It all had to be superficial, a play of colored light across a textured surface. A consummate professional can often get away with this kind of thing, leaving the observer with a sense of more depth than is there; but Ellington was nothing like that, and in the end, in things like the Second Sacred Concert, he has given us not a play of colored lights but a drawing in Crayola on shirt cardboards.

As I have written elsewhere, one of the great problems in art is to match form and content. A tiny idea can shine in a tiny form—witness Duke's charming "Pretty and the Wolf." When content overwhelms form, let us say the death of kings in doggerel ("The King is dead / he said, he said"), the result is comic, bizarre, or grotesque. When form is too large for the content, the work appears obvious, or empty, as when a huge choir and orchestra are shouting out, "Freedom, Freedom must be won / 'Cause Freedom's even good fun"—the form is hopelessly oversized for the content. With words like the ones that Ellington wrote for it, the Second Sacred Concert could not possibly succeed, and it did not.

The Third Sacred Concert suffers from more bad libretto, but the music is a good deal better, and it is therefore at least partially successful. It was sponsored by the United Nations and performed at Westminster Abbey, in London, on October 24, 1973, which had been designated United Nations Day. Duke was excited by the idea of performing at Westminster, one of the world's best-known churches, but the concert was marked by all sorts of problems. The Ellington band had been working at a club called Mr. Kelly's in Chicago, and had been rehearsing for the concert after the evening performances. The band arrived in London early in the morning of the day of the concert and, however weary, had to begin rehearsing immediately with the soloists. Ellington, already fatally ill with the lung cancer that would kill him, was close to collapse. He needed injections to keep him going. To make matters worse, Paul Gonsalves was using drugs—Mercer guessed LSD[9]—which triggered an epileptic fit, and he had to be hospitalized. What with one thing and another, Duke told Mercer, "I have never been so unprepared to do a performance as I am in this case."[10] Under the circumstances, then, it is lucky that anything good came out of the concert at all.

This time Duke had given the concert a loose theme—love—and several of the pieces used the word in the title. There are some good bits and pieces. Alice Babs has an interesting melody in the middle of "Every Man Prays in His Own Language," which has a curious feel of Renaissance music to it, and appropriately enough she is followed by an a cappella recorder solo by Art Baron. Babs returns with quite a simple melody. The piece is marred by Ellington's recitation of more of his heavy-handed writing at the end; but his spoken part is brief, and to my mind this piece, especially the unusual and striking melody Alice Babs sings, is by far the best thing in the concert. Babs has a pure, warm voice, and her intonation is astonishingly good; she is a pleasure to listen to, regardless of what she sings.

But the rest of the concert is quite ordinary, made up of the sort of music that might pass unnoticed in a nightclub, were it clad in secular dress. Once again there is too much form for the content.

Another writer may have a better view of these three Sacred Concerts, but although the first two were performed many times in many places, like the suites, they have never been great sellers. It is my feeling that Duke was invited to perform them in various churches, cathedrals, and other locations more for the publicity than for the musical value in these works. Once again, if mine were a minority view, it would be one thing, but unfortunately it is not. Duke's fans and the loyal jazz press always found good things to say about the Sacred Concerts. Stanley Dance, for example, thinks that the Second Sacred Concert was the best of the three and says that Alice Babs, a well-schooled musician, was "mightily impressed" by the writing in "Supreme Being."[11]

But I have not been able to find support for this position among professional music critics. For the most part, they ignored the Sacred Concerts, as they did the suites. Nor did Ellington's fans at dances and concerts clamor to hear any of the sacred music. Ellington knew what they wanted, and he gave it to them: "Mood Indigo," "Cotton Tail," "Don't Get Around Much Anymore." He never felt required to offer them a medley consisting of "It's Freedom," "TGTT," and "In the Beginning God."

23

The Final Days

Sometime in the spring of 1972, while the band was in Houston, Cootie Williams became ill with a chest ailment. It was decided that the whole orchestra ought to be checked out to be sure that they had not caught something from Cootie. According to Mercer, most of the musicians got a positive result in the preliminary test for emphysema, probably because they had spent so much of their lives in smoky nightclubs, and were told to get follow-up tests. Two of the men, however, were warned that they might have something more serious and that they ought to see their doctors when they got home. They were Harry Carney and Duke Ellington.

Ultimately, doctors made a diagnosis of cancer. Mercer said, "It originated in the lymphatic duct, and it was hitting the bloodstream, and the bloodstream was taking cells out all over the body."[1] Duke was determined that nobody should know how sick he was. Arthur Logan knew, of course, and Ruth was eventually told, but Mercer was not, and he resented it when he finally found out. For Duke it was extremely important always to maintain the image of himself as the strong, competent father who could solve all problems, and he did not want anybody to know that he was failing. But by the time of the trip to London, in October 1973 for the Third Sacred Concert, it was clear that something was seriously wrong.

Duke, in any case, was determined not to die. Somehow he would find a way around the disease, as he had always before found ways around problems that confronted him. So he pressed ahead with the Third Sacred Concert and the tour that was built around it.

While the tour was under way, back in New York on Sunday, November 25, Arthur Logan fell to his death from the Henry Hudson Parkway in

Harlem. To this day nobody really knows what happened. He had just gotten approval from New York City for the removal of a bus depot that would allow him to expand Knickerbocker Hospital, and there were hints that people opposed to the removal killed him. When the police found the body, his car was parked in the southbound lane of the parkway, which suggested that he had gone there of his own volition, and they initially listed the death as a probable suicide. But later, no doubt under pressure from important friends of Logan, they changed the cause of death to "undetermined."

Duke refused to believe it was suicide. Edmund Anderson said, "I haven't the slightest notion of the true cause of his death, but I have to think Logan knew during 1973 that Edward wouldn't live to see his seventy-fifth birthday. And something died in Arthur's soul."[2] (Actually, Duke just barely did live to see his seventy-fifth birthday.)

Logan was buried on November 29, 1973. His funeral was attended by two thousand people, including former Mayor Robert F. Wagner, who spoke. Governor Nelson Rockefeller issued a statement that said in part, "The death of Dr. Logan is a great tragedy and a profound loss to the city."

Mercer found out about Logan's death as the orchestra was returning to London from Zambia. The orchestra had an important command performance to play at the London Palladium, and Mercer and Ruth decided not to say anything to Duke about Logan's death, fearful of his reaction. In fact, so disturbed were they by the prospect of telling him that they put it off for three days. Finally, on the day Logan was buried, back in New York, they told Duke. "That night he cried himself to sleep, and it was the first and only time I had ever seen him cry," Mercer said. "If ever he lost a friend, it was Arthur. I saw him affected by Billy, but nothing like with Arthur."[3] For several days Duke had trouble getting a grip on himself. He kept saying, "Why did he have to die?" and it was clear that he felt not merely bereft but abandoned by the one person he could count on for anything, the person he leaned on for emotional support.

Logan's death, his own illness, personnel shifts in the band, and age would certainly have driven other men into retirement, but Ellington would not quit. He insisted on carrying on his usual heavy schedule of playing and composing. Finally, in January 1974, he collapsed. He went into Columbia Presbyterian Medical Center, and the band's forthcoming engagements were canceled. After two or three weeks he was allowed to go home to be tended by Evie. But Evie herself was sick, and in March she went into the hospital suffering from lung cancer.

Then, in mid-April, Ellington went back into Columbia Presbyterian. An announcement was made that his condition was not serious and that he would "be out in a few days."[4] It was, however, extremely serious. Duke continued to work—he was particularly anxious to make changes in the Third Sacred Concert, and he had other projects in mind as well. For perhaps a month he managed to go on working, but by now he was going downhill rapidly. His seventy-fifth birthday was celebrated around the world with concerts and broadcasts. A special program of pieces from the Sacred Concerts was arranged for the Reverend John Gensel's church, and the band, which had not been working, was brought together to perform. Duke, however, was unable to leave the hospital, and he celebrated his landmark birthday in his room with a small party of family and friends.

In the middle of May, Paul Gonsalves died in London. Free, now that the Ellington band was not working, he had gone to Holland to play a job there and then to London to see friends. He died there from some combination of drugs, drink, and years of hard living. Duke was not told of his death.

For another few days he continued to work as much as he could. Then, on about May 22, he developed pneumonia, "a serious condition for him," a hospital spokesman said.[5] He lingered for two more days. On May 24, early in the morning, he died. His death was a front-page story around the world. The New York Times headed its piece, "Duke Ellington, Master of Music, Dies at 75," and went on to call him "America's most important composer."[6] President Nixon issued a statement that said, "The wit, taste, intelligence and elegance that Duke Ellington brought to his music have made him, in the eyes of millions of people both here and abroad, America's foremost composer. His memory will live for generations to come in the music with which he enriched his nation."[7] That Sunday the Times carried an editorial saying in part, "For in Duke Ellington, American jazz achieved its rightful stature and dignity."[8] The funeral, on May 27, was also a front-page story. It was held at St. John the Divine, where the Second Sacred Concert had first been given. There were ten thousand people in the church, another twenty-five hundred outside. Earl Hines, Joe Williams, and Ruth's husband, McHenry Boatwright, performed, and for the recessional a portion of the Second Sacred Concert was played, with Hodges's saxophone soaring through the high arches of the church over the enormous crowd. Ellington was buried in Woodlawn Cemetery next to his parents. Almost fittingly, within weeks Harry Carney, who had been with the Duke Ellington orchestra for some forty-seven years without a break—longer than anyone but Duke himself—was also dead. Two years later, in April 1976, Evie died, and was buried beside Duke in Woodlawn. Some of the old guard lingered—Barney Bigard until 1980, Cootie Williams until 1985; Lawrence Brown and Jimmy Hamilton were still alive at this writing.

So, finally, it was over. Duke Ellington died possibly the most celebrated musician of his era. His name was known to hundreds of millions of people all over the world, and it is probable that the majority of people alive at the moment of his death, one way or another, knew something about his music.

It was typical of him that he left no will. It was a final act of mischief, of keeping things in the palm of his own hands, that he settled nothing on anybody. The result was that Evie, Mercer, and Ruth had to come to some arrangement about the disposition of the estate, and inevitably there were hard feelings. Evie was provided for, but she died bitter about her circumstances and about the fact that Duke had never married her. Essentially, Ruth ended up with the music publishing company Tempo, and Mercer took over the band, which he continues to lead, playing not only Duke's music, but new pieces as well. But with Duke's death the demand for the orchestra has slackened, and it does not work full-time.

How, then, do we finally assess Duke Ellington? Was he really, as so many have claimed, America's foremost composer? Was he merely a great songwriter? How do we see him as a jazz musician, in view of the fact that he has always been considered a good, but not a great, instrumentalist?

To begin with, the idea that Duke Ellington was one of the great writers of popular songs of the golden age of song writing offers certain problems. Alec Wilder, in his classic work *American Popular Song*, refused to consider Ellington a songwriter at all. He said of his tunes, "Very few of them are essentially songs, nor were they meant to be. They were composed as instrumental pieces to which words have been added and for which simplified releases were often substituted."[9] Perhaps more significant is the fact that the central melodic ideas of virtually all of Ellington's best-known songs originated in somebody else's head. "Black and Tan Fantasy," "Black Beauty," and "East St. Louis Toodle-Oo" were primarily the work of Bubber Miley. "Creole Love Call" was written by King Oliver; "Caravan" and "Perdido," by Juan Tizol. "Mood Indigo" was worked out mainly by Lorenzo Tio, Jr. "Do Nothing Till You Hear from Me" was adapted from "Concerto for Cootie," the main theme of which was written by Williams; "Don't Get Around Much Anymore," "I Let a Song Go Out of My Heart," and "I'm Beginning to See the Light" came from Hodges melodies; "In a Sentimental Mood," "Sophisticated Lady," and "Prelude to a Kiss" were adapted from Otto Hardwick melodies; "I Got It Bad" was adapted from something Mercer wrote; "Satin Doll" and "Take the A Train" were written by Billy Strayhorn. Of all the songs on which Ellington's reputation as a songwriter—and his ASCAP royalties as well—is based, only "Solitude" appears to have been entirely his work. For the rest he was at best a collaborator, at worst merely the arranger of a band version of the tune. Given this, it is hard to see how Ellington can be considered an important songwriter, in a class with Gershwin, Youmans, and Kern.

Yet, paradoxically, Ellington's recorded music is simply awash with melody, tens of thousands of measures of it, much of it memorable, some of it masterly. There can be no doubt that Ellington wrote a huge proportion of this enormous body of melody; ironically, not only do we not know how much but we do not even know which portions. Virtually never can we say with assurance that Duke Ellington wrote *this* particular phrase, line, complete melody. All we can say is that during those thousands of nights on trains and planes, in hotel rooms and empty ballrooms late at night, he wrote thousands upon thousands of bars of music. Much of it has disappeared, but a great deal of that music found its way onto the records. If Ellington was not a great songwriter, he was certainly a melodist of genuine power.

But this is not enough, of itself, to qualify him for the title "America's greatest composer." Once again the question raises certain problems. By "composer" we usually mean somebody who makes up more or less complete works of music that are written down or, today, at least organized on a piece of tape by the creator. Ellington rarely wrote out a composition in complete form, and in many, perhaps most, instances, the work existed on paper only in scraps and pieces, which have long since disappeared.

Furthermore, like that of the songs, the provenance of much of the work is obscure. The men in the sections worked out a lot of the voicings, although in the main from chords supplied by Ellington. Tom Whaley and Juan Tizol often made alterations as they extracted the parts. A great many of the contrapuntal or answering lines were suggested by members of the band, in some cases simply to give themselves something to play while the main line was carried by somebody else. Phrases, snatches of melody, came from everywhere. And, of course, after 1939 Billy Strayhorn contributed a great deal. Given all of this, we are entitled to question not just whether Ellington was America's greatest composer but whether he was a composer at all.

Yet, the simple fact remains that there exists an enormous and important body of music that would not be there without Duke Ellington. If we believe, as I do, that jazz is the most significant musical form of the twentieth century, it is obvious that the music ascribed to Duke Ellington constitutes one of the major bodies of music from that era. Louis Armstrong was probably the most influential jazz musician who ever lived, and he left an impressive body of work. The Armstrong records, however, are mainly valuable for his own playing, despite occasional fine solos by others, and two-thirds of the music on most of his records can be dismissed as only passable jazz. Charlie Parker was almost as influential as Armstrong, but his career was so dented by his waywardness that the body of work he left us is relatively small and uneven.

Duke Ellington was not so influential as either Armstrong or Parker; or perhaps it is best to say that his influence was more diffuse, a matter of musicians incorporating his sounds, ideas, and harmonies into their thinking without being quite aware of doing it. But influence aside, we can safely say that Ellington left a much larger and on the whole much more even body of work than any other musician in the history of jazz, a body of work that includes hundreds of complete compositions, many of them almost flawless.

The key point is that without Ellington none of this would have existed. It is true that Duke drew a great deal from Williams, Miley, Bigard, Hodges, and the rest; but it is equally true that none of these men had important careers in jazz apart from Ellington. Ellington played upon these men as a card shark manipulates the deck. He brought out the best in them. By choosing when and what they would play, he paraded their strengths. Would Bubber Miley have been remembered—or even recorded— if it had not been for the way Ellington used him? Would Cootie Williams ever have taken up the plunger style on which his fame is based, without Ellington? Would Hodges have developed the weaving, sinuous style that made him one of the master jazz musicians, if Ellington had not given him space and used him as he did? Would Tricky Sam Nanton have worked out the method that gave him his place in jazz history, in another band?

It seems to me, then, that it was fair for Ellington to take what he did from these people, because he invented them. He was to one degree or another instrumental in shaping their improvising styles, and he was certainly responsible for choosing from their stylistic repertoires the aspects that would make the best music. This point is crucial in assessing Ellington's final worth: he, and nobody else, created the musical machine that produced the great compositions we know as "Ellington."

We thus have to see Duke Ellington as we see a master chef. The chef does not chop all the vegetables himself or make the sauce with his own hands. But he plans the menus, trains the assistants, supervises them, tastes everything, adjusts the spices, orders another five more minutes in the oven for the lamb. And in the end we credit him with the result.

So it was with Duke Ellington: wherever he got the ingredients, it was his artistic vision that shaped the final product. Hodges, Williams, Bigard, and the rest could not have done any of this, and, when they had their own bands, despite years of observing Ellington's methods, they created little memorable music aside from their own playing. It is Ellington's personal stamp, instantly recognizable, that is on these works. They are not simply display cases for the soloing of Nanton, Miley, or Brown; they are unified pieces in which the personalities of the soloists are subordinated to the artistic purposes of Ellington. Despite the contributions of others, this is not committee music, conglomerate stones of elements tossed helter-skelter into the mix. This is Duke Ellington's music, just as surely as Armstrong's and Parker's solos were their music. And given that, although Ellington did not possess the raw natural gift of some of the other great jazz musicians, his achievement in the end may be the greater, because it consists not merely of jazz solos but of unified works that may include several jazz solos.

If, then, it is Ellington who created these pieces, we must find their source in his character. It is clear enough that if Duke had been a different kind of person, these works would be different and perhaps would not exist at all. Without his utter confidence that what he liked was good, he would not have been able to sort so quickly through the ingredients available to him and settle on what should be used. Without his need to dominate the people around him, and his ability to do so, he would not have been able to bend these fractious and frequently independent-minded individuals to his purposes. Without his willingness to endure disorder—indeed, the quixotic pleasure he took in a certain amount of chaos—the band would not have played with the looseness necessary to the fire and drive that are essential to jazz. Without his need to break rules, to challenge constraints, he would not again and again have found his way to the new, the different, the fresh, the surprising. Duke Ellington's music was not produced simply by an artistic impulse, the almost unconsidered feeling for a certain way of playing, certain types of melody, harmony, and rhythm, as it is with most jazz musicians. It was instead the product of his entire character. It had to be, because he was not manipulating just musical ideas but also people—indeed, whole sets of social circumstances that included musicians, gangsters, nightlifers, show business entrepreneurs, and the culture beyond them. These were his raw material.

Because of this, the way Ellington related to other people was critical. He could be, and frequently was, generous and sympathetic to the people around him. He was loyal to his musicians and often kept them in the band long after other leaders would have fired them. He was devoted to his family, and even more loyal to them than he was to the musicians. But he was also a very private man. He did not let his hair down with many people, did not confess his worries, his failures. One of his musicians once said, "It may sound corny, but I think he's lonely for love, I don't mean lonely for chicks. I mean for somebody he feels will be entirely honest with him. . . ."[10]

Duke Ellington seems to have seen the people around him as a bemused adult views children whose antics he does not quite understand but finds amusing. In a sense he was the ringmaster of a circus, surrounded by elephants, acrobats, seals, clowns, and dancing horses—gay and gaudy dolls he must control by judicious choice of the kind word, the whip, the handful of peanuts. Don George, in a telling phrase, once said that Duke was "an incredible devourer of relationships."[11] He loved people, George said, but "he was evasive at the same time that you could never put your finger on any part of him. . . ."[12] Curious, concerned, loyal, intrigued—but deeply attached to only a very few: Arthur Logan, Billy Strayhorn, his mother, his sister. And those to whom he was attached had to put themselves almost wholly at his service. This capacity to be concerned but removed was essential to Ellington's ability to create his music as he did, drawing it not from the piano but from people.

It is thus not necessary to see Duke Ellington as a "composer" in the narrow sense of the word. I think we can see him as something just as important, an improvising jazz musician. Ellington disliked the term "jazz," partly because he had been raised to middle-class values that did not really approve of that low-class music, and partly because he considered the term limiting. But whatever he thought, he was essentially a jazz musician. Students of jazz all accept this, and while some like to think that he went beyond that category, as he himself would have said, the fact is that his orchestra was a jazz band and that the music it played was mostly jazz.

So he was a jazz musician, and like any jazz musician he worked out his music not in the privacy of a soundproof room but with an instrument in rehearsal halls, ballrooms, recording studios. He made it by trial and error, experimenting with sounds until he came to something he liked. And, like any jazz musician, when he came out on the stage, he felt free to make changes in the spirit of the moment, eliminating this solo, letting that one continue, cutting this part, adding this one. The difference was that his instrument was a whole band.

It follows that if we see Duke Ellington as a jazz musician, rather than as a composer in the strict sense, the "work" must be the recordings, as it is with other jazz musicians, not the "compositions"—that is, written versions of them made either by himself or by later transcribers. It is, of course, perfectly legitimate to make these transcriptions and to perform them, as many bands today are doing. But I insist that this is not "Duke Ellington music" but something else. Ellington made his music on the spot, and only the recordings can reflect it. After all, which of the many versions of, say, "Creole Love Call" is the definitive one? It is impossible to say, just as it is impossible to say which of Louis Armstrong's takes of "Stardust" is definitive, because Ellington was always the improviser.

As will be abundantly clear to the reader by now, I think that the works of Ellington that matter are those hundreds of pieces in the three-minute form of which he was the master: "Black and Tan Fantasy," "Daybreak Express," "Concerto for Cootie," "Ko-Ko," "Main Stem," "Rockin' in Rhythm," and dozens and dozens more—many more than I have been able to discuss in this book—are Ellington's contribution to the art of his time.

It is my belief that his growing interest in the extended pieces was one of the great artistic errors in jazz history. They are not very good; and they drew him away from developing the form he was at home with.

As I have said, the notion of "art" as a special practice with its own principles existing in the abstract, apart from an audience, has become widespread in the twentieth century. We have novelists, painters, dancers, and composers who endlessly produce work whose main function is to be art. Even though few people care about the works in question, many of these artists become celebrated, because what they do can be classified as art.

To the contrary, the reason why jazz is important—why its practitioners are widely discussed and written about—is that millions of people care about it, and often care about it so passionately that they are willing to devote their lives to it. When jazz becomes confounded with art, passion flies out and pretension flies in. I believe that what people in time come to see as the important art of a period always was created out of a wish to act directly and immediately on the real feelings of people—to persuade, influence, entertain, disturb, amuse, or excite at least some people.

Duke Ellington's best work was created to do just that. Those great pieces we so love were functional works meant to accompany dancing, to support singers or dancers, or to excite and entertain audiences at the Cotton Club in New York, the Crystal Palace in Fargo, the Palladium in London. When he forgot this, when, instead of operating on the feelings of people, he created music in emulation of models from the past, which in many cases he did not really understand, he was lost, and his work became empty.

But that, of course, was a choice he had a right to make, and he was hardly alone in making it. In the end it does not really matter, for he left us so large a body of transcendent music that it is the work of a lifetime to explore it thoroughly. His gift to us was immeasurable, and I have no doubt that it will be lasting.

Notes

The following abbreviations are used throughout the notes. "Rutgers" refers to oral histories lodged at the Institute of Jazz Studies at Rutgers University. Where the subject's name is not given, it will be obvious from the text. "Rutgers vert. file" refers to material in the vertical file at the institute. "Yale" refers to oral histories lodged at the Duke Ellington Oral History Project at Yale University. They are identified by code number. "Schomburg" refers to oral histories lodged in The Schomburg Center for Research in Black Culture, in New York City. These oral histories are available on tape only, and it is not possible to locate references exactly. They are identified by code number. "MIMM" refers to Duke Ellington's autobiography, *Music Is My Mistress*. (Garden City, N.Y.: Doubleday, 1973).

1. Childhood

1. Barney Bigard, *With Louis and the Duke*, ed. Barry Martyn (New York: Oxford University Press, 1986), 65.
2. Rutgers, #5, 32.
3. Joel Williamson, *The Crucible of Race* (New York: Oxford University Press, 1984), 45.
4. Ibid., 117.
5. The information about Ellington's paternal line is abstracted from Lincoln County census records.
6. Constance McLaughlin Green, *A History of the Capital, 1800–1950* (Princeton: Princeton University Press, 1962), 149.
7. Ibid., 153.
8. *MIMM*, 17.
9. Ibid.
10. Schomburg, C-451.
11. *MIMM*, 10.
12. Author's interview.

13. Yale.
14. Schomburg, C-451.
15. Ibid.
16. Mercer Ellington with Stanley Dance, *Duke Ellington in Person* (Boston: Houghton Mifflin, 1978), 69.
17. *MIMM*, 10.
18. Ibid., 6.
19. Ibid., 15.
20. Author's interview with Fran Hunter.
21. Schomburg, C-451.
22. *Horizon*, Nov. 1979, 56.
23. Ibid.

2. Introduction to Music

1. Lewis A. Erenberg, *Steppin' Out* (Westport, Conn.: Greenwood Press, 1981), xiii.
2. *Correspondence of F. Scott Fitzgerald*, edited by Matthew J. Bruccoli and Margaret M. Duggan with the assistance of Susan Walker (New York: Random House, 1980), 16.
3. Edward A. Berlin, *Ragtime* (Berkeley: University of California Press, 1980), 147.
4. Interview note, probably by George Hoefer, Rutgers vert. file.
5. Leonard Feather, *From Satchmo to Miles* (New York: Stein and Day, 1972), 52.
6. *MIMM*, 20.
7. Ibid.
8. Ibid., 22.
9. Yale, 550A.
10. Ibid., 539.
11. Rutgers, #4, 51.
12. Ellington, *Duke Ellington in Person*, 19–20.
13. Ibid., 19.
14. *MIMM*, 28.
15. Rutgers, #1, 33.
16. Chris Goddard, *Jazz Away from Home* (London: Paddington Press, 1979), 291.
17. Barry Ulanov, *Duke Ellington* (New York: Creative Age Press, 1946), 14.
18. *Washington Star*, April 23, 1971.
19. Radio interview, Sweden, 1951, Yale.
20. *Ebony*, 1959, in Rutgers vert. file.
21. Derek Jewell, *Duke* (New York: W. W. Norton, 1977), 30.
22. Author's interview.
23. Rutgers, #3, 59.

3. New York

1. Stanley Dance, *The World of Duke Ellington* (New York: Scribner's, 1970), 58.

2. Bigard, *With Louis and the Duke,* 51.

3. Whitney Balliett, *Jelly Roll, Jabbo, and Fats* (New York: Oxford University Press, 1983), 58.

4. Kay Davis interview, Yale 548, 11–12.

5. Rutgers, 253–54.

6. *Melody Maker,* June 24, 1933, 13.

7. *MIMM,* 35.

8. Dance, *World of Duke Ellington,* 62.

9. *New York Clipper,* Nov. 8, 1922, 28.

10. Ibid., Jan. 4, 1924, 25.

11. Author's interview.

12. Thomas Laurence Riis, "Black Musical Theatre in New York, 1890–1915" (Ph.D. diss., University of Michigan, 1981), 73.

13. *Billboard,* Jan. 3, 1925, 50.

14. Ibid., Oct. 4, 1924, 48.

15. Ibid., Oct. 18, 1924, 48.

16. Ibid., Dec. 13, 1924, 94.

17. *MIMM,* 36.

18. Samuel B. Charters and Leonard Kunstadt, *Jazz: A History of the New York Scene* (Garden City, N.Y.: Doubleday, 1962), 210.

19. *MIMM,* 36–37.

20. Du Conge, *Ada Smith, Bricktop* (New York: Longstreet, 1972), 75.

21. Unidentified clipping in Rutgers vert. file.

22. Dance, *World of Duke Ellington,* 66.

23. *Billboard,* Sept. 22, 1923, 55.

24. Ibid., Sept. 3, 1924, 50.

25. *MIMM,* 65.

26. Williamson, *Crucible of Race,* 74.

4. The Move Downtown

1. Robert Sylvester, *No Cover Charge* (New York: Dial Press, 1956), 48–49.

2. *Billboard,* Nov. 3, 1923, 56.

3. George Hoefer notes, Rutgers vert. file.

4. Willie "the Lion" Smith with George Hoefer, *Music on My Mind* (Garden City, N.Y.: Doubleday, 1964), 173.

5. Rutgers, 19.

6. Ibid.

7. Herbert G. Gutman, *The Black Family in Slavery and Freedom* (New York: Pantheon Books, 1976), 507.

8. Charters and Kunstadt, *Jazz,* 171.

9. Ulanov, *Duke Ellington,* 47.

10. Schomburg, C-467.

11. Author's interview.

12. Goddard, *Jazz Away from Home,* 292.

13. *New York Clipper,* Nov. 23, 1923.

14. Nat Shapiro and Nat Hentoff, *Hear Me Talkin' to Ya* (New York: Dover, 1955), 231.

15. Mercer Ellington, *Duke Ellington in Person,* 24.

16. *MIMM*, 70.
17. *Down Beat*, June 7, 1962.
18. Dance, *World of Duke Ellington*, 66.
19. Rutgers.
20. Charles G. Shaw, *Night Life* (New York: John Day, 1931).
21. *Show*, Aug. 1964, 106.
22. Mercer Ellington, *Duke Ellington in Person*, 149.
23. Yale, 527a, 12.
24. Ibid., 507a, 4.
25. Ibid., 523, 13.
26. Dance, *World of Duke Ellington*, 60.
27. Ibid., 163.
28. Mercer Ellington, *Duke Ellington in Person*, 210.

5. Duke Takes Over

1. Rutgers, #3, 48.
2. *New York Clipper*, April 10, 1924, 18.
3. Ibid., April 24, 1924, 19.
4. Dance, *World of Duke Ellington*, 69.
5. *MIMM*, 109.
6. Rutgers, #4, 35.
7. Ibid., #3, 32.
8. *Down Beat*, June 7, 1962.
9. Ibid.
10. Ibid.
11. *MIMM*, 47.
12. Bigard, *With Louis and the Duke*, 72.
13. *Orchestra World*, Jan. 1926.
14. Sylvester, *No Cover Charge*, 45.
15. Quoted in the *Chicago Defender*, Aug. 27, 1927. I have not been able to locate the original story.
16. Dance, *World of Duke Ellington*, 10.
17. Ibid., 132.
18. Schomburg, C-467.

6. Enter Irving Mills

1. Arnold Shaw, *Honkers and Shouters* (New York: Collier Books, 1978), 343.
2. Author's interview.
3. *Billboard*, Feb. 7, 1925, 52.
4. *New York Clipper*, June 13, 1923, 18.
5. Walter C. Allen, *Hendersonia* (Highland Park: Walter C. Allen, n.d.), 61.
6. *Down Beat*, Dec. 26, 1956, 6.
7. Smith, *Music on My Mind*, 149–50.
8. *MIMM*, 89.
9. Ralph Gleason film *I Love You Madly*.

10. Yale, 538, 4.
11. Dance, World of Duke Ellington, 69.
12. Yale.
13. Ibid., 567, 19.
14. Ibid., 21.
15. Ibid., 16.
16. Schomburg, C-467.
17. Ulanov, Duke Ellington, 58.

7. The Cotton Club

1. *Pops Foster*, as told to Tom Stoddard (Berkeley: University of California Press, 1973), 61.
2. Stanley Dance, *The World of Earl Hines* (New York: Scribner's, 1977), 49.
3. Smith, *Music on My Mind*, 136.
4. *Variety*, Jan. 1, 1925.
5. Sylvester, *No Cover Charge*, 45.
6. Ibid.
7. Notes in Rutgers vert. file.
8. Ibid., 5.
9. Sylvester, *No Cover Charge*, 21.
10. Ibid., 103.
11. Cab Calloway, *Of Minnie the Moocher and Me* (New York: Thomas Y. Crowell, 1976), 93.
12. Edward Jablonski, *Happy with the Blues* (Garden City, N.Y.: Doubleday, 1961), 55.
13. Liner notes, *The Early Duke Ellington*, Everest FS-221.
14. *New Yorker*, July 8, 1944, 29.
15. Shapiro and Hentoff, *Hear Me Talkin' to Ya*, 235.
16. Dance, *World of Duke Ellington*, 82.
17. Bigard, *With Louis and the Duke*, 38.
18. Ibid., 42.
19. Ibid., 44.
20. Ibid.
21. Ibid.
22. Yale, 500BC.
23. *Billboard*, Dec. 15, 1923, 102.
24. *Down Beat*, June 7, 1962, 20.
25. Rutgers, #4, 20.
26. Dance, *World of Duke Ellington*, 101.
27. Yale, 580b, 22.
28. Dance, *World of Duke Ellington*, 96–97.
29. *Melody Maker*, June 24, 1933, 9.
30. Rutgers, 168.
31. Ibid., 46.
32. Ibid., 88.
33. Williams interview, Rutgers, 86.
34. Dance, *World of Duke Ellington*, 105.
35. Ibid.

36. Rutgers, 88.
37. *Down Beat*, May 7, 1952, 6.
38. Rutgers, 145–46.
39. Ibid., 250–53.
40. Ibid., #1, 3.

8. Becoming Celebrated

1. Marshall Stearns, *The Story of Jazz* (New York: Oxford University Press, 1970), 184.
2. *MIMM*, 419.
3. Ibid.
4. Ibid., 420.
5. Yale, 538a, b, 1.
6. Bigard, *With Louis and the Duke*, 47.
7. Dance, *World of Duke Ellington*, 217.
8. Rutgers, 130.
9. Ibid., #3, 18–19.
10. Yale, 580A, 20.
11. Ibid., 567, 7.
12. *New Yorker*, July 8, 1944, 29.
13. Bigard, *With Louis and the Duke*, 36.
14. *New York Times*, March 30, 1930, 24.
15. Unidentified clipping in Rutgers vert. file.
16. Personal communication.
17. Yale, 550A, 21.
18. Ibid., 537, 4.
19. Ibid.
20. Author's interview.
21. *Phonograph Monthly Review*, July 1927.
22. Ibid., June 1927.
23. Ibid., Sept. 1927.
24. Ibid., Jan. 1928.
25. Ibid., June 1928.
26. Ibid.
27. Ibid.
28. *Disques*, June 1932.
29. Author's interview.
30. Author's interview with R. D. Darrell.
31. Letter from Edgar Jackson to R. D. Darrell, Sept. 27, 1932, in author's files.
32. Don George, *Sweet Man* (New York: G. P. Putnam, 1981).
33. Rutgers, #3, 28.
34. Ibid., #3, 24.
35. Mercer Ellington, *Duke Ellington in Person*, 47.
36. Ibid., 48.
37. Rutgers, #2, 24.
38. Author's interview.
39. Yale, 37.

40. Unidentified clipping, 1959, in Rutgers vert. file.
41. Ruth Boatwright interview, Yale.
42. *Inter-state Tatler*, May 2, 1930.
43. Author's interview.
44. Nat Hentoff interview, Yale 513, 11.
45. Bernice Wiggins interview, Yale 550, 11.
46. Schomburg, C-451.
47. Mercer Ellington, *Duke Ellington in Person*, 90.
48. *New York Times*, March 29, 1981.
49. *MIMM*, 41.

9. The Ellington Style Takes Shape

1. *Billboard*, Jan. 31, 1925, 50.
2. *Orchestra World*, May 1926.
3. *MIMM*, 49.
4. Schomburg, C-467.
5. *MIMM*, 98.
6. James Lincoln Collier, *The Making of Jazz* (Boston: Houghton Mifflin, 1978), 245.
7. *MIMM*, 97.
8. Yale, 37.
9. Dance, *World of Duke Ellington*, 50.
10. Mercer Ellington, *Duke Ellington in Person*, 159.
11. *Disques*, June 1932.
12. Note in Rutgers vert. file.
13. Harriet Milnes, "The Formation of Duke Ellington's Mature Style" (M.A. thesis, Mills College, 1978).
14. Charters and Kunstadt, *Jazz*, 118.
15. *MIMM*, 106.

10. On the Road

1. Calloway, *Of Minnie the Moocher and Me*, 106.
2. *Chicago Defender*, Nov. 5, 1932, 11.
3. Sylvester, *No Cover Charge*, 58.
4. Ibid., 47.
5. Ulanov, *Duke Ellington*, 151.
6. Linda Dahl, *Stormy Weather* (New York: Pantheon Books, 1984), 125.
7. Yale, 557, 27.
8. Rutgers, #2.
9. Ibid., #1, 6.
10. Ibid., #3, 13.
11. Ibid., #2, 9.
12. Bigard, *With Louis and the Duke*, 70.
13. Rutgers, #4, 36.
14. Ulanov, *Duke Ellington*, 102–3.
15. Ibid.

11. "Mood Indigo"

1. New Yorker, July 1, 1944, 28.
2. Down Beat, Jan. 1937, 10.
3. Schomburg, C-467.
4. Rutgers, 155.
5. MS in Rutgers vert. file, 20.
6. Milnes, "Duke Ellington's Mature Style," 22.
7. Mercer Ellington, Duke Ellington in Person, 151.
8. Jewell, Duke, 101.
9. MIMM, 78–79.
10. Cootie Williams oral history, Rutgers.
11. Bigard, With Louis and the Duke, 64.
12. Ibid.
13. MIMM, 82.
14. Martin Williams, ed., The Art of Jazz (New York: Oxford University Press, 1959), 127.
15. Ulanov, Duke Ellington, 104.
16. Rutgers, #2, 13.
17. Ulanov, Duke Ellington, 111.
18. Rutgers, #4, 32.
19. Alec Wilder, American Popular Song (New York: Oxford, 1972), 413.
20. Liner notes, Reflections in Ellington, Everybodys 3005.
21. Jewel, Duke, 46.
22. Dance, World of Duke Ellington, 16.

12. The Trip to England

1. Ulanov, Duke Ellington, 151.
2. See James Lincoln Collier, Louis Armstrong: An American Genius (New York: Oxford University Press, 1983), 249–52; New Republic, Nov. 18, 1985, 33; James Lincoln Collier, Institute for Studies in American Music, in preparation.
3. MIMM, 434.
4. Ulanov, Duke Ellington, 169.
5. Ibid., 130–32.
6. Melody Maker, June 10, 1933, 2.
7. Ibid., June 24, 1933, 1.
8. Ibid., 2.
9. Ibid., July 1, 1933, 2.
10. Ibid.
11. Ibid.
12. Ulanov, Duke Ellington, 142.
13. Ibid., 151.
14. Constant Lambert, Music Ho! (New York: Scribner's, 1934), 214.
15. See Goddard, Jazz Away from Home, 137.
16. Life and Letters, July 1928, 124–31. Lambert says, "Jazz, in fact, is just that sort of bastard product of art and life that provides so acceptable a drug to those incapable of really coping with either."

17. Jim Godbolt, A History of Jazz in Britain, 1919–50 (London: Quartet Books, 1984), 157.

13. Duke Faces the Swing Era

1. Dance, World of Duke Ellington, 85.
2. Ibid., 271.
3. MIMM, 87.
4. Yale, 550A.
5. Rutgers, #2, 11–12.
6. Author's interview.
7. New Yorker, June 24, 1944, 32–33.
8. Yale.
9. Mercer Ellington, Duke Ellington in Person, 183–85.
10. Personal communication.
11. Martin Williams, ed., Jazz Masters of the Thirties (New York: Macmillan, 1972), 211–15.
12. Shapiro and Hentoff, Hear Me Talkin' to Ya, 206.
13. Williams, Jazz Masters of the Thirties, 210.
14. John Hammond, John Hammond on Record (New York: Summit Books, 1977), 133.
15. Jazzletter, vol. 1, no. 10, p. 4.
16. Ibid.
17. Down Beat, March 21, 1951, 18.
18. Rutgers, 200.
19. Bigard, With Louis and the Duke, 65.
20. Film I Love You Madly.
21. Mercer Ellington, Duke Ellington in Person, 64.
22. Dance, World of Duke Ellington, 60.
23. Schomburg, C-451, Ruth Ellington Boatwright.
24. Author's interview.
25. Mercer Ellington, Duke Ellington in Person, 64.
26. Ibid.
27. Ulanov, Duke Ellington, 164.
28. Washington Tribune, June 1, 1935.
29. Author's interview.

14. Concertos and Small Groups

1. Time, March 22, 1937.
2. Hammond, John Hammond on Record, 159.
3. Author's interview.
4. Author's interview.
5. MIMM, 86.
6. Ibid.
7. Williams, Art of Jazz, 133.
8. Jewell, Duke, 56.
9. Williams, Art of Jazz, 133.
10. Ulanov, Duke Ellington, 166.

11. Yale, 550A, 19.
12. Jim Haskins, *The Cotton Club* (New York: New American Library, 1984), 130.
13. *New Yorker*, July 1, 1944, 32.
14. Ibid., June 24, 1944, 33.
15. Mercer Ellington, *Duke Ellington in Person*, 164.
16. Yale, 562A, 16.
17. Gunther Schuller, *Musings* (New York: Oxford University Press, 1986), 55.
18. Author's interview.
19. Wilder, *American Popular Song*, 414.
20. Lawrence Brown interview, Rutgers, 33–35.

15. New Additions to the Band

1. *New York Clipper*, Oct. 18, 1922, 28.
2. Ibid., Jan. 24, 1923, 30.
3. Ulanov, *Duke Ellington*, 217.
4. *Down Beat*, May 1, 1939, 1.
5. Yale.
6. Ulanov, *Duke Ellington*, 206.
7. Haskins, *Cotton Club*, 109.
8. Ulanov, *Duke Ellington*, 206.
9. *MIMM*, 89.
10. Bigard, *With Louis and the Duke*, 49.
11. Yale, 567, 21.
12. Hammond, *John Hammond on Record*, 139.
13. Yale.
14. Ibid., 550B, 26.
15. Ibid., 525.
16. Ibid.
17. Ibid., 504A.
18. *New Masses*, Sept. 29, 1936.
19. *Down Beat*, May 1939, 14.
20. Ibid., Dec. 15, 1942.
21. Yale, 38.
22. Ibid., 38, 4.
23. Schomburg, C-451.
24. Yale, 46.
25. Ibid.
26. Author's interview.
27. Rutgers, 42–43.
28. Interview at Yale with Helen Saddler Strayhorn and Carol Strayhorn.
29. *Down Beat*, June 7, 1962, 22.
30. Ibid.
31. *Down Beat*, Oct. 1, 1940, 49.
32. Yale, 77d, 69.
33. Dance, *World of Duke Ellington*, 61–62.
34. Yale.

35. Rutgers, 199.
36. Author's interview.
37. Dance, *World of Duke Ellington*, 61.
38. Ulanov, *Duke Ellington*, 235.
39. Charlie Barnet with Stanley Dance, *Those Swinging Years* (Baton Rouge: Louisiana State University Press, 1984), 185.
40. Rutgers, #8, 12–13.
41. Yale, 580B, 24.
42. Ibid., 50.
43. *MIMM*, 156.
44. Mercer Ellington, *Duke Ellington in Person*, 85.
45. *MIMM*, 164.
46. Rutgers, 180.
47. Ibid., #8.
48. Yale, 507a, 8, 19.
49. Rutgers, 180.
50. Ralph J. Gleason, *Celebrating the Duke* (New York: Dell, 1976), 251–52.
51. Schomburg, C-463.
52. Ibid.
53. Interview for Swedish radio at Yale.
54. Schomburg, C-463.
55. Dempsey J. Travis, *Black Jazz* (Chicago: Urban Research Institute, 1983), 374.
56. Jewell, *Duke*, 68.
57. Yale, 550B 41.
58. Jewell, *Duke*, 239.

16. *Black, Brown, and Beige*

1. Russell Sanjek, *From Print to Plastic: Publishing and Promoting Americans' Popular Music (1900–1980)* (Brooklyn: Institute for Studies in American Music, 1983), 22–26.
2. *Down Beat*, Nov. 1, 1940, 16.
3. Yale, 5211, 13–14.
4. *Down Beat*, March 15, 1941, 4.
5. Ibid., Dec. 1, 1939, 14.
6. Ibid., April 15, 1940, 15.
7. Ibid., June 1, 1940, 12.
8. Ibid., June 15, 1940, 12.
9. Ibid., Aug. 1, 1940.
10. Ibid., Feb. 15, 1940, 14.
11. Ibid., May 15, 1940.
12. Ibid., Sept. 1, 1940, 3.
13. *New York Times*, Dec. 9, 1961.
14. Yale.
15. Ulanov, *Duke Ellington*, ix.
16. Dance, *World of Duke Ellington*, ix.
17. Jewell, *Duke*, 52–53.
18. Yale, 550A, 15.

19. Ulanov, *Duke Ellington*, 257–58.
20. *Down Beat*, Feb. 15, 1943, 12.
21. Schomburg, 451.
22. *New York Times*, April 29, 1957, 20.
23. Ibid., Nov. 15, 1948, 22.

17. The Early 1940s Recordings

1. Personal communication.
2. Unpublished paper.
3. André Hodeir, *Jazz: Its Evolution and Essence* (New York: Grove Press, 1956), 79.
4. Jewell, *Duke*, 76.
5. *MIMM*, 153.

18. The Old Hands Begin to Depart

1. Dance, *World of Duke Ellington*, 108.
2. Rutgers, 215–16.
3. Ibid.
4. Ibid., 219.
5. *Down Beat*, May 7, 1952, 6.
6. Ibid., Sept. 1, 1942, 15.
7. *MIMM*, 165–66.
8. Bigard, *With Louis and the Duke*, 77.
9. *Down Beat*, July 15, 1942, 4.
10. Yale, 580a.
11. Ibid., 14.
12. Bigard, *With Louis and the Duke*, 54.
13. Yale, 5211, p. 11.
14. Rutgers, #2, 19.
15. Personal communication.
16. Williams, *Jazz Masters of the Thirties*, 102.
17. *Washington Star*, Aug. 7, 1970.
18. *Down Beat*, Aug. 12, 1946, 9.
19. Dance, *World of Earl Hines*.
20. Yale, 553.
21. Leonard Feather, *The Encyclopedia of Jazz* (New York: Bonanza Books, 1965), 254.
22. Yale, 56AAB.
23. *Down Beat*, Feb. 15, 1944.
24. Ibid., Feb. 11, 1946, 1.
25. Stanley Dance, *The World of Swing* (New York: Da Capo, 1979), 285.
26. Yale, 557, 33.
27. Jewell, *Duke*, 186.
28. Mercer Ellington, *Duke Ellington in Person*, 138.
29. Yale, 525, 13.
30. *Jazz Journal*, March 1986, 8.

19. Decline and Fall

1. *Down Beat*, June 17, 1949, 12.
2. Ibid., 14.
3. Ibid., July 15, 1949, 1.
4. Ibid., Aug. 12, 1949, 1.
5. Ibid., July 30, 1947, 2.
6. Mercer Ellington, *Duke Ellington in Person*, 102.
7. *Down Beat*, May 6, 1953, 1.
8. Rutgers, #4, 36.
9. Ibid., #5, 15.
10. Jewell, *Duke*, 115.
11. *Down Beat*, Jan. 9, 1957, 20.
12. George, *Sweet Man*, 119.
13. Liner notes, *Ellington at Newport*, Columbia 8648.
14. Stanley Dance, personal communication.
15. See above, n. 13.
16. *Down Beat*, Aug. 8, 1956, 17.
17. See above, n. 13.
18. *Down Beat*, Aug. 8, 1956, 17.
19. Ibid.
20. Ibid.

20. The Last Band

1. *Down Beat*, Sept. 19, 1956, 9.
2. *Time*, Aug. 20, 1956, 54.
3. Ibid., Jan. 23, 1956, 65.
4. Yale, 527A, 8.
5. Rutgers, #7, 19.
6. *Down Beat*, July 25, 1968, 21.
7. Ibid.
8. Mercer Ellington, *Duke Ellington in Person*, 131–32.
9. Ibid., 136.
10. Ibid., 140.
11. *MIMM*, 159.
12. Jewell, *Duke*, 72.
13. *MIMM*, 156.
14. Rutgers, #4, 20.
15. Liner notes, Onyx ORI-216.
16. Winthrop Sargeant, *Jazz: Hot and Hybrid* (New York: Da Capo, 1975), 251.

21. The Concert Pieces

1. Jules Edmund Rowell, "An Analysis of the Extended Orchestral Works of Duke Ellington" (M.A. thesis, San Francisco State University).
2. *MIMM*, 183.

3. Schomburg, C-499.
4. Liner notes, *Duke Ellington,* Encore 14359.
5. *MIMM,* 192.
6. *New York Times,* April 29, 1957, 20.
7. Horizon, Nov. 1979, 6.
8. Rowell, "Extended Orchestral Works of Duke Ellington," 415.
9. Author's interview.

22. The Sacred Concerts

1. *MIMM,* 259.
2. Ibid., 260.
3. Unpublished paper.
4. Yale, 557, 24.
5. Barnet, *Those Swinging Years,* 185.
6. Hammond, *John Hammond on Record,* 138.
7. Show, Aug. 1964, 72.
8. Author's interview.
9. Mercer Ellington, *Duke Ellington in Person,* 195.
10. Ibid., 196.
11. Personal communication.

23. The Final Days

1. Mercer Ellington, *Duke Ellington in Person,* 191.
2. Jewell, *Duke,* 224–25.
3. Ibid.
4. *New York Times,* April 14, 1974, 50.
5. Ibid., May 23, 1974, 34.
6. Ibid., May 25, 1974, 1.
7. Ibid.
8. Ibid., May 26, 1974, IV-14.
9. Wilder, *American Popular Song,* 412.
10. Show, Aug. 1964, 106.
11. George, *Sweet Man,* 51.
12. Ibid., 137.

Discographical Note

Duke Ellington's musical output was enormous, and in one shape or another most of his recordings are in print somewhere in the world. In addition, a large mass of concert and broadcast material is available, with more coming on the market constantly. Finally, there are those hundreds of hours of Ellington tape housed in Copenhagen, which may be issued some day. Although a few assiduous Ellington fans have amassed nearly complete Ellington collections, it will be beyond the means of most even to attempt to do so. Among other things, few record stores carry more than a fraction of what is available at any given time. The following, then, is intended merely as a guide to what I consider to be the most important items that are more or less readily available at the moment.

At the heart of any Ellington collection are two sets of "complete" works issued by French companies: the RCA Black and White set called *The Works of Duke Ellington Integrale*, in twenty-four records; and the CBS "Aimez Vous le Jazz" *The Complete Duke Ellington*, in fourteen double albums. Because Columbia and Victor swallowed up most of the smaller companies during the Depression, these sets contain perhaps 90 percent of Ellington's formal recordings from the beginning to the postwar period, including all the small-band recordings of the time. They include as well a number of alternate masters. However, these important sets will be available in record stores randomly, and it may take time to amass complete sets. They are somewhat easier to find in Europe, especially in jazz record stores in London and Paris. It is sometimes possible to find them listed in the catalogs of mail order record companies specializing in jazz.

Far easier to get is a set of three RCA records entitled *The Beginning* (MCA 1358), *Hot in Harlem* (MCA 1359), and *Rockin' in Rhythm* (MCA 1360)—covering the 1920s and early 1930s. These are readily available, and for that reason I recommend them to the reader interested in Ellington's earlier work.

For readers who want only a sampling of Ellington's work, there is a Victor two-record set called *This Is Duke Ellington* (RCA VPM-6042), which contains a good selection of the major pieces from 1927 to 1945. Columbia some time ago issued two excellent boxed sets of material from this period, called *The Ellington Era*, vol. 1 (C3L 27), vol. 2 (C3L 39); these may still occasionally turn up in record stores. Another older compilation that may still be found is *In a Mellotone* (RCN LPM-1364), which includes many of the important items from the early 1940s period. Easier to find is *The World of Duke Ellington* (CG 32564), which contains music from the mid-forties.

Music from Ellington's later period has not been issued systematically. Generally available is a Prestige series of the 1940s Carnegie Hall concerts. CBS has issued a box of its complete holdings for the 1947–52 period (CBS 66607). The Three Sacred Concerts, entitled *Concert of Sacred Music* (French RCA DL 43663), *Second Sacred Concert* (Prestige P24045), and *Third Sacred Concert* (RCA-APLI-0785), are usually available. Also generally available are many of the extended pieces, although it is impossible to know which ones will be in a record shop at a given moment.

Finally, the following items can usually be found with a little searching: *Ellington at Newport* (CL 934); *And His Mother Called Him Bill* (French RCA NL-69166); the 1932 stereo pieces in an album called *Reflections in Ellington* (Everybodys 3005); and *Original Movie Sound Tracks, 1929–35* (Biograph M-2). Record stores will have in stock other Ellington items besides these, but it will be a matter of chance as to what and when.

Index